SAFETY MANAGEME~~NT~~

Ashgate Studies in Human Factors for Flight Operations

Series Editors

R. Key Dismukes, Ph.D.
Formerly Chief Scientist for Human Factors at the NASA Ames Research Center, California, USA

Capt. Daniel E. Maurino
Formerly Coordinator of the Flight Safety and Human Factors Study Programme at the International Civil Aviation Organization (ICAO), Quebec, Canada

Sidney Dekker, Ph.D.
Professor, Griffith University, Brisbane, Australia

Ashgate Studies in Human Factors for Flight Operations is a series dedicated to publishing high-quality monographs and edited volumes which contribute to the objective of improving the safe and efficient operation of aircraft.

The series will achieve this by disseminating new theoretical and empirical research from specialists in all relevant fields of aviation human factors. Its foundation will be in applied psychology, presenting new developments and applications in such established fields as CRM, SA and decision-making. It will also encompass many other crucial areas such as fatigue and stress, the social environment, SMS, design, technology, communication and training.

Submitted work relevant to the objective of the series will be considered for publication by the board of editors. The series is intended for an international readership and so books with a broad geographical appeal are especially encouraged.

Safety Management Systems in Aviation

ALAN J. STOLZER
Embry-Riddle Aeronautical University, USA

CARL D. HALFORD
Contract Engineer, The MITRE Corporation

&

JOHN J. GOGLIA
Senior VP, JDA Aviation Technology Solutions, USA

ASHGATE

Published by
Ashgate Publishing Limited
Wey Court East
Union Road
Farnham
Surrey GU9 7PT
England

Ashgate Publishing Company
Suite 420
101 Cherry Street
Burlington, VT 05401-4405
USA

Ashgate website: http://www.ashgate.com

British Library Cataloguing in Publication Data
Stolzer, Alan J.
  Safety management systems in aviation. – (Ashgate studies
  in human factors for flight operations)
  1. Aeronautics – Safety measures 2. Aeronautics – Safety
  regulations 3. System safety
  I. Title II. Halford, Carl D. III. Goglia, John Joseph,
  .1944–
  363.1'241

  ISBN: 978-0-7546-7304-0 (hbk)
         978-1-4094-1211-3 (pbk)
         978-0-7546-9087-0 (ebk)

Library of Congress Cataloging-in-Publication Data
Stolzer, Alan J., 1960–
  Safety management systems in aviation / by Alan J. Stolzer, Carl D. Halford, and John J.
Goglia.
      p. cm. -- (Ashgate studies in human factors for flight operations)
  Includes bibliographical references and index.
  ISBN 978-0-7546-7304-0
  1. Aeronautics--Safety measures. 2. Aeronautics--Safety regulations. 3. System safety. I.
Halford, Carl D., 1950- II. Goglia, John Joseph, 1944- III. Title.

TL553.5.S743 2008
363.12'47--dc22

2008010405

MIX
Paper from
responsible sources
FSC® C018575

Printed and bound in Great Britain by the
MPG Books Group, UK.

Contents

List of Figures

List of Tables

List of Abbreviations

AC	Advisory Circular
ALARP	As Low as Reasonably Practicable
AQP	Advanced Qualification Program
ASAP	Aviation Safety Action Program
ATOS	Air Transport Oversight System
CFIT	Controlled Flight into Terrain
CFR	Code of Federal Regulations
CRM	Crew Resource Management
DAR	Digital Airborne Recorder
DNAA	Distributed National Archives
EICAS	Engine Indicating and Crew Alerting System
EO	Enabling Objectives
ERC	Event Review Committee
FAA	Federal Aviation Administration
FADEC	Full Authority Digital Engine Control
FMEA	Failure Mode Effects Analysis
FMS	Flight Management System
FOIA	Freedom of Information Act
FOQA	Flight Operations Quality Assurance
FST	Functional Safety Team
FTA	Fault Tree Analysis
ICAO	International Civil Aviation Organization
IEP	Internal Evaluation Program
ISO	International Organization for Standardization
JTA	Job Task Analysis
KPI	Key Performance Indicator
KSA	Knowledge, Skills, and Attitudes
LFL	Logical Frame Layout
LOSA	Line Operations Safety Audit
MOU	Memorandum of Understanding
PADB	Program Audit Database
PDCA	Plan-Do-Check-Act
PDPC	Process Decision Program Chart
PF	Pilot Flying
PM	Pilot Monitoring
PPDB	Pilot Proficiency Database
PRA	Probabilistic Risk Assessment
QAR	Quick Access Recorder
SA	Safety Assurance
SC	Safety Council

SME	Subject Matter Expert
SMS	Safety Management System
SPO	Supporting Proficiency Objectives
SRM	Safety Risk Management
TC	Transport Canada
TEM	Threat and Error Management
TLS	Target Level of Safety
TPO	Terminal Proficiency Objectives
VDRP	Volunary Disclosure Reporting Program

About the Authors

Alan J. Stolzer, Ph.D. is Professor of Applied Aviation Science at Embry-Riddle Aeronautical University, Daytona Beach, Florida, USA. He holds a Ph.D. in Quality Systems from Indiana State University, and several professional certifications: Quality Engineer, Quality Manager, and Quality Auditor from the American Society for Quality; Project Management Professional from the Project Management Institute; Airline Transport Pilot, Flight Instructor with Instrument and Multi-Engine Ratings, and Airframe and Powerplant Mechanic from the Federal Aviation Administration. Dr. Stolzer has several thousand hours in more than 40 makes and models of fixed-wing aircraft. His research interests include safety, quality, flight operations quality assurance, safety management systems, and emergency preparedness. He is a prolific author and has been awarded and managed numerous grants and contracted training programs. Dr. Stolzer is involved in academic accreditation activities and has served as an expert witness and legal consultant on aviation accidents.

Carl D. Halford has wide experience in many aspects of airline operations, including safety and quality, airline flight and simulator instruction, maintenance, management and union representation. Mr. Halford holds an Airline Transport Pilot certificate, with an assortment of type ratings, and has over 9,000 hours of flight time in a variety of aircraft. Mr. Halford has held a variety of airline positions, including Manager of Voluntary Aviation Safety Programs, Manager of Flight Operations Quality Assurance (FOQA), Manager of Aviation Safety Action Partnership (ASAP), and Manager of Part 121 Training. He has also been an Airline Pilots Association Master Executive Committee Chairman and holds several professional certifications. Mr. Halford has completed a Masters degree from DePaul University, with a specialization in Safety Management Systems (SMS). He has assisted in the construction of the Distributed National Archive for airline safety information, and is presently engaged in research with MITRE Corporation in this endeavor.

John J. Goglia is an active consultant, author, and educator in the field of transportation safety. Mr. Goglia served as a Member of the National Transportation Safety Board from August 1995 to June 2004 and was the first Board Member to hold an FAA aircraft mechanic's certificate. As a Board Member, Mr. Goglia distinguished himself in numerous areas of transportation safety. In particular, he was instrumental in raising awareness of airport safety issues, including the importance of airport crash fire and rescue operations and the dangers of wildlife at airports, and played a key role in focusing international attention on the increasing significance of aircraft maintenance in aviation accidents. Mr. Goglia has been recognized many times for his contribution to aviation safety; awarding bodies include the National Air Disaster Alliance, Aviation Week and Space Technology,

Acknowledgements

Authoring a book is no small endeavor—it takes the support and encouragement of many people to accomplish. The authors are appreciative of various colleagues who provided guidance and wisdom, including Michelle Harper, Contract Engineer with The MITRE Corporation, who willingly shared her expertise in Aviation Safety Action Programs, and particularly in the theories and best practices in the development of employee self-reporting systems.

We are also indebted to our friends and colleagues who contributed commentaries from their experiences with aviation safety and SMS—we call these commentaries "SMS in Practice", and they are interspersed throughout the book. Contributors include:

> Darryel Adams, SMS Program Manager, Airport Safety and Operations, FAA
>
> Dr. Tim Brady, Dean, College of Aviation, Embry-Riddle Aeronautical University
>
> Robert Clack, Senior Analyst, Flight Safety/SafeOps, American Airlines
>
> Jerry Dennis, Executive Director, The Medallion Foundation
>
> Jack Kreckie, retired Deputy Fire Chief for Boston Massport Fire & Rescue
>
> Cpt. Lloyd Murray, retired TWA Captain and Company ASAP ERC Representative
>
> Cpt. Hugh Schoelzel, former VP—Corporate Safety, TWA
>
> Mont Smith, Director of Safety, Air Transport Association
>
> Cpt. Bruce Tesmer, retired Captain, Continental Airlines, former Manager, Flight Crew Performance/Safety and President of Foresight Bias Collaborative

We've also included commentaries from FAA executives Marion Blakey, Nicholas Sabatini, and Robert Sturgell, which were excerpted from various public speeches. We appreciate their individual and collective efforts to promote SMS.

Finally, we thank all the men and women who have worked tirelessly to make the aviation industry as safe as it is.

Foreword

Thanks to the extraordinary efforts of thousands of hard-working professionals in the aviation industry over the years, the U.S. airline safety record is the envy of the world. Improvements in safety methods, technology, training, and other factors have resulted in a precipitous decline in the accident rate over the past several decades. Not to diminish the work of those who made this improvement a reality, but we really have discovered the low-hanging fruit in aviation safety, and we're seeing the evidence of that fact in a leveling of the accident rate. Now we need to do more. The number of airline departures has risen dramatically in the past few years. Other countries around the world continue to struggle with their accident rates. We must not become complacent with our own safety record; rather we must employ new methods and programs that can drive down accident rates. Safety Management Systems (SMS) offers the best opportunity to make this happen.

During my tenure on the National Transportation Safety Board just a few years ago, we witnessed high-profile crashes such as USAir Flight 427, TWA Flight 800, EgyptAir Flight 990, and the aviation-related deaths of public figures such as John F. Kennedy, Jr., Payne Stewart, and John Denver. Fortunately, these tragic events are rare occurrences. Even so, we can do better—and we must. This is indeed a critical time for aviation safety.

This book provides insights and elaboration on SMS that other documentation does not. The authors stress that an effective SMS program is based on quality management principles, a position supported by the FAA. But this book goes further—the reader will see the entire discussion of SMS grounded in a quality approach, using quality tools and methods to illuminate SMS.

The authors also offer a persuasive argument for the use of more rigorous, scientific methods for managing safety. It stands to reason that if we've achieved about all we can with current methods, we must do something more. Other industries have embraced tools such as modeling, data mining, and stochastic methods for safety; it is logical to conclude that aviation should similarly benefit from those methods.

Safety Management Systems in Aviation also offers the reader a thorough description of the practical realities of SMS. SMS is not rocket science, it is not a program available only to large, complex organizations, and it is not only for organizations that are *required* to implement it. SMS can benefit any organization that fully commits to it, that recognizes SMS as a *management system*, and that strives to inculcate *SMS-thinking* in the personnel throughout the organization.

I anticipate that this book will be of great value to the student of SMS and aviation safety, whether they be college students or industry professionals. The easier gains have been made, now it is incumbent on us as an industry to change our approach to safety to ensure we drive our accident rate down to as close to zero as we can. SMS can help us achieve that goal.

The Honorable Jim Hall
Former Chair, U.S. National Transportation Safety Board
Managing Partner, Hall & Associates LLC

Preface

Tis the good reader that makes the good book.

Ralph Waldo Emerson

We wrote this book with two audiences in mind. Perhaps obviously, we hope that the aviation safety professional already engaged in the field will find the text helpful as the reality of the global adoption of SMS approaches his or her operation. The term 'aviation safety professional' is in itself very broad, and includes those working in a safety department, managers who are cognizant of their responsibilities to run a safe operation, and regulators who are adopting a new way of oversight. SMS is by its very nature a collaborative enterprise, and so any text on SMS needs to be relevant to all of aviation's stakeholders.

Our other intended audience is especially important, perhaps more so than all of us who are presently engaged in the industry. That other audience is the student of aviation safety, in college, striving to gain the skills and expertise necessary to become employable, and dreaming of making a mark. We especially want to speak to you, for the reality is that we realize the adoption and maturation of proactive and predictive safety will not happen on our watch. In fact, it's likely that the implementation of SMS will progress in fits and starts, with notable success stories, and with failures. Like any other human endeavor, some of the best intentions will become diluted, and some of the greatest thoughts will ossify into institutionalization. We are relying on you to take up the torch, and make these ideas we are struggling with a reality.

Write what you know. That should leave you with a lot of free time.

Howard Nemerov

Trying to explain anything in depth quickly illuminates one's own gaps in knowledge and understanding. In the course of writing this book, we have filled all of that free time Mr. Nemerov refers to by thinking about, researching and debating amongst ourselves the key concepts underlying SMS, a subject which of course extends across all types of operations and professional specializations. In that sense, we hope the message of this work can be applied across the industry, to all 'aviation service providers', to use the FAA term. But in giving examples of the application of SMS, the reader will undoubtedly notice that many of the references and anecdotes in this text are based primarily on the airline industry. There are several reasons for the attention we gave to airlines. First, this segment of the industry is highly visible and extremely important to the national interest and, thus, deserves particular attention. Second, the airline industry has arguably progressed further down the path toward SMS than other segments of the aviation industry, so there is a richer body of information which can serve to illuminate SMS. And finally, the majority of our cumulative experience is in the airline industry. These points notwithstanding, SMS is important and relevant to all sectors of the industry, and we trust we've adequately stressed that throughout this book.

> Make sure you have finished speaking before your audience is finished listening.
>
> *Dorothy Sarnoff*

We have striven to take Ms. Sarnoff's advice seriously, and so we have not attempted to say everything there is to say about SMS. The reader will note that we make frequent reference to the primary sources in the field of SMS, those being the ICAO and FAA documents cited in the bibliography. We strongly recommend that the SMS practitioner becomes very familiar with their contents. We have tried to extract the important principles described in these sources, and have gone into detail where we think such detail is warranted. But we have purposely tried to not just re-present the content of those documents; those writers already said it well the first time.

We have also included references to other suggested reading in the text. We especially recommend John Kotter's *Leading Change*, and Peter Senge's *The Fifth Discipline*. We must face the fact that implementing SMS requires transformational change, and Kotter's work provides an excellent blueprint for guidance as to how to do that. Senge's work illuminates the philosophical basis of SMS, systems thinking. Understanding and applying Senge's message will assure that an SMS does not merely satisfy regulatory requirements but is based on sound principles.

Perhaps the most important recommendation of all that we wish to relate to those already engaged in this global transformation of aviation safety, or to those who aim to become a part of it, is to become proficient in, and disciples of, quality. Primary references in this field are too numerous to cite, and we would not recommend that the serious reader use a summary approach to learning about quality anyway. Dive into it. Obtain professional certifications such as offered by the American Society for Quality. Developing an understanding and mastery of quality management and quality engineering is challenging but very rewarding, and those skills have clear application to the direction in which SMS needs to evolve.

> Why shouldn't truth be stranger than fiction? Fiction, after all, has to make sense.
>
> *Mark Twain*

The reader will note that this book begins and ends with a fictional narrative—the first part of the narrative is presented in the Prologue, and the remainder appears in the Epilogue. We have included this narrative so that we could attempt to breathe life into the concepts presented in the expository text, to present how a fully functioning SMS might actually work. It is fictional, and we make all of the usual assertions and declarations about it—it doesn't represent any company, living or dead, the equipment malfunctions are completely made up and might very well be impossible, and we cast no aspersions on any person, place, thing, organization, country, group ... you get the idea. But we encourage the reader to engage in the thought experiment that transported us to the idea of including such a fictional tale, the same thought experiment that really was the origin of this entire effort. Imagine, if you will, a company, yours perhaps, five years from now. During those five years the company has embraced SMS, and has successfully implemented the transformational change necessary to have a true safety management system. What would it look like? What would a normal work day be like? What would the interactions be like? Engage fully in this thought experiment, filling in all the details you can.

Now, go build it.

Prologue—Quest Airlines

Tiller sat at a desk in his spacious office and relaxed. He just finished gathering together a few items he planned to take with him this evening on QAL Flight 222 to Paris for some much needed rest and relaxation. Tiller was waiting for his wife to arrive at his office; the plan was to head over to the airport together. He didn't want to be late; the airline's policy was to be the on-time airline, and not wait for tardy passengers, even if one of the passengers was the president of the airline.

Appointed six months ago by the board of directors of Quest Airlines (QAL) as president and CEO, Ken Tiller brought a wealth of management expertise to the airline. A former chief executive at a major car company, Tiller brought a focus on quality management to the airline that was sorely lacking before his arrival. He was a strong proponent of quality, having witnessed it transform a struggling car company into a world class performer. Tiller believed it could do the same for QAL, and the board of directors was counting on him to make it happen.

While he was waiting for his wife to arrive, Tiller decided to review the numerous reports provided to him on a daily basis from his management team. He clicked on the dashboard on his computer and drilled down to the reports he was looking for. The reports varied from financial performance to human resource matters to operational statistics. Tiller marveled at the quantity of data being gathered, but knew that the airline was falling short of putting all that information to effective use in managing the airline. Just a few months prior, he had gathered his senior staff together and challenged them to create an airline management system that would serve as the model for how the airline would be operated. He was determined to change the traditional silo structure so common in the industry. His new safety guy, Glenn Seyfat, preached to everyone he could about crossing boundaries, and how important this was to safety. Tiller knew the challenge was even bigger than Glenn's world. He had vowed that he would allow himself to retire the day after he had a concise, meaningful Integrated Airline Management System dashboard on his computer, succinctly displaying the performance of all of the functions, and especially the cultures, he needed to manage. He knew he had quite a few more years to wait for his retirement party.

Tiller was very concerned about safety, and he studied the safety reports on his desk with great interest. Tiller believed that the safety program at QAL had improved substantially in the past few months as a result of the airline's adoption of a Safety Management System (SMS) as an integral component of his Integrated Airline Management System (iAMS) project.

Tiller made an excellent decision to start off his tenure as president—he hired Glenn Seyfat as the Vice President for Safety and Director of Safety (Part 121). A former Airbus captain, Seyfat flew for a competitor airline until five years ago when he lost his medical certificate due to an undiscovered but benign (except to the FAA) heart abnormality. Tiller believed that with Seyfat's background as a union safety officer, he could provide the qualities necessary to build an industry-leading safety program at the airline.

Tiller shuffled through the reports until he found the historical safety summary he had requested. The structure of the report itself caught his eye first, and spoke volumes about the challenge ahead.

Actually it was well done—the management team before his was quite professional. But it was entirely a forensic report—a thorough analyses of observations taken at the scene of the crime, broken down by year, geographic region, airplane type … he suspected somewhere in there was a breakdown by the color of the captain's hair. He searched through the document and couldn't find a single page that spoke to strategic safety planning. Tiller was fond of reminding his team that pilot seats are usually bolted to the aircraft so as to face in the direction of flight. That was also his standard for management reviews—for every project, he wanted to see the flight plan, and the navigation log. At least Glenn was aware of the problem, and had been apologetic in the email accompanying the report.

He was especially interested in the summaries of the two major accidents that blighted QAL's 77 year history as an airline. The first was in 1938 when one of the Waco 9's it operated in airmail service crashed, killing the pilot. Tiller noted that the company accident report was submitted less than two days following the crash, and was signed by the airline's chief pilot. Tiller surmised that safety during that era was a part-time responsibility of the chief pilot. He quickly read the brief report, which had an unsatisfying conclusion.

> …weather conditions at the time of the crash were for overcast and light rain. It was nearly dusk. The pilot misjudged his speed and was unable to make it to the runway, crashing just short. The doctors reported that the pilot died instantly. There were no other factors to be found. The cause of this crash was pilot error and, as a result, no action is deemed necessary. Investigation closed.
>
> Signed,
>
> Charles Smith
>
> Chief Pilot

Tiller wondered how in the face of those factors, anyone could conclude that no action was necessary. Thankfully, times have changed and most people realize the limitations of those methods.

The second accident summarized in the report was the 1975 midair collision of a QAL Boeing 727 and a general aviation Piper Cherokee. Ninety-three people were killed in the crash. An investigation concluded that the cause of the crash was the failure of the Boeing crew to maintain visual separation from the Piper on departure, which it had earlier reported seeing. He was heartened to see a much more thorough analysis of the contributing factors to the crash. One comment jumped off the page. "Interviews with other crews revealed complaints about the complexity of the departure procedure. One captain related a similar incident involving another airline in which a collision was narrowly avoided." His safety guru Glenn had been preaching the other day about how 1974 was a pivotal year in the safety business. Tiller scribbled a sticky note, "Glenn—dog and pony about the 70s, next management retreat."

Just as he was finishing the report, Tiller's wife burst in the room. "On y va! On y va!," she cried.

Tiller smiled. "Okay. Let's go to Paris."

Boston: 22:23 UTC (5:23 P.M. EST)

Day 1

"QAL Flight 222, cleared for takeoff", a Logan tower controller said.

"Roger, cleared for takeoff, QAL 222," repeated First Officer (F.O.) Tim Evans.

With the authority of nearly 90,000 pounds of thrust courtesy of Pratt & Whitney, Flight 222 took off at 5:25 p.m. EST in the Boeing 757 for an on-time departure from Boston to Charles de Gaulle International Airport in Paris. Scheduled flight time was 6 hours 40 minutes for the flight across the Atlantic; it was a trip Captain Bob Sanders and F.O. Evans had made many times. Seated in the jumpseat was the International Reserve Officer (or "film critic" as QAL pilots called the position), F.O. Jim Tyler, who was relaxing after reviewing the latest flight plan information.

Sanders and Evans were expecting virtually clear skies and a smooth ride for the 3,500 mile flight; they had rarely experienced such good weather on the long trip.

The autopilot on the Boeing leveled the plane off at cruise altitude and the autothrottles adjusted the power to compensate.

Evans accomplished the items on the checklist flow, ran through the checklist to verify that he hadn't missed anything, and the two pilots settled in for the flight.

"Cruise checklist complete," Evans said.

Over the Atlantic: 01:12 UTC (8:12 PM EST)

As Sanders was finishing another cup of coffee and discussing "the mess in Washington and the upcoming elections" with Evans, the "ding" of the Master Caution interrupted the debate. Sanders saw that the A/T DISC annunciator was illuminated, and heard the disturbing sound of both engines spooling down to idle. Engine instruments confirmed his perception.

"WHAT THE …!" Sanders gasped as he heard the sound of the Pratt & Whitneys spooling down to idle.

"What's going on, Bob? Did … did we do something?" asked Evans.

The captain spent a second or two shaking himself out of the strange paralysis he suddenly felt, punched the Master Caution light off, regrouped, and took command. After quickly assessing the status of the engines, he confirmed they were running, but only at idle power. He moved the throttles back and forth—they might has well have been toys. No response.

"Okay, time to earn our keep," Sanders said. "Tim, call Gander and tell them we're declaring an emergency and turning right to one-eight-zero. We're going to need lower."

"Center, QAL Flight 222, we've got a … uh … problem up here. It looks like we've got a power … partial power loss. We're going to need lower. We're turning right heading one-eight-zero. And we'll go ahead and declare an emergency now," said Evans.

"Get Jim up here," Sanders said, and seconds afterward he heard the film critic's voice on the cabin interphone. "What's up?" Jim asked. Tim buzzed him in, unlocking the security device on the cockpit door.

"We're trying to figure that out," said Sanders. "The autothrottle disconnected, both engines went to idle, and are now unresponsive to throttle movement." He demonstrated that fact by moving the throttles up and down through their full range of movement. Nothing.

A bell chimed. Ignoring the call from the cabin, Sanders weighed his options as the nauseating thought of ditching a fully loaded 757, at night, in the Atlantic Ocean came over him. The cabin could wait another minute. He repositioned the throttle levers again. No response. As the 757 rolled out on a southerly heading, he said "Tim, get on the radar and start playing with the tilt. Find us a ship. We would have to be on the Victor track tonight." Victor was one of the northernmost of the eastbound North Atlantic Tracks, hundreds of miles away from the shipping lanes.

Another call from the cabin. This time Sanders picked it up.

"How bad is it?" came the question from the lead flight attendant.

"June, sorry for not answering the first time. I want you to quietly get your team together, and have them review ditching procedures. We have 20 minutes left in the air, we'll use 5 to get ourselves ready, 10 to prepare the passengers. So we'll be ready in 15. Don't say anything yet to the passengers. When you're confident your team is focused, come on up here. See you in 3 or 4 minutes."

"Jim, help me think this through. You get on the horn with dispatch and get them up to speed. Try to figure out which damn checklist might help. I'll take care of getting us ready for our swim."

As June entered the cockpit, Sanders felt the nose begin to pitch up as the power on both engines began to increase. Two minutes and two seconds after the mysterious power reduction, an equally mysterious power increase brought the power setting back to normal.

The pilots were simultaneously relieved and anxious. They leveled off at their new altitude and reset the power to cruise.

Sanders took a deep breath. "Well, let's assess... We had a severe loss of power on both engines at cruise altitude. It lasted for about two minutes. Power seems to be restored and operating normally. All engine indications are normal. We're three out of Boston with over three and a half hours to go. What do you think?"

"I think we should divert or return to Boston. Definitely not continue to Paris."

"Agreed. Let's call dispatch for their assessment. Sanders punched up a page on the CDU. Looks like Gander is our closest. Tim, start laying our alternate into the FMS."

Sanders recapped the entire incident to QAL dispatch over the next two minutes.

"Dispatch concurs. We're diverting to Gander, Newfoundland," Sanders announced.

"Dialed in and ready to verify," Evans immediately replied.

"I'd better talk to the passengers." Sanders picked up the handset and connected it into the PA.

Ladies and gentlemen, this is the captain. As you noticed, we had a little problem sustaining cruise power on the engines a few moments ago. Everything is operating just fine now, but to be on the safe side, we're going to divert to Gander, Newfoundland. We should be on the ground there in ... Sanders turned to Evans who mouthed the answer ... *40 minutes. QAL will arrange for accommodations for all of you for the night, and a new airplane will be dispatched for the continuation to Paris tomorrow. We apologize for the inconvenience, but we're sure you understand that we want to be cautious. Sit back and relax and we'll have you safely on the ground soon.*

Ken Tillman clasped his wife's hands to reassure her, though she wasn't particularly nervous. Tillman was certain there was more to the event than what was just explained by the captain, and he was eager to get the full story once they landed. *The crew seemed to be doing a commendable job in handling this situation*, Tillman thought, and he was determined not to distract them from their work.

Evans retrieved the Gander approach charts, though he anticipated a visual approach on such a clear night. With the FMS now fully programmed, Evans maintained a watchful eye on the EICAS systems for any further sign of trouble. None was forthcoming.

Boston: 02:02 UTC (9:02 P.M. EST)

Glenn Seyfat looked down at his pager. It didn't go off often, but when it did it was always something he needed to know.

QAL 222, BOS to CDG, diverting to YQX after momentary partial power loss on both engines. Landing at 02:40 UTC.

Seyfat studied the screen of his pager. *Now that's curious*, Seyfat thought. Seyfat knew that all key personnel at QAL were receiving the same message from Systems Operations Control (SOC), including the Director of Maintenance (DOM), the Director of Operations (DOO), and program managers of the various safety programs such as Aviation Safety Action Program (ASAP), Flight Operations Quality Assurance (FOQA), and others.

Seyfat had established a procedure to conference call on incidents of this level, so he expected that the Director of SOC, John Simmons, would be calling soon. Just then the phone rang. "Hi, John."

"Hi, Glenn. Well, this one is curious, isn't it? Hold on a minute and I'll get the others on the line."

In a few moments, Seyfat, Simmons, DOO Don Doppermeyer, and DOM Todd Jacks were on the telecon. Simmons briefly described what he knew, which wasn't much more than he had just sent via the pager.

"Don, what do you think?" asked Seyfat.

"Well, I'm not sure. A dual engine power loss? Who was the captain, Jack Savage? I think we need some answers," replied DOO Don Doppermeyer. A veteran airline manager, Don had been employed at QAL in various positions for more than 25 years, and had seen it all. Almost all.

"Jack Savage? You've been watching too many old movies! I agree about the answers. An interesting side note to this, I remember Ken saying that he was going to Paris with his wife. I'm just certain they were on that plane. Anyway, I assume we'll be dispatching a go-team to Gander to take a look. Is that right, Todd?"

"We have a contractor on the field at Gander and I'll have them take a look, but I'd also like to send our own team up there. John, are you sending a ferry plane for the passengers? If so, let's put our team on it from St. Louis."

"Good plan. I've already authorized the plane. We're accommodating the passengers for the night, but we need to have them on their way to Paris by mid-morning. That means a plane needs to be on its way to Gander within the next couple of hours. Can you have your team ready by then?" asked Simmons.

"Done—I'll get right on it."

"We really need to get that plane back in service as soon as possible," Simmons said, stating the obvious.

"Agreed, but we also need to have some answers about what caused the problem. We want to make decisions based on facts, not on a 'could not duplicate' finding," said Seyfat.

"I think we'll have more than that," Jacks interjected. "Let's let the team get there and take a look. I'll ask them for an initial reading as soon as possible."

"I predict that we're all going to have a busy day tomorrow. Anything else? See you then," said Seyfat.

"Good. I'll send out another alert when the plane's on the ground. Goodnight, everyone," Simmons said.

Approaching Newfoundland: 02:45 UTC (00:15 P.M. NST)

"QAL Flight 222 is cleared to land," came the comforting words from the Gander tower.

After landing Sanders guided the Boeing to the arrival gate, and the passengers were offloaded and shuttled to nearby hotels. After their in-flight adventure, most of the passengers seemed pretty happy just being on the ground.

The crew met in the airport conference room for a debriefing as Sanders had ordered. Tillman joined them while his wife waited in the lounge.

"I just spoke with maintenance," Sanders explained. "We have a contracted maintenance facility here on the field, and they're going to take a look at the plane.

Regardless of what they find, a ferry bird will arrive tomorrow for the passengers as I indicated earlier. Our own maintenance go-team will be on the plane. The company will decide tomorrow whether we're flying home or whether we'll be dispatched someplace else. For now, we're checking into the crew hotel. Everyone get some rest, and good job tonight."

"My wife and I will continue on to Paris tomorrow. Probably wouldn't look good if the president of the airline didn't get back on the plane tomorrow with the rest of the passengers. Good work everyone," Tillman said.

At the hotel, Sanders, Evans and Tyler conferred one more time about the flight and their handling of the strange event. Finally, they separated and went to their respective rooms. Sanders plopped his bags on the floor next to the door and looked longingly at the bed. But he decided he had one more task to complete. He broke out his laptop, connected to the QAL safety website, and filed an ASAP report. Three rooms down the hall, Evans did the same.

Gander Airport: 03:30 UTC (01:00 A.M. NST)

As Jim Jacobs turned into the parking lot at DA Aviation Services, he saw the QAL Boeing 757 being towed into the hangar. A qualified 757 technician, Jacobs had gotten a call from his supervisor forty-five minutes earlier asking him to return to work to diagnose an engine problem. Jacobs had clocked out at midnight after an eight-hour shift, and now, tired and hungry, he was back on the job. He clocked in, grabbed a cup of coffee, and rolled the maintenance computer workstation over to the big airplane.

Jacobs turned on the computer, scrolled to the 757 maintenance procedures, and double-clicked. While that was loading, he climbed into the 757 to retrieve the maintenance log.

That was strange, Jacobs thought, as he read the captain's entries. *Both engines? Simultaneously? So the cause had to be something common to both engines.* Following the procedures on the screen, Jacobs checked a host of computers, systems, and components.

Jacobs completed all systems tests. *Nothing.* Everything seemed to be operating correctly. Jacobs was puzzled. *Common to both engines*, he though. *Perhaps something in the throttle quadrant—couldn't hurt to look.* Jacobs pulled some tools from his box and climbed back up to the flight deck.

After a few minutes of disassembly, the technician inspected the interior of the throttle quadrant and immediately noticed a foreign substance. "What the heck is that?" Jacobs exclaimed to no one but himself.

Inspecting further, Jacobs felt a sticky substance covering the inside of the throttle quadrant. *Perhaps a liquid was poured in there and dried*, Jacobs thought. *Not sure what it is, but there's a lot of it. No harm in removing it.*

After a few more tests called out in the maintenance procedures, Jacobs decided he had done all he could do to solve the mystery. His supervisor had told him earlier that QAL's guys would be arriving early in the morning. They would no doubt replace some of the components with spares, and send the replaced parts back to the shop for further testing.

Only thing left is the maintenance entry, Jacobs thought. '*Procedures followed, could not duplicate' will be the essence of it.*

At 4:15 a.m., Jacobs was headed home, again.

Boston: 12:00 UTC (07:00 EST) QAL Headquarters—'Morning Call'

Day 2

"It's 7 o'clock so if everyone's here, let's get started," said Seyfat. As Director of Safety, Seyfat chaired the morning call every day. In the room or on the phone were the principle people involved in safety for QAL: DOO Don Doppermeyer, DOM Todd Jacks, SOC John Simmons, ASAP manager Joe Quick, FOQA manager Lisa Tada, Boeing 757 fleet Chief Pilot Bill Ledder, and safety representatives from the pilot and maintenance unions. Also joining the discussion as usual, via phone, were two FAA inspectors: the Principle Operations Inspector (POI) from the FAA's Boston Certificate Management Office (CMO) Sandy Peters, and Inspector Tom Grunch who recently joined the FAA and was still in training.

Seyfat began with his customary briefing on the purpose of the morning call— to review the previous day's activities and discuss any anomalies that need to be considered by the safety team. He gave his traditional introduction to the meeting:

"I know you all have heard me say this a hundred times now, but I don't care." He looked around the room with the usual grin on his face. "We can't let ourselves get lost in the details of the post-mortem. Our focus is the Risk Management Plan. Let's learn what we can from yesterday, and make sure our RMP has no holes in it. Tom, this is your first morning call with us—have you had a chance to review the RMP yet?"

The POI spoke up. "We've been talking about it over here."

"Good," said Seyfat. "We'll stick with tradition then and do the 3 minute RMP brief next Monday like we always do. Let's see—Lisa it's your turn next week, right?"

"Yes," said the FOQA manager.

"Okay, let's get on with it," and Seyfat plunged in. "We all know we have a big event to discuss, but let's do the other stuff first." For the next five minutes Simmons assumed his role as Director of Systems Operations Control and went through the usual litany of events from the preceding day—a bird strike in ABQ, a flight attendant with a sprained ankle following a turbulence encounter, weather delays and a diversion in the southeast U.S.

"Let's move on to QAL 222. For those of you who may not know, 222 was a Paris-bound 757 that experienced a partial power loss on both engines at cruise lasting for about two minutes. They diverted to Gander, and we sent a go-team there last night on a ferry bird. The passengers should be on their way to Paris shortly. Todd, what have we heard from our maintenance crew?"

"Glenn, our team landed about two hours ago so they haven't done much yet. Our contractor, DA Aviation Services, took a quick look last night and couldn't find anything. Our guys are into it now. They called me about 30 minutes ago and said that so far they haven't found the smoking gun. They took plenty of spares, so they'll get it going once they pinpoint the problem. We should know something in a few hours. It's nose number 123, go figure. No history of recent engine problems, 11,000 hours airframe time, about 2,000 on the left engine, 1,200 on the right following a FOD event, bulbs and brakes since then."

"I saw the page last night and came in early this morning to check the reports," explained Joe Quick. "Both the captain and first officer filed ASAP reports last night. I called and woke up the union and Federale ERC reps this morning, and asked them to review the reports. Tom, we have a secure website that allows them to do that. The reports have already been accepted into ASAP."

"Good," replied Seyfat. "So we all understand that the investigation we're about to do is covered under ASAP, correct?"

"Lisa, I'd like your team to analyze the FOQA data as soon as possible. The crew checked the box on the ASAP form to agree to that, right Joe? Todd, I assume that the go-team is pulling the information?" asked Seyfat.

"Absolutely, we'll get it to safety and maintenance by mid-morning."

"I know that we all know this, folks, but just a reminder... Only two departments are authorized to look at the data, okay?" reminded the pilot union representative.

"We're all clear on that," offered Seyfat.

"We've got a couple of planes down, so we sure could use 123 in Miami as soon as possible," said Simmons.

"Understand," said Seyfat. "But we need answers first. This was a hell of a strange and potentially serious event that, at the moment, we can't explain. I don't want to put anyone on that airplane until we can explain what happened and be assured that it won't happen again."

"Agreed," said Doppermeyer. "Or at least have taken every reasonable precaution."

"Okay, folks. Let's learn all we can in the next few hours and reconvene at 2 o'clock," said Seyfat.

"So, Todd," began Tom Grunch with a hint of indignation in his voice. "I'm not really hearing a plan yet. Aside from troubleshooting the plane, what specifically are you going to do before putting it back into service?"

Sandy Peters appeared to be a little chagrined at his younger colleague, but didn't say anything.

The DOM chimed in. "Well, Tom, as Glenn said earlier, our plan is to make decisions based on solid information. We don't have enough information to formulate a plan as of yet, but we should know more soon. What more would you like for us to do?"

"I think we should agree that the plane won't be flown until you can tell us what happened," suggested Grunch.

Sandy shifted in his seat. "Hmm. That's an interesting suggestion, Tom, let's talk about that off-line in a few minutes."

"Okay, see everyone at 2", said Seyfat, and the meeting was concluded.

After the call was over, the POI turned to his new investigator. "Just to clarify, the way this works is that we're invited in to observe how the airline makes its decisions, and the processes they use for making them. We constantly assess whether those processes are in accord with their SMS, and the interface with our oversight responsibilities. The fact is, they haven't made any decisions about moving the airplane, they've handled the appropriate paperwork, they seem intent on gathering information before reaching any conclusions and, so far, they've kept us in the loop. I'm satisfied with that. Let's see where they go from here."

"Well, perhaps. Other inspectors have told me that it's really our jobs to either agree or disagree with their plan—effectively to approve it or not. I know the SMS discusses that relationship, but come on, we're still the ones with the Congressional mandate to oversee the safety of the national airspace system."

"I understand the mandate, Tom, but we do that a little differently today than in the past. The airline has responsibilities for safety as well. An SMS provides that mechanism wherein we can all manage safety in an effective way. Let's meet with them this afternoon and see how they move forward."

At about the same time nearly 1,000 miles away, Tillman, his wife, and two hundred thirteen other passengers were taxiing out in their replacement 757 for Paris. From his seat in first class, Tillman could see the QAL maintenance crew working on the engines of the airplane that had stranded them in Gander. Tillman was by no means a mechanic, and he knew he wouldn't understand the technical jargon of the maintenance write-up, but he was looking forward to a layman's explanation of what caused his plane to power down. *Soon enough*, he thought. For now it's off to Paris—finally.

Director of Maintenance Todd Jacks had a hands-on style, and had been in phone contact with his maintenance team periodically throughout the day, and each call left him a little more discouraged than the last. The computer readouts from the various black boxes were revealing *what* happened, but failed to shed any light on *why* it happened. Jacks had begun preparing himself for that unwelcome outcome.

Boston: 19:00 UTC (02:00 P.M. EST) QAL Headquarters

Seyfat convened the meeting with the same cast in attendance. "Okay, everyone, this meeting is specifically about 123, so let's get to it. What do we know?"

Jacks spoke first. "The team downloaded the DFDR and with concurrence of the ASAP guys, downloaded and examined the QAR as well. Tom, we did that because when we started FOQA we all agreed to use the DAR side of the box and use a 512 word-per-second LFL, focusing on engine parameters. But with the equipment they have on-site, they're unable to determine the cause. They've R&R'd all the likely components, throttle position sensors, Fuel Control Units, FADEC, etc., with the spares they had with them, and have shipped the components to the depot in St. Louis for more extensive analysis. Our team here has run the analysis on the data they pulled from the QAR and it's still a mystery. There are no definitive indicators of what caused the power loss, only that one occurred."

"No good news from FOQA either," replied Lisa. "We scrutinized it, but our analysts didn't see anything definitive. There is a data loss on some parameters right at the time of the event. No idea why yet."

Jacks continued, "They've run up the engines and done all the ground checks possible. Everything checks out." He paused. "Based on that analysis, the airplane is able to be returned to service."

"So we have a 'could not duplicate'," Seyfat sighed.

"It seems to me our choices are return to service or wait until the shipped components can be analyzed at the depot. That could be a few days," said Jacks.

"Well, nobody wanted the 'could not duplicate', but that's what we have," Simmons stated. "Maintenance says the airplane is ready to go, and we need it in Miami tomorrow morning."

"Okay, I'd like everyone to chime in on this one," Seyfat said. "Recommendations."

Simmons reiterated the need for getting the plane to Miami to meet schedule. The Director of SOC reminded the group of the cost of keeping a Boeing 757 out of service for a day, much less three or four, while components were analyzed. He encouraged a return to service decision.

Doppermeyer was next. While not enthusiastic, he concurred with Simmons.

"If it was just a 'could not duplicate', I'd be uncomfortable," Jacks began. "But we followed procedure by the book and have replaced far more hardware than required. The problem should not reoccur. My guys will sign it off and it'll be ready. We'll continue the investigation when we get the components and, if necessary, we'll send them to the manufacturer for analysis."

Seyfat turned to Bill Ledder. "Bill, we have a crew there and they're well rested by now. Are you comfortable launching them for Miami?"

"I believe so. I'll call Bob Sanders and brief him. He was the captain of the flight. He may want to talk with maintenance for a rundown of what has been done. I'll talk to him about route of flight. I suppose the crew could refuse, but we'll cross that bridge if we come to it."

"I've already asked the International Manager on Duty to generate a flight plan that keeps the aircraft over land all the way to MIA." Simmons offered.

"Okay, I gotta say from Safety's perspective I'm not comfortable, but we don't have a no-fly recommendation. Don, you're the DOO. You're the guy. What do you say?" Seyfat asked.

Don took a moment, then said, "Let's fly it. Todd, I assume our maintenance guys will be in back?"

"You're not asking for a ferry permit, correct?" asked Sandy Peters.

"That's correct. We have a signed off, serviceable airplane. No permit needed," assured Jacks.

Grunch might be the new inspector on the block, but he seemed to have no hesitation in expressing his opinion. "Wait a minute. Have we done everything we can here?"

"Well ..." Jacks voice slowed down and dropped an octave. Everyone who knew him knew what that meant. "We could buy a new airplane, put this one up on eBay.

Would you concur with that plan?" He had great confidence in his maintenance crew on the ground. They had a good airplane, and he had things to do.

The DOO stepped in before Grunch could respond. "Guys, this is what we get paid the big bucks for. What else, specifically, should we do before we ferry 123 to MIA?"

There was silence. Doppermeyer said, "Okay, we fly. John, have your planners do what they have to do to keep 123 off the Atlantic route for a while. Sandy, not to put you on the spot here, but as the POI, any advice?"

Peters said, "Not at this time. Don, don't put 123 up on eBay just yet. You know we're not happy until you're not happy. Keep us in the loop." He decided that a discussion with his new inspector was in the cards for the near future.

"The ERC meets tomorrow morning," Quick interjected. "The timing would work out to conduct a phone interview with the crew. That could be important in this investigation, but we need to get some things on the table right now. We all know we need to share whatever we learn, inside this group, at least. But it will be the crew that decides to what extent that happens. And we need to move forward with the assumption that the ERC will determine if any corrective action is needed for the crew. No company discipline, no FAA action. Agreed?"

"Agreed," said the Director of Ops.

"But Joe," said the POI. "You know we can't say this is a sole source report. So I will not rule out FAA action. If the ERC says LOC or LOW, that's what we'll do."

A Letter of Correction or Warning wasn't as bad as having a certificate yanked, but as ASAP manager, Joe knew that issuing such letters could inhibit the flow of information from the pilot group. He had worked hard to build trust, and he was intent on defending it.

"I know, Sandy, I know, but I want to go into the meeting asking both the ERC and the crew to work toward a decision that will allow us to share their report with this group. Some crews consider that risky business, so I need to hear from you all a commitment to not play Whack-A-Mole with this crew. You give me that assurance here, I'll relay it to them tomorrow."

The Director of Operations offered, "Joe, I fly the line too. You might be covering my a... I mean my rear someday. You've got my support."

"Thanks Don," said Joe. "And our vigilant overseers at the FAA...?"

"Captain Quick, our job is to support FAA policy, and FAA policy is to trust the ERC. That's what we'll do."

"Excellent," Seyfat concluded. "I bet we'll hear an interesting story tomorrow. Let's reconvene then. In the meantime, everybody, think RMP. What impact does this event have on our present Risk Management Plan? Lisa, you're at bat next Monday. Impress us with your insights in your RMP review. Okay, let's go see if anything else is happening besides 123."

Note to Reader: This fictional story will continue in the Epilogue. Following its conclusion, we'll challenge you to think about where SMS was exhibited in the story, where you detected a positive safety culture, the management interventions and processes that solved the mystery, and what role oversight played in this case. But for now, it's time to delve into SMS!

Chapter 1

Introduction to SMS

Ah, this is obviously some strange usage of the word "safe" that I wasn't previously aware of.

Douglas Adams

This is a good time to be reading a book about Safety Management Systems (SMS) in aviation. Regulatory authorities, safety experts and industry leaders have proclaimed that SMS represents the future of safety management in the aviation industry. SMS has been prevalent in other countries for years, and is now gaining traction in the United States. SMSs provide organizations with a powerful framework of safety philosophy, tools, and methodologies that improve their ability to understand, construct, and manage proactive safety systems. Exciting opportunities will be available for people who are knowledgeable and skilled at SMS.

In the past aviation safety improvement was characterized by a fly-crash-fix-fly approach. We would fly airplanes, have the occasional unfortunate crash, and we would investigate the cause(s) to prevent it from happening again. Sometimes the causes would be weather-related or a mechanical failure, but more often the cause would be determined to be human error—usually the pilot. Essentially, the prevailing philosophy was once the cause was determined to be the pilot, we simply needed to encourage other pilots not to make the same mistakes.

Today we realize that it is much more productive to engineer a system in which, to the extent possible, causes of failure have been *designed out*. As one might imagine, there are many elements to this engineering effort, and many of these will be discussed in this book. The modern, well-informed aviation safety practitioner must have a working understanding of hazard identification, risk management, system theory, human factors engineering, organizational culture, quality engineering and management, quantitative methods, and decision theory.

SMSs are not just for aviation—they are found in a wide variety of diverse industries, such as chemical, oil, construction, occupational health, food, highway, electrical, fire protection, and others. SMSs are not new concepts in these industries—references to SMSs in the literature of some of these industries can be found as far back as the early 1980s. Many of these industries had historically poor safety records and have benefited from the philosophy and structure SMSs provide.

SMSs are not just in the U.S. Many people mistakenly think that the United States always leads when it comes to aviation safety. While the U.S. does have an enviable safety record, other countries are considerably farther along in their efforts to develop and implement aviation SMS programs. Transport Canada committed to the implementation of SMS in aviation organizations in 2005. Europe and New Zealand, to name two others, have moved forward with SMS more quickly than the U.S.

ICAO definition of SMS

The International Civil Aviation Organization (ICAO),[1] a specialized agency of the United Nations, codifies the principles and techniques of international air navigation and fosters the planning and development of international air transport to ensure safe and orderly growth. ICAO has mandated that its 190 member States develop and implement SMS programs to achieve an *acceptable level of safety* in aviation operations. This requirement presently applies to Annex 6—Operation of Aircraft, Annex 11—Air Traffic Services, and Annex 14—Aerodromes, of the statutes. In response, the Federal Aviation Administration (FAA) issued AC 120-92 (dated 06/22/06), *Introduction to Safety Management Systems for Air Operators*. The advisory circular (AC) introduces the concept of a safety management system (SMS) to aviation service providers (for example, airlines, air taxi operators, corporate flight departments, pilot schools), and provides guidance for SMS development by these organizations. The AC applies to both certificated and non-certificated air operators that desire to develop and implement an SMS.

ICAO has required that its member States develop and implement SMS programs to improve safety, and the FAA is encouraging aviation service providers to develop an SMS. Of course, the overarching goal is to improve safety, and the experts representing ICAO believe that deployment of an SMS is the best means of accomplishing that goal.

ICAO's definition of "SMS" is "an organized approach to managing safety, including the necessary organizational structures, accountabilities, policies and procedures" (ICAO, 2006, 1-2). The following paragraphs will decompose the term Safety Management Systems to better understand it, and present a definition that attempts to capture the essence of SMS.

SMS defined

Safety

Safety means different things to different people. In the Merriam-Webster Online Dictionary, the definition for "safety" is given as follows: "the condition of being safe from undergoing or causing hurt, injury, or loss" (Merriam-Webster Online Dictionary, 2007). How this definition is applied is, in part, a function of our circumstances. For instance, if you *live* near a nuclear power plant, safety means that whatever happens in such a facility doesn't adversely affect your health and

---

1 The International Civil Aviation Organization (ICAO) is a specialized agency of the United Nations and was created with the signing in Chicago, on December 7, 1944, of the *Convention on International Civil Aviation.* ICAO is the permanent body charged with the administration of the principles laid out in the Convention. It sets the standards for aviation safety, security, efficiency and regularity, as well as for aviation environmental protection, and encourages their implementation. ICAO's membership comprises 190 Contracting States. Its headquarters are in Montréal and it has regional offices in Bangkok, Cairo, Dakar, Lima, Mexico City, Nairobi and Paris.

well-being. To those *constructing* the nuclear power plant it means efficient control of the nuclear chain reaction, proper cooling of the reactor core, and prevention of the release of radioactive materials. If you are a downhill skier, you want to reach the bottom of the slope without a broken ankle, sprained arm, or a head injury. In the context of Webster's definition of safety, that is, "freedom from danger or injury", did the downhill skier embark on a *safe* activity when he took off down the slopes? Was he *free* from danger or injury? In that context, is *anything* safe? Most of us drive to work or school every day. However, more people are killed or injured in this country in automobile accidents (approximately 44,000 deaths per year) than any other activity. Surely we're not all considered "unsafe".

To the traveling public, the term "safety" means, at its most fundamental level, that we want to reach our destinations without getting hurt. Since people do get hurt on occasion, it is logical to conclude that we are willing to accept some risk in traveling. Whether consciously or subconsciously we know that there is some chance, albeit a minute one, that we could be hurt or killed while traveling.

Today we average about 50 accidents in commercial airliners in this country each year, as "accident" is defined by the National Transportation Safety Board (the averages are about 2 "major", 3 "serious", 20 "with injury" and 25 "with damage"). Despite the horrific images and 24/7 press coverage that major accidents attract, the traveling public is sophisticated enough to realize that when the odds of any one flight being your last one are so remote (that is, 1 to 4.9 million), "safe" is a reasonable word to apply to commercial aviation.

But of course as safety professionals, we have to be considerably more sophisticated in the use of that word. *Safety* is defined by ICAO as "the state in which the risk of harm to persons or of property damage is reduced to, and maintained at or below, an acceptable level through a continuing process of hazard identification and risk management" (ICAO, 2006, p. 1-1). (Actually, ICAO's definition might best be thought of as relating to safety *management*.) This definition recognizes that the risk in the activity is not reduced to zero, but rather to an acceptable level. It also suggests that safety of the activity is measured against the acceptable level. And it explains that we maintain safety by a process. That process involves identifying the hazards that impede safety, and managing risks.

So for safety professionals, the very word "safety" implies constant measurement, evaluation, and feedback into the system. Safety is a verb, and an active one at that.

At the simplest level, we collect data about events and try to discern trends. We will get into greater depth later concerning the appropriate use of statistical tools in SMS, but for now let's take a look at some statistical charts to help understand the *state of safety* in our system today. First, Figure 1.1 depicts the number of fatal accidents for U.S. air carriers from 1987 through 2006 (14 CFR 121, scheduled service) (NTSB, 2007a, Table 6). The dashed line is a best fit regression which comfortingly indicates that the trend during this period seems to be decreasing. Of course these are raw numbers and, consequently, they do not really tell us if we're becoming more or less safe.

Figure 1.2 shows the accident *rate* per 100,000 air carrier *departures* (14 CFR 121 scheduled service) from 1987 to 2006 (NTSB, 2007a, Table 6); thus, it normalizes the data by taking into account the increase in air travel. The figure shows two

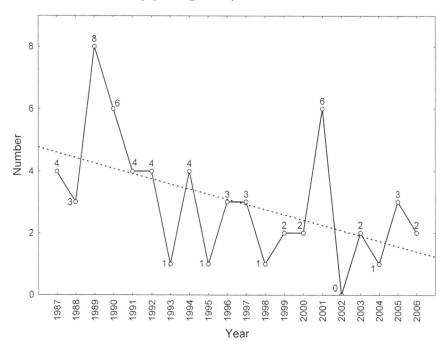

Figure 1.1   U.S. airline accidents with fatalities from 1987–2006, 14 CFR 121 scheduled service

rates—one for all accidents and one for accidents with fatalities. The "all" accidents line (top) shows a slight increase over time, while the "with fatalities" line (bottom) shows an overall decreasing rate. Most people might examine this chart and conclude that these data support the use of the word "safe", considering the ICAO definition.

SMSs will affect all aspects of aviation—not just airlines, so let's take a look at general aviation safety statistics (see Figure 1.3) (NTSB, 2007c, Table 10). As opposed to the airline safety data which were based on number of departures, the general aviation statistics use number of flight hours. Again, the (dashed) trend lines (all accidents rate is the top line, fatal accident rates is the bottom) are in a downward slope, which is good, but that still doesn't tell us whether we're safe.

Finally, it's worth noting the *relative* safety among airline (14 CFR 121, scheduled), air taxi (14 CFR 135, scheduled) (National Transportation Safety Board, 2007b, Table 8), and general aviation operations, as shown in Figure 1.4. Clearly, general aviation has a significantly higher accident rate (although it has been steadily decreasing) than either air taxi or air carrier, and air carrier is the lowest of the three. Probably everyone that views this chart will have a different perception about the level of safety that exists in each of these operations, the trends associated with each, and the reasons for the differences.

This discussion underscores the point that as safety professionals or others interested in safety as a discipline, we must understand the concept of safety as complicated, and only having real meaning when considered in light of processes designed to control the outcome.

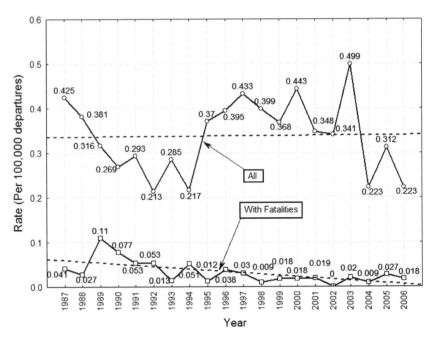

Figure 1.2   **U.S. airline accident rate per 100,000 departures from 1987–2006,
"all" and "with fatalities", 14 CFR 121 scheduled service**

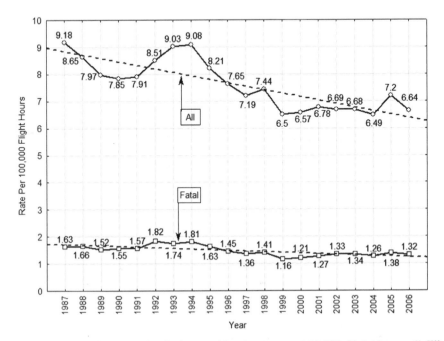

Figure 1.3   **U.S. general aviation accident rates per 100,000 flight hours, "all"
and "with fatalities", from 1987–2006**

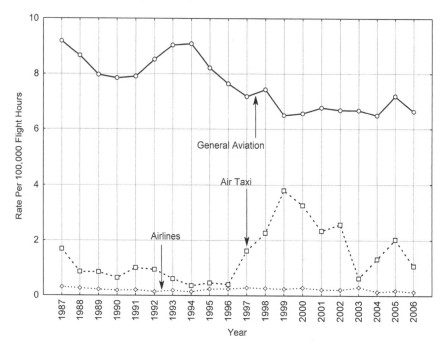

Figure 1.4   Comparison of accident rates per 100,000 flight hours among airlines (14 CFR 121, scheduled), air taxi (14 CFR 135, scheduled), and general aviation in the U.S. from 1987–2006

Management

A generally accepted definition is that *management is the process of getting activities completed efficiently and effectively with and through other people.* The functions normally associated with management are planning, organizing, staffing, directing, controlling, and (sometimes) budgeting. *Management* is leading and directing an organization or an activity through the deployment *and manipulation of resources* (something managers do), whether the resources are human, financial, intellectual, material, or other.

Systems

The dictionary defines "systems" as "a regularly interacting or interdependent group of items forming a unified whole" ("systems". Merriam-Webster Online Dictionary, 2007). A system is more than the sum of its parts. A useful way to think about the concept of systems is that it is an amalgam of people, procedures and processes, and equipment that are integrated to perform a specific function or activity within a particular environment.

Definition of SMS

The following is offered as a comprehensive definition of SMS: *A dynamic risk management system based on quality management system (QMS) principles in a structure scaled appropriately to the operational risk, applied in a safety culture environment.*

This definition and its components will be examined in some detail throughout this book. This section includes only a cursory overview.

Risk management systems   An SMS system is, at its core, a dynamic risk management system. A review of the current guidance in risk management is revealing, and is an indication of how paradigms in the safety community are still in the process of shifting, even among the proponents of SMS. We will first review current risk management theory as promoted by the FAA and ICAO, and then describe an alternate view.

In both FAA and ICAO guidance documents, *risk* is described as a measure of the expected losses which can be caused by an undesired event, factored with the probability of the event occurring; that is, risk equals severity x likelihood, or:

$$R = S \times L$$

Even the best safety analyses a few decades ago were forensic in nature. Note that this definition of risk is also. The two measures on which this traditional calculation of risk is based both depend upon an analysis of undesired events. Moreover, the data from which these calculations are drawn are historical. For example, suppose that a hard landing occurs. A forensic approach to risk analysis would have the safety department look into the various safety databases maintained by the airline, and review the "hard landing" reports on file. After review of those reports, subject matter experts would assign a measure of severity to the reports, and then aggregate those assignments into an index that describes the severity of the hard landing event. Then an attempt would be made to calculate a rate statistic (the number of hard landings divided by the exposure statistic, in this case the total number of landings in the system), thus deriving the likelihood of occurrence index. Using these two indices, a final "risk index" would be obtained by referencing a risk matrix. A typical risk matrix is shown in Figure 1.5 (FAA, 2006, p. 15).

Most operators have a management guidance document that describes appropriate mitigating action and allowable timelines for corrective and preventive actions, based upon this risk index.

Accomplishing this process on the various types of undesired events experienced in operations also would give the management team the ability to prioritize actions based upon the relative value of the risk indices assigned to each event type.

This analytic approach applied to understanding undesired events is a great improvement over that utilized in the past. However, this traditional "severity *x* likelihood = risk" calculation is by its very nature backward-looking, and does not by itself capture the essence of SMS. An SMS also accomplishes risk analysis at the *constituent element* level of a system, where hazards are identified. In its most sophisticated form, risk analysis is based on model-building, in which estimates of the range of potential severities, possible likelihoods, and measures of the effectiveness of those controls put in place to mitigate hazards are allowed to interact with each other over and over in scenario-modeling software, with the result being a prediction of the most probable outcome of events. Forensic analysis of undesired events is an important method of identifying hazards, but not the only one.

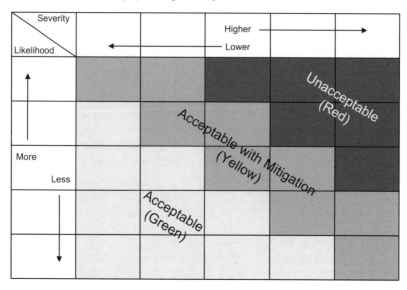

Figure 1.5   Risk matrix

Risk and reliability   As we have described in the classical view of risk management, the focus is on the event—the evaluation of its severity and the likelihood of its occurrence. These considerations remain active in an SMS, but a concept from quality engineering is added; that is, reliability. Reliability is a measure of a system's ability to operate without defects or errors, and is consciously *designed into* a system. A reliability approach to risk management uses quality engineering techniques to modify system design, adding parallel subsystems, redundancy, alerts, barriers, and so forth. Reliability will be covered in greater depth in Chapter 3.

Risk management   Risk management is the process of measuring risk and developing strategies to manage it. These strategies usually include reducing the negative effect of the risk. In the forensic risk analysis equation above, changing the severity [S] or likelihood [L] would accomplish that task. A quality engineered approach will include a rigorous analysis of the system of interest—identifying hazards, understanding the interactions between these hazards, and engineering detection systems, incorporating parallel and/or redundant systems when appropriate, and determining clear go/no go decision points. Finally, as SMS is incorporated into an integrated management system, strategic risk planning will include transferring the risk (for example, to insurance carriers), avoiding the risk, and/or accepting the consequences—in whole or in part—of the risk (see Figure 1.6).

It is important to note the following regarding risk management strategies:

1. They are not mutually exclusive. Choosing one of them doesn't mean you can't also choose others. In fact, often these strategies will be mixed and combined to varying degrees.
2. The individual strategies are not an all-or-nothing proposition. Strategies can be and often are partially deployed.

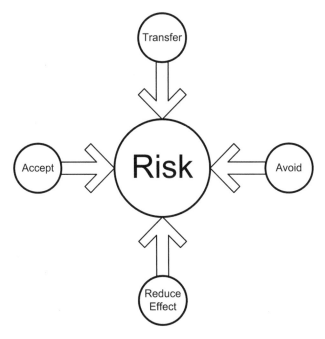

Figure 1.6 Strategic risk management

3. The strategies are somewhat of a balancing act.
4. The decisions regarding risk management must be made by the organization's management.

Production versus protection Risk is evaluated in the context of the *production* versus *protection* concept. Production refers to the product or service that is the objective of the organization. Production could be the air traffic services, flight training, airport services, maintenance services, or other activities, depending on the nature of the organization. It is the successful production of the intended service that enables an organization to remain in business.

Because there are hazards in aviation, a consequence of production is safety risk. This risk necessitates the creation of a *protection* system for users and stakeholders, which is a responsibility of the aviation service provider (most directly) and the regulating authorities. This protection system is fundamentally what an SMS should provide.

The production and protection goals must be balanced by the management of an organization. Often this balance is fragile; too much production may compromise safety and too much safety may compromise financial performance.

The purpose of a risk management process is to identify hazards and attendant risk associated with those hazards, and to manage and reduce the risks. A widely used process, and one espoused in the FAA's AC 120-92, includes the following steps (FAA, 2006, pp. 12–17):

1. *Systems and task analysis.* System design is the cornerstone of risk management. A documented systems and task analysis should thoroughly

describe and explain interactions of the components of the system, including people, hardware, software, and environment.

2. *Hazard identification.* Considering the system described in the previous step, hazards must be identified, documented, and controlled.

3. *Risk analysis and assessment.* As discussed above, risk is evaluated by its two components: likelihood of undesirable event occurring, and severity of the occurrence.

4. *Severity and likelihood criteria.* The tool normally used for this is a matrix with severity along the x-axis and likelihood along the y-axis.

5. *Risk Acceptance.* The risk matrix allows for categories of acceptance to be graphically depicted as, for example, acceptable, acceptable with mitigation, and unacceptable.

6. *Other risk assessment tools for flight and operational risk management.* In the last decade, a number of tools have been developed for the air carrier world that can be used to provide additional assessment of risk. These tools—Voluntary Disclosure Reporting Program, Aviation Safety Action Program, Flight Operations Quality Assurance, Maintenance Operations Quality Assurance, Internal Evaluation Program, Advanced Qualification Program, and Line Operations Safety Audit—will be explored in detail in later chapters.

7. *Causal analysis.* Root cause analysis is performed to determine why risks are assigned certain levels and as a first step in developing means to reduce risks to lower levels.

8. *Controlling risks.* Examples of controls include: new or modified procedures, new or improved hardware or software aids, changes to training, new or modified equipment, or other controls. This is the heart of the improvement.

9. *Hierarchy of controls.* A typical hierarchy of controls is: design the hazard out through system modification; physical guards or barriers (such as guards on certain switches); warnings, advisories, or signals of the hazard; procedural changes to avoid or mitigate the hazard; and training. The process of selecting the appropriate controls should be approached in a structured manner.

10. *Residual or substitute risk.* This step involves an assessment of the controls to ensure new risks are not being introduced into the system and that the control selected is likely to be effective.

11. *System operation.* When the controls are implemented, the system is placed in operation and monitored to ensure effectiveness.

Returning to our definition of SMS—a dynamic risk management system based on quality management system (QMS) principles in a structure scaled appropriately to the operational risk, applied in a safety culture environment—let's briefly consider QMS principles.

Quality Management System (QMS) principles

QMSs are systems that outline the policies and procedures necessary to improve and control the various processes that will ultimately lead to improved business performance. *SMSs are based on QMS principles.* These principles can be found throughout an effective SMS program. One of the primary organizations that promotes quality is the International Organization for Standardization (ISO),[2] which is a non-governmental, international standards setting body composed of 157 member countries. A brief overview of the principles of QMS as articulated by ISO includes the following (ISO, 2007):

- *Principle 1 Customer focus.* Organizations depend on their customers and must understand current and future customer needs. Organizations should meet customer requirements and strive to exceed customer expectations.
- *Principle 2 Leadership.* Leaders establish unity of purpose and direction of the organization. Effective leaders create and maintain an environment in which people can become fully involved in helping the organization achieve its objectives.
- *Principle 3 Involvement of people.* People are the essence of an organization and their full involvement serves to benefit the organization.
- *Principle 4 Process approach.* Managing activities and resources as processes enable desired results to be achieved more efficiently.
- *Principle 5 Systems approach to management.* Identifying, understanding, and managing interrelated processes as a system contributes to the organization's effectiveness and efficiency in achieving its objectives.
- *Principle 6 Continual improvement.* Continual improvement of performance must be a permanent objective of the organization.
- *Principle 7 Factual approach to decision making.* Analysis of data and information leads to effective decision making.
- *Principle 8—Mutually beneficial supplier relations.* An organization and its suppliers are interdependent and a mutually beneficial relationship enhances the ability of both to create value.

These eight principles should be kept at the forefront of any effort to develop and manage SMS programs.

Our definition also includes the phrase *scaled appropriately to the operational risk.*

Scaled appropriately to the operational risk.

Clearly, one size will not fit all when it comes to SMSs. These safety management programs must take into account the operational risk that exists in the particular aviation organization. Various factors will influence the operational risk, including nature of the production activity, and size of the organization. The primary objective of the SMS—safety—should be achieved regardless of where the organization is on the risk continuum or its size.

---

2 Founded on February 23, 1947, the International Organization for Standardization (ISO) is a non-governmental, *international* standard-setting body composed of representatives from *national* standards bodies. ISO sets world-wide industrial and commercial standards which often become law through treaties or national standards.

Further, many risks must be managed on a scale beyond any one organization's boundaries. For example, runway incursions remain consistently near the top of everyone's list of scary occurrences. When one looks at the list of stakeholders involved in this issue, and at the list of contributing factors, it is clear that a true fix of the runway incursion problem requires action on the part of many organizations—airlines, charter operators, maintenance organizations, airports, catering services, etc. An SMS designed to mitigate this risk must therefore be appropriately scaled to include all stakeholders as active participants, with common goals and shared accountability. The challenge of designing a management system that can be effective in such collaborations will be discussed in later chapters.

Finally, some safety issues require attention all the way from the bottom to the top of the food chain. These issues, national or even global in scope, are being addressed in many creative and promising programs, such as the Commercial Aviation Safety Team and its component Joint Implementation Measurement and Data Analysis Team, the Joint Planning and Development Office, and the Distributed National Archive. These programs are evolving into central components of a national Safety Management System.

Finally, from our definition, an SMS is *applied in a safety culture environment.*

Safety culture environment.

Culture is defined as the values, beliefs, and norms shared by a group of people that influence the way they behave. We are all influenced by cultural issues. Organizational psychologists tell us that there are three distinct cultural environments that we need to understand (Helmreich, 1998):

1. national culture encompasses the value system of particular nations,
2. organizational/corporate culture differentiates the behavior found in various organizations, and
3. professional behavior differentiates the behavior found in different professional groups.

These various cultures set boundaries for acceptable behavior and provide a framework for decision making. It is within the intersection of these environments that a *safety culture* evolves, and it is generated from the top down.

A safety culture is regarded as a fusion of these desirable cultures within an organization:

- *Informed culture:* People are knowledgeable about the human, technical, organizational and environmental factors that determine the safety of the system as a whole.
- *Flexible culture:* People can adapt organizational processes when facing high temporary operations or certain kinds of danger, shifting from the conventional hierarchical mode to a flatter mode.
- *Reporting culture*: People are prepared to report their errors and experiences.
- *Learning culture*: People have the willingness and the competence to draw conclusions from safety information systems and the will to implement major reforms.

- *Just culture*: People are encouraged, and even rewarded, for providing essential safety-related information. There is a clear line that differentiates between acceptable and unacceptable behavior.

Chapter 11 will cover safety cultures in greater depth, and describe the inextricable tie between a strong safety culture and successful implementation of SMS.

The four pillars of SMS

As described in Advisory Circular (AC) 120-92, SMS is structured upon four basic components of safety management: policy, safety risk management, safety assurance, and safety promotion. All four structural elements must exist and must be robustly executed in order for an SMS to be effective. In AC 120-92, the FAA has chosen to represent these principles as the "four pillars", and so it is important, especially for the reader in the U.S., to understand the concepts behind the image. The following description of the four pillars borrows heavily from AC 120-92, with some additions and edits for clarity or expansion of concept.

Pillar 1—Policy

Every type of management system must define policies, procedures, and organizational structures to accomplish its goals. An SMS must have policies and procedures in place that explicitly describe responsibility, authority, accountability and expectations. Most importantly, safety must be a core value for the organization.

Safety and quality   SMS uses quality management principles, but the requirements to be managed by the system are based on an objective assessment of safety risk, rather than customer satisfaction with products or other conventional commercial goals. These requirements must be explicitly referenced in SMS policy documentation, and must be fully integrated into the organization's mission and vision.

Roles, responsibilities, and relationships   In today's complex operational environment, many organizations and agencies are charged with some aspect of maintaining the highest levels of safety. SMS acknowledges this shared responsibility, and specifically describes the roles, responsibilities and relationships between all stakeholders involved in maintaining safe operations. In SMS, each interface between production and operation, on the one hand, and oversight on the other, is clearly identified, and each subsystem is designed to provide the interfacing agency or organization everything it needs to perform its role.

Executive management involvement   A primary characteristic of an SMS is its absolute clarity in defining that the key factor for success is top management's personal, material involvement in safety activities. While all members of the organization must know their responsibilities and be both empowered and involved with respect to safety, the ultimate responsibility for the safety of the system cannot be delegated down from top management. SMS identifies key behaviors that demonstrate this involvement, such as inclusion of safety goals into strategic plans, and regular management review of the SMS. Executive management involvement is a key requirement in SMS policy documentation.

Procedural frameworks SMS policy must include clear requirements for all operational departments to document their procedures, controls, training, process measurements and change management systems.

Pillar 2—Risk management

A formal system of risk identification and management is fundamental to controlling risk to acceptable levels. A well-designed risk management system describes operational processes across departmental and agency boundaries, identifies key performance indicators and regularly measures them, methodically assesses risk, and exercises controls to mitigate that risk.

Systems analysis and engineering Risk management requires a detailed understanding of operational systems. The system consists of the organizational structures, processes, and procedures, and the people, equipment, and facilities used to accomplish the organization's mission. Systems analysis is the heart of quality engineering, and a well-done systems engineering analysis will explain the interactions among the hardware, software, people, and environment that make up the system in sufficient detail to identify hazards and perform risk analyses.

Hazard identification Once processes are well understood, hazards in the system and its operating environment can be identified, documented, and controlled. The first step in the process, hazard identification, is based on a thorough understanding of the system, emphasizing the importance of the previous steps concerning system description. Once the system is well-understood, one can review the written system description or the process workflow diagram and at each component of the workflow, ask the question "what if...". What if this component failed? What if that threat appeared? What if the other error was made? As with system and task descriptions, judgment is required to determine the adequate level of detail. While identification of every conceivable hazard would be impractical, aviation service providers are expected to exercise due diligence in identifying significant and reasonably foreseeable hazards related to their operations.

Risk analysis and assessment SMS encourages risk assessment decision-making and acceptance through use of a consistently applied process, such as that described in the ICAO Safety Management Manual. Later chapters will cover risk assessment in detail.

Risk acceptance Operations are never undertaken without some level of risk, so the correct approach to risk management is the development of risk acceptance procedures, including acceptance criteria and designation of authority and responsibility for risk management decision-making.

Causal analysis   Risk analyses should inevitably lead to causal analyses, which in turn are provided to the operational managers for process modification, or fed back into the safety assurance component of SMS. Causal analysis provides the basis for continuous improvement.

Controlling risk   Once the preceding steps have been completed, risk controls must be designed and implemented. These may be additional or revised procedures, new controls, changes to training, additional or modified equipment, changes to staffing arrangements, or any of a number of other system changes. SMS requires that clear lines of responsibility and authority be drawn that assign the task of controlling risk.

System operation   The risk management component of SMS should be designed to not only continuously monitor, assess, analyze and control risk, but also provide the next component, safety assurance; an efficient means of auditing, analyzing, and reviewing the results of its efforts. Risk management works in concert with safety assurance to ensure effective functioning in a changing operational environment.

Pillar 3—Safety assurance

Once policies, processes, measures, assessments, and controls are in place, the organization must incorporate regular management review to assure safety goals are being achieved. Solid change management processes must be in place to assure the system is able to adapt.

The relationship between Safety Risk Management and Safety Assurance   In SMS, an organization's effectiveness in managing risk is derived from an objective assessment of risk in the organization's operation. While this differs somewhat from the criteria used to evaluate a quality system (that is, customer expectations), the safety assurance functions in SMS have their origins in the international quality management standard, ISO 9000. In the U.S. airline environment, a significant part of the safety assurance function is assigned to the Internal Evaluation Program (IEP) outlined in Advisory Circular 120-59.

Information for decision-making   Safety assurance uses information from a variety of sources; audits, investigations of safety-related events, monitoring of key process indicators in routine operations, and information submitted by employees into employee reporting systems. A key concept in SMS is that these various oversight systems should feed into a system of management review.

Internal audits   SMS assigns immediate responsibility for the safety of every process within an organization to the owner of that process. Process owners are the domain technical experts in any organization and thus the most knowledgeable about the technical processes involved. Managers within operational departments are assigned the responsibility for monitoring their own processes through an internal auditing program.

Internal evaluation   SMS also defines an additional audit function at the organizational level. This level provides a quality assurance function to assure that the more in-depth and technical reviews accomplished by the departmental internal audits are accomplishing organizational goals by assessing and mitigating risk. In U.S. airline operations, this is the Internal Evaluation Program, or IEP. These audits provide executive management the information for decision-making required for the evaluation of the overall SMS.

Integration of regulatory and voluntary programs   In many aviation organizations there exists a mixture of both voluntary safety programs and ones required by regulation. SMS does not supplant those programs required by law, nor does it eliminate the value of others established voluntarily. Instead, SMS provides a framework for all of these programs to integrate into a coherent safety assurance strategy.

External audits   External audits provide yet another level of safety assurance. These audits may be required by regulation, or may be third-party audits initiated by the organization to provide an objective evaluation of its processes. Once again, SMS does not supplant the need for these external oversight systems, but rather considers these audits as another information source for management review.

Analysis and assessment   Perhaps the most important part of any continuous improvement process is the consistent application of management review. If management review is not a routine part of the organization's calendar, all of the other components of the SMS system are useless. In addition, management review must include well-defined change management processes, so that intelligence gained from analysis and assessment can be applied to decrease operational risk.

Monitoring the environment   Just as assessment of the business environment must be a regular part of strategic planning, SMS acknowledges a similar need to continuously monitor the operational environment to assess new threats and monitor existing ones. The safety assurance component must incorporate such assessments on a routine basis.

Pillar 4—Safety promotion

Finally, the organization must continuously promote safety as a core value with practices that support a sound safety culture.

Safety cultures   One of the most challenging elements of SMS is the creation and nurturing of a safety culture, in which every person, from CEO to new-hire, understands his or her role in maintaining a safe operation, and actively participates in controlling and minimizing risk.

Creating a safety culture begins at the top of the organization, with the incorporation of policies and procedures that cultivate a *reporting culture* (where structures are in place that allow safety-related information to flow from all levels of the organization into a system empowered to correct problems), and a *just culture* (in which individuals are both held accountable for their actions and treated fairly by the organization). Maintaining a safety culture requires constant attention by every layer of management and every department within the organization. A central tenet of SMS is this realization—that the safety department does not *own* safety, rather it is owned by every employee.

Communication   To support a reporting culture, the organization must cultivate the willingness of its members to contribute to the organization's understanding of its operation. Since some of the most valuable reports involve self-disclosure of mistakes, the organization must make the commitment to act in a non-punitive manner when those mistakes are not the result of careless or reckless behavior. An SMS must have mechanisms to allow employees to submit reports on safety deficiencies without fear of reprisal.

An SMS must also have robust mechanisms to disseminate information to its workforce so that each employee has timely access to safety-related information. Knowledge Management Systems support SMS by identifying the type of information each employee needs, and providing targeted means to disseminate that information.

Organizational learning   Information has no value unless an organization learns from it. An SMS must incorporate controls to assure that lessons learned influence the design of its systems. An SMS must be a closed-loop system, in which an audit trail exists to demonstrate that a discovery in the risk assessment and analysis process leads to causal analysis, which is then used in a preventive/corrective action process to modify the operation and reduce risk. It further requires that lessons learned be regularly incorporated into a continuing qualification program for relevant employees.

Emergency response

In both ICAO and FAA documentation, emergency response is included as an integral part of SMS. For readers already familiar with existing emergency response requirements in ICAO and FAA regulations, and with existing emergency response programs at large air carriers and airports, the inclusion of this topic in SMS planning and implementation can immediately arouse suspicion. Why, one might ask, do we once again need to revisit something that is already very highly regulated, which already requires significant resource assignment within the organization, and which already works pretty well? A common concern is that any additional requirements imposed by an SMS system will only be burdensome and increase complexity, with little return on investment as to the quality of emergency response.

To that criticism we would point the concerned reader to a component of our own definition of SMS, as a program "scaled appropriately to the operational risk'. The natural evolution of safety management in our industry has driven the reactive response to disasters such that emergency response *is* already well-developed in areas of potentially high operational risk, such as at Class I airports or at major air carriers. Anyone involved in safety planning at a hub airport or large airline knows that existing ERPs (emergency response plans, as ICAO designates them) are very well developed and extensive, and by regulation regularly tested.

For those operators, it is very likely that existing ERPs will fulfill all SMS requirements, so fluster or panic is not necessary. For those existing well-developed programs, the extent of burden in incorporating their ERPs into an SMS framework will probably be very low. But we ask patience of the reader with this particular orientation, because, as mentioned earlier, SMS is intentionally a scalable system, whose principles apply for both the large and the small service provider. Therefore the general outlines for emergency response in SMS are worthy of consideration, with the knowledge that some levels of operation already have robust systems, while others will benefit from a review.

Chapter 11 of the ICAO Safety Management Manual is devoted to emergency response planning, and is in our experience the best single source of reference for a service provider to use to review the fundamentals of their own programs. There are of course specific regulations governing levels of emergency planning and response, dependent upon the location, scale and type of operations involved, but the purpose of our review here is to highlight the essences. Exhaustively covering the topic of emergency response is far beyond the scope of this book, and for a detailed review of the essentials the reader is referred to the ICAO document. But a quick review is in order, so that the SMS practitioner can understand how the ERP fits in to the larger philosophies and techniques of SMS.

The ICAO Safety Management Manual states that the purpose of an ERP is to ensure that there is (ICAO, 2006, p. 11–1):

1. orderly and efficient transition from normal to emergency operations,
2. delegation of emergency authority,
3. assignment of emergency responsibilities,
4. authorization by key personnel for actions contained within the plan,
5. coordination of efforts to cope with the emergency, and
6. safe continuation of operations or return to normal operations as soon as possible.

The purpose of requiring that an ERP be a part of an SMS is to ensure that a service provider has thought through each one of the enumerated items above, and has established a plan of operations prior to the need to use the plan. This purpose is entirely driven by the same underlying motivation that energizes SMS in the first place—the control of risk. In this case, the risk being controlled is not specifically aimed at the circumstances that led to the emergency (though SMS would drive the need to consider corrective action to prevent the emergency in the future, of course). Rather, the risk that is mitigated by having the ERP is that associated with handling the emergency itself.

An emergency is an event that is by its very nature high risk, certainly for those victims at the immediate scene, but also for first-responders, for those assisting those responders, and especially for those other customers who continue to receive services from the organization while the emergency is in progress, even if those customers are a thousand miles away from the scene. An ERP exists to control the organizational response to the emergency in such a way as to minimize the risk for all facets of the operation. An ERP is a control mechanism.

The ICAO document defines the following sections as constituent elements of a well-designed ERP:

- *Governing policies*. An ERP should have explicit references to the regulations governing emergency response in the organization's operational environment, and should contain the company policies and procedures that determine how the organization will respond to the emergency.
- *Organization*. Emergency response is a process, and ideally should be created using the same discipline as applies to the creation of any process under SMS (see Chapter 8). The ERP should describe who has responsibility and authority in various aspects of the response, how that response is conducted, what resources will be available, and so on.
- *Notifications*. The ERP should contain a very clear notification process, so that assistance is available when needed. Not to be neglected, of course, is the terrible task of notifying relatives of those involved in the event. Other steps in the ERP will also address the responsibilities the operator has to the families involved.
- *Initial response*. The initial response to an emergency is potentially a very high risk environment. This section should be especially well considered, keeping first-responders in mind.
- *Additional assistance*. The ERP should be designed such that backup is immediately available when needed. All available resources should be considered. This step feeds back into the notifications step.
- *Crisis management center*. A well managed emergency requires special infrastructure—communications, methods of coordination, quick command and control decision-making. Planning for a crisis management center is essential.
- *Records*. There are both regulatory and practical requirements for good record-keeping during an emergency. The ERP planning team should assure that all record-keeping requirements are identified, and that someone is assigned the responsibility for maintaining these records.
- *Accident site*. The accident site itself is an extremely high risk environment, and the operator must assure that no further harm is done in responding to the event. That means access control must be a part of the plan, and protective equipment must be available for first-responders. There are regulatory responsibilities the operator has concerning protection of the site, and those responsibilities must be assigned.
- *News media*. It is inevitable that an operator involved in a serious emergency will have contact with the media. Having a plan to control that contact might not immediately seem like risk management, but it is. The media interfaces with other groups the operator clearly has responsibilities to, such as the families of victims and employees. Not the least of the reasons to have a media plan in an ERP is to assure that those actually managing the crisis are isolated from a barrage of questions and requests by the media, so that they can do their jobs.

- *Formal investigations.* The operator needs to plan on how to support the formal investigations that are an inevitable part of post-incident operations. The time required to support such investigations can be quite significant, and good planning beforehand can help assure that company interests are represented without removing critical personnel from routine operations.
- *Family assistance.* The operator clearly has a responsibility to the families of victims; not only a moral one, but a legal one. Those responsibilities include setting up family assistance services, travel accommodations for family members, financial assistance in some circumstances, and especially satisfying the need for accurate and up-to-date information concerning the event.
- *Post-critical incident stress counseling.* The effects of a serious emergency do not end with the cleanup of the accident site, or even the closure of the investigation. Emergency events can be by their very nature traumatic, and the operator has a responsibility to consider the human factors involved in emergency response, such as duty times during the event, time off afterward, and especially the provision of post-incident counseling should it be necessary.
- *Post-occurrence review.* The essence of SMS is continuous improvement. As such, an ERP should include plans to debrief everyone involved in the event, and should require a post-incident review of activity.

Readers familiar with ERPs existing at major air carriers or airports will recognize these elements as already existing in the emergency planning documentation required by regulation. Smaller operators would be well served to review their own procedures in light of these ICAO suggestions. An ERP that covers these issues will satisfy all the requirements in SMS—as long as one other step is included.

Management review is one of the most important steps in any quality process, and since SMS is exactly that—a quality process—it is essential that an ERP contain within it the requirement for regular management review of the plan. And with something as serious as the ERP, that review cannot be only a document review. It is necessary to exercise the plan on a regular basis. Large operators and airports already have such a requirement mandated by regulation. For smaller operators embracing SMS, it is very important that the ERP is actually taken off the shelf at regular intervals, and run in a simulated environment.

For those in the U.S. the Department of Homeland Security has created outstanding resources for operators to use to create a schedule for emergency response exercises. There is no need to reinvent the wheel—a smart management team will take advantage of this excellent work, and appoint someone in the organization to become fully certified in the HSEEPS program (Homeland Security Exercise and Evaluation Program). This training is designed to support emergency management, and a well-designed toolkit exists to assist in the creation of all levels of emergency response practice—from table top drills, to functional practice, to full scale exercises.

How to recognize an SMS when you see one

The previous section exposed the reader to what (in the U.S. at least) might be considered the orthodox disquisition of SMS, through the four pillars. While conceptually sound, the SMS practitioner needs an in-depth understanding of the fundamentals, a comprehension deep enough to be able to enter any organization, at any level, and recognize the elements of a successful SMS as they might exist, in many different forms.

Throughout this book we will use every opportunity we can to take apart SMS and lay the components out on the table in front of us—examining those pieces in detail, and then putting it all back together only to take it apart in a different way. It's important for the reader to understand that in doing this we are not suggesting that the conceptual structure the FAA has created in the four pillars, or the outline used by ICAO, is the wrong way to describe SMS. Just as any complex system can be viewed from a variety of perspectives, each contributing to our understanding of the whole, deconstruction of the components of SMS can help us assure that we have a solid grasp of the discipline. It is incumbent upon the SMS student or practitioner to comprehend not just the large components, but the details.

Recognizing an SMS by looking at the organization's documentation and records

Suppose you walk into an aviation service provider's office, and have three hours to find evidence that the organization has an SMS. What would you look for?

Policy   This is the same word as is used in the first pillar, but with a distinction. A careful reading of the four pillars guidance reveals that other important concepts are included under the heading of policy. In addition to references to the importance of clear policy guidelines in SMS, there is also a discussion of process definition. Policies and processes are two different concepts. And while there is an acknowledgement of the necessity of record-keeping in the advisory circular, we will elevate this topic to equal that of policy.

Policies are the shalls and shall-nots of the organization, and tend to be more fixed than process descriptions. Policies reflect the strategic vision and commitment to the values of the organization. Policies also provide guidance for the creation of new processes, and standards against which processes or process measures can be evaluated. For example an organization might (should!) have a policy stating "All process descriptions will identify one or more Key Process Indicators (KPIs) through which the performance of the process can be evaluated." Or perhaps a policy might specify that "All processes will clearly define the roles of responsibility for and authority over that process."

Policy documentation is extremely important to SMS. Just as a Quality Management System must have a Quality Policy Manual, an SMS must have the equivalent of a Safety Policy Manual. You can recognize an SMS by its documentation.

Process descriptions   An organization with an SMS will understand what you mean when you ask to see examples of its process descriptions. Process descriptions can be as simple as a set of instructions for an employee to use to do his job, or as complex as a multi-departmental process workflow diagram. The best process descriptions will follow a standardized format, so that no matter which one of the organization's many processes you examine, you can readily tell who is responsible, or how they measure the success of the process, or which records must be kept. We assert that quality based process descriptions are the distinguishing feature of a mature SMS.

Process measurements   Just as a quality organization knows that it must establish measures within its processes to enable continuous monitoring of performance, so must an SMS have measures within processes to determine whether those processes are meeting their safety targets. In an SMS, measures are directed at those points within the process that are most revealing of risk. An SMS does not collect data in order to collect data. The SMS practitioner in that organization can readily answer why a particular process measure has been established.

Record-keeping   An organization with an SMS is good at keeping records, and can readily answer why it does so. And that reason is not in order to be prepared for audits. Of course there are regulatory reasons for keeping many records, but from an SMS perspective records are kept in order to facilitate management review. Those records include the process measurements described above, but also include narratives submitted in an employee self-reporting system, results of internal and external audits, and even those parameters not directly associated with safety issues, such as routine operational performance numbers (flights per day, fuel logs, maintenance schedules, and so on).

But perhaps most importantly, an SMS carefully records, and frequently references, the decision-making processes involved in management review. For incidents and events (reactive safety), this kind of record includes categories such as what happened, why did it happen, what was the effect, how are we going to decrease the risk of such an event, who is responsible for the action, and, critically, did it work? For proactive and predictive safety efforts, the record includes what *might* happen, why it might happen, etc., down to how will we tell if our intervention is working? Management review requires the availability of good records, and an SMS will be able to readily produce them when needed.

Risk assessment   An organization's SMS practitioners will be able to immediately answer when asked the question "How do you assess risk?" Their answer will reveal that they have a process for that assessment, not just a guess. That is not to say that every SMS must have software to run Monte Carlo simulations, or use Probabilistic Risk Assessment, or stochastic modeling. Not every organization's methodology need be the same, though guidance is available upon which to build a risk assessment process. What all SMSs will have in common is a considered, rational and thoughtful way to assess and prioritize risk.

Recognizing an SMS by asking the most fundamental question of all—How do you manage change?

Even though this is only Chapter 1 of this book, we have already made the following suggestion, and you can count on seeing it frequently from this point forward: none of the preceding characteristics, methods or techniques have value at all in an SMS unless there is an effective safety change management process in place. A safety change management process is one that takes the results of all the work described thus far, and *acts* on it. A mature SMS change management process will be established and governed by policy, defined in a clear process description, and itself monitored in a management review tasked with assuring that successful action is an inherent part of the SMS. An organization with an SMS can not only describe its safety change management process, but can point to success stories that resulted from its application.

Recognizing an SMS by observing the organization's safety programs

Another characteristic of an organization with an SMS is that if you say to one of its SMS practitioners, "Tell me about your safety programs ...," you might as well find a seat and settle in for a long presentation. It is the nature of an SMS to be proactive, and the SMS practitioner has a natural proclivity to actively seek sources of new information and new methods of risk control. Chapter 2 of this book will cover a brief history of proactive safety programs in the U.S. (focused on airline operations for reasons we outlined in the Preface)—an SMS will likely have most if not all of them.

The characteristic of a safety program within an SMS is its proactiveness. The SMS practitioner in charge of such a program does not wait for events to happen, but rather uses every technique available to discover the information necessary to anticipate areas of increased risk, before they happen. A safety program manager within an SMS is proud of this fact, and will relate success story after success story, if you have the time. It's worth the investment to listen.

Recognizing an SMS by talking to the organization's employees

Picture yourself in the break room of an aviation service provider, in the middle of a group of its employees taking a short respite from their labors. These people are not executives, nor members of the organization's safety department, but they could be any other work group employed by the organization. Ask a few of them three questions, and from their answers you will begin to know whether the organization has a mature and well-functioning SMS. Those questions are:

1. What are the three greatest areas of risk in your work, and what do you do to mitigate that risk?
2. When was the last time that you or one of your fellow workers were asked to help figure out how to make the job and the company's products safer?
3. What happens to you when you make a mistake?

Everyone complains about their job now and then. Overlooking this fact of life, the employees of an organization with a mature SMS will be able to point out where the risk is in their work, because the organization has invested in ways to communicate that information to each employee. And not communicating just generic safety information, but information relevant to that specific employee's work. Those in charge also know that the most accurate and informed sources of risk information for every process within that organization are the employee groups performing that process. Therefore there will be mechanisms in place to tap this vital source of intelligence.

This is one of the most important features of an SMS. In an SMS, *the responsibility for safety is pushed out onto the shop floor.*

Finally, employees of an organization with a mature SMS understand that they are fully accountable for their actions, but not punished for unfortunate but natural human error. To the question of what happens when they make a mistake, the employees would answer that they would probably feel bad, maybe ashamed that they did it, but not enough to keep them from participating in the self-reporting systems the company has created. They understand that they are not responsible for being perfect, but are responsible for striving for continuous improvement, and one of the best ways to reach for that goal is to submit a report.

The remainder of this book will immerse the reader into significantly more detail about the history and components of, and the theory underlying, SMS. But once one is familiar with the concepts, recognizing a vibrant SMS is similar to distinguishing great art—you know it when you see it. Verification of the existence of an SMS is not presently accomplished (nor probably should it ever be) by merely the achievement of having 8 of 10 boxes checked on the "Is There an SMS Here?" form. SMS is far more organic and integral to the fabric of an organization, and there is no one-size-fits-all SMS. But once you are an SMS practitioner yourself, spend a short time visiting an organization with a mature program, and you'll know, because safety management is everywhere you look.

SMS in Practice

Nicholas Sabatini, FAA Associate Administrator for Aviation Safety, recently gave his perspective on the value he believes operating under an SMS provides an organization:

What is the next organizational step to improve an already excellent record?

Let me give you a three-word answer to that question. Safety Management Systems, or SMS. Safety Management Systems enable organizations to identify and manage risk. Managing risk is fundamental, and Safety Management Systems enable us to manage risk far better than before. With this formalized approach, we can identify issues, fix them, and ensure that they stay fixed.

Operating under a Safety Management System assures a disciplined and standardized approach to managing risk. The best part is we can review past experience and address known hazards and at the same time we can look ahead and rigorously apply Safety Risk Management principles to any changes or introduction of new elements.

Furthermore, under an SMS, the whole process—identifying potential problems and putting corrections in place—is ongoing and the procedure is continuously assessed to make sure it is working.

SMS is rigorous. It is measurable. And, it is repeatable.

In this era of competing demands, tight budgets, and high expectations, SMS enables all of us to focus our limited resources on the highest priority hazards. It will help us find, understand, prioritize, and fix problems early—when it is less expensive in both lives and dollars.

I have described Safety Management Systems in terms of process. Yet, what is equally important is that this disciplined approach to hazard identification, risk management, mitigation and measurement goes hand in glove with a safety culture.

Organizations that operate under an SMS are committed to safety. They know that success requires more than procedures, more than mitigations, more than measurement. It requires that safety be a way of thinking—a mindset.

Source: http://www.faa.gov/news/speeches/news_story.cfm?newsId=7509. (Excerpted statement of Nicholas Sabatini, Associate FAA Administrator for Aviation Safety to the Bombardier Learjet Safety Standdown 2006, October 4, 2006.)

Review questions

1. Explain the relative nature of the term "safe". Is commercial aviation getting more or less safe?
2. What is meant by the term forensic aviation safety management?
3. Why is it important that an SMS program is "scalable"? What are the possible consequences of the program *not* being scalable?
4. Why is it important that SMS programs be supported by top management?
5. Explain the concept of "safety being pushed out to the shop floor" in an SMS program.
6. Explain why a risk management system must be "dynamic" in order to be a part of an SMS.
7. Who is responsible and accountable for safety in an organization?

References

Federal Aviation Administration [FAA] (2006). *Introduction to Safety Management Systems for Air Operators.* Advisory Circular 120-92. Retrieved December 3, 2007 from http://rgl.faa.gov/Regulatory_and_Guidance_Library/rgAdvisoryCircular. nsf/0/6485143d5ec81aae8625719b0055c9e5/$FILE/AC%20120-92.pdf.

Helmreich, R. (1998). Building Safety on the Three Cultures Of Aviation. Proceedings of the IATA Human Factors Seminar, 39-43. Retrieved December 5, 2007 from http://homepage.psy.utexas.edu/homepage/group/HelmreichLAB/Publications/pubfiles/Pub236.pdf

International Civil Aviation Organization [ICAO] (2006). *Safety Management Manual (SMM),* 1st edn. (Doc 9859 AN/460). Montréal, Canada: ICAO.

International Organization for Standardization [ISO] (2007). *"Quality Management Principles."* Retrieved December 3, 2007 from http://www.iso.org/iso/qmp.htm.

National Transportation Safety Board [NTSB] (2007a). *Table 6. Accidents, Fatalities, and Rates, 1987 through 2006, for U.S. Air Carriers Operating Under 14 CFR 121, Scheduled Service (Airlines)*. Retrieved December 3, 2007 from http://www. ntsb.gov/aviation/Table6.htm.

National Transportation Safety Board [NTSB] (2007b). *Table 8. Accidents, Fatalities, and Rates, 1987 through 2006, for U.S. Air Carriers Operating Under 14 CFR 135, Scheduled Service*. Retrieved December 3, 2007 from http://www.ntsb.gov/ aviation/Table8.htm.

National Transportation Safety Board [NTSB] (2007c). *Table 10. Accidents, Fatalities, and Rates, 1987 through 2006, U.S. General Aviation*. Retrieved December 3, 2007 from http://www.ntsb.gov/aviation/Table10.htm.

"safety". Merriam-Webster Online Dictionary (2007). Retrieved December 3, 2007 from http://www.merriam-webster.com/dictionary/safety.

"systems". Merriam-Webster Online Dictionary (2007). Retrieved December 3, 2007 from http://www.merriam-webster.com/dictionary/system.

Chapter 2

History and Evolution of Safety

The safety of the people shall be the highest law.

Marcus Tullius Cicero

SMS in Practice

Dr. Tim Brady, Dean of the College of Aviation at Embry-Riddle Aeronautical University, writes about Daedalus, Icarus, and SMS:

How can we apply SMS principles to the first aviation fatality that "occurred" in Greek legend, that of the death of Icarus, the son of Daedalus?

If one were to establish a timeline, the accident occurred about 3,700 years ago near the island of Crete. The accident report, however, was not filed until Ovid reported the accident around the turn of the century, the first century that is. Ovid (Publius Ovidius Naso) was a Roman poet who was born 43 years before the birth of Christ and died in 17 AD. Clearly Ovid failed to visit the accident site, interview witnesses (who had passed on seventeen centuries earlier), or plot the flight path of Icarus. Nevertheless he did give us a limited description of the vehicle:

> Now Daedalus, the carpenter, had made a pair of wings
> Contrived of wood and feathers and a cunning set of springs

Our next bit of forensic evidence about the accident comes from John G. Saxe, an American poet and lawyer who, in the mid 1800s, describes the cause of the accident by relating the admonition of Icarus' father Daedalus:

> "My Icarus," he says, "I warn thee fly
> Along the middle track: not low nor high;
> If low thy plumes may flag with ocean's spray,
> If high, the sun may dart his fiery ray."

Ovid completes the report by describing the structural failure of the vehicle:

> and, bold in vanity, (Icarus) began to soar,
> rising upon his wings to touch the skies;
> but as he neared the scorching sun, its heat

softened the fragrant wax that held his plumes;
and heat increasing melted the soft wax—
he waved his naked arms instead of wings, . . .

There are several lessons that one can take away from this accident, the first is that perhaps all aircraft accident investigators should receive training as poets; the second is that a more formalized accident reporting system could have filled in the gaps represented by the 37 or so centuries between the accident and the data analysis, and the third is that neither Ovid nor Saxe had a clue about radiant energy and its scientific effect on wax.

But none of these observations relate to SMS which uses data collection and analysis to defeat the accident before it occurs, so let's return to the question posed in the first paragraph. How can we apply SMS principles to Icarus' accident?

We can surmise that no event reporting system existed at the time. If there had been one, it would have discovered that Daedalus had a penchant for scientific discovery which seemed to race ahead of his sense of family values. Daedalus was an accomplished engineer. He is reported to have invented both the saw and the sail, the latter of which, of course, is an airfoil. He was also accused of pushing his nephew off the top of a large Greek building in Athens. Some say he did it in a fit of jealous rage, jealous of his nephew's popularity compared to his own. But others say that the nephew's body was found at the base of the building somewhat enshrouded in a curious cloak of feathers and wax. From that point on, a bird similar to a dove was referred to throughout the Greek world by the nephew's name, Talus.

An alert SMS professional would have determined that Daedalus was performing unauthorized flight experiments and that his nephew, Talus, was in fact a test pilot killed while performing an experiment in aerodynamics. The SMS professional would have shared this data with others, particularly with colleagues on the island of Crete where Daedalus fled with his son Icarus. There, in the service of King Minos, Daedalus built a maze. Perhaps the SMS event reporting system eventually alerted King Minos that Daedalus was a threat to sound safety practices because Minos imprisoned Daedalus in the maze that he, Daedalus, had constructed. But because Minos did not correctly analyze the data and take stronger corrective actions, the system failed to prevent the mad scientist, Daedalus, from conducting one more experiment, this time with his son, Icarus. After all, the only way Daedalus could escape was to leap from the side of the cliff which intersected the maze with a set of wings that would support flight. But first he had to get the design right. He coldly observed the attempted flight of his son Icarus which ended in his death then redesigned his own set of wings and flew successfully.

The first fatal aviation accident

The date commonly attributed to the birth of aviation is December 17, 1903. It was during that year that bicycle builders Orville and Wilbur Wright took to the skies in a heavier-than-air, powered, and (somewhat) controllable craft they had constructed called the Wright Flyer.

The first aircraft fatality occurred only 1,736 days later with Orville at the controls. He had traveled to Fort Myer, Virginia, to demonstrate the Wright aircraft to the Army in September 1908. Orville was dissatisfied with one of the propellers so, on September 17th, he replaced it with a new one that had never been flight tested. A twenty-six year old Army Lieutenant, Thomas E. Selfridge[1], was the passenger onboard with Orville on the test flight. After a few circuits around the field at Fort Meyer, the end of the propeller blade flew off. The aircraft nose-dived from a low altitude; Orville was seriously injured, and Selfridge died only hours later. There were about 2,500 hundred witnesses to the crash, including famous aviator and friend of the Wright brothers, Octave Chanute. An investigation was conducted into the crash, and an accident report was submitted on February 19, 1909. The report stated, in part (Defense Technical Information Center, 1999):

> I examined most of the witnesses whose testimony is given above, immediately after the accident, on the field I was present when the Aeronautical Board made it's [sic] examination on the following day, September 18th, and talked at various times with Mr. Wright, Mr. Chanute, Professor Zahm, and others relative to the accident. At the time of the accident I was holding my horse and watching the machine from the upper end of the field near the starting point. When the machine struck, I galloped at once to the spot.
>
> On September 17th, Mr. Wright was almost ready to begin his official trials so he put on a set of new and longer propellers that day for the purpose of tuning up the speed of his machine preparatory to making his official speed trial. These propellers were probably 9 feet in diameter; the ones in use up to that time were probably 8 feet 8 inches in diameter.
>
> Lt. Selfridge was to leave for St. Joseph, Missouri, for duty in connection with Dirigible No. 1, on September 19th and was very anxious to make a flight before leaving, so Mr. Wright, at my suggestion, had said a few days before that he would take him up at the first opportunity. On September 15th and 16th, high winds prevented his making a flight. On September 17th, the instruments at the aeroplane shed recorded a northeast wind of four miles an hour. At 4:46 p.m. the aeroplane was taken from the shed, moved to the upper end of the field and set on the starting track. Mr. Wright and Lieut. Selfridge took their places in the machine, and it started at 5:14, circling the field to the left as usual. It had been in the air four minutes and 18 seconds, had circled the field 4 ½ times and had just crossed the aeroplane shed at the lower end of the field when I heard a report then saw a section of

---

1   Lieutenant Thomas Etholen Selfridge was born in 1882 and was graduated 31st in a class of 96 from the U.S. Military Academy at West Point in 1903. One of his classmates was General Douglas MacArthur, who graduated 1st in the class. Selfridge was the U.S. government representative to the Aerial Experiment Association, which was chaired by Dr. Alexander Graham Bell (inventor of the telephone). Selfridge is buried in Arlington National Cemetery, only a few hundred yards from where he crashed.

the propeller blade flutter to the ground. I judge the machine at the time was at a height of about 150 feet. It appeared to glide down for perhaps 75 feet advancing in the meantime about 200 feet. At this point it seemed to me to stop, turn so as to head up the field toward the hospital, rock like a ship in rough water, then drop straight to the ground the remaining 75 feet. I had measurements taken and located the position where the machine struck, 304 feet from the lower cemetery gate and 462 feet from the northeast corner of the aeroplane shed. The pieces of the propeller blade was picked up at a point 200 feet west of where the aeroplane struck. It was 2 ½ feet long, was a part of the right propeller, and from the marks on it had apparently come in contact with the upper guy wire running to the rear rudder. This wire, when examined afterward, had marks of aluminum paint on it such as covered the propeller. The left propeller had a large dent, and the broken piece of the right propeller had a smaller dent indicating that the broken piece flew across and struck the other propeller. The upper right had [sic] guy wire of the rear rudder was torn out of the metal eye which connected it to the rear rudder. I am of the opinion that due to excessive vibration in the machine, this guy wire and the right hand propeller came in contact. The clicking which Mr. Wright referred to being due to the propeller blade striking the wire lightly several times, then the vibrations increasing, it struck it hard enough to pull it out of its socket and at the same time to break the propeller. The rear rudder then fell to the side and the air striking this from beneath, as the machine started to glide down, gave an upward tendency to the rear of the machine, which increased until the equilibrium was entirely lost. Then the aeroplane pitched forward and fell straight down, the left wings striking before the right. It landed on the front end of the skids, and they as well as the front rudder were crushed. Both Mr. Wright and Lieut. Selfridge were on their seats when the machine struck the ground, held there by wire braces which cross immediately in front of the two seats. It is probable that their feet struck the ground first, and as the machine dropped nearly head first, they were supported by these wire braces across their bodies. When I reached the machine, the mounted sentinels at the lower end of the field were entering at the left hand end between the two main surfaces, which were now standing on their front edges. I found Mr. Wright lying across the wires mentioned above, trying to raise himself, but unable to do so. He was conscious and able to speak, but appeared very badly dazed. He was cut about the head where he had struck the wires, and possibly the ground. Lieut. Selfridge was lying stretched out on the wires, face downward, with his head supported by one of these wires. He died at 8:10 that evening of a fracture of the skull over the eye, which was undoubtedly caused by his head striking one of the wooden supports or possibly one of the wires. He was not conscious at any time. With the assistance of a couple of enlisted men I removed Mr. Wright from the machine and placed him on the ground where he was immediately taken charge of by Army surgeons, among them Major Ireland, who were among the spectators at the time of the accident. Lieut. Selfridge was carried out immediately and similarly cared for. At least two civilian surgeons among the spectators, whose names are not known, assisted in caring for both of them. Within ten minutes they were carried to the post hospital on litters by hospital corps men and were placed on the operating table. Captain Bailey, Medical Corps, U.S. Army, was in charge of the hospital at the time. He was assisted in the operating room by the surgeons mentioned above.

In the meantime the mounted sentinels had been placed around the aeroplane to keep back the crowd, a very difficult matter at the time. Mr. Wright was found to have two or three ribs broken, a cut over the eye, also on the lip, and the left thigh broken between the hip and the knee. He was in the hospital at Ft. Myer for six weeks under the care of Major

Francis A. Winter, and at the end of that time went to his home at Dayton, Ohio. Lieut. Selfridge was buried with full military honors at Arlington Cemetery on September 25th.

The wings on the right side of the machine were not badly damaged, those on the left side which struck the ground first were crushed and broken. Apparently the front rudder, skids, and left wings received most of the force of the fall. The rear rudder as shown on the accompanying photographs, exhibits "C", "D", and "E" was thrown down on the rear end to the skids and on the main body of the machine probably due to the shock on striking the ground. The gasoline tank was damaged sufficiently to allow the gasoline to leak out. The water cooler of the engine was somewhat twisted; the engine itself was not badly damaged and could probably be very easily put in running order again. I had the aeroplane taken to pieces and removed to the aeroplane shed the evening of the accident. It was afterward shipped to Dayton, Ohio, by Mr. Wright's direction.

In his testimony, Chanute stated he examined the propeller blade and believed that the wood was "brittle and over-seasoned, or kiln dried".

That was the essence of the report of the first airplane crash with a fatality. It is fascinating to read this report from the perspective of a century of aviation safety evolution, and recognize in the reporter's work the same painstaking attention to detail and objective analysis that we have come to expect from present-day NTSB reports. In the description one can see the progenitors of many of our present-day accepted practices in forensic analysis—crowd control and the principle of preservation of evidence, description of "witness" marks in the wreckage, identification of probable cause. We see in this report the essence of reactive safety analysis, necessarily reactive because as yet there was not sufficient experience to answer what-if questions and raise the level of safety to being proactive or predictive.

The problems identified in the report were corrected, and the U.S. Army signed to purchase the plane in 1909.

Government efforts to improve safety

The U.S. government played little role in promoting or regulating safety in the early days of aviation. As the growth of the aviation industry resulted in increasing public awareness of incidents and accidents involving aircraft, Congress eventually passed the Air Commerce Act of 1926. This legislation charged the Department of Commerce with the operation and maintenance of the airway system, and to provide safety through a system of regulation. It also granted authority to the Secretary of Air Commerce to investigate, record, and make public the cause of accidents in civil air navigation. In 1931 and 1937, strengthening of the legislation and associated regulations established the first standardized methodology for the investigation of accidents and incidents.

In 1938, the Civil Aeronautics Act was passed, establishing three agencies to oversee aviation:

1. Civil Aeronautics Authority—The Civil Aeronautics Authority's role was to legislate the safety and economics aspects of the air transportation industry.
2. Administrator of Aviation—The Administrator's role was to carry out the safety policies of the Civil Aeronautics Authority.

   3. Air Safety Board—The Air Safety Board's role was to investigate aircraft
      accidents.

In 1940, an amendment to the Civil Aeronautics Act reduced these three entities
to two. The Civil Aeronautics Board (CAB) was established as an independent
agency to exercise judicial and legislative authority over civil aviation, and to
control the economic regulations applicable to air carriers. The CAB's Bureau
of Aviation had direct responsibility for the investigation of aircraft accidents.
The second agency established in 1940 was the Civil Aeronautics Administration
(CAA), which was placed under the Department of Commerce. The CAA's
responsibility under this legislation was the execution of safety regulations,
including enforcement and promotion of aviation safety.

   Predominantly as a result of several mid-air collisions, including a spectacular
crash involving a TWA Constellation and a United Airlines DC-7 over the
Grand Canyon, and other factors, Congress enacted the Federal Aviation Act in
1958. This legislation was similar to the Civil Aeronautics Act in many ways,
but differed in that it greatly expanded the government's authority over aviation
safety. The former CAA became an independent Federal Aviation Agency. The
safety rulemaking powers were transferred from the CAB to the Federal Aviation
Agency, resulting in that agency having both rulemaking and enforcement
authority—a broad power that persists to this day. The CAB retained its role in
accident investigation under this Act, as well as the economic regulation of air
carriers.

   In 1966 the Department of Transportation was formed and the Federal Aviation
Administration (FAA) was incorporated into this new cabinet level agency. The
CAB was relegated to a role responsible only for the economics of the industry
(until its phase-out in 1985), and a new agency, the National Transportation
Safety Board (NTSB) was formed. The NTSB became a fully independent agency
in 1975, and is the single entity responsible for the conduct of transportation
accidents.

   Though the specific agency responsible for aviation safety has changed
through the years, and the sophistication of the tools available to the investigator
has increased tremendously, up until recently the basic methodology had changed
little. From the Secretary of Air Commerce, through the CAA and CAB, through
the FAA and now the NTSB, the primary method of research concerning the
mitigation of risk in aviation has been reactive—post-event analyses of incidents
and accidents. Many significant advances in safety have resulted from this
methodology: decreases in serious wake turbulence encounters due to greater
in-trail spacing, improved cargo compartment smoke detection systems, ATC-
based Mode C transponder intruder conflict alerting systems, improved windshear
detection systems at airports; the list of advances is long indeed, and proves the
worth of rigorous post-accident investigation. Several events would happen,
though, that would point to the need for a more rigorous, scientific, and proactive
approach to aviation safety. Two of these events—the crash of TWA Flight 514
and the Challenger Space Shuttle disaster—are discussed below.

Turning points

TWA flight 514

On the snowy Sunday morning of December 1, 1974, TWA Flight 514 was inbound to Washington's Dulles Airport. TWA Flight 514 originated in Indianapolis, with an intermediate stop in Columbus, Ohio, and had originally been scheduled to land at Washington National Airport. The flight had to divert to Dulles because of high winds at National. The crew received an approach clearance for a VOR/DME runway 12 at Dulles 44 miles from the airport. At 11:09 a.m., the Boeing 727 crashed into Mount Weather, Virginia, about 25 miles from Dulles, destroying the aircraft and killing all 92 people aboard.

The NTSB analysis of the accident revealed a number of systemic problems that directly contributed to the event (NTSB, 1975):

1. The failure of the FAA to take timely action to resolve the confusion and misinterpretation of air traffic terminology although the agency had been aware of the problem for several years;
2. The issuance of the approach clearance when the flight was 44 miles from the airport on an unpublished route without clearly defined minimum altitudes; and
3. Inadequate depiction of altitude restrictions on the profile view of the approach chart for the VOR/DME approach to runway 12 at Dulles International Airport.

But the most significant fact that the NTSB uncovered during this investigation was that this was not the first time this type of event had occurred. As the NTSB report described:

Ironically, approximately 6 weeks before the TWA accident an air carrier flight [a United Airlines flight], after being "cleared for the approach", descended to 1,800 feet while outside of the Round Hill intersection during a VOR/DME approach to runway 12 at Dulles. The carrier involved had implemented an anonymous safety awareness program, was in fact made aware of the occurrence, and subsequently issued a notice to its flight crews to preclude the recurrence of a near-fatal misinterpretation of an approach clearance. The Board is encouraged that such safety awareness programs have been initiated. It is through such conscientious safety management that the expected high level of safety in air carrier operations can be obtained. In retrospect, the Board finds it most unfortunate that an incident of this nature was not, at the time of its occurrence, subject to uninhibited reporting and subsequent investigation which might have resulted in broad and timely dissemination of the safety message issued by the carrier to its own flight crews.

The NTSB noted in the recommendations section of the final report that the FAA had already implemented one of its proposals in the creation of the Aviation Safety Reporting Program (ASRP). Details of the program had been outlined in FAA Advisory Circular (AC) 00-46. Interesting politics were at work behind the creation of this AC.

In the aftermath of TWA 514, the FAA was quick to accept the need for the creation of some sort of national safety reporting system, even before the publication of the NTSB final report on the accident. But as the drafts of the program were developed problems were immediately apparent. After decades of adversarial dealings with the FAA, pilots were extremely wary of submitting any report that could potentially be used against them or their colleagues. It became clear that the only way the system would work was if a neutral, *trusted broker* of voluntarily submitted information could be found.

In 1976, to answer the findings of the NTSB report, the FAA entered into a Memorandum of Agreement with NASA that created the Aviation Safety Reporting System (ASRS). NASA would be responsible for the design, data collection, report de-identification, and aggregate analysis of submitted safety reports. NASA would also be responsible for the dissemination of intelligence gathered from the aggregate analysis. The FAA would remain the source of funding for the system.

This structure has served the aviation community, particularly general aviation, but has not provided airlines with the data sharing mechanism described in the NTSB report on Flight 514. It was not until the last decade of the 20th century that this mechanism began to be built.

By the 1990s, investigators and regulators alike were coming to the realization that there was a limit to the effectiveness of post-hoc fixes to safety problems, and that limit was based upon relatively simple math.

Airline flight safety

Decreasing returns, increasing challenges

Figure 2.1 illustrates the overall effectiveness of the safety initiatives undertaken by government and industry in the last fifty-six years of airline operations. This figure clearly shows the spectacular success that decades of dedicated work had created—a precipitous decrease in the U.S. airlines fatal accident rate through the time period depicted (left *y*-axis) (ATA, 2007b). A best-fit line reveals the leveling off of the rate around 1980, which is, incidentally, the first year where there were no fatal U.S. air carrier accidents. Note that with the decreasing rate there is also a corresponding reduction in variability of that rate.

The same figure also shows a dramatic, almost uninterrupted growth in air travel in the U.S. from 1950 through the present date as indicated by the number of departures (right *x*-axis) (ATA, 2007a).

For the regulator and safety professional of the 1980s and 1990s, the combination of the relative flattening of the accident rate and the projections of substantial growth of the volume of air travel, resulted in a simple but sobering prediction—a projected increase in the number of fatal accidents in the U.S. This would be unacceptable to the traveling public. The track record of the airlines in 1994 would bring these worries to a climax.

Thirteen tragic months

Table 2.1 depicts the details of the airline crashes that resulted in fatalities during the thirteen-month period leading up to January 1995 (NTSB, 2007).

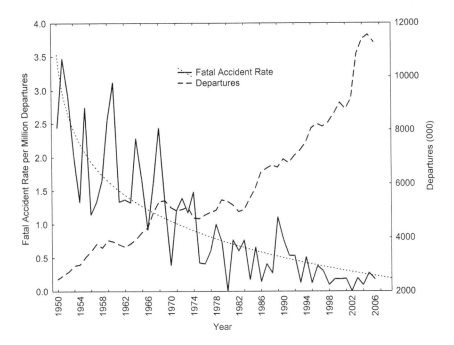

Figure 2.1   **Fatal accident rates per million departures and departures—U.S. air carriers operating under 14 CFR 121—1950 through 2006**

Table 2.1   **U.S. airline crashes with fatalities (CFR part 121 and 135, scheduled service) from December 1993 to December 1994**

Source: NTSB, 2007

Date	Carrier	Aircraft	Location	Fatalities
12/01/1993	NW Airlink	Jetstream 31	Hibbing, MN	18
01/07/1994	United Express	Jetstream 41	Columbus, OH	5
07/02/1994	US Air	Douglas DC-9	Charlotte, NC	37
09/08/1994	US Air	Boeing 737	Aliquippa, PA	132
10/31/1994	American Eagle	ATR-72	Roselawn, IN	68
11/22/1994	Trans World Airlines	Douglas DC-9	Bridgeton, MO	2
12/10/1994	Ryan Air Service	Cessna 402C	Elim, AK	5
12/13/1994	American Eagle	Jetstream 31	Morrisville, NC	15

SMS in Practice

FAA Administrator, Marion Blakey, talked about the importance of SMS given the commercial aviation accident rates in a speech before the 2006 International Safety Forum:

> We need a rigorous and formalized approach to identifying hazards, assessing the related risk, and identifying and prioritizing the best way to intervene. Then, we measure the effectiveness of our actions. It's a continuous loop. That's your basic safety management system. Make no mistake about this one: Safety Management Systems are the way to surmount those inevitable walls that seem impenetrable, the walls that seem to come out of nowhere, some of them below the surface just waiting to be discovered.

> It is tough to do, but I don't know that we really have much of a choice. Right now, the commercial fatal accident rate in the United States is about two fatal accidents for every 10 million takeoffs. The forecasts anticipate that we should expect a doubling or tripling of the amount of traffic in the system over the next 10 to 20 years.

> The question is elementary: Is it acceptable to us, or the flying public, if the number of accidents double or triple as well? I don't think so. We know that the passenger numbers continue to climb beyond a billion by 2015.

Source: http://www.faa.gov/news/speeches/news_story.cfm?newsId=7529. *(Excerpted statement of Marion C. Blakey, FAA Administrator to the 2006 International Safety Forum, November 2, 2006.)*

With a total of 282 fatalities during this thirteen-month period, the pressure on regulators from a wary and concerned public was intense. Of even more concern was the fact that the investigations of these incidents were not leading to a small set of common causes. The factors ranged across the spectrum; from training practices, to engine and airframe design, to faulty procedures; the list of things to fix was long, and growing. To all involved in the industry, it was becoming clear that a new approach was needed.

The 1995 Aviation Safety Summit

On January 9th and 10th, 1995, Federico Peña, then-Secretary of the Department of Transportation, called industry delegates from all over the nation together in the first ever Aviation Safety Summit. During the two day session, more than 950 representatives from airlines, unions, manufacturers, and regulators met to discuss the formulation of new initiatives to improve safety and increase public confidence. Peña and then-FAA Administrator David Hinson encouraged cooperation to reach a goal of zero accidents. Workshops and breakout sessions resulted in the identification of 540 issues by the delegates. In response, the FAA issued an Aviation Safety Action Plan on February 9, 1995, that included 173 safety initiatives.

This meeting stands as the single most significant event in recent history in terms of its effect on the way airline safety is conducted in the U.S. A host of new programs and structures were put into place: new requirements for a director of safety position at all airlines, requirements for Part 135 regional airlines to meet the same safety standards as their larger Part 121 counterparts, the creation of a new FAA Office of System Safety, new requirements for advanced flight data recorders—the list is long. A key outcome of the 1995 safety summit was a set of new airline safety programs, now known as proactive safety.

Focus on events in airline safety

Before beginning a description of airline-specific voluntary safety programs, it should be noted that these programs are primarily based on event analysis. Just as in Orville Wright's day, event analysis is still important; it has been the impetus for the creation of most of the safety programs we are about to discuss, but it will not be the most significant part of the future of SMS. SMS is not a forensic pass-time. Deeply rooted in quality, SMS demands of its practitioners the ability to honestly assess today's performance, compare that performance to a vision and a plan, and then move forward ever closer to those goals. The most important role of the SMS practitioners of the future will not be their analysis of a particular event; rather it will be in uncovering the precursors of such an event; engineering quality into the system, and measuring process indicators to detect when the system is in a state of control that prevents such an occurrence, or when it begins to stray.

That being said, the fact is that the aviation industry, at least the operational side of it, has not yet reached the point in which process measurement and control far outweigh fault or defect detection as a means of determining the state of quality of the system. Just as it took scores of years for the manufacturing sector to understand and embrace quality principles, the same is true for flight operations. Part of this time lag on the flight operations side is due to parochialism. After all, flying is "leading edge" (even that term is borrowed from us). What do we have to learn from widget makers?

Well, quite a lot. If you ask most modern widget maker product design teams what their Quality Function Deployment plan is, they will hand it right over to you. The same is true of their process capability measures—these are estimated even before the first production run. But for us—what is our process capability index for airspeed control from 1,000 AGL to touchdown?

"Don't know, we fly jets, not make widgets."

Maybe we *should* know.

But again, all of the above being said, the fact is that for the present state-of-the-art in flight operations, fault or defect detection remains, and will remain, an important component of this aspect of our quality management system (read *SMS*). In the defense of safety practitioners, the challenge we accept every day is an amazingly complex one, with hugely varying initial conditions, very precise and unforgiving tolerances, and high consequence of failure.

Events matter, we need to know about them, and thus the importance we place on understanding our core event detection systems in SMS, which make up the core of the modern safety department. In the U.S., these programs are often referred to as the *voluntary safety programs*.

Not all of the voluntary safety programs focus on the event. ATOS, AQPs, IEPs, and LOSAs are process-oriented programs, and FOQA can be used in process measurement analyses. Chapters 4 through 7 will detail the distinction between event analyses and process measurement analyses.

Another important point to make is that as the voluntary programs have emerged from the traditional forensic approaches to safety into the developing philosophy of SMS, they have brought along those issues that were so formative at their inception—de-identification and data sharing. We will return to these issues after a brief introduction to the programs.

In the previous chapter, we presented a high-level review of the government's regulatory approach to aviation safety. Notice the pattern in the evolution of these regulations. From aviation's beginnings through 1966, with the formation of the NTSB, there was an ever-increasing separation between the entity responsible for promoting and overseeing the operational aspects of aviation, and that entity responsible for analyzing the causes of its failures. This makes intuitive sense. The evolution toward independence was driven by the increasing clarity of the realization that objective evaluation requires independence. This conclusion is as true today as it was in 1966 (witness present-day FAA advisories concerning the need for independence in the management of Internal Evaluation Programs). And similar to the organizational evolution at the national level, this separation of responsibilities was taking place within corporate borders. Over time, independent safety departments were increasingly the entities responsible for event investigation.

The common theme in proactive safety

This common theme in proactive safety distinguishes it from the dominant methodology of the past, that of reactive investigation. The difference is essentially between descriptive and inferential analysis. When an aircraft crashes and an investigator arrives at the scene, the bulk of the data is, tragically, laid out before him. The task is to discover the clues that will eventually allow the detailed description of the event, and from that description, new layers of protection can be developed to prevent the same sequence from happening again.

In contrast, proactive safety programs use inferential analysis to describe a potential reality that is not yet manifest. As a first step in the solution of problems, reactive programs deduce the details of past events. Proactive programs infer the future from present observation. This distinction, not at all yet fully recognized within the aviation industry, requires a very different set of skills and tools than those existing in most safety departments today. Today's typical safety professional has risen through the operational ranks in the organization, and is a consummate subject matter expert. That expertise is a necessary but not sufficient qualification for quality work in a proactive safety program. Equally important is the ability to form hypotheses concerning how best to study and therefore predict areas of risk, design well-crafted information-gathering tools that collect relevant observations, and then apply appropriate statistical tools to the analysis of the aggregate data. Proactive safety, then, closely resembles scientific inquiry.

Proactive airline safety programs

The programs commonly accepted as having directly resulted from, or benefited from, the 1995 Aviation Safety Summit, and are considered to be a part of proactive safety are discussed in the following paragraphs.

Advanced Qualification Program   Advanced Qualification Program (AQP) changed the paradigm in airline flight training from a programmed-hours-of-instruction model to a train-to-proficiency model (FAA, 2006c). Central to the functioning of an AQP program is the Pilot Proficiency Database (PPDB). The PPDB is the repository for measures of pilot performance during training sessions. A requirement for every AQP program is the demonstration by the airline that it conducts regular analysis of this aggregate data to determine trends, and make appropriate modifications to the training program when necessary. Also required is the definition of mechanisms that incorporate into the training curricula lessons learned in other safety oversight programs.

Air Transport Oversight System   Air Transport Oversight System (ATOS) was a major change in the way the FAA conducts its oversight responsibilities (FAA, 2006a). Airline operations are divided into seven systems, based on processes rather than departments. Safety Attribute Inspections look at written procedures and determine whether important traits such as responsibility, authority, controls, process measurements, etc., are defined, and compliance with these requirements is measured in a standardized way. Similarly, Element Performance Inspections are accomplished to assure operational behavior is consistent with procedures and regulations. Both measures are entered into a national ATOS Database for aggregate analysis.

Aviation Safety Action Program   An Aviation Safety Action Program (ASAP) provides a mechanism for the observations of potential safety hazards by employees engaged in routine operations to filter up to decision-makers (FAA, 2002a). Designed to be non-punitive, robust protection mechanisms are built into the program to assure reporters are not penalized by reporting inadvertent errors. Every ASAP program is required to have some system to aggregate information extracted from reports and analyze that information to uncover trends.

Flight Operations Quality Assurance   Flight Operations Quality Assurance (FOQA) is regarded as the most objective of the proactive safety programs, in that it collects data recorded by an aircraft's flight data acquisition and recording systems and aggregates it into a database that incorporates a part or all of an airline's fleet (FAA, 2004). Routine flight operations are then analyzed by sophisticated software that identifies exceedances and trends. Every approved program must demonstrate some means of using the intelligence gathered from this analysis in the mitigation of risk.

Internal Evaluation Program   An Internal Evaluation Program (IEP) is an internal audit program that is required to possess two important characteristics (FAA, 2006a). First, there is strong encouragement for the IEP to adopt the same principles, and use the same checklists, that are a part of the FAA's oversight system, ATOS. Some means of aggregate analysis must be defined, so that overall trends can be identified. Secondly, the IEP program must be independent of the departments it is charged with oversight of. IEPs must report directly to top management within the organization.

Line Operations Safety Audit   In a Line Operations Safety Audit (LOSA), highly trained observers ride in the jumpseat of an air carrier during routine scheduled flights for the purpose of collecting safety-related data on flightcrew performance, environmental conditions, and operational factors (FAA, 2006d). The program relies on confidential data collection and non-jeopardy for flight crewmembers; that is, assurance that action will not be taken against those individuals observed to commit errors. LOSA is based on a Threat and Error Management (TEM) model, which is a conceptual framework for understanding operational performance in complex environments such as that found in commercial aviation. LOSA samples all activities in normal operations, as well as problems encountered during the flight and how the crew managed those problems. According to AC 120-90, LOSA is important for the following reasons (FAA, 2006d, pp. 3–4):

- Threats in the airline's operating environment can be more readily identified.
- Threats from within the airline's operations can be identified.
- The degree of transference of training to the line can be assessed.
- The quality and usability of procedures, such as crew callouts, can be checked.
- Problems in the human/machine interface can be more readily identified.
- Pilot shortcuts and workarounds can be identified.
- Safety margins can be assessed.
- A baseline for organizational change can be determined.
- A rationale for the allocation of resources can be determined.

Voluntary Disclosure Reporting Program   Under a Voluntary Disclosure Reporting Program (VDRP), a certificate holder (a company) that becomes aware that a potential violation of regulations has, or might have, occurred, immediately notifies its FAA office and discloses that fact, along with any corrective actions that have been taken to assure continuing safe operation (FAA, 2006b). The FAA then reviews the facts of the situation, and decides whether the incident was due to careless or reckless disregard for safety on the company's part. Seldom is that the case, and so usually the FAA accepts the report and agrees to not pursue fines or certificate action against the company, provided that the company follows up with a "comprehensive fix" that addresses the underlying causes of the event.

The VDRP allows a participating aviation service provider to report a potential violation and receive some protection from prosecution. In a sense, a VDRP is a vinculum that exemplifies the partnership between *production* and *oversight*, in SMS parlance. The FAA assumes good will and honesty from the certificate holder, and the certificate holder assumes that the FAA will not punish the company. Both sides assume that they hold a critical goal in common: safe operations.

We will be discussing non-punitive *just cultures* in depth later in this book; the VDRP is a symbol of such a just culture.

One element that all of these programs have in common is the fact that they are all voluntary. No operator is required by regulation to participate in any of these programs. While the International Civil Aviation Authority (ICAO) has established an international standard for the inclusion of many of these programs, and while the European Joint Aviation Authorities had required all large aircraft operators to establish one of these programs (FOQA) by January, 2005, the FAA has continued to assert that keeping these programs voluntary is the appropriate model for the U.S. The great concern the industry and its associated unions have with mandatory programs is that regulators would be empowered to unilaterally dictate data sharing mechanisms. Keeping these programs voluntary rather than mandatory has been a central goal of the industry throughout the decade of negotiations with the FAA.

Each program is clearly distinct, and has its own area of focus: for AQP, training; for ATOS, national oversight of the airline system; for ASAP, tapping into the observations and wisdom of the workforce; for FOQA, using exquisitely detailed data to paint an objective picture of routine operations; and for IEP, the measurement of management systems. These distinctions allow the various proactive safety programs to be used in concert, each revealing a particular aspect of the reality of line operations. But while these areas are separate in their specializations, the shared concept is what defines them as proactive: each uses its own dataset and methodology to draw inferences about the universe it is observing, and hoping to control.

ASAP—a deeper examination

ASAP is by far the most successful of all the voluntary programs, and is widely accepted and embraced by flight crews, dispatchers, maintenance technicians and flight attendants. In addition to being informative about the program itself, examining the history of ASAP will provide us with an understanding of a few key concepts that influence all the voluntary programs, and indeed will influence the evolution of SMS.

American Airlines pioneered the Aviation Safety Action Program in 1994. A concise description of ASAP is contained in the FAA's order that established ASAP as a program to be protected by Part 193. The description from that document is excerpted below. (The excerpts provided below are portions of full paragraphs in the order.) Note the commitment by the FAA to protect ASAP information from disclosure, and especially note the FAA's assumption that ASAP information will be submitted to the agency (FAA, 2002b):

> An Aviation Safety Action Program (ASAP) is entered into voluntarily through a Memorandum of Understanding (MOU) signed by the FAA, an air carrier or a repair station (referred to in this notice as "certificate holder"), and, if applicable, an employees' labor union. The intent of the program is to encourage defined groups of certificate holder employees to report possible violations, safety issues and events to an ASAP Event Review

Committee (ERC) comprised of one representative from each such party. Because of its capacity to provide early identification of needed safety improvements, an ASAP offers significant potential for incident and accident avoidance. FAA experience to date has clearly established that an ASAP can produce safety-related data that is not available from any other source. FAA limits enforcement actions it takes against employees covered by an ASAP to encourage them to report possible violations and safety problems. In order for a possible violation to be covered under an ASAP, the employee's ASAP report ordinarily must be submitted within a time limit specified in the MOU, any alleged violation must be inadvertent and must not appear to involve an intentional disregard for safety, and the reported event must not appear to involve criminal activity, substance abuse, controlled substances, alcohol, or intentional falsification. ...

For ASAP reports involving alleged violations, the ERC investigates to determine if [independent] information from FAA sources is available concerning the event (e.g., air traffic control tapes), and whether the reporting employee may have previously reported similar violations under the ASAP. Except for ASAP reports involving possible criminal activity, substance abuse, controlled substances, alcohol, or intentional falsification, [regulations] protect the content of all ASAP reports in the possession of the FAA from public disclosure. Similarly, any other information received by the FAA from the [certificate] holder concerning the content of such ASAP reports, including for example statistical analyses, periodic program review reports, and trend information will be protected from disclosure under this designation, unless the certificate holder authorizes the FAA to disclose that information. Voluntarily provided information ... will be protected from disclosure under this designation.

Certificate holders participate by executing an ASAP MOU with the FAA, and by voluntarily sharing information from the ASAP with the FAA. Employees covered under the ASAP MOU participate by submitting ASAP reports in accordance with that MOU.

No certificate holder is required to participate in ASAP, and no employee is required to submit reports even if his or her employer participates in ASAP. An ASAP MOU may be terminated at any time by any of the parties to the MOU.

The FAA anticipates that information from a certificate holder's ASAP will be shared with the FAA.

The citation above best summarizes the present status of the ASAP programs in the U.S. because it comes from the Notice of Proposed Order that defined ASAP as eligible for protection under Part 193. This designation is the culmination of what was the lengthy process of negotiations between the FAA and industry, through the issuance of another contentious Advisor Circular (AC 120-66B Aviation Safety Action Programs), and through the creation of the ASAP-FOQA Aviation Rulemaking Committee. The three emphasized lines in the above citation essentially define the proposed contract between the industry and the FAA concerning ASAP and, by extension, all proactive safety programs:

1. FAA limits enforcement actions it takes against employees to encourage them to report possible violations and safety problems.
2. Voluntarily provided information will be protected from disclosure under this designation.

3. The FAA anticipates that information from a certificate holder's voluntary safety programs will be shared with the FAA.

These three rules establish the working agreement that now exists for the development of all proactive safety programs in the U.S. For those programs constituted in conformance to the regulations defining the voluntary program, the FAA has promised to answer the two great concerns voiced by industry and its unions, those being the misuse and disclosure of information. In turn, industry has promised to share that information with the FAA.

But now, with the political questions close to resolution, comes perhaps the greatest challenge of all. What, precisely, is the meaningful information that needs to be shared? We are now at the crux of the matter. How can we apply the methods of scientific, inferential inquiry to the study of proactive safety information?

Data sharing

From the birth of proactive safety programs in the 1990s, there has been the assumption that information and intelligence gained from one operator's program would somehow be integrated with that of others, and that the result would be a greater understanding of the issues and risks associated with the question under study. The exact method that this sharing should take, though, has been perhaps the most controversial issue in the short life of these programs, and more than once has threatened their very existence.

The FAA has been generally direct and unapologetic concerning its motives for desiring the submission of aggregate data from proactive programs. For example, in the preamble to 14 CFR 13.401, the FOQA rule, the FAA directly states one of its motives (FAA, 2001):

> One of the principal benefits to the FAA and to public safety of aggregate FOQA data submission will be the opportunity it affords to target the limited resources available for FAA surveillance to those areas where it is most needed. The FAA fully anticipates that it will conduct physical surveillance for that purpose in areas identified by FOQA aggregate trend data.

The industry has been extremely resistant to the idea of "submitting" data or information from these programs to the FAA. Two concerns were behind the resistance. First, there was worry that the FAA might use such information in a punitive action against the reporter. Second, the legal staffs of both airlines and unions were deeply concerned about the possibility that any information submitted to the federal government would be available to the general population under the Freedom of Information Act (FOIA).

Part 193   To answer these concerns, the FAA enacted 14 CFR Part 193, Protection of Voluntarily Submitted Information, in 2001. This regulation provides protection for safety information voluntarily submitted to the FAA from both misuse by regulators and, in most instances, from release to third parties under FOIA.

The concerns of the industry and unions regarding misuse of safety data by the FAA were understandable. In the years leading up to the safety summit, most industry professionals felt that the FAA had demonstrated a propensity to use punitive measures such as fines and certificate action as its primary levers by which it attempted to assure safe operations. It has taken over a decade for the industry to begin to replace this suspicion with the realization that the leadership of the agency had made a serious long-term commitment to changing its approach from being the sheriff to being a partner in safety. This commitment has now been continuously demonstrated through multiple changes of leadership at the FAA, and the reasonable observer has concluded that this enlightened partnership approach to safety is well on its way to becoming firmly institutionalized.

With protective regulation such as Part 193 in place, many of the original objections to information sharing on the part of industry and the unions were answered, but there was still a considerable disagreement as to the appropriate method that sharing should take. The regulations (specifically the FOQA rule) put in place were purposely vague about sharing methodology, stating only that the sharing must take place "in a form and manner acceptable to the Administrator". This vagueness in the guidance contained in the federal rules resulted in a somewhat disjointed evolution of the national data-sharing initiative, but there was no better way to proceed. That very vagueness was necessary to allow industry and regulator the time to develop dialog and trust, and time to explore which methods would prove most likely to result in meaningful data-sharing.

Directly after the FOQA rule was put into place, with its mandate of data-sharing for those with approved programs, an Aviation Rulemaking Committee, or ARC, was established to determine how best to create that "form and manner" of sharing. During months of discussion and negotiation within the ARC, sharing was accomplished in another venue—regular "InfoShare" meetings, in which members of the community would present the results of studies from their proactive programs, primarily from FOQA and ASAP. The ARC process, being charged with the creation of policy recommendations, was frequently contentious and difficult, but InfoShare was consistently remarkably open. It was InfoShare that better represented the true desires and motivations of industry, union and regulator.

In 2004, the FOQA/ASAP ARC decided to begin a rather bold initiative in which ASAP and FOQA data, voluntarily provided by airline partners, would be shared in a Distributed National Archive, or DNA. The distributed nature of the network allowed proprietary data to remain on company property, while still allowing researchers access. NASA was invited to build the program due to its experience in FOQA research, and in turn invited the University of Texas at Austin's Human Factors Research Project to assist in the creation of the ASAP archive.

Purposely limited to a two year demonstration project, NASA successfully demonstrated that the DNA could function and deliver meaningful studies on national safety issues. More important than the specific conclusions of those studies was the experience of the various stakeholders in the project as they worked together to produce the studies. The FAA continued to demonstrate its enlightened approach to partnership and non-punitive action, and by the time the demonstration project was complete, the next steps were ready to be taken.

As this book reaches publication, a new program called ASIAS is emerging to take the place of the demonstration project. The Aviation Safety Information Analysis and

Sharing system is a new component of the FAA's safety directorate, AVS. ASIAS will be the repository of the many sources of safety information from the public sector already collected by the agency, and will also house the DNA. The MITRE Corporation has been chosen to manage the system. As a Federally Funded Research and Development Center independent from federal agencies, MITRE has inherited the role of trusted broker for the sensitive and proprietary safety information contained in the DNA. Through a collaborative effort between MITRE, the FAA and an increasingly well-represented sample of the industry, policies and procedures are being built to allow these remarkably rich sources of safety information to be used in a protected manner, while allowing the full power of the analytic capabilities of MITRE and other research partners to be brought to bear on the most important safety issues of our time.

But another component of this new structure is perhaps the most important aspect: the relationship between ASIAS and another relatively new but very successful example of partnership between industry and regulator—the Commercial Aviation Safety Team, or CAST. Composed of representatives from all of the primary stakeholders in the commercial aviation industry, CAST uses a collaborative decision-making approach to determine the best methods of intervention, and has been given significant power by the FAA to establish new initiatives.

Over the first ten years of its existence, CAST was assigned the very aggressive goal of decreasing the commercial aviation fatal accident rate in the U.S. by 80 percent by the end of 2007, and it nearly met that target. Considering the data sources available to CAST at the onset of the program, the analysis accomplished by its research component (the JIMDAT, or Joint Implementation Measurement Data Analysis Team) was of necessity reactive in nature, but through a very thorough and methodical approach that has examined hundreds of accidents and incidents, JIMDAT has developed an extensive list of "problem statements" that describe contributing factors to the accidents and incidents studied. From those problem statements have come intervention strategies called "safety enhancements", or SEs. A large number of CAST SEs have been enacted during its tenure, including improvements in MSAWs (minimum safe altitude warning systems), TAWS (terrain avoidance alerting systems), CFIT and ALAR (controlled flight into terrain, and approach/landing accident reduction) procedural modifications, and many others.

Through ASIAS, CAST now has a tool to move the national model of safety intervention from its traditionally reactive model to a firmly proactive approach. ASIAS serves a safety risk assessment function for the larger national SMS, and by incorporating the information gained through the proactive programs existing within its airline partners in the DNA, ASIAS will play a significant role in the evolution from reactive to proactive.

Finally, thirty years after the crash of TWA 514, the stage is set for the creation of institutional means to share vital safety information, *before* rather than after events that result in damage, injury or death. The lessons of 514 have been learned, and through a sometimes tortuous path systems have been built so that stakeholders can detect hazards, describe high-risk operations, and identify weak controls, share that knowledge with other stakeholders, and most importantly work together toward a solution. These are the essential components of proactive safety, the absence of which was illuminated by the TWA crash.

SMS in Practice

Retired TWA Captain Lloyd Murray discusses his remarkable connection with the tragic beginning of the data-sharing initiative, TWA 514, and one of its outcomes, ASAP:

> Thirty-plus years is a long time to remember details, but some are vividly etched in my mind, particularly my almost-fatal connection with TWA 514. As a very junior flight engineer in LAX, I had, I thought, finished the month of November 1974 by maxing out my time. Sometime on the morning of the 30th I received a call from crew scheduling regarding an assignment leaving that night. I reminded them that I was out of time. After some discussion they instead deadheaded me on that same flight (LAX to MCI—which was the beginning of the pairing for TWA 514 the next day). I was to go to the hotel and be on standby for the Kansas City domicile the following day.
>
> As I checked in, I met the captain of the flight, Pat Brock, who I had flown with previously. We exchanged greetings and when he found out I was going to be on standby at MCI, he suggested we meet for dinner the next night since he was returning there from Washington, D.C.
>
> During the night I was called by crew scheduling and given a flight assignment that left early the next morning from MCI. After we landed at our first stop, the outbound crew taking the aircraft from us was already on the jetway discussing something intently. They had a list of names and asked if I knew any. I said "Sure, I just flew with them last night." They told me 514 had just crashed on an approach into Dulles. I was stunned.
>
> With the information that followed over the next few days, we discovered that ATC was not required to issue an altitude restriction prior to reaching a portion of the published approach. This was news to many pilots since we always assumed separation was provided. There was also discussion that another carrier had done the same thing (but missed Round Hill) in the preceding weeks. We now know that UAL disseminated that information to its pilots, but no mechanisms existed to inform other operators of this vital information.
>
> Tragically, 'information sharing' has been the exception rather than the rule in aviation until recently. In the late 90's we attempted to start an ASAP program at TWA, in addition to using the ASRS. It took some perseverance, but finally ASAP was established in 2000. What's interesting to me is that I, who was providentially spared from TWA 514, found myself as the TWA rep for the ASAP program until the airline ultimately merged with AA.

We now find ourselves at the same point of evolution of proactive safety that Octave Chanute found himself in as an investigator of that first fatal crash, as reactive and forensic techniques began to be applied.

ICAO makes a useful discrimination between reactive, proactive and predictive safety, and we will explore those definitions in much more detail in later chapters.

In a mature SMS, all three techniques are applied to mitigate risk. The investigation of the Selfridge accident was (necessarily) a model of the reactive approach, while the NTSB's findings in TWA 514 began the path toward the proactive. Twelve years after TWA 514, another disaster was witnessed by millions of television viewers, high in the skies over Florida's east coast, tragically illuminating the need for even more advanced methods of risk management.

The Challenger space shuttle

On January 28, 1986, the Challenger space shuttle, STS-51-L, exploded in the sky over Florida just 73 seconds into its flight. The proximal cause of the accident was the failure of a rubber O-ring seal in a solid rocket booster (SRB), which resulted in a flame leak that caused the structural failure of the external fuel tank, the destruction of the orbiter, and the deaths of seven astronauts. The post-accident investigation, conducted by a commission appointed by the president, revealed that the ambient temperatures on the night prior to the launch were well below the minimum temperature necessary for the O-ring to remain effective at sealing the joints of the SRB. Further, engineers at Morton Thiokol, the contractor responsible for the SRBs, had informed NASA managers about their concern during a pre-launch teleconference. The concern of its engineers notwithstanding, the contractor recommended that the launch proceed the next morning as scheduled.

The investigating commission found that contributing causes of the accident included the failure of both NASA and Morton Thiokol to respond adequately to the flaw in the design of the O-ring sealing system. The report was also critical of the decision-making and management processes used by NASA and its contractors. The report concluded that "failures in communication ... resulted in a decision to launch [the shuttle] based on incomplete and sometimes misleading information, a conflict between engineering data and management judgments, and a NASA management structure that permitted internal flight problems to bypass key Shuttle managers".

The commission produced many findings and recommendations. Among the findings were the following (NASA, 2007):

- Organizational structures at Kennedy and Marshall have placed safety, reliability and quality assurance offices under the supervision of the very organizations and activities whose efforts they are to check.
- As the [shuttle program's] flight rate increased, the Marshall safety, reliability, and quality assurance work force was decreasing, which adversely affected mission safety.
- Problem reporting requirements are not concise and fail to get critical information to the proper levels of management.

Key recommendations of the commission included:

- NASA should establish an Office of Safety, Reliability and Quality Assurance to be headed by an Associate administrator, reporting directly to the NASA Administrator. It would have direct authority for safety, reliability, and quality assurance throughout the agency. The office should be assigned the work force to ensure adequate oversight of its functions and should be independent of other NASA functional and program responsibilities.

• NASA should establish an STS Safety Advisory Panel reporting to the STS Program Manager. The Charter of this panel should include shuttle operational issues, launch commit criteria, flight rules, flight readiness, and risk management. The panel should include representation from the safety organization, mission operations, and the astronaut office.

The Challenger tragedy spoke vividly about the many system failures in communication, engineering safety, decision-making, and organizational safety structure. Most significantly from our perspective, the National Research Council produced a report entitled "Post-Challenger Evaluation of Space Shuttle Risk Assessment and Management," which emphasized the need for a more sophisticated method for assessing risk in the highly complex undertaking of space flight. The Committee, chaired by Retired General Alton Slay, issued 11 recommendations, including using Probabilistic Risk Assessement (PRA), establishing an agency-wide Systems Safety Engineering function, and performing Failure Mode Effects Analyses (FMEAs) on software (and including human factors considerations in the FMEAs). PRA as a tool in predictive safety assessment is covered in Chapters 5 and 10.

Our short review of the history of aviation safety has focused on three exemplar accidents which represent the evolution of safety thinking: reactive, proactive and predictive. Up to now it has been an unfortunate but inevitable fact that disaster has been a driving force in that evolution. Our mandate in SMS is to learn from all three approaches, and to act before the next one occurs.

SMS in Practice

Then-FAA Administrator, Marion Blakey, discussed the important role of data sharing in a speech before the 2006 International Safety Forum:

> ... data sharing is an important part of the safety message. Sharing safety data is essential to achieving a stronger future for aviation safety. Today, we don't even know how much safety information is out there. Operators, manufacturers, repair stations, suppliers—all the way across the aviation community board. Nick Sabatini, the head of the FAA's aviation safety organization, maintains that we collect barely five percent of the available data. Where's the other 95? Good question. If we're going to continue to put downward pressure on the accident rate, we need far more information about emerging trends, precursors. We need to know more about what is going on every day in the operating, maintenance, and manufacturing environments.

> When we share this information, we put ourselves in the place where diagnostics becomes prognostics. Remember, the low-hanging fruit is gone. Sharing information on what we see, what we find, that's the way of the future.

Source: http://www.faa.gov/news/speeches/news_story.cfm?newsId=7529. (Excerpted statement of Marion C. Blakey, FAA Administrator to the 2006 International Safety Forum, November 2, 2006.)

Review Questions

1. Explain how the government's role in aviation safety over time has been reactive in nature. Give examples.
2. Explain the impact the 1995 Aviation Safety Summit had on commercial aviation safety.
3. Explain the difference between process-based and event-based aviation safety.
4. What is the "common theme in proactive safety"? Discuss descriptive and inferential analysis.
5. Explain the importance of data sharing on aviation safety. Discuss the current state of data sharing in aviation safety.
6. What role does CAST play in the national SMS?

References

Air Transport Association [ATA] (2007a). *"Annual Traffic and Ops: U.S. Airlines."* Retrieved December 3, 2007 from http://www.airlines.org/economics/traffic/Annual+US+Traffic.htm.

Air Transport Association [ATA] (2007b). *"Safety Record of U.S. Air Carriers."* Retrieved December 3, 2007 from http://www.airlines.org/economics/specialtopics/SafetyRecordOfCarriers.htm.

Defense Technical Information Center (1999). The First United States Army Aircraft Accident Report (September 1908) (Report Number ADA382312). Retrieved November 15, 2007, from http://stinet.dtic.mil/cgi-bin/GetTRDoc?AD=ADA382312&Location=U2&doc=GetTRDoc.pdf.

Federal Aviation Administration [FAA] (2001). *Flight Operational Quality Assurance Program*, (Federal Register, Volume 66, Number 211). Retrieved December 3, 2007 from http://www.epa.gov/fedrgstr/EPA-IMPACT/2001/October/Day-31/i27273.htm.

Federal Aviation Administration [FAA] (2002a). *Aviation Safety Action Program (ASAP)*. Advisory Circular 120-66B. Retrieved December 3, 2007 from http://rgl.faa.gov/Regulatory_and_Guidance_Library/rgAdvisoryCircular.nsf/0/61c319d7a04907a886256c7900648358/$FILE/AC120-66B.pdf.

Federal Aviation Administration [FAA] (2002b). *Document Action: Notice of Proposed Order Designating Information as Protected from Disclosure,* (Docket No. FAA-2002-13236). The Federal Register. Retrieved December 3, 2007 from http://www.thefederalregister.com/d.p/2002-09-05-02-22270.

Federal Aviation Administration [FAA] (2004). *Flight Operational Quality Assurance.* Advisory Circular 120-82. Retrieved December 3, 2007 from http://rgl.faa.gov/Regulatory_and_Guidance_Library/rgAdvisoryCircular.nsf/0/40c02fc39c1577b686256e8a005afb0a/$FILE/AC120-82.pdf

Federal Aviation Administration [FAA] (2006a). *Air Carrier Internal Evaluation Programs.* Advisory Circular 120-59A. Retrieved December 3, 2007 from http://rgl.faa.gov/Regulatory_and_Guidance_Library/rgAdvisoryCircular.nsf/0/fd8e4c96f2eca30886257156006b3d07/$FILE/AC%20120-59a.pdf.

Federal Aviation Administration [FAA] (2006b). *Voluntary Disclosure Reporting Program*. Advisory Circular 00-58A. Retrieved December 3, 2007 from http://rgl.faa.gov/Regulatory_and_Guidance_Library/rgAdvisoryCircular.nsf/0/85eb126d9daf2461862571e800667468/$FILE/AC%2000-58A.pdf.

Federal Aviation Administration [FAA] (2006c). *Advanced Qualification Program*. Advisory Circular 120-54A. Retrieved December 3, 2007 from http://rgl.faa.gov/Regulatory_and_Guidance_Library/rgAdvisoryCircular.nsf/0/1ef8eee828670517862571a20064a40b/$FILE/AC%20120-54a.pdf.

Federal Aviation Administration [FAA] (2006d). *Line Operations Safety Audit*. Advisory Circular 120-90. Retrieved December 3, 2007 from http://rgl.faa.gov/Regulatory_and_Guidance_Library/rgAdvisoryCircular.nsf/0/013a142c839ea74086257162006cc27d/$FILE/AC%20120-90.pdf.

National Aeronautics and Space Administration [NASA] (2007). *"Report of the Presidential Commission on the Space Shuttle Challenger Accident: In compliance with Executive Order 12546 of February 3, 1986."* Retrieved December 3, 2007 from http://science.ksc.nasa.gov/shuttle/missions/51-l/docs/rogers-commission/table-of-contents.html.

National Transportation Safety Board, [NTSB] (1975). *Aircraft Accident Report, Trans World Airlines, Inc., Boeing 727-231, N54328, Berryville, Virginia, December 1, 1974*. (Report No. NTSB-AAR-75-16). Retrieved December 3, 2007 from http://amelia.db.erau.edu/reports/ntsb/aar/AAR75-16.pdf.

National Transportation Safety Board, [NTSB] (2007). *"Database Query, Accident/Incident Information"* (U.S. Airline Crashes with Fatalities (CFR Part 121 and 135, Scheduled Service) From December 1993 to December 1994). Retrieved December 3, 2007 from http://www.ntsb.gov/ntsb/query.asp.

Chapter 3

Principles of Quality Management

Quality is not an act. It is a habit.

Aristotle

Quality management

Recall the definition of SMS from Chapter 1: SMS is a dynamic risk management system based on *quality management system (QMS) principles* [emphasis added] in a structure scaled appropriately to the operational risk, applied in a safety culture environment. Quality management is the underpinning of safety management systems. In the words of the FAA Associate Administrator for Aviation Safety (Sabatini, 2005):

> When effectively combined, the SMS and QMS systems assure us of safe and quality product. Stated simply: SMS needs a quality management system because SMS requires documented, repeatable processes. The quality management system provides the strong foundation upon which an SMS is built. Aviation Safety's QMS will be the springboard to our SMS.

To engage in the study or practice of SMS one must have a strong foundation in quality management systems (QMS). There are many aspects to QMSs, and there are innumerable books dedicated to discussing them. This chapter will begin with a brief history of quality management and will then present some of the concepts regarded as most critical to SMS, such as quality tools; the quality management system including strategic planning, deployment, performance measurement, and quality information system; leadership and management; and documentation. A short section on project management is presented. Finally, a very brief overview of reliability is provided.

Overview and history[1]

Managing for quality in the U.S. can be traced back to the earliest days of the country. Gaining independence from England meant that the U.S. had to establish its own manufacturing capability. Up to that time, colonists had been dependent on England for their manufactured goods.

Artisans   Like their European ancestors, apprentice artisans in the U.S. learned their craft from more experienced artisans, called masters. The master trained the apprentice in how to make a product, and the master would inspect the product to

---

1   The principle reference for this section is Juran, 1995.

ensure that it was of sufficient quality. When the apprentice had learned his craft well enough, he could set out on his own. This concept of quality was important because these products were usually sold within the community, and news of poor workmanship could travel very fast.

The Industrial Revolution   Artisans and independent shops were largely made obsolete by the dawn of the Industrial Revolution and the factory system. The Industrial Revolution began in Europe sometime before 1800 and came to the U.S. shortly after the turn of the century, and it represented a major shift in technological and socioeconomic conditions during that time. Whereas artisans typically worked in small shops or out of their homes, the factory system brought various new machines under one roof where products could be made more efficiently. This, of course, revolutionized how products were made. Workers who were expert at making a product were given narrower, more specialized tasks. Craftsmen typically became workers on the factory floor, while master artisans and shop owners became production supervisors. This latter group was still typically responsible for ensuring quality. Larger factories had supervisors dedicated to the inspection of products, but while our capacity for production increased dramatically, the quality of products tended to suffer in this new paradigm.

Scientific management   In the early 1900s, the U.S. began to adopt many of the teachings of Frederick W. Taylor, an American engineer, who developed a management method to improve industrial efficiency. Taylor's system consisted of four principles: 1.) Conduct a scientific study of each task, and use the results to replace old rule-of-thumb methods, 2.) Scientifically select, train, teach and develop workers rather than allow them to train themselves, 3.) Cooperate with the workers to ensure the work is being done in accordance with the scientifically developed principles, and 4.) Divide work more equitably among management and workers, allowing management to apply scientific management principles. His concept was to separate planning the work from execution of the work, and to assign those tasks to those best equipped to accomplish them. In Taylor's model, engineers would plan, and supervisors and workers, who typically lacked technology literacy or cognitive ability, would execute the plans. Productivity indeed did rise dramatically following the implementation of Taylor's principles and his time and motion study methods, but again, quality generally suffered as a result of this increased focus on productivity.

To improve quality, central inspection departments were created and headed by a chief inspector. Through sampling inspection of raw materials and goods throughout the manufacturing process, the task of the inspection department was to prevent defective products from leaving the facility. Paradoxically, the production department's job was to produce the product, and the inspection department's job was to ensure the quality of the product.

Statistical quality control   Statistical quality control (SQC) was introduced by Walter Shewhart, a Bell Labs statistician, who pioneered some statistical tools to improve the quality of telephone products. Shewhart knew that industrial and manufacturing processes produce data, and that the data does not always follow a normal, or Gaussian, curve. He theorized that there were two kinds of variation at work in a process; chance causes (more commonly referred to as "common causes" today) and assignable causes (also known as "special causes"). Chance causes exist in every process, including in stable, in-control processes. Some processes exhibit assignable cause variation that yields an unstable, out of control process. Based on this Shewhart devised a chart that is designed to detect when a process is out of control and, therefore, is a candidate for improvement. These charts are called "control charts" and are discussed later in this chapter. In sum, statistical quality control, now referred to as "statistical process control" or SPC, uses statistical tools to measure and analyze the degree of variation in a process.

W. Edwards Deming, a statistician with the U.S. Department of Agriculture and Census Bureau, became a proponent of Shewhart's SQC methods and later became a leader of the quality movement in both Japan and the United States.

Quality—World War II   After the U.S. entered World War II, the priority for all manufactured products was given to the military, and the demand for products was immense. The emphasis remained on inspecting and testing these products for conformance to specifications, but there also was an effort placed on employing sampling methods to reduce problems associated with inspecting the enormous volume of product. Bell Labs assisted in the development of military standards for sampling tables.

After the War   When the war ended in 1945, there was a large unmet demand for civilian products. In an effort to satisfy the demand as quickly as possible and capture market share over their competitors, manufacturers emphasized quantity over quality. The tendency to place greater importance on meeting delivery dates at the expense of quality could be seen through the latter part of the century.

As quality in the U.S. suffered in the decades following the war, Japanese companies set about improving the quality of their products. Ironically, it was primarily through the influence and instruction of two Americans, W. Edwards Deming and Joseph Juran, that the Japanese quality revolution occurred. It was not until the improved Japanese products penetrated the U.S. marketplace in the 1970s that some U.S. businesses turned once again to quality. Deming and other quality gurus were called upon to help lead the U.S. out of its own quality crisis. Some companies achieved world-class quality in the 1980s, and the popular label for managing for quality at the time was Total Quality Management (TQM).

Programs such as the Malcolm Baldrige National Quality Award emerged in the late 1980s and offered companies a means of self-assessment. At the same time, ISO 9000 was established as a quality management standard by the International Organization for Standardization (ISO). Just twenty years later, the list of U.S. companies using the Baldrige criteria and/or applying for ISO 9000 certification is extensive.

Many experts believe that the U.S. has made significant improvements in product quality and is once again poised to lead the next world-wide quality revolution.

Quality tools

Within every organization there is room for improvement. Organizations that strive to improve must set about doing so in a structured, consistent, and systemic manner. If the right data is not collected, problems may be misidentified. If the wrong solutions are implemented, the actual problems may get worse and the organization will suffer.

There are several well-known and widely regarded problem-solving or process improvement tools. These tools have been used by organizations around the world to improve quality. Seven of these are known as the *basic quality tools*, and seven are known as *management and planning tools*.

Basic quality tools

Quality guru, Kaoru Ishikawa, once stated, "As much as 95 percent of all quality-related problems in the factory can be solved with seven fundamental quantitative tools" (Ishikawa, 1985). The seven basic quality tools include the following:

1. Flowcharts.
2. Pareto charts.
3. Cause-and-effect diagrams.
4. Control charts.
5. Check sheets.
6. Scatter diagrams.
7. Histograms.

Most if not all of these tools will be familiar to many readers, but since they are such valuable tools, each one will be discussed briefly and an example of its use provided. It is worth noting that almost all of these tools are considered quantitative in nature; flowcharts and cause-and-effect are the exceptions. All of these tools are graphical depictions.

The basic quality tools are most commonly used in quality control rather than quality assurance applications; that is, their greatest utility is in monitoring, tracking, and analyzing data.

Flowchart   The purpose of a flowchart is to provide a graphical representation of a process. It enables the observer to understand the components, activities, and tasks associated with the process. There are many different types of flowcharts, including top-down, detailed, cross-functional, work flow diagrams, and deployment charts.

There are several steps in preparing a flowchart:

- *Determine the start and stop points.* In other words, determine the boundaries of the process being examined.
- *List the major elements of the process, including decision points.* Elements must be listed in sequential order.
- *Document the process.* Use standardized symbols.
- *Review the results.* Compare the flowchart with the actual process and check for errors and omissions. Having someone else check the validity of the flowchart is a great idea.

Standard symbols for a flowchart are shown in Figure 3.1.

A simple example of a cross-functional flowchart for an internal audit process is shown in Figure 3.2.

Pareto chart   The purpose of a Pareto chart is to provide a graphical representation of the factors having the greatest cumulative effect on the system, thus enabling the analyst to separate the "vital few" factors from the "trivial many".

The Pareto chart is based on the "80/20 rule" postulated by the Italian economist Vilfredo Pareto[2]. Pareto observed that 80 percent of the country's land was held by 20 percent of the population. The concept was adapted later to apply to quality applications to suggest that 80 percent of quality problems were a result of 20 percent of the causes.

The Pareto chart is essentially a rank-ordered (highest to lowest) bar chart.

Focusing on the most important causes of quality problems just makes sense. It allows organizations to get the most bang-for-the-buck in terms of quality improvements.

The basic steps in preparing a Pareto chart are as follows:

* *Rank order the columns or categories of data.* Starting with data from a check sheet or a histogram, order the columns from highest frequency on the left to lowest frequency on the right.
* *Prepare the chart.* The left-side vertical axis is labeled "frequency". The right-side vertical axis, if used, is the cumulative percentage (0 percent to 100 percent). The columns or bins are labeled according to the group names of the response, or dependent, variable.
* *Calculate and draw cumulative sums.* Add the subtotals for the first and second categories, and place a dot above the second bar indicating that sum. Add to that the subtotal for the third category and place a dot above the third bar for that new sum. Continue the process for all the bars. Connect the dots, beginning at the top of the first bar and ending at the 100 percent mark on the right vertical axis.

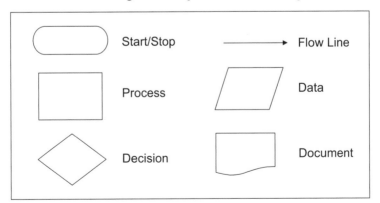

Figure 3.1   Flowchart symbols

---

2   Born in Paris in 1848, Vilfredo Pareto moved to Italy at the age of 10. He earned degrees in mathematical science and engineering, and lectured on economics and management for much of his life. Pareto died in Switzerland in 1923.

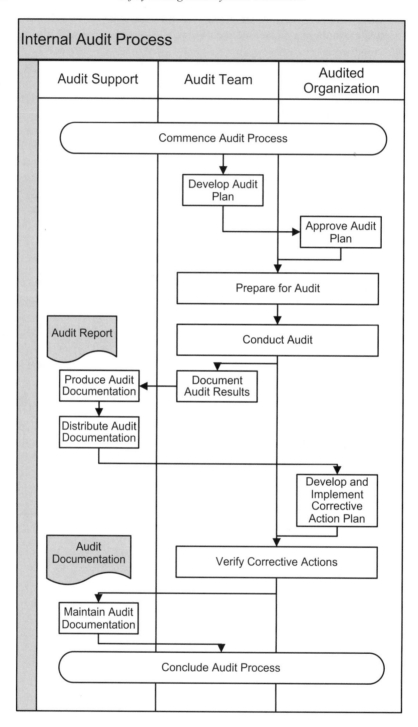

Figure 3.2   Cross-functional flowchart

An example Pareto chart showing the number of defects on a hypothetical fleet of military transports over a given period of time is depicted in Figure 3.3.

Cause-and-effect diagram The cause-and-effect diagram, also known as the Ishikawa diagram or fishbone diagram, is simply a tool to determine and understand the causes of a certain event.

Cause-and-effect (C-E) diagrams are used in problem-solving situations to help analysts identify factors that may cause a given effect, and in situations where analysts need to discover factors that may lead to process improvement.

The following steps are often used in developing a C-E diagram:

- *Identify the single problem or opportunity that is to be analyzed.* A short descriptor of this problem or opportunity is placed in a rectangle or box on the right side of the diagram. The "spine" of the fishbone extends to the left from the rectangle or box.
- *Identify the major causes of the problem or opportunity.* To aid in grouping causes, major categories of causes are often identified as methods, machines (equipment), people (manpower), materials, measurement, and environment. These groupings are represented as the major bones extending from the spine of the C-E diagram.
- *Identify the minor causes associated with each major cause.* Minor causes are identified and represented as additional skeletal structure associated with the major cause they are related to.
- *Continue to identify additional causes.* This process continues until all causes are identified and documented.

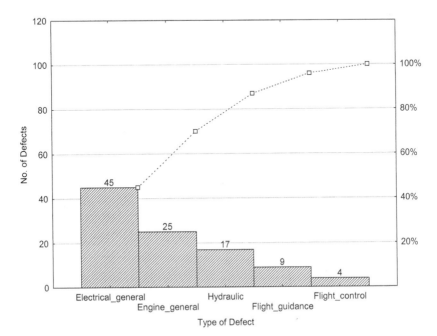

Figure 3.3   Pareto chart

An example of a C-E diagram to discover the root cause(s) of a tire failure is shown in Figure 3.4.

Control Charts   Control charts are produced as part of a methodology called Statistical Process Control (SPC). SPC is quantitative problem-solving, with the primary intent being to determine whether processes are in or out of statistical control. SPC is a powerful tool for communicating information to personnel within the organization, and to assist them in troubleshooting and decision making.

Variation   Control charts plot the variation in a process (a repeatable sequence of events or operations) over time and compare measured characteristics against calculated standards of variation. These calculated standards of variation are derived using principles of probability. The primary use of control charts is to detect causes of variation that are not random, or common; that is, causes that are assignable, or special. Assignable causes are not considered part of the system, and should be identified and corrected.

It is important to understand this issue of variation since it is the enemy of quality and plays such a large role in process improvement. Variation exists in all processes—every one. As we stated earlier, there are fundamentally two types of variation—common and special cause variation. Common cause variation includes a wide range of unidentifiable causes; they are considered inherent in a process. Attempts to eliminate common cause variation usually result in more variation. Special cause variation is not natural to a process. This type of variation, if observed by the operator, can usually be removed or adjusted.

Thus, the real purpose of control charts is to assist the process operator in recognizing special causes so that correction can be applied to bring the process back in statistical control.

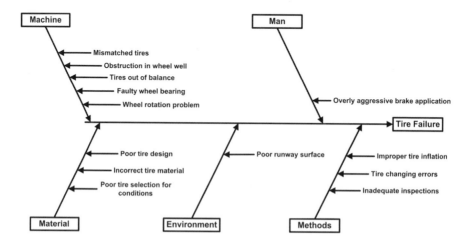

Figure 3.4   Cause-and-effect diagram

Variable selection A critical part of control charting is selecting the variable of interest. In manufacturing applications, that variable might be a critical dimension or weight of the product or component. In other cases, the variable selected for monitoring might be a "leading indicator" of special causes; that is, one that detects special causes before others do. We'll discuss the very important concept of "leading indicators" for SMS applications in Chapter 10.

Sample selection Another important consideration for control charting is selecting samples of the variable being monitored. The goal is to detect any process shift that may take place, so minimizing within-sample variation and maximizing between-sample variation is desirable. This rational subgroup method must be applied with care to ensure the same process is producing each item.

Types of charts—variables charts The most prevalent control charts are $\overline{X}$ and R charts. These are variables charts because the data to be plotted result from a measurement on a variable or continuous scale. The $\overline{X}$ chart primarily indicates any changes in the mean value of the process, while the R chart indicates the changes in the variability of the process. Another variables chart is the $\overline{X}$ and s chart. Since standard deviation is a better measure of dispersion than the range value, the $\overline{X}$ and s chart is regarded as more precise than the $\overline{X}$ and R chart. While the standard deviation may be more difficult to calculate than range, that consideration is obviated by the use of modern software tools normally used to prepare these charts.

Other types of variables control charts include: Individuals and Moving Range, Median, and Moving Average Moving Range. These charts are beyond the scope of this book.

Control charts for attribute (or count) data are also important to the safety professional. Attribute data is data that falls into categories, such as good or bad, conforming or non conforming, and non defective or defective. Attribute charts that deal with the number of defects or non conformities are called *c* charts, and those that deal with the proportion of defects or nonconformities are called *p* charts. A summary of attribute charts follows:

Types of charts—attribute charts

- *c* Chart—Used for measuring defects when sample size is constant. This chart is useful when the defects are rare events and, thus, the control limits are based on the Poisson distribution.
- *u* Chart—Used for measuring the rate of defectives in units of varying size.
- *np* Chart—Used for measuring the number of defectives. This chart is not based on the distribution of rare events, but rather on the binomial distribution. The *np* chart should be used when the occurrence of defectives exceeds about 5 percent of the units inspected.
- *p* Chart—Used for percentage measurements, such as percentage of parts defective.

Control limits   Control limits are calculated based on the data from the process. The formulas for determining upper and lower control limits for the $\bar{X}$ and s chart are listed below (the constants are widely available in texts and other sources).

- Upper control limit for the averages chart: UCL $\bar{x} = \bar{\bar{X}} + A_3 \bar{s}$
- Lower control limit for the averages chart: LCL $\bar{x} = \bar{\bar{X}} - A_3 \bar{s}$
- Upper control limit for the standard deviation chart: UCL $s = B_4 \bar{s}$
- Lower control limit for the standard deviation chart: LCL $s = B_3 \bar{s}$

Control chart analysis   Each of the control limit formulas is based on data from the analysis, and these limits are established at $\pm 3\sigma$ from the mean. Each data point is compared with the distribution that was used to create the control limits. Recall from statistical theory and, specifically, the central limit theorem, that if a data point falls outside the control limit we can state that there is a 99.72 percent likelihood that the data point didn't come from the distribution upon which the control limits were based. In other words, the process has changed, and the presence of assignable (non-random) causes is highly likely.

Aside from detecting data points that fall outside the control limits, there are other indicators in a control chart that the process may be out of statistical control. Various texts do not agree completely on this list of factors, but the following serves to illuminate possible indicators of problems when analyzing control charts:

- Any point more than 3σ from the centerline (discussed above).
- Nine points in a row on the same side of the centerline.
- Six points in a row steadily increasing or decreasing.
- Fourteen points in a row alternating up and down (this may indicate that two processes are being measured).
- Two out of three points more than 2σ from the centerline (same side).
- Four out of five points more than 1σ from the centerline (same side).
- Fifteen points in a row within 1σ of the centerline (either side).
- Eight points in a row more than 1σ from the centerline (either side).

It is worth noting that a control chart is essentially a graphical hypothesis test. The null hypothesis is that the process hasn't changed. What we're doing with control charts is gathering evidence to see if we can reject the null hypotheses and conclude that the process has changed.

For a simple example of an attribute chart—a *p* chart, suppose that an analyst in the safety department wanted to plot the number of defectives, or instances where the crew failed to properly follow the initial descent checklist. This data was collected in the Line Operations Safety Audit program, and includes the "defectives", the number of total observations (that is, "sample size") made in a particular time period, and the resultant proportion defective ("fraction"). The data collected is shown in Table 3.1 and plotted in a control chart (that is, a *p* chart) as shown in Figure 3.5.

Note that there are two instances that fall outside of the control limits on the control chart (denoted on the line by the large open circles at time period "3" and "10"), suggesting that there is a *special* cause for this variability that should be investigated. It should also be noted that the figure depicts *moving* (upper and lower) *control limits* (indicated by the irregular dashed lines; this is due to the variability in sample sizes.

Table 3.1   Line oriented safety audit data

Defectives, np	Sample Size	Fraction, p
25	175	0.14
14	185	0.08
11	210	0.05
9	130	0.07
9	99	0.09
11	104	0.11
15	115	0.13
13	100	0.13
23	155	0.15
55	205	0.27
23	175	0.13
10	150	0.07
18	140	0.13
29	199	0.15
11	185	0.06
19	155	0.12
18	161	0.11
22	155	0.14
23	145	0.16
17	139	0.12

Check sheets   The purpose of a check sheet is to record a tally count of event occurrences.

Check sheets are simple, generic tools that are designed for a specific task, and can be adapted for a wide variety of purposes. The steps in completing a check sheet are as follows:

- *Determine what event or problem will be observed.* Develop operational definitions appropriate for the particular application.
- *Design the check sheet for the application.* Information that should be included on the form includes: a description of the event or problem being observed, duration of the data collection period, individuals responsible for the process, and individuals responsible for the data collection. All spaces on the form should be properly labeled. The form should allow for simple symbols, such as an "x", tick mark, dot, etc., to indicate an event occurrence.

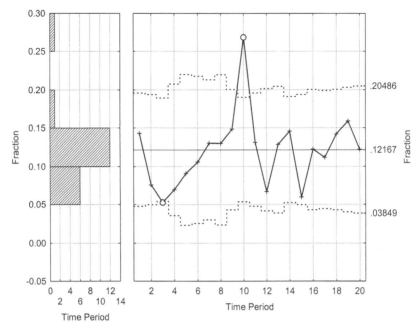

Figure 3.5   Control chart (p) for line operations safety audit data

The form should also include a space for remarks.

- *Record the data.* Each event occurrence results in a symbol being added to the check sheet.
- *Analyze results.* Data collected via check sheets are often used to initiate process improvements, or to inform other quality tools such as histograms or Pareto charts.

An example of a check sheet is presented in Table 3.2.

Scatter diagrams   The purpose of a scatter diagram is to graphically indicate the relationship between two variables.

Scatter diagrams can be used when there is a suspected relationship, or correlation, between numerical variables. The variables are plotted on an x-y graph and the resulting pattern is examined for correlation. There are five broad possible outcomes for an analysis of the scatter diagram as exhibited by Figure 3.6.

The steps in completing a scatter diagram include:

- *Select two variables of interest.* The two variables should have a suspected correlation.
- *Collect the data.* Normally the data is input into a statistical software program.
- *Generate scatter diagram.* The software program will automatically select the appropriate scale for the display.
- *Evaluate the results.* Evaluate the results to identify any relationships that may exist. Additionally, many software programs have the capability to report a correlation coefficient, which numerically indicates the strength of the relationship.

Table 3.2   Check sheet

Tugs found parked without parking brake applied	Days				
	Monday	Tuesday	Wednesday	Thursday	Friday
Concourse 1 W	II		I		
Concourse 1 E		III			
Intl Concourse	IIIIII	IIIII	III	II	III
South Ramp	I			II	
Staging		II			

Total

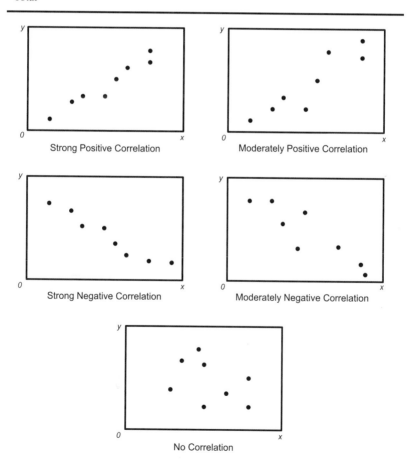

Strong Positive Correlation

Moderately Positive Correlation

Strong Negative Correlation

Moderately Negative Correlation

No Correlation

Figure 3.6   Scatter diagram analysis

Suppose a safety analyst wanted to understand the relationship between safety training and the number of runway incursion errors (not necessarily involving an aircraft) committed by airport maintenance crews. Data was collected on the number of hours of safety training received by maintenance crews, and number of runway incursions recorded. The data are as shown in Table 3.3.

Based on this data, the scatterplot would appear as shown in Figure 3.7.

A regression line has been placed on the scatterplot. There appears to be a linear relationship between the two variables, and the correlation coefficient ("r") is -0.6714, which indicates a moderately strong negative correlation; that is, the more training hours the fewer errors. It is important to note that causation cannot be determined from this analysis—only that there appears to be a relationship between the two variables.

Table 3.3   Safety training data

Crew Number	Hours	Errors
Crew1	17	3
Crew2	19	2
Crew3	15	3
Crew4	12	3
Crew5	25	1
Crew6	11	3
Crew7	9	5
Crew8	7	6
Crew9	11	4
Crew10	13	3
Crew11	19	0
Crew12	12	3
Crew13	20	4
Crew14	19	5
Crew15	14	4
Crew16	14	4
Crew17	18	3
Crew18	14	5
Crew19	19	1
Crew20	22	0

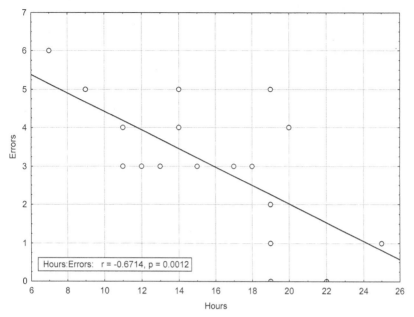

Hours:Errors: r = -0.6714, p = 0.0012

Figure 3.7   Scatterplot of safety training data

Histograms   The purpose of a histogram is to graphically depict frequency distributions.

Similar in appearance to a bar chart (but with no spaces between the bars), histograms are used to visualize how a set of data are distributed relative to each other. The vertical axis (y axis) of the graph depicts frequency, and the horizontal axis (x axis) depicts categories or groups of data. By examining a histogram, it is possible to determine whether the output of a process is distributed approximately normally.

To prepare a histogram, the following steps are normally followed:

- *Collect the data.* Gather and record at least 50 data points from a process.
- *Determine the number of columns or groups to be used.* Software normally does this automatically. Rules of thumb for determining this number manually are as follow: 50 to 100 data points—use 6 to 10 columns; 100 to 250 data points—use 7 to 12 columns; over 250 data points—use 10 to 20 columns.
- *Prepare the graphic.* Use the software to prepare the graphic. Provide a descriptive title, provide a measurement scale for each axis, and label the columns.

As an example, a safety study was commenced involving runway touchdown zones. Data was collected on distances from actual aircraft touchdown from the beginning of the touchdown zone. The data are shown in Table 3.4 and a histogram is presented in Figure 3.8.

Table 3.4   Runway touchdown zone data

Obs. No.	Dist.	Obs. No.	Dist.	Obs. No.	Dist.	Obs. No.	Dist.	Obs. No.	Dist.
1	500	11	40	21	400	31	920	41	650
2	420	12	470	22	410	32	750	42	490
3	380	13	320	23	320	33	820	43	350
4	-50	14	270	24	170	34	740	44	810
5	680	15	90	25	190	35	280	45	250
6	1120	16	50	26	520	36	110	46	270
7	450	17	130	27	500	37	250	47	360
8	680	18	250	28	410	38	450	48	410
9	410	19	320	29	310	39	350	49	400
10	380	20	30	30	300	40	700	50	380

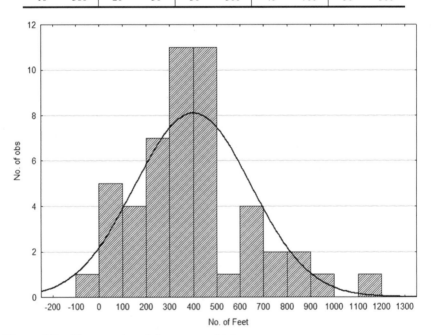

Figure 3.8   Runway touchdown zone histogram

Use of the basic quality tools in safety assurance

As described in Chapter 1, Safety Assurance is a key component of SMS, and identified by the FAA as one of the four pillars. AC 120-92 describes the role of safety assurance as follows (FAA, 2006, p. 17):

Safety Assurance: Managing the Requirements. The safety assurance function applies the processes of quality assurance and internal evaluation to the process of making sure that risk controls, once designed, continue to conform to their requirements and that they continue to be effective in maintaining risk within acceptable levels. These assurance and evaluation functions also provide a basis for continuous improvement. ... safety assurance uses many of the same practices as those used in quality management systems (QMS). In an SMS however the requirements being managed relate to ensuring risk controls, once designed and put into place, perform in a way that continues to meet their safety objectives.

Diagrammatically (using one of the basic quality tools, the flowchart), the FAA depicts SA as shown in Figure 3.9 (FAA, 2006).

A mature SMS will utilize the seven basic quality tools extensively throughout its safety assurance function. One tool is especially fundamental to SA—the flowchart. Note the purpose of SA—to assure that controls, once designed, are effective in

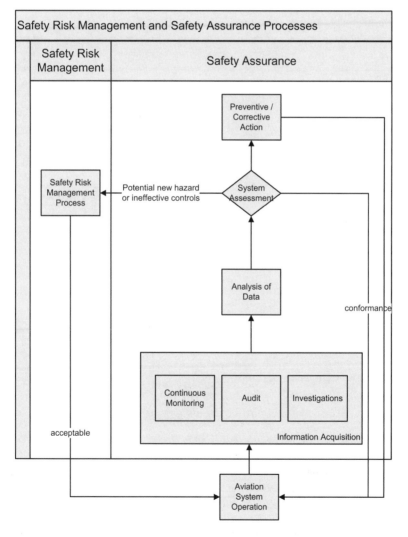

Figure 3.9   Safety risk management and safety assurance processes flowchart

achieving their goal of mediating risk—requires that process measurements are strategically designed to measure control effectiveness. The best way to accomplish this is through the use of flowcharts.

Let's examine some of the controls in place to mediate the risk of midair collisions due to altitude deviations (see Figure 3.10):

Note that the controls in this flowchart are the decision diamonds. Preparing a flowchart helps to clarify exactly where the controls are in a process, and additionally helps to identify how an SA data collection and analysis process would go about measuring the effectiveness of controls. We suggest that the reader review the flowchart once again, and from that review design a check sheet that a LOSA auditor might use to record control effectiveness for this process.

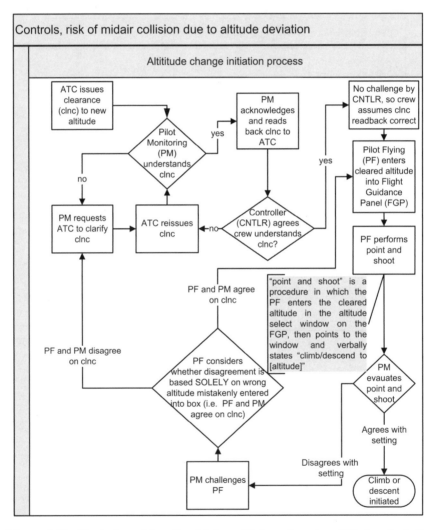

Figure 3.10 Controls, risk of midair collision due to altitude deviation flowchart

The flowchart and associated check sheets are the basic tools for SA data collection. Flowcharts can of course take many forms and levels of sophistication, as can check sheets. But all forms are fundamentally the same; the flowchart is used to assure that the SMS practitioner understands the process to be monitored, and the check sheet provides a standardized method of collecting data concerning the processes performance.

As implied in the presentation of the other tools, their application to SA analysis is limited only by the SMS practitioner's imagination.

Management and planning tools

There are also seven tools known as *management and planning tools*. These tools are used primarily for planning projects, communicating information, problem solving, and promoting innovation. These tools include:

- Tree diagram.
- Affinity diagram.
- Activity network diagram.
- Interrelationship digraph.
- Matrix diagram.
- Priorities matrix.
- Process decision program chart.

To explain and illustrate these tools, let's consider a scenario of a small air ambulance operation desiring to improve its safety program.

Tree diagram   A tree diagram is used to break down objectives or tasks into progressively greater detail, much like a work breakdown structure in project management (discussed later in this chapter). The process of executing a tree diagram aids the individual or team in understanding the individual tasks that must be accomplished in order to achieve the objective. Our air ambulance operation is using a horizontal tree diagram to more fully understand the breakdown structure of certain tasks, in this case, transporting a patient to a medical facility for treatment (see Figure 3.11). Of course, a thorough, well-developed tree diagram will be considerably more extensive than the figure shown here.

Affinity diagram   An affinity diagram is used to organize large amounts of data into groupings based on natural relationships. Often this data is generated during brainstorming processes and then, using affinity diagram techniques, these data are organized into groups so they can be better analyzed. When affinity diagramming is used in conjunction with brainstorming, it tends to stimulate innovation and breakthrough ideas.

Affinity diagrams can be created using software programs or simpler methods such as Post-It® notes and poster boards. Figure 3.12 shows the results of our fictitious air ambulance organization brainstorming for ways to improve safety. The ideas generated were placed into logical groupings; that is, "training", "equipment", "management", and "programs".

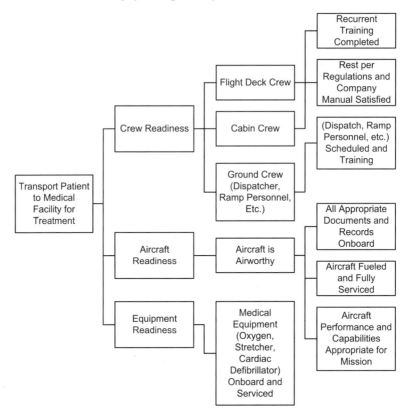

Figure 3.11   Tree diagram

Activity network diagram   The activity network diagram (AND) is used for particularly complex projects that are time-limited. Producing an AND assists in determining which tasks can be accomplished in series and which can be done in parallel and, thus, how long the project will take and what resources are needed and when. When used as a project management tool, the AND reveals the critical path, which is the longest path through the series of activities that must be completed to finish the project. Figure 3.13 depicts a typical structure for an AND, where the analysis includes the tasks to complete between scheduling an air ambulance transport activity and commencing the flight. The activities on the bottom row represent the critical path since the sum of these activities is greater than the sum of the activities listed in the top row. If reducing the start to finish time was important, the air ambulance provider might consider providing additional resources, as appropriate, to the critical path to reduce that time.

Interrelationship digraph   An interrelationship digraph indicates the relationships that exist among critical issues. It is frequently used to show the relationships between the groups generated during an affinity diagramming process.

The relationships are indicated by drawing an arrow from the issue that is the cause to the issue that experiences the effect. Dashed lines can be used for weak relationships and solid and heavy solid lines for progressively stronger relationships.

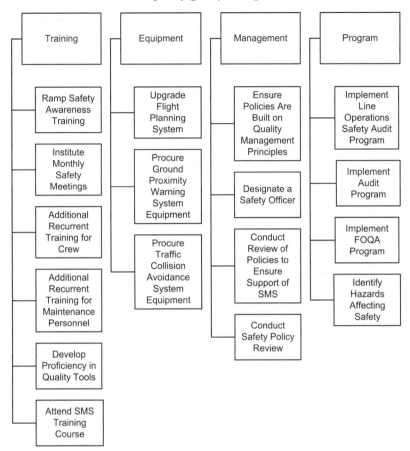

Figure 3.12 Affinity diagram

Figure 3.14 shows the beginnings of an interrelationship digraph to explore the safety problems faced by our air ambulance organization.

Matrix diagram   A matrix diagram is useful when comparing two sets or lists of items to understand the various relationships between the items. There are several types of matrix diagrams, including:

- L-shaped—shows the relationship of two groups of items.
- T-shaped—shows the relationship of three groups of items, where the second and third groups are related to the first but not to each other.
- C-shaped—relates three groups of items simultaneously using three dimensions.
- Y-shaped—relates three groups of items, where each group is related to the other two in a circular layout.
- X-shaped—relates four groups of items, where each group is related to two other groups in a circular layout.
- Roof-shaped—relates one group of items to itself.

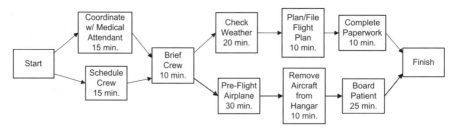

Figure 3.13   Activity network diagram

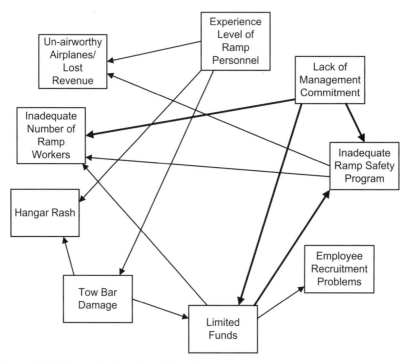

Figure 3.14   Interrelationship digraph

In a simple L-matrix, one of the sets of items becomes the columnar set and the other becomes the row set, and a value or symbol is used to show the strength of the relationship between the items. An example of an L-matrix indicating the relationship between some of the safety issues and organization's personnel is displayed in Figure 3.15.

Prioritization matrix   The prioritization matrix is a tool that enables problems or alternatives to be ranked by particular criteria, which assists in choosing between several options.

The criteria are listed on both the vertical and horizontal axes of the matrix. The criteria are then compared and a weighted score is assigned based on the relative importance of that criteria. The factors are then assessed and scores are recorded. The

	Maintenance	Ramp	Dispatch	Flight Ops
Unairworthy Airplanes/ Lost Revenue	◯	◉	△	△
Inadequate Number of Ramp Workers	◯	◉	△	△
Hangar Rash	◯	◯	△	△
Inadequate Ramp Safety Program	△	◯	◯	◯
Limited Funds	△	◉	◉	◉

△ = Weak   ◯ = Medium   ◉ = Strong

Figure 3.15 L-matrix diagram

final scores for the criteria are a function of the weightings assigned to them and the individual scores. The alternatives can then be rank-ordered based on the final scores. The prioritization matrix allows our air ambulance organization to help determine where it might get the most return on investment (ROI) of its safety dollar. This matrix is an excellent tool for evaluating potential ROI based on expert estimate of cost of implementation and effectiveness of the solution. Figure 3.16 shows a small portion of what a prioritization matrix might look like for our aviation service provider. Based on this analysis, the air ambulance service would designate a safety officer, develop proficiency in quality tools, and conduct ramp awareness safety training.

Process decision program chart   This powerful tool is used for contingency planning for situations that may cause failure of a project. Contingency plans can then be developed to address those situations.

Items to prioriitze \ Criteria	Low cost Wt. = 3		High Results Wt. = 5		Final Score
Conduct ramp awareness safety training	5	15	6	30	45
Designate a safety officer	4	12	7	35	47
Conduct safety policy review	4	12	2	10	22
Upgrade flight planning system	1	3	7	35	38
Implement audit program	3	9	6	30	39
Develop proficiency in quality tools	4	12	7	35	47

Figure 3.16 Prioritization matrix

Projects are broken down into tasks, which are evaluated to determine possible failures. For each possible failure, a contingency plan is determined. By completing a thorough analysis using the process decision program chart (PDPC), our air ambulance provider can apply countermeasures that provide a greater likelihood of success of achieving its objective. An example PDPC, based on the tree diagram presented earlier, is shown in Figure 3.17. Note also that PDPCs will be used extensively in our discussion of Safety Risk Management (SRM) in Chapters 4 through 6.

Additional tools

In addition to the tools discussed above, there are many other tools and methods used by quality professionals to improve processes. Two of these tools regarded as vital to process improvement efforts will be discussed here: Plan-Do-Check-Act and SIPOC analysis. Two additional tools used for analyzing designs and processes for potential failure—Failure Mode Effects Analysis (FMEA) and Fault Tree Analysis (FTA) are also briefly presented.

Plan-Do-Check-Act Simple yet remarkably effective, the Plan-Do-Check-Act (PDCA) cycle is a structured method for carrying out change in a process. The PDCA cycle, or Shewhart cycle after its originator, is based on the premise that quality lies in having clear, repeatable processes. Figure 3.18 depicts a PDCA cycle.

The first phase of the tool is *plan*. In this phase the problem or improvement opportunity is clearly defined and understood. Various tools, such as root cause analysis, can assist in getting to the heart of the issue. In addition, it may be a good

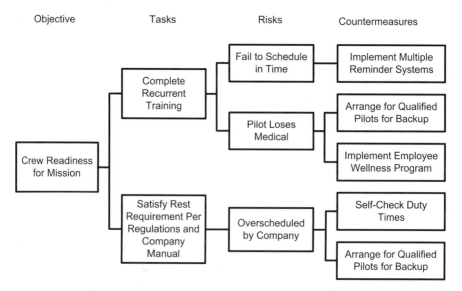

Figure 3.17 Process decision program chart

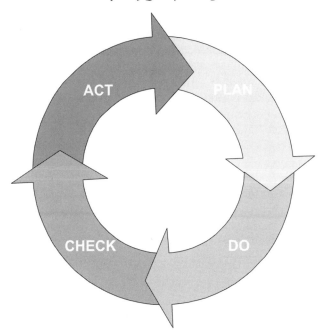

Figure 3.18 Plan-Do-Check-Act cycle

idea to map the process to ensure that all involved have a grasp of the issue and the processes surrounding it. Alternatives are explored and a plan is developed in this phase. In conjunction with the selection of an alternative, a means to measure the effectiveness of the solution is developed.

The second phase is *do*. This phase involves implementing the plan. For very complex situations when time is available, it is often a better approach to pilot test the plan to determine its efficacy. Information learned from this limited implementation can be used to inform and improve the plan phase.

Check is the third phase of the PDCA cycle. In this phase we study the results of the implementation of the plan. If we were pilot testing the plan, we might modify the plan based on these results.

The final phase is *act*. If the results were effective, the solution would be institutionalized in this phase. If the results yielded less than what was desired, the plan would be modified. In any event, the cycle would be continued to achieve further improvements in the process.

Many leading organizations in the world use the PDCA cycle on a daily basis with great success to achieve process improvement and to solve problems. This is a tool that organizations should attain some proficiency in using.

SIPOC analysis It is essential that processes be understood from a process management perspective before improvements are attempted. SIPOC (Suppliers–Inputs–Process–Outputs–Customers) is a tool that is used to identify all the elements of a process improvement project prior to initiating the project. The team uses this tool to identify the suppliers of a process, the inputs to the process, the process that needs to be improved, the outputs of the process, and the customers of the process. Figure 3.19 depicts the framework of a SIPOC diagram.

Failure Mode Effects Analysis The FMEA provides a systematic means of identifying and assessing potential failure modes, understanding the root causes of those failures, and determining the actions necessary to eliminate the potential failures. (See Chapter 10 for a detailed description of FMEA.)

Fault Tree Analysis FTA is a graphical tool for analyzing complex systems to determine potential failure modes and the probabilities that these failures might occur. (See Chapter 10 for a detailed description of FTA.)

Quality management system

Components of Quality Management Systems (QMS) typically include strategic planning (i.e., what organizations should be doing to strengthen their business positions), strategic plan deployment (i.e., determining the best means of implementing those plans), and quality information systems, or QIS, (i.e., improving the strategic plan deployment). Let's look at each one of these concepts in turn.

Strategic planning

Strategic planning is a formal process undertaken by an organization to plan for its future. There are several elements to this. First, it is a formal process; you should know when it is being done. Typically there are one or more planning teams engaged in the process, and the teams are given specific charges. Second, strategic planning should be objective oriented; that is, the organization should know what it wants to be. Third, strategic planning must be a continual process since the business environment is always changing. Fourth, strategic planning should be inclusive; that is, individuals throughout all levels of the organization should participate in the process.

Several models have been developed to aid in the strategic planning process. A commonly used 10-step process is presented in Figure 3.20 (Westcott, 2006, p. 94). In this model as in others, planning is thought of as strategic, tactical, and operational. Strategic is the highest level and involves the determination of what the organization wants to become in the future. Tactical planning is focused on implementation—the steps the organization needs to take to implement strategic plans. Operational plans, also called action plans, break planning down further into specific tasks that need to be accomplished on a day-to-day basis to fulfill the organization's strategic vision.

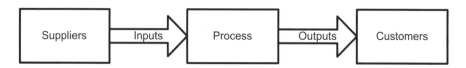

Figure 3.19 Framework of a SIPOC diagram

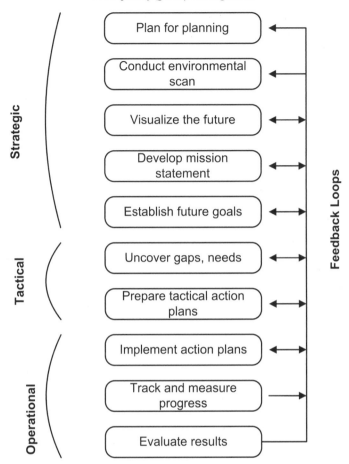

Figure 3.20 10-step strategic planning process

Hoshin planning

Hoshin[3] planning is an alternative to the traditional strategic planning model presented above. Hoshin planning is a systemic planning methodology developed in Japan and based on Management by Objectives and the Plan-Do-Check-Act cycle for continuous improvement. Hoshin planning provides an organization the opportunity to achieve breakthrough results by both defining long range key business objectives and ensuring the implementation of business fundamentals required to operate the organization successfully.

The process begins with envisioning the future about three to five years hence. The Hoshin planning team then develops innovative ideas about how the organization

---

3 Hoshin in Japanese translates to "shining metal pointing direction". In Hoshin planning, the metal can be thought of as the needle of a compass, which is metaphorically pointing in the direction the organization should move.

can achieve the goal(s). These ideas are then distilled into specific strategies. Three tools are then used to analyze these strategies: the Interrelationship Digraph, the Gap Analysis, and the Criteria Matrix. This analysis process enables the planning team to reach consensus. Cross-functional teams are then formed to further investigate the viability of each strategy and to develop action plans. Strategies are approved and implemented. Importantly, the Hoshin planning team meets regularly to measure progress on each initiative, and to make any adjustments in the plan that are deemed necessary.

The Hoshin plan is hierarchical in nature, and cascades throughout the organization by linking strategies at one level to objectives at another level. Thus, every member of an organization is involved in Hoshin planning. And, by virtue of this involvement, Hoshin is a very effective tool for communicating the direction the organization is moving.

One of the challenges in Hoshin planning is maintaining the balance between trying to achieve breakthrough results against managing the business fundamentals of the organization. Breakthrough results—Hoshin objectives—become the focus when the business fundamentals are in control. When business fundamentals are not in a state of control, the organization must focus on these first before pursuing the higher Hoshin objectives. An important point is that most of time available to dedicate to breakthrough activity is time that would previously have been spent on out of control business fundamentals.

As mentioned, the Hoshin process ensures that the strategies and action plans cascade up and down the organization until approved. One of the distinct advantages of the Hoshin method is that the action plans are inherently developed in this process, thereby greatly enhancing the ability of the organization to deploy the plan that is created.

See Figure 3.21 for a depiction of the Hoshin planning processes in a functional flowchart (Wescott, 2006, p. 96).

SWOT

A valuable tool for strategic planning is the SWOT analysis. SWOT is an acronym that stands for the following:

- **Strengths**—(internal) features of an organization that are helpful to achieving the objective.
- **Weaknesses**—(internal) features of an organization that are harmful to achieving the objective.
- **Opportunities**—(external) conditions that are helpful to achieving the objective.
- **Threats**—(external) conditions that are harmful to achieving the objective.

SWOT is a tool used for understanding the internal and external environment in which the organization operates. The results of a SWOT analysis are used to inform the various parts of the strategic planning process.

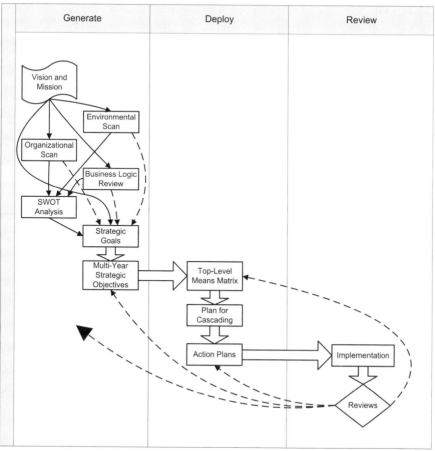

Figure 3.21 Hoshin planning process

Benchmarking

Benchmarking is an important tool for the quality manager, particularly in strategic planning. Benchmarking is a systematic process for identifying and utilizing knowledge of best practices and processes of others to assist an organization in improving its processes or performance.

This important quality tool allows managers to comprehend what processes are working well for others, and to help set realistic and attainable goals for their own organizations. It can foster a culture of learning and innovation as organizations gain insight into what methods are working well for others.

Benchmarking requires that the inquiring organizing has a thorough understanding of its own processes, and has established boundaries around the processes to be studied.

There are various types of benchmarking, including internal, competitive, functional, generic, and collaborative. *Internal benchmarking* involves examining similar processes between business units to identify best practices. In *competitive benchmarking* an organization seeks to compare its performance against that of one or more competitors. Of course, an organization needs to understand who its competitors are before this type of benchmarking can be accomplished. *Functional benchmarking* focuses on comparing performance or processes to other organizations with similar processes in the same function, but outside the industry. The goal of *generic*, or *best-in-class benchmarking*, is to identify the processes that are the best performing regardless of the industry in which those processes are found.

Generally, benchmarking involves the following steps:

- Identify process to be benchmarked.
- Identify and train the team that will accomplish the benchmarking activity.
- Identify benchmarking partners.
- Collect and analyze benchmarking information.
- Compare performance against benchmarking partner.
- Assess how upgrading process will impact the organization.
- Establish new process.
- Monitor the results.
- Improve the process as appropriate.

Strategic plan deployment

Many organizations do a good job of strategic planning, but these efforts fail due to lack of a deployment strategy. This usually results in the strategic planning document sitting on a shelf gathering dust, disenchanted workers who won't take the next strategic planning exercise seriously and, importantly, lost opportunities for positioning the organization to achieve its objectives. Developing and implementing a deployment strategy should be thought of just as important as the planning phase discussed previously.

Deploying a strategic plan means making the strategic objectives actionable, implementing them, and measuring their effectiveness.

Action plans

Action plans are derived from strategic objectives created during strategic planning. There may be one or more action plans developed for each objective. Action plans normally include:

- Project name and description.
- Strategic objective being addressed.
- Start and due dates.
- Project objectives.
- Scope of the project.
- Deliverables.
- Measurement criteria.
- Resources needed (not just money, but time, personnel, supplies, facilities, etc.).
- Gantt chart with the work broken down into manageable units, persons responsible identified, dependencies listed.
- Other items as appropriate.

The astute reader may have read through the list above and recognized that it looks like a project plan, and that's exactly what it is! In reality, action plans are mini-projects and should be treated accordingly. This means that those teams developing and executing action plans need to have a good understanding of project management theory and practice. (A brief introduction to the topic of project management is found later in this chapter.)

Performance measurement

In the past, organizational performance was assessed based almost entirely on financial results. In sharp contrast to that, modern quality management theory states that a number of factors must be measured to understand how the organization is performing.

There are several reasons why performance measurement is important. First, performance measurement ensures that there is organizational alignment in terms of strategies and actions. We must measure what we value rather than what is easy to measure. As well, the areas we measure should be in harmony with our organizational strategies. If we have an organizational strategy pertaining to, say, ramp safety, we should measure our performance in that area. This helps ensure that behaviors align with strategies and values. Second, we measure performance to know what success is and when we've achieved it. This is accomplished by gathering the best data available in accordance with the system we've created for that purpose. Third, we measure performance to improve. The data is then used to drive improvement.

Important areas to measure are:

- Outcomes customers desire.
- Outcomes customers wish to avoid.
- Product, service, or process characteristics customers desire.
- Outcomes the organization desires.
- Outcomes the organization wishes to avoid.
- Product, service, or process characteristics organizations desire.

Typical performance measurement tools include sales figures, production reports, customer survey reports, safety reports, and, of course, financial reports.

As we've stressed elsewhere in this book, managers would be well-served by refocusing their attention from outcomes to processes. Focusing on processes will help to ensure that repeatable and reliable outcomes are achieved. From that perspective, one can immediately see the value in having closed-loop versus open-loop processes. Closed-loop processes are those that are designed to feed information back into the process to enable the process to be monitored. Only a process that is monitored and measured can be improved.

Closed-loop processes have two outputs:

1. the intended change in the input(s) from the application of a particular operation, and
2. information gleaned from the process that can be used to manage, control, and improve the process.

Open-loop processes typically have only the first one. Thus, closed-loop processes produce data. This data is used to inform the decision making necessary to achieve improvement.

Balanced scorecard

One popular method of measuring performance is the balanced scorecard. The purpose of a balanced scorecard is to provide a comprehensive measure of performance in terms of the organization's vision and strategies. This method does not in itself aid in the creation of the strategic plan; rather it is a management system used in the deployment process. By encouraging the organization to think beyond just financial measures, the balanced scorecard helps focus attention on other important perspectives of performance, such as the customer, internal business processes, and learning and growth, and to define appropriate metrics for measuring progress in these areas. This "balanced" approach to measuring performance assists the organization in achieving its strategic goals and results by developing and managing appropriate objectives, measures, targets, and initiatives for each of these four perspective.

Learning and growth   Organizations must learn and innovate in order to achieve their goals—this is the learning and growth perspective. Metrics in this area should measure the ability of the organization's employees and information systems to attain corporate improvement and adapt to change.

Customer perspective   The customer perspective is a fundamental tenet of quality, and is a key perspective of the balanced scorecard method. This perspective focuses on satisfying those who receive an organization's products and services. As obvious as this may seem, this area is often overlooked because some organizations find it difficult to measure. Even when the precision attainable in measuring customer satisfaction is not high, organizations must strive to determine the appropriate objectives, measures, targets, and initiatives, and to identify leading and lagging indicators of customer satisfaction.

Internal business perspective   The internal business process perspective includes strategic management, and those that apply to mission-oriented and support processes. Metrics are developed that tell management how the operation is running, and whether the products or services it is producing are meeting customer requirements.

Financial perspective   Obviously, the financial perspective is also important. Managers must have timely and accurate data regarding financial matters to make effective decisions.

Once the objectives are determined via the strategic planning process, the balanced scorecard method can be used to transform these objectives into measurable, reportable indicators of performance. Used in this method, the strategic plan, the action plans, and the balanced scorecard all interact to become a powerful means of ensuring that an organization achieves its purposes.

Dashboard

A (digital) dashboard is similar in some ways to a scorecard, but different in substantive ways as well. Dashboards are software-based reporting mechanism that aggregate and visually display metrics and key performance indicators via components such as gauges and dials. They are software-based, and usually have drill-down capabilities to allow users to obtain only the level of information necessary. Dashboards report information in virtually real-time as opposed to scorecards which report information in prescribed intervals.

While scorecards are management systems, dashboards are measurement systems. Often easier to deploy than a scorecard, dashboards can be setup for a single business unit or the organizational as a whole. Dashboards frequently use the metrics derived from a balanced scorecard and, thus, are a powerful tool for communicating organizational performance.

Quality information system

Many organizations have developed a quality information system (QIS) and rely on that QIS for helping to achieve quality and make better decisions. A specific type of management information system, the QIS is a computer database system that can process and store large amounts of quality information, and is designed to learn from that information. The QIS stores and analyzes such information as customer requirements, measurement data, specifications, processes, and so on. An effective QIS is fully integrated with other management information systems, including marketing, finance, sales, and manufacturing. A QIS can be a powerful tool for tracking problems and corrective actions, generating solutions, and supporting and driving quality improvement efforts in an organization.

Documentation

Documentation is a critical component of a quality program. Documentation must be clear, accurate, and reflect compliance with standards or regulations. Quality documentation has several purposes:

- To define—standards, quality assurance procedures, policy and procedure manuals.
- To verify—records, data sheets, meeting minutes.
- To explain—manuals, instructions, training.

The quality manual describes the quality management system of an organization. The organization's plans for achieving its quality goals and objectives are documented in the quality manual.

Figure 3.22 depicts the typical quality documentation hierarchy.

The top tier, Tier 1, represents a policy statement, which is typically the opening statement in the quality manual. The policy statement is management's policy and objectives for quality.

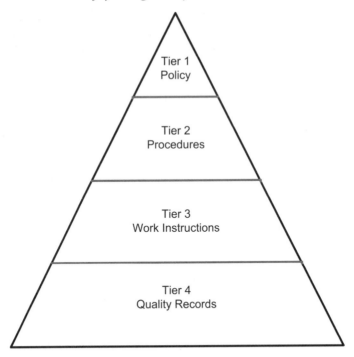

Figure 3.22 Quality documentation hierarchy

Tier 2 consists of procedures. Procedures are sometimes contained in the quality manual, but more often are distributed throughout the organization in other ways. Procedures can be thought of as how an organization actually does its business. Good procedures explain who is to accomplish the procedure, what the procedure is, when it is to be accomplished and, if applicable, where it is to be accomplished. Procedures should refer to work instructions.

Work instructions constitute Tier 3. Work instructions provide specific details about the manner in which work is accomplished, usually based on a specific job title.

Tier 4 is quality records. These are the results obtained through the quality system. It is these results that enable an organization to verify that it is doing what it says it is doing.

Document control allows authorized copies of manuals to be distributed wherever they need to go. Modern document control tools enable the management of all documents throughout their life cycle. Many of these tools facilitate document generation, approval, routing, revision control, access, and audit capabilities.

Common problems related to quality documentation include redundancy and complexity. Some quality experts believe that company documentation can be reduced by 50 percent or more just be eliminating the redundancy that exists in the documentation. For example, enumerating policies on procedures documents, including exhibits in procedures, including verbiage included in other documents rather than referring to that document, are common errors that simply add bulk to the documents with no value-added.

Complexity often results from organizational efforts to generate documentation that aren't well coordinated. Failure to approach this task from a systems perspective results in various departments or units creating similar, overlapping, and sometimes contradictory documents.

Project management

> It must be considered that there is nothing more difficult to carry out nor more doubtful of success nor more dangerous to handle than to initiate a new order of things.
>
> *Machiavelli*

It is difficult to image a complex project being accomplished today without following a project management approach. Building a new baseball stadium, repaving a length of interstate highway, producing a movie, and launching a new operating system for your computer are all examples of projects that require a high level of planning and execution to be successful.

But the project approach is being used in the workplace every day in nearly every organization for much smaller projects as well. Business is about rapid change in product or service, and change requires the tools and skill sets found in the project approach.

Some businesses employ the services of project management specialists. Many organizations, though, so value project management skills that they provide such training to their regular workforce, arguing that nearly everyone is engaged in project management at some level.

The growth and interest in the discipline of project management has increased at a terrific rate in the past several years. A great illustration of that is the growth in membership in the largest professional association focused on project management— Project Management Institute (PMI). Ten years ago, PMI had a membership of about 24,000; today membership in PMI exceeds 240,000 in 160 countries (PMI, 2007)! That is a clear indication of the business community's recognition of the importance of project management knowledge and skills in today's business environment.

Project management skills are essential for quality management professionals; in fact knowledge and skills in this discipline are included in the body of knowledge for quality managers (i.e., American Society for Quality's Certified Manager of Quality/ Organizational Excellence).

So, too, are these skills necessary for individuals engaged in the management of safety systems. In every sense, efforts to improve safety systems can be characterized by specific objectives, a defined life span, multiple units participating, the triple constraints of time/cost/performance, and the fact that the specific effort has never been done before. Indeed, these are the very factors that make a project a project!

Definition of a project

A project is a "complex, nonroutine, one-time effort limited by time, budget, resources, and performance specifications designed to meet customer needs" (Gray & Larson,

2008, p. 5). This definition emphasizes the imperative to understand the customers' needs. Failure to address their needs is a sure recipe for not meeting them!

Role of the project manager

The role of managers is to plan, staff, organize, lead, and control. That is essentially what project managers do, but instead of managing a company or a business unit, they manage a specific project.

There are some factors that make being a project manager quite different from traditional management roles. First, the members of a project management team are often on-loan from their functional departments where their actual supervisors are, and where their allegiances lie. This often results in the project manager having less influence over the employee than is enjoyed by the functional manager. Second, the resources available to a project manager are often very limited and are often provided by functional areas. Third, project managers rarely possess the technical expertise of the functional manager, so they have to rely on the talents and abilities of those assigned to the project team for that expertise. These factors, among others, make the role of a project manager dynamic and challenge, and not for the faint of heart!

Nearly every project is limited by the triple constraints of time (when it can begin and when it must end, as well as schedule milestones), cost (budgetary limitations), and performance (characteristics of the project fulfilling requirements). Often one or more of these constraints can be traded off for others. For example, for more money we can reduce the time it takes to complete the project. To increase performance we can increase time and/or cost. The task of a project manager, then, is to balance these constraints to achieve the project objectives.

Project life cycle

Projects typically pass sequentially through four phases: defining, planning, executing, and delivering. Since resources needed and project focus varies according to what stage the project is it is essential for the project manager to understand these phases.

The first phase is *defining*. Many managers believe that the defining phase is the most important part of the project, since that is where goals, specifications, and objectives are established, and major responsibilities are assigned. This phase is usually completed fairly early in the project.

The second phase is *planning*. The planning phase is where schedules, budgets, and resources are determined in order for the project to meet its objectives. Risks to the project are determined and assessed in this phase. Planning begins in earnest after the defining phase, and continues throughout the majority of the project.

Executing is the third phase. This phase involves reporting on status, change management, quality, and forecasting. The executing phase is the most resource intensive and extends virtually from the beginning to the end of the project.

The fourth and last phase is *delivering*. Delivering includes transferring the product or service to the customer, training the customer on its use, transferring required documentation, releasing project personnel, and recording lessons learned.

Unfortunately, delivery is often a poorly performed aspect of the project due to participants' eagerness to move on to other work. As its name implies, delivery almost entirely resides at the end of the project.

Project selection

Every project undertaken should have a direct link to the organization's strategic plan, otherwise, why do it? Projects should reflect the organization's priorities and help it achieve its business objectives. As discussed earlier, the deployment of the strategy is accomplished through projects.

Many organizations manage project selection through a *portfolio management system*. Businesses use various systems for classifying projects according to what makes sense for them, but generally, projects fall into three classifications: compliance, operational, and strategic. Compliance-based projects are those that must be done to remain in compliance with a regulation, standard, law, or other directive, and where failure to do so may result in a penalty to the organization. Operational projects are those that are undertaken to not only sustain the operations of the business, but also to improve those operations in some way. Strategic-based projects support new endeavors of the organization, such as a new product or service. Some organizations employ complex financial models and other criteria to determine whether proposed projects are accepted or rejected and, if accepted, prioritized.

Defining the project

As we mentioned, the first step in the life cycle of a project is to define the project. Defining the project has several components. Two of the most significant components—project scope and the work breakdown structure—will be discussed.

Project scope   Think of the project scope as the end result or purpose of the project. It is what the customer will have upon successful completion of the project. The project scope is developed by the customer and project manager, and must be clearly and carefully documented into a scope statement. Scope statements include deliverables, timelines, milestones, technical requirements, and exclusions. Success of the project is measured against this document.

Unfortunately, project scope is often overlooked and underemphasized. Research has shown that a poorly defined scope statement is the most common cause of project failure.

Work breakdown structure   Projects begin with a scope statement, which is broad statement describing the objective of the project. For any work to be accomplished, though, this objective must be broken down into greater detail such that individual tasks can be accomplished. The work breakdown structure (WBS) is the outcome of this process, and is a detailed map of the project. The lowest level of a WBS is a work package. A work package is a definable element of work that has a beginning and end point, specific resource needs, and a cost. There can be hundreds of work packages in complex projects, and the sum of all the work package costs represents the total project costs.

Planning the project

The project management plan is "a formal, approved *document* that defines how the project is executed, monitored and controlled. It may be summary or detailed, and may be composed of one or more subsidiary management plans and other planning documents" (PMI, 2004, p. 369).

Now that the project has been defined, it must be planned. This includes planning for what the project is expected to cost, how long it will take, and will be accomplished at the end of the project.

Project costs and time   Based on the work packages, costs can be estimated. There are several types of costs in projects, including direct costs (i.e., labor, material, equipment, and other), project overhead costs (connected directly to specific projects), and general and administrative overhead costs (not connected directly with specific projects). Costs and budgets are not synonyms. Costs become budgets only after they are time-phased to the project.

There are numerous models for estimating costs, ranging from the company's own database, macro methods (upper level managers' estimates), consensus methods (similar to the Delphi method), ratio methods and apportion methods. The ratio method derives cost and time estimates from a formula, such as knowing that renovations of commercial property in a certain area costs x per square foot, and the property to be renovated is y square feet, the product of those factors becomes the ratio estimate. The apportion method is similar to the ratio method, and assumes that future project costs and time will follow past experience, so estimates are derived based on that past experience applied to the current project.

No project ever goes according to plan; something always causes estimates to be off-the-mark. Project managers should resist the temptation to overestimate to account for overruns; that's the purpose of contingency funds and time buffers. There are models and methods for contingency planning, but the rule is: the greater the uncertainty in the estimates, the greater the contingency funds and time buffers that are needed.

The project network diagram

The project network diagram is developed from the WBS, and is used for planning, scheduling, and monitoring project progress. It is very similar in purpose and appearance to the Activity Network Diagram discussed earlier. The project network depicts the project activities including the order in which they are completed, the relative times to complete each task, and the interdependencies of the tasks. In addition, the network diagram reveals the critical path of the project, which is the longest pathway through the project. Network diagrams indicate when resources are needed and, thus, assist in the scheduling of labor, equipment, and other resources.

Risk management

It is inevitable that in any complex project there are going to be multiple risks to its successful completion. Risk is an uncertain event that, if it occurs, can have a positive or negative effect on the project.

Prudent project managers will develop a risk management plan for their projects. A risk management plan attempts to *proactively* identify the risks, assess the risks, develop a response to the risks, and control the risk response. This may include the provision of contingency funds. The key to an effective risk management plan is to do this planning proactively when time, cost, and an array of technical solutions are at the disposal of the project manager.

Contingency plans should recognize that the likelihood and costs of risks occurring are *not* distributed evenly throughout the project life cycle. In fact, the likelihood of a risk event occurring is much greater in the beginning of the life cycle and much less at the end. Conversely, the cost of a risk event is minimal at the beginning and maximum at the end of the life cycle. Intuitively, this makes sense. For example, in the early stages of a project there are nearly an infinite number of possible events that may occur, but if they do occur, there is ample time to implement a contingency solution at low cost.

Risk identification Risk identification attempts to generate a listing of all possible risks to the project. This should almost always be accomplished by a team using brainstorming methods.

Risk assessment The risks determined through identification should then be assessed for significance. Some of the risks can usually be discarded. Others require significant attention. A common tool used at this stage is called the risk severity matrix where the likelihood and severity are the two factors of the matrix. The Failure Mode Effects Analysis discussed earlier extends the matrix by including ability to detect the failure into the matrix. From either tool a risk value is calculated.

Decision trees and Program Evaluation and Review Technique (PERT) are additional tools that are used to assess risk. A PERT simulation uses statistical distributions to determine an optimistic and pessimistic likelihood of completing the project on time and on budget.

Risk response Developing a response to the risk usually involves mitigating the risk (either through reducing the likelihood of the event or the severity of the event), avoiding, transferring, sharing, and retaining.

Risk response control Executing the risk management plan and monitoring indicators of triggering events are part of the risk response control.

Project execution Project execution is also an area where many projects stumble. This should not be surprising since you'll recall that project execution spans nearly the entire project life cycle. From a project management perspective, project execution can be characterized by evaluation and control of the project.

Project monitoring information systems (PMISs) are used to track progress. Determining which data to collect and the appropriate measurement metrics are the keys to an effective PMIS). The PMIS is then used to report progress.

Project control generally involves four steps: establishing a baseline plan regarding cost and schedule, derived from the WBS; measuring progress and performance which, for cost related measures, is accomplished using *earned value* (EV) formulas; comparing plan against actual to detect deviations or gaps; and acting to close those gaps.

A crucial point to understand is that any evaluation must be made against a time-phased baseline plan. This is where the importance of the EV system emerges. Using the time-phased baseline, comparisons can be made between the actual and planned time schedule and costs. While a thorough treatment of EV is beyond the scope of this book, the following definitions are provided for the convenience of the reader.

- EV   =   Earned Value is the percent complete times the original budget.
- PV   =   Budgeted Cost of the Work Scheduled.
- AC   =   Actual Cost of the Work Performed.
- CV   =   Cost Variance is the difference between the EV of work performed and the actual cost.
- SV   =   Schedule Variance is the difference between the EV and the PV.
- CPI =   Cost Performance Index is the EV divided by the AC.
- SPI =   Schedule Performance Index is the EV divided by the PV.
- BAC =   Budget at Completion (i.e., project budget).
- EAC =   Estimate at Completion.
- ETC =   Estimate to Complete.
- VAC =   Variance at Completion.

Delivering the project

Every project ends in some manner, whether it is due to successful completion, cancellation, or postponement. Project delivery ensures that proper closeout procedures are executed depending on what type of closure was initiated.

Delivering the project to the customer on time and within budget is the most desirable circumstance, but that is not always possible. Sometimes projects simply don't work due to lack of planning, changed priorities of the organization, unanticipated events, or other reasons.

Team member and project manager evaluations should be completed in a timely fashion. All billing should be accomplished. Key information from the project along with lessons learned should be recorded in the organization's database. Documentation should be delivered to the customer. These are just some examples of the many tasks necessary in the final phase of the project life cycle.

Reliability

Any system that depends on reliability is unreliable.

Author Unknown

We've all done it. We've pulled the holiday decorations out of the attic or basement, untangled the inevitable knots in the Christmas lights, plugged them in and—nothing. No light. They just don't work when you expect them to. Or, you tug on the starter rope of the lawn mower—nothing. We can all think of many examples of when items just don't work as intended. Some examples of things not working as intended are a flat tire, a drippy water faucet, a taxi that never shows up, and an airliner that arrives too late for you to make your connecting flight.

In everyday life, we tend to think of reliability as "when stuff just works". Well, more precisely, reliability is the probability that a product or service will continue to perform its intended function without failure for a specified period of time under stated conditions. Reliability is important for many of the same reasons that quality is important:

- The company's reputation is a function of the product or service being available when it is needed.
- We want satisfied customers who we can retain as customers.
- We desire to reduce our warranty and repair costs.
- Having an effective reliability program can give us a competitive advantage.

While it is not the purpose of this book to delve into the formulas and underlying theories of reliability, we do believe it is useful for the student and practitioner of safety management to have a comprehension of the *basic* theories.

System reliability

In a *series* system, there are *n* components or subsystems connected in a series (see Figure 3.23). In this kind of system, the failure of any component results in the failure of the system. The reliability of a series system is simply the product of the reliabilities of each of its components, as represented by the following formula:

$$R=P(x_1)P(x_2)...P(x_n)$$

where $P(x_i)$ is the reliability of component x_i.

If Component 1 had a reliability of .95, Component 2 was .90, and Component 3 was .85, the reliability for this series system would be .73.

In a *parallel* system, failure of a component in the system would not necessarily cause the failure of the system since there are other paths that may perform properly. A parallel system is represented by the following formula:

$$R=1-P(1-x_1)P(1-x_2)...P(1-x_n)$$

where $P(x_i)$ is the probability of failure of component x_i. Figure 3.24 depicts a parallel system.

Figure 3.23 Series system

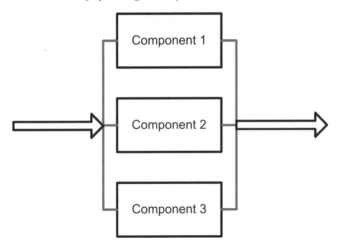

Figure 3.24 Parallel system

If Component 1 had a reliability of .88, Component 2 a reliability of .85, and Component 3 a reliability of .90, the reliability for this parallel system would be .9982.

In reality the design of a given system is typically composed of combinations of series and parallel systems.

Measures of reliability

Reliability is quantified by three functions: the reliability function, the probability density function, and the hazard rate function.

The reliability function at a certain time *(t)* is the probability that a component will survive a time greater than *t*. The formula for the reliability function is:

$$R(t) = \frac{(n-x)}{n}$$

where *x* = number of observed failures, and *(n—x)* equals survivors.

The probability density function represents the failure probability at a certain point in time (rather than the cumulative failure probability up to a certain time *(t)*. The formula is:

$$f(t) = \lambda e^{-\lambda t}$$

where λ is the constant hazard rate.

Finally, the hazard function, also known as the instantaneous failure rate function, is represented by the following formula:

$$h(t) = \frac{f(t)}{R(t)}$$

Various textbooks more focused on reliability will provide examples of the use of each of these formulas.

Perhaps the most common measures of reliability are the mean time to failure (MTTF) and the mean time between failures (MTBF). MTTF is used when the system is non-repairable (e.g., a light bulb), and MTBF is used when the system is repairable (e.g., an airplane).

When the failure rate is constant the MTTF is simply the reciprocal of the failure rate. When the assumption of constant failure rate cannot be made, the following formula applies:

$$MTTF = \frac{1}{n}\sum_{i=1}^{n} t_i$$

The Bathtub curve

It is important to note in the definition provided above that reliability is a function of time. This element of time is important in the context of failure *rate* models, such as the *bathtub curve* (see Figure 3.25). The bathtub curve depicts failure rate versus time, and has three distinct regions. The first region is the early life or infant mortality region, which is characterized by a decreasing failure rate over time. Failures in this region are typically a result of manufacturing defects or shipping. The second region is the constant failure rate region. Failures in this region occur in a random pattern over time. The third region is known as the wear-out region, which is characterized by an increasing failure rate over time.

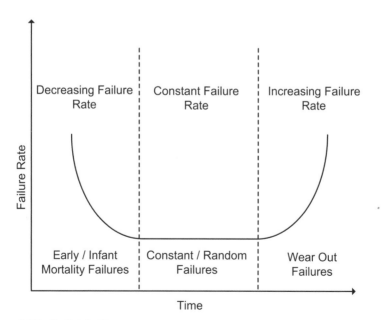

Figure 3.25 Bathtub Curve

The bathtub curve does an excellent job of representing the failure rate of many, but not all, types of items.

Reliability engineering

The goal of reliability engineering is to ensure that a system will operate in its intended manner under specified conditions. Reliability engineering has been applied most commonly to manufacturing settings, but it is applicable to all systems.

In systems where reliability is vital, a reliability program plan is often developed. The reliability program plan specifies customer requirements with respect to system reliability; the organization's strategy to attain that reliability; the tools, methods, and procedures that are used; interfaces with various stakeholders; a reliability responsibilities matrix; and documentation regarding testing, analysis, and input to related functional areas, such as safety engineering, program management, and others.

As with quality, reliability must be designed into the system. There are numerous techniques for designing for reliability, but an important starting point is modeling. Reliability modeling provides a graphical depiction of the relationships between different parts of the system, and aids reliability engineers in determining strategies for improving reliability by reducing or eliminating failure points, providing for system redundancy, and other techniques. Modeling can be as simple as creating block diagrams depicting the nature of the system, such as series, parallel, etc., to more advanced simulations methods, such as Monte Carlo, Markov, and others.

Review questions

1. What are the seven basic quality tools? Why are they important?
2. Explain the concept of variation (what is it, where does it exist, what types are there, etc.)
3. What is the difference between attribute and variables control charts?
4. Explain why correlation between two variables does not necessarily imply causation.
5. Explain safety assurance.
6. What is the PDCA cycle and when is it useful?
7. Explain the Hoshin planning process.
8. Describe the various types of benchmarking.
9. Describe the four phases of projects.
10. Explain the significance of a bathtub curve.

References

Federal Aviation Administration [FAA] (2006). *Introduction to Safety Management Systems for Air Operators*. Advisory Circular 120-92. Retrieved December 3, 2007 from http://rgl.faa.gov/Regulatory_and_Guidance_Library /rgAdvisoryCircular.nsf/0/6485143d5ec81aae8625719b0055c9e5/$FILE/ AC%20120-92.pdf.

Gray, C., and Larson, E. (2008). *Project Management: The Managerial Process*, 4th ed. New York: McGraw-Hill.

Ishikawa, K. (1985). *What is Total Quality Control?* Englewood Cliffs, NJ: Prentice Hall.

Juran, J. (ed.), (1995). *A History of Managing for Quality: The Evolution, Trends, and Future Directions of Managing for Quality*. Milwaukee, WI: ASQC Quality Press.

Project Management Institute [PMI] (2004). *A Guide to the Project Management Body of Knowledge*, 3rd ed. Newtown Square, PA: Project Management Institute.

Project Management Institute [PMI] (2007). *"Who We Are."* Retrieved December 3, 2007 from http://www.pmi.org/WhoWeAre/Pages/Default.aspx.

Sabatini, N. (2005). "SMS: I'm a Believer." *Safety Management Systems Symposium*. McLean, VA.

Westcott, R. (ed.), (2006). *The Certified Manager of Quality/Organizational Excellence Handbook,* 3rd ed. Milwaukee, WI: ASQ Quality Press.

Chapter 4

Hazards

Insisting on perfect safety is for people who don't have the b*lls to live in the real world.

Mary Shafer

SMS in Practice

In a speech at the International Safety Forum in 2007, Robert Sturgell, Acting FAA Administrator, offered his perspective on SMS:

> So how are we going to raise the bar? The answer to that, I think, is simple to say but a challenge to implement. The answer is SMS—safety management systems—and the challenge I'm here to issue today is for each of the people in this room to become activists for safety management systems. If your operation, or organization, or your nation, doesn't have one in place or isn't yet moving toward developing one, that needs to change.
>
> The challenge for you is to return to your cockpit, your workplace, your country, and push hard for SMS. Aviation no longer is in the business of combing through ashes and wreckage to find answers. SMS will give us the intelligence we need before the problem reaches the headlines. When it comes to risks, the low-hanging fruit is long gone. SMS uses hard data to point us in the direction we need to go. We don't have to wait for something bad to happen.
>
> Here in the United States, fatal air carrier accidents have dropped 65 percent since 1996. That works out to one fatal for every 4.5 million departures. Internationally, the numbers are dropping as well. If the 1996 accident rate had remained the same through last year, there'd have been almost three dozen major accidents. The actual number of fatal accidents was 11.
>
> Yet, from an international perspective, accident rates vary considerably, with some regions doing well and some not so well.
>
> So, the point is that collectively, we all still need to take a step up, and I'm including the United States of America in that group as well. The safety management system approach will enable us to do that. SMS enables you to keep your eye on the ball every single day. Ultimately, we don't want to just meet ICAO minimums. Ultimately, our goal is to raise the bar worldwide no matter where you go. No matter what flag's on the tail. From takeoff to touchdown and all points in between, we want to ensure a consistent level of safety.

At its most fundamental level, a safety management system helps organizations identify and manage risk. It does not wait for something to happen. It doesn't rely on anecdotal information. It is based on hard data. Safety management systems help us manage risk far better than we have, because it's a disciplined and standardized approach to managing risk. We can review past experience and address known hazards at the same time we can look ahead and rigorously apply safety risk management.

At the very core of the SMS is the need to identify potential hazards and then analyze risk. After that, the next steps are to rank hazards and assess risk, and then identify mitigation options. It's a closed-loop process where identified risks are mitigated and the mitigations are monitored to provide continuous system safety.

Our Air Traffic Organization is adopting a Safety Management System for its operational policies, processes, and procedures.

Our Aviation Safety organization is moving to an SMS construct. Last year, Nick Sabatini's organization developed an SMS doctrine and now his group is moving surely to implementation. The next logical step to enhance safety is what I see as the evolution from "inspecting safety" to taking a systems approach with SMS.

What's important in this construct is that SMS is being implemented in accordance with ICAO standards that are themselves being changed to apply a systems approach to aviation safety in all aviation domains, including air carriers and airports.

That's a fundamental difference with the SMS approach—the process itself is overseen. The burden is on the service provider to ensure the safety of the products and services it provides—whether it is design and production of aircraft, air carrier operations, or air traffic control. In this way, both regulator and service provider can better target resources based on risk.

Perhaps the best way to characterize the safety management system is to say that it is a structure of voluntary, non-punitive reporting methods set up with an organization to foster safety awareness all across the board. Even small bits of information can point to a larger problem before that large problem can become a catastrophe.

Source: http://www.faa.gov/news/speeches/news_story.cfm?newsId=10032. (Excerpted statements of Robert A. Sturgell, Acting FAA Administrator to the 2007 International Safety Forum, November 29, 2007.)

SMS is a dynamic *risk management system* based on quality management system (QMS) principles in a structure scaled appropriately to the operational risk, applied in a safety culture environment. Chapters 4, 5, and 6 focus on the components of safety risk management: hazards, risks and controls. Before beginning the discussion, it is helpful to put all three concepts in context by taking a brief look at Safety Risk Management (SRM).

The 30,000 foot view of SRM

Let's begin our description of the SRM model with two very high-level summaries, as provided by the FAA and ICAO. First the FAA:

A. Safety Risk Management

1. SRM shall, at a minimum, include the following processes:
   a. system and task analysis;
   b. identify hazards;
   c. analyze safety risk;
   d. assess safety risk; and
   e. control safety risk.

B. The SRM process shall be applied to:

1. initial designs of systems, organizations, and/or products;
2. the development of operational procedures;
3. hazards that are identified in the safety assurance functions (audits, self-reporting systems, operational data analysis, etc.); and
4. planned changes to the operational processes to identify hazards associated with those changes.

ICAO presents a graphical description of the SMS risk management model in Figure 4.1 (ICAO, 2006, p. 5–7). Not surprisingly, there are strong similarities between the FAA and ICAO descriptions. The ICAO version graphically illustrates the cyclical nature of SMS.

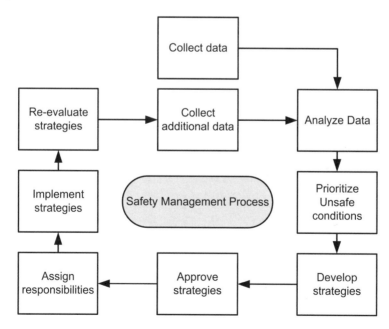

Figure 4.1   Safety management process—ICAO

The ICAO and FAA descriptions are associated in Table 4.1.

Though the FAA and ICAO choose to emphasize different components of SRM (each description detailing important pieces), they both describe a three-step process:

- Identify hazards.
- Assess risk.
- Control risk.

In our discussion below we will not choose one high level description over the other, but rather will refer to this general three-step process as the essence of SRM. Our intent is not to advocate one agency's perspective, but rather to clarify the elements they have in common, and to identify areas where both need further explication.

Before we begin with a discussion of hazard identification, it is worthwhile to note one difference in the FAA and ICAO descriptions. In the final steps described in the ICAO process, it is clear that the "re-evaluate control strategies" and "collect additional hazard data" illustrate that ICAO is advocating continuous improvement through a feedback process. Though the FAA overview of SRM noted above does not explicitly list continuous improvement as a part of SRM, Advisory Circular 120-92 is clear in its inclusion of quality feedback control mechanisms as a critical part of SMS. This is just a matter of presentation—both ICAO and the FAA strongly state that continuous improvement is a necessary part of SMS. We will later relate this continuous improvement feedback process advocated by both ICAO and the FAA to the central idea in a quality-system, Plan-Do-Check-Act (PDCA). This is the *management* in safety management. We'll return to this concept in Chapter 11 when we discuss horizontal change management through *Functional Safety Teams*—our term for Safety Action Groups (ICAO) or Safety Action Teams (FAA)—and vertical change management through the Safety Council.

Table 4.1   Comparison of high level safety risk management process descriptions—FAA and ICAO

FAA	ICAO
System and task analysis	Identify hazards
Identify hazards	
Analyze safety risk	Assess risks
Assess safety risk	Prioritize risks
Control safety risk	Develop elimination/mitigation strategies
	Approve control strategies
	Assign responsibilities
	Implement control strategies
	Re-evaluate control strategies
	Collect additional hazard data

In order to reach our goal of clarifying SRM, we will proceed through descriptions of the components of the "standard model" of SRM as presently put forward by most reference material. That presentation will contain descriptions of hazards, controls, risks, severity, likelihood, the risk matrix, risk indices, and ALARP (as low as reasonably practicable). These are the components of that standard model, but if one ponders the essential elements of SRM above—identify hazards, assess risk, control risk—one can see that the entirety of SRM encompasses a much larger challenge and effort than is implied by this short list of tools. The SMS practitioner needs to understand what this standard model encompasses, but more importantly he or she needs to understand that true SRM is that larger task, the PDCA of safety management.

Note that this presentation and explanation of the elements of the SMS risk management process will be in a conceptual order, starting with hazard identification and proceeding through the steps we will outline below. But be alert for a pitfall. We are at this point *not* trying to describe *how to implement* SMS. We are attempting to build the theoretical understanding of a *model* of risk management. As with trying to understand any model, it can help to describe a system by stating "first A, then B, then C", but the actual functioning of the system will be much more dynamic. So while it is true that in this section we will be presenting the elements of risk management in SMS in a logical stepwise sequence, don't mistake this as our prescription for SMS implementation.

It is important to understand the conceptual basis for SMS before moving into implementation strategies, and that is what this section will attempt to convey. But it is equally important to know that we as an industry will be implementing SMS into an already very complex and fully functional system, that in many ways and for many years has identified hazards and mitigated risks with a high degree of success. We are not starting from scratch, but rather re-engineering a system to conform to new models of risk and quality management. That re-engineering will *not* be best accomplished by artificially imposing the order of engagement described in this theoretical discourse. We will later describe in detail the intricacies of applying these concepts—as you review the fundamentals in this chapter, be sure to keep in mind that an application of this theory into present-day aviation operations is more complicated than a high-level conceptual discussion.

Hazards explained

In order to generate risk measurements, against which strategies can be created and prioritized, and through comparison to Target Levels of Safety (TLS) progress can be measured, it is necessary to first start with a more basic concept, hazard identification. From a conceptual perspective the derivation of SMS's risk management process depends upon an accurate and consistent method of hazard identification.

So understanding the process of hazard identification will be our first task in understanding the larger SMS process. We're going to take a close look at hazard identification, even to the extent of parsing the phrase down to the level of definitions for each word. Far from being just an intellectual exercise, we think that there are important concepts to bring out of these words—ones that will guide our later suggestions for practical SMS implementation strategies.

Definitions

We will begin our exploration with the first concept in the SMS process flow, that of "hazard". We'll try to keep the conceptual discussion of SRM sequential, consistent with the process outlined above, but in order to get a firm handle on the definition of hazard, it will be helpful to contrast it with the definition of risk offered by ICAO and the FAA.

Hazard: definitions

Both agencies provide similar definitions of hazard:

- Hazard (ICAO)—"Condition, object or activity with the potential of causing injuries to personnel, damage to equipment or structures, loss of material, or reduction of ability to perform a prescribed function." (ICAO, 2007a).
- Hazard (FAA)—"any existing or potential condition that can lead to injury, illness, or death to people; damage to or loss of a system, equipment, or property; or damage to the environment. A hazard is a condition that is a prerequisite to an accident or incident." (FAA, 2006, Appendix 1, p. 2).

The operative words in both of these definitions speak to potentialities. The word hazard itself is both an identification and a classification of conditions that exist prior to or associated with another occurrence, and which are precursors or contributing factors to that condition.

Let's contrast these definitions with the agencies' definitions of risk:

Risk: definitions

- Risk (ICAO)—"The likelihood of injury to personnel, damage to equipment or structures, loss of material, or reduction of ability to perform a prescribed function, measured in terms of probability and severity." (ICAO, 2007a).
- Risk (FAA)—"The composite of predicted severity and likelihood of the potential effect of a hazard in the worst credible system state." (FAA, 2006, Appendix 1, p. 3)

While hazard speaks to abstract potentialities, risk deals with consequences, and their probability of occurring. It's an important distinction, best illustrated by examples.

Examples of hazards versus risks

In its discussion of the distinction between hazard and risk, ICAO gives a good contrast:

- A crosswind blowing from a direction that is perpendicular to the runway at 15 knots is a good example of a hazard.
- The potential of an aircraft departing the side of the runway during the landing roll, as a result of inadequate compensation for that crosswind, is a good example of a risk.

Another way to think of the difference is to associate hazards with contributing factors, and risks with consequences, and measures of "scariness" of the state of things, as hazards are (or are not) controlled. If you encounter a description of a hazard that speaks to the state of something, for example:

- A hard landing,
- A skid on an icy surface,
- An incorrect maintenance procedure applied,
- A bent towbar,
- An aircraft off assigned altitude,

then you are most likely seeing the description of a risk rather than a hazard. Think "contributing factor" when identifying hazards.

Identification equals classification

Earlier we suggested that in order to understand the central meaning of "hazard", we would parse the phrase "hazard identification" in some detail. We'll do that now, in order to drive home the point that hazard identification has inherent within it a process of classification. Given that, we should be conscious and intentional about the taxonomy we use to classify the hazards we identify. We will gain much by being consistent.

First, it is important to recognize a subtle but important point about the use of the word hazard. Before we ever get to the point of making a finer distinction on the types of hazards we see in aviation operations, by the very fact of discriminating "pre-existing conditions" into "hazards" and "not-hazards", we are engaged in the act of classification. We are either consciously or subconsciously deciding that some of those pre-existing conditions have inherent within them the potential to influence an outcome so as to increase operational risk. We make these judgments upon the basis of experience.

An interesting study was accomplished several years ago at the University of South Florida in which pilots were grouped by levels of experience, and then asked to review and then classify ASAP-like reports into types of hazards encountered and the severity of the resulting situation (Prince, 1999). Not surprisingly, the group with the highest experience level was most consistent in its classifications and in its severity assignments. In contrast, the group with the least experience was less consistent, and more importantly, mis-understood or mis-classified high-severity hazards.

Prince securely established a principle that must be observed when identifying hazards in SMS; that is, the only group that can identify hazards consistently, accurately and dependably are those engaged in the operation under study. In SMS, hazard identification cannot be an ivory tower exercise—it requires that the "E" in SME (subject matter expert) be a part of the team. As you recall from the discussion of the principles of quality management, the most effective management is one that pushes decision-making out onto the shop floor, in this case using the real world experience of the front line employees to name for us those hazards they live with every day.

Information gain and loss during classification

There is another interesting contradiction to consider in a discussion of hazard identification. It has to do with the fact that since identification equals classification, we both gain and lose information when we identify.

To illustrate this contradiction, we'll stray briefly from our field, but not too far—let's look at a conversation between two ornithologists:

Bird Guy 1:	What's that bird?
Bird Guy 2:	What's it look like?
Bird Guy 1:	It has bright red plumage. And a little tuft on its head. It's medium size. And has an orange beak with a black face. And ...
Bird Guy 2:	Aha. It's a cardinal.

Information gain   The interesting thing about identifying something by classifying it is that now we know a lot more about that bird, knowledge that is not directly based upon the information we extracted from that one brief encounter. We know that its mother was not bright red, but instead a reddish gray. We know it eats mostly seeds, grains and fruits. We know that this bird will not migrate next winter, but will tough it out with us during the cold weather. By identifying (classifying) the bird as a cardinal, we can know much more about it than we would otherwise know by simply observing it. Identification is an information gaining process.

Information loss   But it also can be a lossy process. What Bird Guy 1 was about to say just before Number 2's aha moment was, "and it has little yellow feathers at the tip of its wings." This one fact, inconsistent with the "classic" definition of cardinal, might be inconsequential for most purposes, but essential for others. If the bird guys ever want to study this topic, or if they later find that the rate of speciation is relevant to the original question they were investigating in the first place, the fact of the yellow tipped wings is important. But since it doesn't fit into their pre-existing identification definitions, there is a risk of losing this information.

Taxonomies and information gain   This contradiction has much to do with the issue at hand—hazard identification. The first point to be made is that there is much for us as a community to be gained by giving serious thought to, and coming to consensus on, a common hazard language. Just as the bird guys added to their knowledge of that individual bird when they were able to identify it as a cardinal, we can extract useful information from the careful work and study that the development of a common taxonomy requires, when using that taxonomy to identify specific hazards in specific operations. There are other powerful reasons for the entire aviation community to come to consensus on the adoption of a common hazard and risk taxonomy (not the least of which is the extreme difficulty of accomplishing aggregate analysis without that commonality—especially important given that such analysis is the basis upon which to calculate likelihood of occurrence), but even at the individual event level, we gain when using consistent language.

Guarding against information loss   But there is another side of that contradiction—the little yellow feathers.

In the dim recesses of the authors' past, we were closely enough associated with Airline X to be aware of a couple of interesting events, both occurring on the same day, in fact in the same general geographic location. In these events, separated by a few hours, two aircraft of the same make and model were transitioning an area of convective activity, well above the tops of the cumulonimbus clouds. During this transition, both experienced transient dual air data computer losses and generator trips, along with communication and navigation problems. In both cases, normal functioning was regained after a few short-but-riveting minutes, and the flights proceeded to their destinations without incident.

In the home-grown and somewhat tortuous classification schema that Airline X used in its event reporting program, these two events were classified as "aircraft malfunctions" and "static discharge events". It just so happened, though, that one of us had just read a fascinating article about "*red sprites*" and "*blue jets*" (Heavner, 2004).

Red Sprites and Blue Jets

Sprites are massive but weak luminous flashes that appear directly above an active thunderstorm system and are coincident with cloud-to-ground or intracloud lightning strokes. Their spatial structures range from small single or multiple vertically elongated spots, to spots with faint extrusions above and below, to bright groupings which extend from the cloud tops to altitudes up to about 95 km. Sprites are predominantly red. The brightest region lies in the altitude range 65–75 km, above which there is often a faint red glow or wispy structure that extends to about 90 km. Below the bright red region, blue tendril-like filamentary structures often extend downward to as low as 40 km. Sprites rarely appear singly, usually occurring in clusters of two, three or more. Some of the very large events, such as shown in [Figure 4.2] seem to be tightly packed clusters of many individual sprites. Other events are more loosely packed and may extend across horizontal distances of 50 km or more and occupy atmospheric volumes in excess of 10,000 cubic km.

Figure 4.2   Red sprite extending above top of distant cumulonimbus

High speed photometer measurements show that the duration of sprites is only a few ms. Current evidence strongly suggests that sprites preferentially occur in decaying portions of thunderstorms and are correlated with large positive cloud-to-ground lightning strokes. The optical intensity of sprite clusters, estimated by comparison with tabulated stellar intensities, is comparable to a moderately bright auroral arc. The optical energy is roughly 10–50 kJ per event, with a corresponding optical power of 5–25 MW. Assuming that optical energy constitutes 1/1000 of the total for the event, the energy and power are on the order of 10–100 MJ and 5–50 GW, respectively.

Blue jets are a second high altitude optical phenomenon, distinct from sprites, observed above thunderstorms using low light television systems. As their name implies, blue jets are optical ejections from the top of the electrically active core regions of thunderstorms. Following their emergence from the top of the thundercloud, they typically propagate upward in narrow cones of about 15 degrees full width at vertical speeds of roughly 100 km/s (Mach 300), fanning out and disappearing at heights of about 40–50 km. Their intensities are on the order of 800 kR near the base, decreasing to about 10 kR near the upper terminus. These correspond to an estimated optical energy of about 4 kJ, a total energy of about 30 MJ, and an energy density on the order of a few mJ/m^3. Blue jets are not aligned with the local magnetic field.

Intrigued, we queried the database for other similar events, but since there was no bucket in the classification schema for red sprite or blue jet, the search was a labor intensive one, reading through the narratives of many "static discharge" events to hunt for similarities.

Indeed, we did find a few. They uniformly reported being well above the tops of cumulonimbus clouds, and reported transient electrical, computer, communication and/or navigation problems.

We mention this anecdote to illustrate a point. In this case, red sprites and blue jets might have a lot in common with our cardinal's yellow feathers. The classification schema in use did not capture what might be the most important information in the event, information that might lead to the identification of an as-yet-unrecognized hazard.

Our purpose is not to announce the discovery of another peril of the skies. These phenomena might represent another hazard to be aware of when flying. They might not. But if we generalize from this one anecdote, we can readily see that hazard identification accomplished only through classification into a standardized taxonomy will inevitably lead to an inability to discover new threats.

The need for two approaches to hazard identification

The lesson is that we need to develop two parallel approaches to hazard identification, especially associated with operational observations. One uses a standard common taxonomy to group like hazards together, and provides a shorthand method of understanding the contributing factors to potentially risky states, or real-world events. The other approach must be much more flexible and exploratory, and requires that the SMS practitioner have a full and complete a record of the original data collected from the event, be that narrative reports, raw flight data, weather information, or other.

If we accept the need to develop the capability for exploratory hazard identification, then we must build the technical, analytic and governance infrastructure to support that development. Specifically:

- Our databases that house safety information must be robust, and designed to maintain not just space-efficient classification information, but also the raw data associated with the event. Our IT infrastructure must support storage and querying of terabytes of safety data.
- Data mining must be developed as an integral tool in the SMS practitioner's kit.
- Given our litigious society, it is understandable why many companies have data retention policies that mandate the destruction of information after a fairly short period—two years is not uncommon. (In the past, short retention periods may have been driven by technological limitations, but that justification is quickly vanishing.) The unfortunate fact is that however justified for defensive reasons, destruction of safety-related data will compromise our ability to find new or previously unrecognized hazards. Since our objective in SMS is to improve the performance of a system that is already functioning very well (in terms of mitigating risk), the need to maximize our ability to detect and measure rare hazards is a very high priority. Legislators and regulators must understand the motivations that drive short data retention periods, and create mechanisms that protect safety-related data from inappropriate use in litigation.

Methods of hazard identification

We just mentioned the need to develop two parallel approaches to hazard identification, especially associated with operational observations.

The FAA's definition of SRM gives us a good starting point to understand when hazard identification, as a part of risk management, needs to be used (FAA, 2006, Appendix 1, p. 9):

- B. The SRM process shall be applied to:
  1. initial designs of systems, organizations, and/or products;
  2. the development of operational procedures;
  3. hazards that are identified in the safety assurance functions; and
  4. planned changes to the operational processes to identify hazards associated with those changes.

In our discussions thus far we have alluded to one method of hazard identification; that is, the analysis of data collected from operational observations—for example, when an Event Review Committee or an analyst in an ASAP program examines a report and from that report identifies one or more hazards. This is one of two methods we will explore—hazard identification through the analysis of data derived from operational observations. The other method is hazard identification through process analysis.

Line B. 3. above refers to the operational observations method. Line B. 1. refers to the process analysis method. (In the real world, all of these areas of SRM application would use a blend of operational observation and process analysis. Remember right now we're trying to pin down the concepts, not describe implementation, so for the moment let's stick with the idea that the two methods are distinct.)

Hazard identification through operational observations   In our discussion of identification methods, we will start on the observational side, in contrast to the presentation of hazard identification offered by ICAO and the FAA, which both focus on process analysis. Both are valid methods, but by far the more common method that will be used in the real world will be identification through operational observation. That will especially be true, as we will see, during the initial stages of SMS implementation. (Hazard identification through process analysis is a hallmark of a mature SMS, and we will find that the FAA delays emphasis on process analysis until phase 3 of SMS implementation.)

Using information from data collected from the operation (whether routine or non-routine) to identify hazards is by no means a new idea. This is part and parcel of the traditional, forensic approach to safety investigation. When an incident or accident happens, the safety investigator uses all the means at his or her disposal to understand the environment, equipment status, cultural milieu, or other—all of the potential contributing factors to the event. He or she is observing the operation (or a historical snapshot of it) to identify hazards. In the voluntary safety programs such as ASAP and FOQA, the same thing is true, except that these programs do not wait for the incident to occur. This method of hazard identification is the traditional one; it is and always will be with us, and must be embraced by SMS as a key method.

This method must possess certain attributes as it begins to be used in an SMS, including rigor, consistency, and flexibility. One way to determine what is different in hazard identification in SMS is to consider why we are doing this in the first place. The simple answer to this question is of course that we identify hazards so as to subsequently enumerate the risks associated with the hazards. But that answer leaves the SMS practitioner waiting with bated breath, awaiting the next step. Perhaps a more concise way to ask the question is—how are we going to go about identifying hazards in such a way as to enable us to move to that next step, and do so consistently in ways that we can describe and justify?

This gets us (finally) to a significant difference between hazard identification in traditional forensic safety investigation, and hazard identification in SMS. When an SMS practitioner approaches the question of identifying hazards, he or she is constantly aware that the work that is associated with a single event or investigation must tie in to a larger protocol. The observations at the event level must immediately relate to and interface with the system of observations that has been developed to capture *all* of the hazard information about the operation. The practitioner of SMS is a believer in the concept that individual events are just worldly manifestations of a much larger mechanism that lies underneath the day to day operation, a mechanism that has rules and laws and complicated clockwork that determines the successes, and failures, of controlling risk. *That* is the subject of the SMS practitioner's study. The SMS practitioner's work is building a model of that mechanism, so as to then be able to find its weaknesses, fix them before they are manifest as an event, and improve safety.

Given the complexity of this underlying mechanism, real rigor is required in that work, and knowing that the observations concerning today's event must relate to yesterday's, and tomorrow's, there must be strong consistency in the ways information is gathered, and in the taxonomy used to describe it. And finally, the SMS practitioner knows that no matter how well the model of Safety Risk Management has been detailed, there will be encounters with the unexpected, so the Safety Information System must be flexible enough to store new and detailed information about the event, not just check boxes in a schema.

So we are here making another argument for something we have asserted before—hazard identification in SMS must be based upon a taxonomy commonly and consistently used, and that taxonomy must itself be based upon an underlying theoretical model. We will make the case for using Threat and Error Management as that underlying model, and the Common Taxonomy the schema.

Hazard identification through process analysis   Both ICAO and the FAA give examples in their coursework and publications that describe hazard identification through process analysis as the primary method of hazard identification, though they do not use our term. We'll support the idea that this method is central to a mature SMS, though once again remember we are talking concept here, not implementation. Let's take the first steps of a walk through the ICAO and FAA method of SRM, in order to understand how hazard identification through process analysis is a key component of SMS.

Let's start with the ICAO outline first, since it's the simpler of the two. The basic "working unit" for SRM risk assessment in the ICAO process (actually in the FAA process too) is a group of subject matter experts (SMEs) assigned the task of assessing risk for a particular part of the operation. The selection, control, governance and empowerment of this SME group is what in the final analysis makes or breaks an SMS, but we will discuss organizational structure later—right now we'll stick with the SRM process itself.

The first step in the SRM process as described by ICAO and the FAA (which, remember, we are calling "hazard identification through process analysis") is for the SME group to brainstorm, discuss, and eventually settle upon a list of hazards that the group thinks is relevant to the task at hand. ICAO offers the tool depicted in Figure 4.3 to facilitate this step (ICAO, 2007a).

To complete this form, the SME group would first take a look at the overall activity they are being asked to assess, and break it down into a list of sub-activities that in combination make up the larger task. Then, for each of these sub-activities, the group would generate a list of hazards that might potentially threaten the successful completion of that sub-activity. Once the generic hazard list is generated for each sub-activity, the group would examine each generic hazard identified, and produce a further breakdown of the components of each hazard.

For example, an airline SME group might produce an SRM for a projected addition of a new destination to its schedule. A small portion of this example is presented in Figure 4.4.

No.	Type of Operation or Activity	State the generic hazard (hazard statement)	Identify specific components of the hazard

Figure 4.3   Hazard identification form

No.	Type of Operation or Activity	State the generic hazard (hazard statement)	Identify specific components of the hazard
1			Increased volume of traffic
2	Air Traffic Services	Air traffic considerations associated with single runway operation	Separation Issues
3			Runway congestion
4			Controller workload
....			....
		....	
	....		

Figure 4.4   Hazard/components process decision program chart, example 1

To give you a sense of where this is going and why this tool is designed the way it is, the tool depicted in Figure 4.5 (note again that this is a process decision program chart, as described in Chapter 3) is used in the next step of the ICAO SRM process, the one which eventually yields the risk assessment (ICAO, 2007b).

Note that the first three columns in this second risk assessment tool are identical to the columns in the first one, the hazard identification form. The fourth column in the hazard identification form—"Identify specific components of the hazard"—will be later used to assist in expressly describing the risks associated with each hazard. Essentially this column is used to make notes concerning why it is that the group has identified this item as a hazard, and these notes will later help in describing the various ways that the hazard can manifest itself in the real world as risk.

In a general sense, Figure 4.6 relates how each sub-activity (Operation I, Operation II, etc.) has multiple child-hazards associated with it, which in turn have multiple child-components.

It doesn't take too much imagination to visualize the length and complexity of a hazard list for many of the typical tasks in aviation, each of which frequently have high levels of complexity in themselves. We are beginning to sense the need for automation support in SRM, lest we get lost in reams of hazard lists. Figure 4.7 depicts what a resultant risk assessment tool might look like as the (perhaps extensive) list of hazards is imported into it. Associated risks and mitigation strategies are also noted in the figure.

No.	Type of operation or activity	State the generic hazard (hazard statement)	Risk(s) description	Current measures to reduce risk, and risk index	Further action to reduce risk, and resulting risk index

Figure 4.5   Hazard/risk process decision program chart, example 1

No.	Type of Operation or Activity	State the generic hazard (hazard statement)	Identify specific components of the hazard
1			Component (1)
2		Hazard A	Component (2)
3	Operation I		Component (3)
4			Component (1)
5		Hazard B	Component (2)
6			Component (1)
7		Hazard C	Component (2)
8			Component (3)
9			Component (4)
10			Component (1)
11		Hazard A	Component (2)
12	Operation II		Component (3)
13			Component (1)
14		Hazard B	Component (2)
15			Component (3)
16			Component (4)

Figure 4.6   Hazard/risk process decision program chart, example 2

Let's now briefly consider a functional area that most would agree is in need of serious SRM in airline operations—the gate arrival/departure task. It's clear with only brief reflection on this task that it is composed of scores of sub-activities, each of which probably has no less than five hazards associated with them, and each of those hazards has again multiple (three, five, a dozen?) ways in which risk can be manifest. And hopefully most of those risks have redundant mitigation measures already in place. It's not difficult to imagine an SRM spreadsheet for gate arrival/departure with hundreds of entries.

No.	Type of operation or activity	State the generic hazard (hazard statement)	Risk(s) description	Current measures to reduce risk, and risk index	Further action to reduce risk, and resulting risk index
1				Current Measure (a)	New Measure (a)
2			Risk (1)	Current Measure (b)	New Measure (b)
3				Current Measure (c)	New Measure (c)
4		Hazard A	Risk (2)	Current Measure (a)	New Measure (a)
5				Current Measure (b)	New Measure (b)
6	Operation I			Current Measure (a)	New Measure (a)
7			Risk (3)	Current Measure (b)	New Measure (b)
8				Current Measure (c)	New Measure (c)
9				Current Measure (a)	New Measure (a)
10			Risk (1)	Current Measure (b)	New Measure (b)
11				Current Measure (c)	New Measure (c)
12				Current Measure (d)	New Measure (d)
13		Hazard B		Current Measure (a)	New Measure (a)
14			Risk (2)	Current Measure (b)	New Measure (b)
15				Current Measure (c)	New Measure (c)

Figure 4.7   Hazard/risk process decision program chart, example 3

Let's remember that we are working up a conceptual picture of how SRM is constructed. A smaller scale service provider (for example, small FBOs, repair shops) should not be discouraged by the potential complexity of the hazard identification or risk management process. A key feature of SMS, woven into our definition of the concept, is that it is scalable, with a complexity appropriate to the organization. A small operation can certainly contemplate SRM record-keeping using commonly available tools such as Microsoft's® Excel or Access, or even Word. But larger service providers, especially those on the scale of major airlines, should take this lesson to heart—SRM, done well, will require a *Safety Information System*, or SIS. It is important to begin growing a respect for the challenge, and therefore understand the importance of adopting methods to keep the task under control.

One method is readily apparent, and is parallel to our previous discussion of the use of taxonomies in hazard identification. We have just established that a reasonably complex SRM might have hundreds of entries for a given task of reasonable scale. With some thought we realize that there will undoubtedly be duplication in the entries. For example, consider the entries shown in Figure 4.8.

Here we have two quite distinct sub-activities—an aircraft approaching the gate, and baggage carts being towed into position by a tug—with identical generic hazards and similar component lists. Clearly what is needed by our SME group is a standard taxonomy to refer to when filling out our form, not only to make its job a little easier, but also to enable effective aggregate analysis in our SIS. Nothing confounds automated processing more than the use of slightly different terms for the same concept.

No.	Type of Operation or Activity	State the generic hazard (hazard statement)	Identify specific components of the hazard
1			Decreased braking authority
2	Final taxi for gate arrival	Clutter (ice, slush, standing water) on ramp	Splash/refreeze on moving components
3			Obstructed ramp markings – stripes, stop lines, warning areas
4	...	...	...
...			...
			Decreased braking authority
	Baggage carts positioned near cargo door	Clutter (ice, slush, standing water) on ramp	Splash/refreeze on moving components
	...		Obstructed ramp markings – stripes, stop lines, warning areas

Figure 4.8   Hazard/components process decision program chart, example 2

Thus, the same arguments we cited earlier asserting the importance of adopting a common taxonomy for hazard identification apply when the method of hazard identification is process analysis. A common hazard taxonomy (in fact a common taxonomy for hazards, risks and controls) will assist in the entire SRM process, no matter what method we employ to identify hazards. In fact, when we consider the benefits of being able to share safety information across the industry—not just narratives, but the analyses of events or processes—it becomes even clearer that adopting a common taxonomy for use in SMS is a high priority action item. It is apparent that SMS practitioners have some homework to do before handing over an SRM analysis assignment to the SMEs.

The ultimate hazard identification tool—SRM-enhanced JTAs   Before concluding this section, let us briefly discuss an important reference in the FAA Advisory Circular. When we started this exploration of hazard identification through process analysis, we decided to begin with the ICAO version because it was a bit simpler. Let's take a minute to examine the FAA iteration of hazard identification—we'll find a hint in the agency's presentation which points to the end-state of a mature SMS. That hint is contained in the phrase "task analysis".

Consider once again the FAA and ICAO descriptions of SRM found in Table 4.1. Notice in the very first step the FAA includes—before the process of identifying hazards—the need to accomplish system and task analysis. This is not to make too fine a point of it—ICAO would certainly agree that system and task analysis is part and parcel of process analysis. But for those who have been associated with proactive safety in the U.S. over the last 10 to 15 years, the phrase "task analysis" when used by the FAA calls to mind a well-defined process in and of itself. It is doubtful that the inclusion of that specific phrase by the FAA was accidental, for it hearkens back to the first of the set of voluntary programs that now make up the constellation of proactive safety—the Advanced Qualification Program (AQP).

A mature organization that has been in the aviation business for years already has an existing training program, a program which has passed all of the regular checks and evaluations accomplished by the regulator to assure that the training program produces employees who are qualified to do their job. The mature state of aviation training, especially in the airline flight crew sector, is no accident or happenstance, but rather the result of the systematic development and application of the discipline of instructional design.

Training system design is a well-developed discipline. A task analysis is performed, goals and objectives of the training are set, methods of skill and knowledge measurement are designed, qualification standards are established, and finally a curriculum is engineered. Most airlines have experience in applying this discipline in their adoption of AQP.

Accomplishing the Job Task Analysis, or JTA, is the first step in AQP. A JTA (sometimes called the Supporting Task Analysis, or STA) is already in many ways oriented toward hazard identification. The identification of probable threats and areas of common errors are already part of developing the Terminal Proficiency Objectives (TPOs), Supporting Proficiency Objectives (SPOs), Enabling Objectives (EOs), and the associated Knowledge, Skills and Attitudes (KSAs) that are a part of every approved AQP program. Interestingly, though an understanding of the hazards encountered during flight is critical to the development of a comprehensive AQP task analysis, the JTA process in AQP explicates not the hazards themselves, but rather the *controls* used by crews to mitigate those hazards.

That is understandable, of course, since it is the mastery of those controls that is the goal of the training process. A well designed AQP program has very detailed and explicit descriptions of these controls, their function and application during specific phases of flight, and very importantly, references to the organizational documentation (for example, operating manuals, policy manuals) where these controls are explained.

AQP is database driven. The Program Audit Database, or PADB, contains the data structure in which the details of a program's TPOs, SPOs, EOs, and KSAs reside. With minimal modification to existing AQP PADBs, tables could be added to the JTA to contain the hazards (and risks) associated with each procedure (the controls) described in the training program. We'll call this modification *SRM-enhanced JTAs*.

When one remembers that another part of the data structure inherent in AQP is the Pilot Proficiency Database, or PPDB, the elements of a very powerful and comprehensive system begin to emerge—indeed, the core of a fully functional SIS. The PPDB is the repository in which measures of pilot performance in the training environment are stored—test scores, maneuvers validation, Line Oriented Evaluations, and the like. With the combination of the PADB and PPDB, AQP already has within it closed feedback loop in which training performance directly circles back to the design of the system in the PADB, which itself contains references to organizational documentation. An SRM-enhanced JTA could be the missing link, connecting operational observations of hazards and risks with the rest of the system. Figure 4.9 illustrates how the components of an existing AQP structure might interface with and become an integral part of an SRM process.

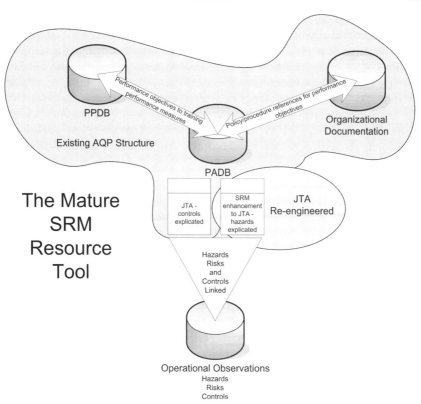

Figure 4.9   The mature SRM resource tool

Hazard identification—summary

Thus far we have established that the first component of SRM, hazard identification, is in itself an area that needs careful development in order to best support subsequent risk assessment. We have also defined two methods of hazard identification—one acccomplished through operational observation, and the other through process analysis. Both are necessary in a mature SMS, but both ICAO and the FAA agree that the best place to start is with operational observation. In both of these methods, we have also discussed the importance of using parallel approaches in hazard identification. In one approach the SMS practitioner examines the activity through the filter of a standardized taxonomy of hazards. This approach provides a structure which can be consistently applied to all activities under consideration, and facilitates later aggregate analysis. The other approach (most closely associated with the operational observation method) is more exploratory, using narrative, demographic or parametric databases to discover previously unidentified hazards. Once those new hazards are identified and validated as continuing, the best programs would create new fields in the existing taxonomy in order to monitor trends and evaluate the effectiveness of controls aimed at mitigating the risks associated with the hazard.

We have also discussed the critical importance of taxonomies in SRM. SMS always places events in the context of the larger operation, and a consistently applied classification schema facilitates analysis of hazard information collected from the operation. We suggest that Threat and Error Management taxonomies should be used for first person reporting programs such as ASAP. More work needs to be accomplished to identify the best taxonomies for other types of data collection and analysis.

Finally, we covered the potential for linking existing task analyses to SRM by re-examining JTAs from the perspective of hazard identification. Such linking would allow the connection of observationally derived risk assessment with existing training curricula based on those JTAs.

Our next task in SRM is to understand how hazards interface with real-world operations.

Review questions

1. Define Safety Risk Management. What processes does SRM include?
2. Define hazard.
3. Why is it important to develop two parallel approaches to hazard identification? What are those approaches?
4. Explain the different sources of information used in hazard identification through operational observation, and hazard identification through process analysis.
5. What are the benefits of using standard taxonomies when identifying hazards?

References

Federal Aviation Administration [FAA] (2006). *Introduction to Safety Management Systems for Air Operators.* Advisory Circular 120-92. Retrieved December 3, 2007 from http://rgl.faa.gov/Regulatory_and_Guidance_Library/rgAdvisoryCircular. nsf/0/6485143d5ec81aae8625719b0055c9e5/$FILE/AC%20120-92.pdf.

Heavner, M. (2004). *"Red Sprites and Blue Jets."* Retrieved November 26, 2007 from http://elf.gi.alaska.edu/.

International Civil Aviation Organization [ICAO] (2006). *Safety Management Manual (SMM),* 1st edn. (Doc 9859 AN/460). Montréal, Canada: ICAO.

International Civil Aviation Organization [ICAO] (2007a). "SMS Training, ICAO SMS Module 04—Hazards." Retrieved December 3, 2007 from http://www.icao. int/anb/safetymanagement/training/training.html

International Civil Aviation Organization [ICAO] (2007b). "SMS Training, ICAO SMS Module 10—Hazards." Retrieved December 3, 2007 from http://www.icao. int/anb/safetymanagement/training/training.html

Prince, A. (1999). The effect of experience on the perception of decision scenarios: A field study (Doctoral Dissertation, University of South Florida, 1999). *Dissertation Abstracts International,* DAI-B 60/08.

Chapter 5

Risks

A ship is safe in harbor, but that's not what ships are for.

William Shedd

Thus far in our discussion of Safety Risk Management (SRM), we have dealt with the process of hazard identification, which at a fundamental level is a process of observation, description and classification. While not without its own complexities, hazard identification is a simple task, compared with our next topic, risk assessment. In our pursuit of forging a process of risk assessment that is worthy of being a part of the "discipline" of SMS, we will be forced to confront some difficult questions:

- What *exactly* are we assessing when we assess risk?
- Since an assessment is a judgment of value or scale, against what standard are we comparing whatever it is that we are assessing?
- What qualifications must one have in order to make an assessment?
- How repeatable are our assessments—will two *qualified* people make the same assessment of whatever it is that we are assessing?
- Do our assessments have *meaning*, and what do we mean by that?
- If we build our risk assessment process to be relatively simple to use, will it produce anything of worth? Alternatively, if we build a comprehensive and complete risk assessment model, will it be so complex as to be impractical, and therefore worthless in a different way?

To add to our difficulties, we need to understand our assignment. As we have asserted before, all indications are that SMS is here to stay, and that it is time to begin to develop the sophistication and clarity into SMS such that it will legitimately qualify as being an academic discipline, possessing all the attributes that this entails—a basis in theory, statistical legitimacy, repeatability of measures and observations, and so on. We also need to understand that SMS is not now, nor should ever be, exclusively the realm of academics. Whatever the edifice we build to support SMS, it has to be practical, understandable by the (trained!) SMS practitioner, and especially, scalable, so that both the fixed-base-operator (FBO) with three rental aircraft and an ICAO member-State can claim to have a functioning SMS. What is ahead of us is no small task.

Definitions

Let's begin our journey with definitions—always a good place to start. You will recall our previous reference to the definitions of risk offered by ICAO and the FAA:

- Risk (ICAO)—"The likelihood of injury to personnel, damage to equipment or structures, loss of material, or reduction of ability to perform a prescribed function, measured in terms of probability and severity." (ICAO, 2007).
- Risk (FAA)—"The composite of predicted severity and likelihood of the potential effect of a hazard in the worst credible system state." (FAA, 2006, Appendix 1, p. 3)

One can see that the ICAO definition is more casual and conversational, relating the broad meaning of the word. On the other hand, the FAA definition is functional, indicating not only their two components of the term (severity and likelihood), but also what it is being measured (the potential effect of a hazard), and when to measure it (in the worst credible system state). The ICAO definition introduces the student to an overview of the mathematics of risk, while the FAA presents the algorithm.

But before we get into the math, let's make sure that we have a very firm, intuitive understanding of what it is we are trying to manage. When trying to really grasp the nucleus of a concept, it is often helpful to refer to etymology, the study of the linguistic roots of words or phrases. We will return to the ICAO and FAA definitions once we have that intuitive understanding.

The root of our English word *risk* dates from the mid 17th century, derived from an older French root— *risqué*—which in turn hearkened from a much older Italian word *riscare*—"to run into danger" (Online Etymology Dictionary, 2007). A more complete mental image of *riscare* might be "to run, unprepared, into danger".

To illuminate the unstated components in this etymology, let's study an example of a medieval Italian merchant, moving his wares from city/state to city/state— say, from Gubbio to Perugia (admittedly, somewhat off the topic of aviation, but we'll start from simple and move to complex!). A young, naïve, or not-so-smart merchant might load up his cart and donkeys, and run, unprepared, into danger, either ignorant or reckless regarding the ever-present hazard of thieves along the road. A more prudent merchant would have maintained good relationships with the ruling family of Gubbio, and for a fee enlisted an armed guard to accompany him along the way. The prudent one understood *riscare*, and prepared for the possibility of attack.

To understand risk, one must grasp the continuum between the extremity of the hazard and the protection of the control—the presence of the crooks and the effectiveness of the armed escort. Controls, or the lack of them, are implicit in an understanding of risk, and so a full definition of risk needs to explicitly address this fact.

So in order to support our new SMS discipline, we want to augment the previous definitions of risk by overtly referring to the importance of controls, right in the definition. We're just about ready to formulate the definitive sentence. But our merchant has another consideration to offer, as real to him as are the profits awaiting him in Perugia.

Let's suppose that the thieves and brigands in Umbria are of a pilfering but non-violent sort. Our merchant therefore does not fear for his life, but is quite concerned about the possibility of loss of his merchandise (or we could make the scenario more realistic by saying that the merchant hires a peasant to transport his goods, so we don't have to depend upon the good nature of the robbers). His merchandise has a certain value to him. Offsetting that value, though, is the cost he is obliged to pay for the service of protection from the lords of Gubbio. If the cost of protection is too high, at some point the merchant will decide to take his chances, and run the donkeys and carts full trot, hoping for the best.

The point is that risk is not assessed in a vacuum. The merchant might calculate that the risk of loss is high, but so is the cost of control. His *assessment*, which is what guides his decision-making, is based upon his weighing the cost of the potential loss against the cost of the control.

Let's not kid ourselves that we do not make those same decisions in aviation operations. Every year scores of flight attendants are injured, sometimes seriously, during turbulence encounters. Most of those turbulence encounters are associated with convective activity. We could eliminate the vast majority of those injuries if we were to make (and enforce!) a rule prohibiting flight operations within 100 miles of convective activity. We have not done that, and that is because effectively we have calculated the risk, calculated the costs of controls (this one, at least), and assessed that the risk of flight attendant injury (and subsequent loss when that risk becomes manifest in an event) does not warrant the cost of such an extreme control.

Note: We are not suggesting that the industry *should* adopt such a control. Clearly such a 100 mile limit would be crippling to air commerce, which is exactly the point: the cost of the control is unacceptable. (Of course left open is the question of what is an acceptable cost—where that balance is.)

Conceptual definitions: risk and risk assessment

We are now ready to offer our own definitions to use in the discipline of SMS:

- Risk—an estimate of the effectiveness (or lack thereof) of hazard controls in preserving the value of an asset in a given scenario.
- Risk assessment—the valuation of the potential loss associated with a risk, as compared with the cost of effectively controlling that risk.

We introduced our merchant from Gubbio stating that we were going to start with simple concepts, and work our way toward the complexities of risk and risk assessment in present day aviation. But our merchant friend has one more contribution to make to our understanding, one that illustrates that risk assessment is an intricate art, even when starting from down-to-earth examples.

Our merchant, being the prudent one, was aware of the existence of thieves along his route, and had the foresight to prepare for the option of purchasing protective services from his lord. But he is not omniscient; he does not know the exact extent of the threat—how many thieves exist along the path, whether they have formed temporary alliances and work together, the lethality of their armament, and so on.

The range of the severity of the threat posed by the thieves and the likelihood of an attack by them is something he needs to estimate, with incomplete information.

In addition, he knows that a generally safe ratio of defenders to attackers is 2 to 1, and a ratio of 3 to 1 is a powerful deterrent. He knows how much each guard will cost him, and what his likely profit will be in Perugia. But again, he does not know for sure the extent of the threat. So he must make an assessment. How many guards to hire?

Success for our 13th century merchant required him to, frankly, wing it. Experience was of great importance, and the wise merchant would seek the advice of others who confronted the same problem. Also important was the best intelligence he could get concerning the day-to-day extent of the threat. The collective wisdom of Gubbio's merchant class would have generated "standards" for such estimation, which represented the best subject matter expert opinion available. It was in all probability pretty good, similar in many ways to our own ability to estimate and assess the risk in flight operations based upon our collective experience.

Speaking of probability, our 13th century merchant predated 1654, and so did not have available to him the intellectual product that resulted from a dispute between two gamblers. Antoine Gombaud was a French nobleman with a predilection for, among other things, gambling. He got into what was undoubtedly a very polite dispute with a gambling acquaintance concerning the best strategy to use in a popular dice game.

Gombaud happened to be friends with the famous mathematician Blaise Pascal, and posed the problem to him. Pascal, in turn, corresponded with another of his friends who was an equally famous mathematician, Pierre de Fermat. The combined dialog of this correspondence resulted in the first formulation of the fundamental principles of probability theory.

During the 300 or so years since Gombaud's *risqué* business, probability theory has matured into a fundamental component of science. Risk analysis, as a subset of probability theory, has also matured into a separate discipline unto itself, and now is the foundation of a central part of quality management, fact-based decision-making. As SMS becomes a recognized discipline itself, we will transition from present-day risk assessment techniques (not far removed from that used by our merchant) to a scientifically sound methodology.

Before we return to further describe the present state of the art and the toolset used to assess risk, we will pay our merchant one last visit, bestowing on him the gift of three centuries of mathematical thought. We'll do this in order to use his relatively simple problem to illustrate how one can apply probabilistic risk assessment, or PRA, to make truly informed decisions in risk management.

We're jumping over where we are (the present-day ICAO and FAA tools) to where we want to be—PRA—for a reason. We are assuming that readers of this text will be leaders of tomorrow's aviation Safety Management Systems. It is therefore important to instill a clear vision of where SMS needs to be in order to join other industries in the application of these sophisticated tools; many of these industries are significantly more advanced in the use of these techniques than is aviation. But, more importantly, if one understands the theory underlying the advanced tools it is then possible to understand how to apply simpler, more efficient tools in a consistent manner.

From Gubbio to Monte Carlo

Through the magic of textbook authorship, we have now anachronically given our 13th century Italian merchant a laptop computer, PRA software (in this case, Crystal Ball by Oracle®), and a battery of sufficient power to keep the equipment going while he learns to use it. He is now ready to apply 21st century Monte Carlo modeling technology to his *riscare* problem.

Very similar to our sketch of the first steps in SRM, his initial task is to identify the hazards. In the real world this task would be more complex than in our thought experiment in that he would identify the threats of hooligans, terrain and night travel or encampment. It would also behoove him to identify error type hazards that might be committed by his guards—falling asleep, not paying attention, or other (if we carried this far enough we would find ourselves arguing for a Threat and Error Management model for medieval trade). In our simplified thought experiment, we will only be using the most obvious of the hazards, the existence of the hooligans, and how many of them the guards might have to face at any one encounter.

So far, this process is the same as described earlier in the hazard identification section; in fact we could use the same form as shown in Table 4.3.

Next, though, we will add a new level of complexity to the model to make it representative of the real world, or perhaps more accurately, representative of the range of what we think the real world might be like. Remember, our merchant does not know the actual extent of the threat, but only a general estimate of the number of thieves. He will represent this by producing a distribution of the likely number of thieves the guards will have to confront at any one time. In this case, a lognormal distribution is most representative of the intelligence he has been able to gather, with three the most likely number, and with the probability quickly falling off with larger numbers (see Figure 5.1).

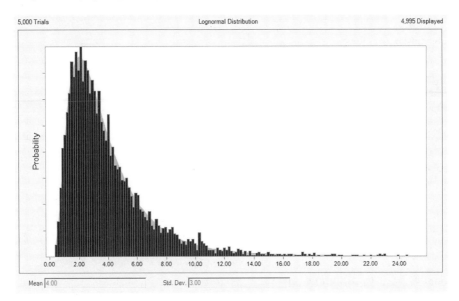

Figure 5.1   Number of thieves (screenshot)

Our merchant also needs to create a "battle odds" table, which gives a range of probabilities of victory when X number of guards confront Y number of thieves (that is, a conditional distribution). The model will take the information from this table and calculate the loss for each tested combination of guards and thieves. Figure 5.2 shows a graphical depiction of a "battle odds table"; this is essentially a piecewise continuous function.

In order to know how many guards he can afford, and eventually make the assessment, he needs to estimate his gross income from selling his goods; this estimate is shown in Figure 5.3. Approximately 166 lire appears to be the mean.

Finally, he is told by his lord how much each guard will cost (the majority of which of course will go to the lord). He has no control over this number, which in this case equals 12 lire.

Equipped with these figures, he can now have the software run a Monte Carlo simulation of 5,000 hypothetical trips from Gubbio to Perugia, each simulation based on a random selection of values from the population distributions he fed into the model. Figures 5.4, 5.5, 5.6, 5.7, and 5.8 display the results of this simulation, showing the mean profit, overall probability of not losing money (expressed as "certainty" near the bottom of the chart), and the distribution of probabilities for all profit values, for a guard number of from four to eight.

A study of these charts reveals that the safest choice for our merchant is to employ six guards. There is a probability of nearly 90.47 percent that he will not experience a complete loss with six guards, and the average profit across 5,000 trials with that level of protection is nearly 76 lire.

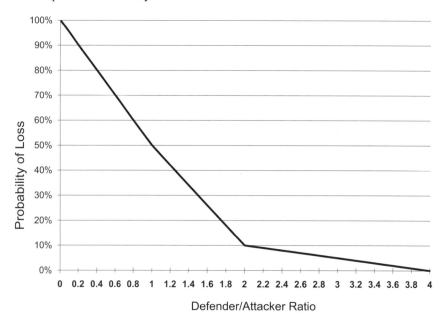

Figure 5.2   Battle odds table—graphical depiction

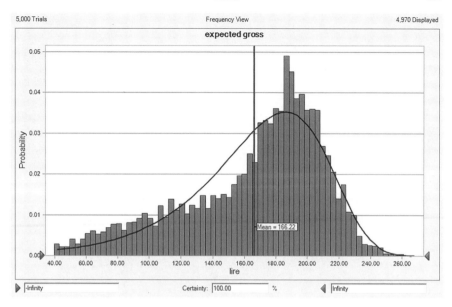

Figure 5.3   Gross income (screenshot)

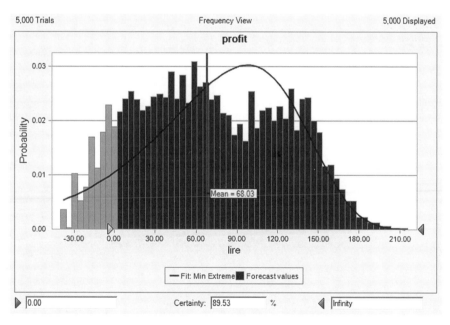

Figure 5.4   Gubbio merchant—four guards (screenshot)

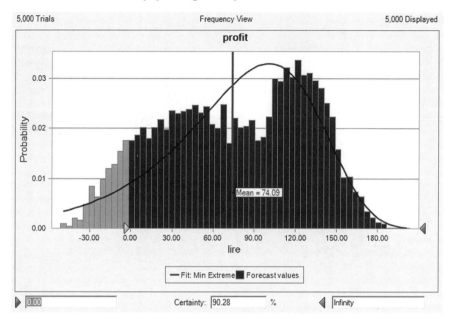

Figure 5.5   Gubbio merchant—five guards (screenshot)

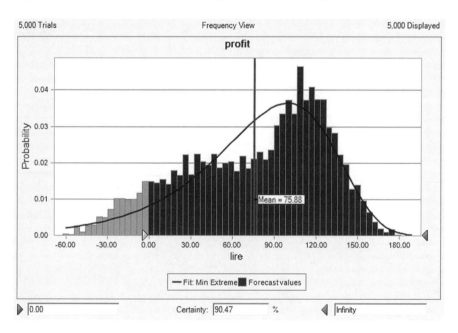

Figure 5.6   Gubbio merchant—six guards (screenshot)

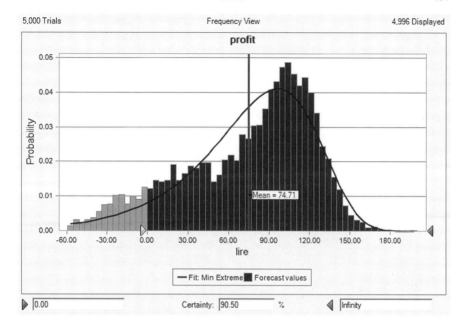

Figure 5.7   Gubbio merchant—seven guards (screenshot)

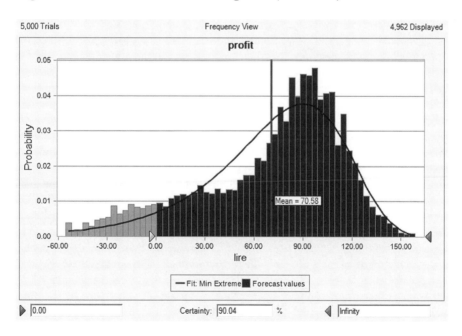

Figure 5.8   Gubbio merchant—eight guards (screenshot)

The following is a summary of what we have learned about risk assessment from our thirteenth century friend:

- Understanding the risk associated with an activity requires the understanding of the hazards surrounding it.
- It is extremely unlikely that a full measure of the severity or probability of occurrence of a hazard will be available. Calculation of risk is inherently an estimation.
- Knowledge of the severity or probability of occurrence of a hazard is best described not by a single value, but by a best estimate of the distribution of potential severities or likelihoods.
- In all but the simplest, most naïve activities (ones in which you run, unprepared, into danger), a calculation of risk requires not only consideration of hazard, but also consideration of the effectiveness of the controls you have adopted to mitigate that hazard.
- Similar to the measurement of hazards, a measurement of the effectiveness of controls is also inherently a process of estimation, and such measures are best described by distributions, not single values.
- One cannot realistically assess risk without also evaluating the cost of controls.
- Risk assessment is the balancing of the potential for loss against the cost of controls.

If we extend what we have learned from the Gubbio merchant into our task of SRM in aviation operations, we see that the ideal risk assessment process is based upon modeling. The ideal model will incorporate each of the principles described in the above bullet points, with hazard severity and likelihood, and control effectiveness and cost, represented by distributions which we then run in our simulation dozens, hundreds, even thousands of times. We then study the results of the running of the model, and make our decisions based upon that intelligence.

The most capable and accurate methods of SRM require sophisticated software based modeling tools, used in PRA. The knowledgeable SMS practitioner understands that *this* is how to do SRM—all other methods are less precise substitutions.

But there is nothing wrong with substituting. The reality is that a well-done PRA study is not a trivial task. It requires well-trained specialists, good software, and the resource investment needed to fully describe the scenario to be studied along with the relevant hazard/control distributions. Frequently these assets will not be available to the SMS practitioner. In these cases there is no option other than to use simpler tools.

As a matter of fact it is probably the rule rather than the exception that SRM will be accomplished in the real world of safety departments through means other than PRA most of the time. And that is perfectly appropriate. The challenge for the SMS practitioner is to keep in mind the rigorous principles required in sophisticated SRM while applying those simpler tools. Doing so will allow the analyst to take advantage of the efficiency and economy of the simpler methods, while remaining cognizant of their limitations.

We are now ready to introduce the core element of that simpler SRM toolset, the risk matrix. Over the past decade or so, this tool has become fairly standardized, and is a component of both the ICAO's and the FAA's guidance documentation concerning SRM methods. The SMS practitioner in a large organization might use PRA a few times a year, and those in smaller organizations perhaps never, but both will use the risk matrix on a daily basis. The SMS guru understands that the PRA model is running in his head as his fingers move along the axes of the matrix.

The Risk Matrix

We'll start with a glimpse at the standard risk matrix, as presented in FAA Advisory Circular 120-92, but for now only a glimpse, because once seeing the components of the matrix, we need to get a firm grip on what those components are before using the matrix to come up with the measure of risk.

The matrix actually has two components, a table (see Table 5.1) (ICAO, 2006, pp. 6–7) and a chart (see Figures 1.5 and 5.9).

Table 5.1   Sample severity and likelihood criteria

Source: ICAO, 2006

	Severity of Consequences			Likelihood of Occurrence		
Severity Level	**Definition**	**Value**	**Likelihood Level**	**Definition**	**Value**
Catastrophic	Equipment destroyed, multiple deaths	5	Frequent	Likely to occur many times	5
Hazardous	Large reduction in safety margins, physical distress or a workload such that operators cannot be relied upon to perform their tasks accurately or completely. Serious injury or death to a number of people. Major equipment damage.	4	Occasional	Likely to occur sometimes	4
Major	Significant reduction in safety margins, reduction in the ability of operators to cope with adverse operating conditions as a result of an increase in workload, or as result of conditions impairing their efficiency. Serious incident. Injury to persons.	3	Remote	Unlikely, but possible to occur	3
Minor	Nuisance. Operating limitations. Use of emergency procedures. Minor incident.	2	Improbable	Very unlikely to occur	2
Negligible	Little consequence	1	Extremely Improbable	Almost inconceivable that the event will occur	1

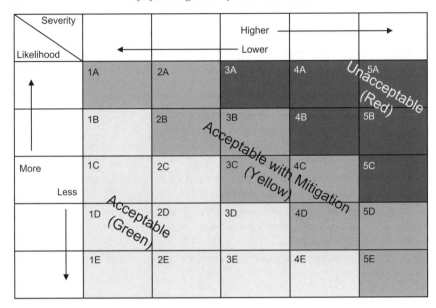

Figure 5.9   Risk matrix with cell labels

We'll begin our exploration of the risk matrix with a brief examination of the chart, even though it is part of the second step in deriving a risk index. We'll do so because it is important to understand why the risk matrix exists in the first place, which is that it provides a consistent means to drive management decision-making.

First notice that the matrix depicted in Figure 1.5 is composed of five rows by five columns, consistent with the five levels of severity and of likelihood, as described by the preceding table. Both ICAO and the FAA use this 5x5 design, but there is nothing magic to this structure. Neither agency demands that risk matrices have a particular number of rows or columns—4x5, 5x4, 3x3; all are perfectly acceptable. The point is that whatever the chosen structure for the matrix, the operator should clearly define an equivalent number of levels of severity or likelihood.

In some matrices, severity and likelihood measures increase as the scale goes up (1 to 5, A to E, etc.). Some matrices have the values reversed. Again, there is no standardization here; an organization can design its own matrix any way it chooses.

To use the matrix, the SMS practitioner would calculate the severity (S) and likelihood (L) of occurrence for an event, and then using the matrix derive which cell corresponds to that level of S and L. We'll use the same matrix we showed you in Figure 1.5 (except we've added cell labels) to explore how the derivation of that resultant cell drives subsequent action (see Figure 5.9) (FAA, 2006, p. 15).

Once having calculated the S and L values and identifying the cell at the intersection of those values on the matrix, if the resultant cell is green, the risk associated with that event, operation, or component of operation is acceptable and (if appropriate to the analysis or question) operations may continue. If it is yellow, careful consideration must be given to the existing risk controls, and if practical, additional controls should be put into place. If the resultant cell is red, an unacceptably high level of risk exists, and controls must be adopted so that a subsequent iteration of the risk index calculation results in the arrival at a yellow or green cell.

A final concept must be introduced before we can talk about how the risk matrix drives decision-making. That is ALARP—meaning that a risk has been mitigated to the extent that is "as low as reasonably practicable". It's critical to note that the word is *practicable*, and not *possible*. The concept of ALARP includes the consideration of practicality. In ALARP, there is no requirement that a risk mitigation strategy result in the lowest possible risk—such a goal is unobtainable. But there is a requirement to obtain the lowest level that can be derived, using those resources reasonably available to the operator.

For decision-making purposes, the risk matrix is used in two contexts discussed below.

Applying the risk matrix in system design   One application of the risk matrix usually involves the SMS practitioner, either as a decision-maker or as a facilitator assisting a team in the design of risk controls. In this context, three rules apply as the team evaluates the risk in components of a system:

- The final cell one lands on when applying the matrix cannot be red. If so, apply and/or create new controls, and reassess.
- If the cell is yellow, give very careful consideration to adding additional controls. ALARP applies, but the scale significantly tips toward mobilizing the resources necessary to provide additional controls.
- If the cell is green, ALARP *still* applies. The cost of controls holds much more influence in a green cell, and consideration of such cost can reasonably result in the decision to accept the risk. But creativity is expected—the SMS practitioner should lead the group toward deriving cost-effective ways to move the risk even lower.

Thus, in the system design process, the risk matrix gives the design team a way to methodically and consistently decide whether the system may be implemented in its present form, or whether additional work needs to be done.

The use of the risk matrix in operational or executive decision-making   The second context in which the risk matrix is used in an organization that has adopted SMS is in driving safety related decisions made by operational or executive level managers. The professional SMS practitioner/specialist may or may not be directly involved in this decision-making, and so it is extremely important that the entire system be designed so as to provide consistent, believable and appropriate guidance for these decisions. When a risk is computed to be a "red" risk, there should be little room for doubt or question as to the appropriateness of that ranking.

For example, let us suppose that an audit is accomplished in which fuel quality is tested at an FBO's various fuel storage sites, and the audit reveals water contamination in multiple tanks in the facility. An in-depth review is accomplished, and the review team determines that based upon its best determination of severity and likelihood of recurrence, the risk index for the study is red. In this case, there should be clear mechanisms for the entire management chain responsible for fuel quality—that is, from the depot manager all the way up to the CEO—to be aware of the results of the study, to know that corrective and preventive action is a requirement, and that such action must be accomplished within a predetermined period.

If the team were to have assigned yellow to the risk, the extent of involvement of the full chain of command might be defined by the organization as to not require the attention of the CEO, and for green the top level involvement might be capped at an even lower level. The organization is once again free to design the system in whatever way makes the most sense within their operation. Some service providers, for example, have decided to have five color-coded levels rather than three, in order to have a greater ability to discriminate escalation within their management structure.

A mature SMS program will have very clear policies that mandate management and executive action to mitigate risk, based upon the risk index assigned to the situation. Those policies must cover three components of response:

- Notification—there should be a well-defined and frequently tested method for notifying appropriate levels of management when risks are found in the operation. Many organizations use pagers to accomplish this function. Most operational managers and executives are very familiar with this—in large organizations the owners of those pagers often receive tens of pages per day notifying them of operational irregularities. Though this infrastructure provides a means for fast intervention, the designers of these notification systems need to be cognizant of the danger of complacency when managers are bombarded with notification after notification. The message recipients are forced to read through the entire message and then make a determination themselves whether the event is high risk. The best notification systems apply some sort of triage process, and preface higher-risk alerts with a clear indicator that tells the recipient to pay particular attention to the message following the indicator when the issue is serious.

- Prioritized requirements for intervention after initial discovery—a mature SMS will have policies in place that require process owners to respond to discovery of risk within clearly defined time intervals, the length of which is determined by the level of risk. The most extreme levels of risk might require immediate intervention by the highest levels of management within the organization, while lower levels might give longer periods for lower level management to respond. For these requirements to be accepted, this graduated response protocol must make sense to all of the management levels touched by the protocol. The best systems will be calibrated with the recognition that all levels of management are already very busy. Not everything in safety must be fixed today, but some issues do require immediate action.

- Prioritized requirements for response to corrective action requests—many organizations assign a risk index to findings that result from routine studies or audits of the operation. Most such organizations use the standard technique of attaching CARs or CPARs (Corrective Action Requests or Corrective/ Preventive Action Requests) to these findings. A good audit system will standardize the requirements for responses to these requests, based upon the risk index assigned to the finding.

Notice that the SMS practitioner is most likely involved in the *design* of these management policies and processes, and not in the individual decision-making associated with each situation or event. As a member of this policy/process design team, the SMS practitioner should continually ask the question: "what is it that we want our manager or executive to do when notified of this level of risk"? The entire purpose of color-coding risk indices is to make it easy for the manager to know what to do, so very careful thought must be put into these policies.

A final thought on the design of policies that address management response to risk: the policies must have teeth. There must be a very clearly stated requirement that managers have a duty to respond to risk in a manner set forth by these policies, and that a lack of response will not be tolerated. This intent to enforce risk management policy must come from the very top—from the "accountable executive" in ICAO terminology. The policy must have a very clearly defined mechanism to escalate notification of failure to comply up to the next levels of management above the manager who failed to meet the requirement. And when the first occurrence of lack of compliance with this policy happens, there must be consequences. Accountability is a central concept in SMS, and there needs to be a history of the organization taking this concept seriously.

To summarize, the risk matrix—composed of the individual cells (the risk indices) and the color codes associated with those cells—exists for one purpose, to drive decision-making and action. This fact needs to be clearly understood before moving on to the next part of our discussion, which concerns the algorithms used to derive how we compute risk. Our algorithms must result in a risk index that makes sense, that will be appropriate to the situation at hand, and that the consensus of subject-matter-expert managers will support. Nothing will kill SMS faster than a system of bureaucratic requirements that seem to mandate action that is inadequate on the one extreme, or silly on the other. Since estimations of severity and likelihood are the determiners of the risk index in this "standard model" (we will present an additional dimension— effectiveness of remaining controls—later), let's keep a practical perspective in mind as we discuss the next components of risk calculation, severity and likelihood.

The severity and likelihood criteria table

Let's consider the severity and likelihood (S/L) criteria shown in Table 5.1, this time made consistent with our matrix discussion above (recall that there is no required design for the table or matrix—we can make it however we want as long as it works).

Many service providers that have already adopted the risk matrix have invested a significant amount of work to add clarity to the definitions in the S/L table. In the authors' experience, severity definitions are becoming quite specific and sophisticated, and are relatively easy to discriminate. Likelihood definitions are generally a bit less developed, although some have added quantitative metrics to the table.

The use of the S/L table in design or process-based risk assessment We know from our previous discussion of Probabilistic Risk Assessment (PRA) that the SMS practitioner must view the risk matrix as a shortcut tool, substituting for the more accurate modeling approach because of its efficiency. In the real world (or more accurately our model of it), severity would be represented not as a point estimate, but as a distribution of probable severities. The S/L table demands that a point estimate of that population distribution be made. In ICAO and FAA parlance, that point estimate is called the "most serious credible outcome". Credible is of course in the eye of the beholder—in system design, we must rely on our appointed subject matter experts to make this determination, educated by data on hand but also in their knowledge of the potentialities of the system.

There are empirical questions that have not yet been answered concerning the valuation of the "most serious credible outcome". Will two or more groups of equally qualified SMEs come up with similar definitions of credible? Even within one group, will that group consistently apply the same standards of estimation across time? We don't know the answers to these questions yet; this is an area in need of academic research. Clearly there is wide variation in how different groups of highly qualified SMEs define "credible". But until the time that answers to this problem are available, users of the risk matrix technique have no choice but to rely on the judgment of their chosen group of SMEs. Given this potential for variance, the savvy SMS practitioner will attempt to control the problem by trying to keep the membership of any one SME group assigned to accomplish risk assessment fairly stable. Our guru should discuss the issue of calibrating the group's judgment openly and frequently, and should encourage civil debate between the members of the group. While we do not yet have good techniques to calibrate judgments between groups, the internal dynamics of a well-facilitated SME group will result in a group that self-calibrates, and comes to a reasonably consistent consensus when assigning a point-estimate severity index.

If the L dimension has been defined in the table through reference to a quantitative metric, then L is best derived by data. If not, L must otherwise be estimated by SMEs. The same cautions concerning repeatability apply here, as they did for the valuation of the severity measure. Lacking a PRA approach, these decisions must be made on the basis of the best information at hand, and especially on the experience of well-qualified SMEs. Just as the SMS practitioner may be quietly running a PRA model in his head to assist in these estimates of severity and likelihood, so the SME relies on a career's worth of experience to put these judgments in context. There is absolutely no substitute for experience in risk assessment.

Acknowledging all of the admitted cautions that one needs to keep in mind when using the risk matrix, in many situations it functions quite well, and provides solid guidance for process design. Let's consider an example where it works. Suppose a team of SMEs from an aircraft servicing ramp operation is assigned the task of assessing the risk of adding a new work stand to assist in engine servicing. The working surface of this stand can be set anywhere from two to ten feet above the ramp surface. The team's assignment is to identify all hazards associated with the stand's use, and create controls to mitigate those hazards. We'll follow their decision-making as they consider just one hazard they have identified: slips and falls.

The team decides to evaluate the risk of injury due to falls at the lowest, middle, and highest setting of the work surface. They note that the corrugated surface of the work area is designed to be non-slip, but they establish that if engine oil is spilled on it, the surface becomes treacherous. They also note that the fence around the platform is four feet high, sufficient to protect from most inadvertent falls from the platform, but the gap between the work surface and the first horizontal rail of the fence is more than enough for a person to roll through.

The team concludes that the likelihood of a fall induced by spilled oil is reasonably low, but they have seen such a slip (at ground level, luckily) three times in the last year. They assign a likelihood index of C to this outcome of this particular hazard (see Figure 5.9).

Next they consider severity. While the team decided that the likelihood was probably constant no matter what the height setting of the stand was, they quickly conclude that the severity of a fall increases dramatically with height. Following some heated debate among the team members over whether the severity should be 4 or 5 (says one team member, "OK, so the result doesn't meet the definition of catastrophic written in the table. So what—it's catastrophic to my union brother that rolls under that rail and falls 10 feet!") the group finally decides on 4.

A 4C could be determined to be "acceptable with mitigation", but our team is appropriately aggressive, and decides that 4C is unacceptable. So they work on ways to mitigate the risk, and decide that their recommendation is for the maintenance department to weld a screen onto the lower two feet of the fence around the work area of the stand. Doing so reduces their severity index down to a 2 (some still argue for 3, but finally concede), irrespective of the height of the surface. The members of the team who were lobbying for a 3 now remind the rest of the group about ALARP, and suggest that an enclosed oil can container be fastened onto the platform as well. Now they have reduced the likelihood as well, by controlling the oil spill.

Through their work on mitigating this risk, they have reduced their assessment from the initial 4C to 2D. They declare "ALARP!", and victory, and publish their determination. The guy who requisitioned the new stands is not too happy about having to spend more money on the modifications, but the team has done its job. The risk matrix has guided this team well, through a number of decisions, and the operation is safer because of it.

But now let's contrast this very positive outcome of applying the risk matrix with another real world example that will not be quite so clear. We'll consider runway overruns.

Our new SME team is composed of performance engineers, check airmen, and safety representatives at a small airline. Following a number of recent incidents in the news, the Safety Council at the airline decided to take another look at this risk.

The team painstakingly identifies a number of hazards that might be associated with the outcome of a runway overrun—unstable approaches, brake failures, ice on the runway. With each they ask the required question: "what is the most serious credible outcome of this scenario"? The answer in every instance: level 5. Catastrophe. A runway overrun can, and unfortunately has, resulted in a number of catastrophic events.

The team moves on to likelihood. They examine their FOQA data, and with clever manipulation of the data determine that the likelihood is quite low indeed, certainly lower by multiple factors of ten compared to the magnitude of scale that our previous ramp SME group was considering.

Should these two groups be using the same matrix, or methodology?

If the whole purpose of the risk matrix is to drive decision-making, one has to wonder about the efficacy of the technique when assessment after assessment results in a risk index of 5E, using our table above. If all points are clustered together in a decision-support tool, it is difficult to see how this supports decision-making.

The fact is that for most calculations involving airborne aircraft, the highest level of severity is very often the correct one to assign. Similarly, given the long and successful history of controlling risk in our industry, most of these outcomes have already been driven down to the point where likelihood for those high severity events is in the neighborhood of 10^{-7} to 10^{-9}. Yet in order to continue moving to the next level of safety, these are exactly the issues we must examine.

We must find new and different ways to assign risk indices to these types of issues. The standard risk matrix is quite valuable, and should not be discarded. But as every carpenter or mechanic knows, to do the job right, use the right tool. We need more risk assessment tools in our toolkit, to supplement our trusty risk matrix.

Risk assessment in operational observations

We ended our discussion of the use of the risk matrix in process design on a slightly discordant note, stating that it is not the perfect tool for all circumstances. Our discussion of risk assessment in operational observations will begin using that same chord.

The use of the risk matrix in determining risk associated with operational observations is often quite confusing. After all, from the process design point of view, it makes intuitive sense that one should start by identifying the hazards first, and move from there to potential outcomes, the risk of those outcomes (through estimates of S and L) and then the application of controls. That's not how risk assessment in the operation presents itself. Here, one starts with reality, with risk manifest, and works backward toward that goal which we have stated repeatedly is the primary focus of the SMS practitioner—using data from the real world to build an accurate model of the operation so as to be able to predict risk.

The complications present themselves immediately. It is likely true that every ASAP manager in existence has mediated a debate among the Event Review Committee (ERC) concerning what level of risk to assign to a particular ASAP report. One ERC member, for example, might judge that the risk associated with a particular heading deviation was quite low—nothing untoward happened, after all. Another member of that same ERC might argue that there was nothing inherently different between the event in question and another one in which being off course resulted in a controlled flight into terrain (CFIT) accident. Who is right? This question essentially asks which of our ERC members is assigning the correct value to "the most serious credible outcome". Credibility, to an unfortunately great extent, depends upon what has most recently been in the news.

Notice a more fundamental issue in this discussion between ERC members, though, one we alluded to just a moment ago. They both are starting their assessment from an event, not from a hazard. They are presented with risk manifest, and now must work their way backwards to identify both the hazards and the controls involved in the event. It is the interplay of those hazards and controls that resulted in the specifics of the event they are evaluating, and eventually they want to identify the relevant hazards and controls from those details, but our suggestion is, start with the event, with the risk assessment of that specific event.

Calculating the likelihood of a past event that actually happened in the real world

In the "standard" method of risk assessment, one determines S and L. This works, frequently quite well, in process design. In operational observations, you are looking at the *result* of S and L, so our best tactic is to keep that focus.

Doing otherwise creates another layer of problems. Let's look again at the course deviation event that our ERC members were arguing about as they tried to determine S. After they tire of arguing about that, they now need to consider L.

One states "Course deviations are our second most common event type. L has to be pretty high on this one." The other says "Look at the particular circumstances here. How many times do we see one of our aircraft deviating and placing themselves on an intercept course for Air Force One?" (Needless to say, this would be an interesting crew debrief).

We suggest that one can take a common sense approach to this quandary. Here is a true statement:

The probability of this particular event occurring was … 1.0

It happened! When processing an event in SMS SRM, the L value is always maxed out.

Calculating the severity of an event   This makes part of the process of risk assignment considerably easier. For ASAP reports, indeed for any operational observation in which an event is at the center of the study, it is only the severity measure that determines the risk index (well, not quite, more in a bit). Recall from our discussion of the S/L table that most organizations take considerable care to describe in detail the various definitions of the severity scale. Using those definitions, the assignment of S is usually straightforward.

Estimating the effectiveness of remaining controls   So far we have determined that in order to do a risk assessment of an event-type operational observation, assign L at the highest level (probability = 1.0), and take the definitions of S at their face value, and assign as written. But there is one last step we must consider. We have to think about how close we came to something more serious.

Two aircraft land on different runways. Each runway has a coat of ice, with braking action nil on a significant part of the surface. Each aircraft brakes well initially, but once on the ice, both glide and glide, until each eventually comes to a full stop, both mercifully still on the runway.

One runway was 15,000 feet long, and that aircraft finally stopped with 6,000 feet remaining. The other runway was 9,100 feet long. The crew of the aircraft on the shorter runway had a few moments during the final deceleration that were considerably more exciting than the other crew.

Clearly, one situation was riskier than the other. The difference is all in controls. From our assignment of the S value from the table, we know how bad it actually was. The final question to ask ourselves is—what controls existed that were still potentially effective in keeping the situation from getting worse?

In our runway scenarios, the length of the longer runway was a very effective control for mitigating the risk of runway overrun. That control kept the situation from becoming any worse. So the S assignment for that event would be determined solely by the actual severity of the outcome. Perhaps the nose gear was damaged by hitting a runway light—whatever the S definition indicated, that would be the S value, perhaps a 2, using our table.

Let's say the other aircraft had identical minor damage. That is where we would start on the table, and then ask ourselves how many controls still existed and were in place to keep the situation from getting worse, and if that answer is few or none, we would then make the determination of what would have happened if the situation were just slightly more unfortunate. In this case, the severity would quickly escalate to a 3 or 4.

Using this technique in risk assessment for events gives due respect to an essential component of any realistic risk calculation, that component being the existence and potential effectiveness of remaining controls. We will discuss this greater emphasis on controls in Chapter 6.

Summary

How to assign risk to an event

In summary, to assign a risk index to an event:

- Since it happened, the likelihood of it having happened is 1.0. Pretty simple, that determines the L value.
- Take the situation as it is, evaluate any injury, damage, or any other criteria built into your severity definitions, and start from that S value, then -.
- Take a serious look at the controls still in place. If there are redundant layers of effective controls remaining, the S value from step 2 will do. If only one or two controls remain, increase the severity index. Evaluate the remaining controls as to their type—engineered controls are more effective than warnings, which are more effective than human monitoring and cross-checks, etc. Control types will be discussed in the next chapter.

Some might argue that this technique focuses too much on the individual event, rather than looking at the incidence of the event type in the total operation. As we noted in a previous discussion of hazard assessment:

When an SMS practitioner approaches the question of identifying hazards, he or she is constantly aware that the work that is done associated with a single event or investigation must tie in to a larger protocol. The observations at the event level must immediately relate to and interface with the system of observations that has been developed to capture *all* of the hazard information about the operation. The practitioner of SMS is a believer in the concept that individual events are just worldly manifestations of a much larger mechanism that lies underneath the day to day operation, a mechanism that has rules and laws and complicated clockwork that determines the successes, and failures, of controlling risk. *That* is the subject of the SMS practitioner's study.

Far from being a reactive technique that focuses too much on this particular event, we would argue that it is *through* focusing on the particulars of the event in question that one can, bit by bit, accurately describe the aggregate. Risk assessment in ASAP, or in incident analysis, or in any program where the event is the focus of the study, is not the closing argument in a trial. It is the laying out of the evidence, one step at a time, upon which that eventual closing argument can be made.

Identifying and quantifying hazards in an event   There is a final point to emphasize in risk assessment through operational observation. Recall we started with the event, and then assessed the risk by looking at severity and controls. What about hazards?

Every mature operational program has mechanisms for illuminating the contributing factors associated with the event. If one examines the threat/error taxonomy, for example, one can see that the Event Type is equal to the outcome on which risk is assessed in the standard risk matrix, and Threats and Errors are equal to hazards. Most such operational observation programs, therefore, already do identify hazards. The question is what to do with them once identified.

One can quickly figure out what *not* to do with them by thinking through the predicament you would put yourself in by assuming the same protocol as is used in process design risk assessment. That protocol starts with the hazard. Let's consider what would happen if we did that for operational observation programs.

For example, use that standard protocol (describe scenario → identify hazard → list potential outcomes → assign S and L → derive risk index → mitigate through controls → re-evaluate until ALARP achieved) on the following hazard: fatigue. Specifically, the challenge is to create an exhaustive list of potential outcomes to the hazard of fatigue, and to take the process all the way to conclusion for all outcomes; in other words, create a meaningful association between fatigue and risk. Using the standard protocol is just plain unworkable in this case.

But finding that meaningful association between the hazard and the risk is exactly our assignment as SMS practitioners. The way to accomplish our task is to focus on a consistent method of assigning risk to events (the methodology discussed above), and in using a standard taxonomy (threat and error management) for hazards associated with the event. Once there is a sufficiently large database containing these fields—hazards ⇔ event types ⇔ risk indices—one can then apply statistical techniques to illuminate which hazard or set of hazards are most closely associated with high risk events. It is here that Principle Components Analysis can help.

The best system will be the one that can, in addition to associating hazards (threats/errors) with event types, also weight those identified hazards proportionate to an assessment of those most influential to the outcome of the event. Such weighting could then also factor in to the determination of which hazards are most contributory to risk. This would be the best system, but our practical side must temper our zeal for perfection. It would be one more thing to classify for the already overworked analyst, and one more thing to attempt to standardize and calibrate between analysts. We should keep the goal in mind, but keep it simple for now.

SMS in Practice

Robert Clack, Senior Analyst, Flight Safety/SafeOps at American Airlines, discusses risk mitigation programs at his airline:

SafeOps is the name given to American Airlines' SMS flight safety program. It provides an effective means of working through safety concerns using data collected from FOQA, ASAP, CERS [Corporate Event Reporting System], LOSA, and FAA ATOS reports. Once each month, flight safety concerns are presented to a review board composed of managing directors from flight operations, flight training, flight dispatch and safety.

The level of management visibility provided by SafeOps ensures that safety concerns are carefully defined and measured by available resources.

Three times per year safety concerns, resolved and pending, are presented to the vice president in charge of operations. This schedule and management participation ensures that these issues receive appropriate attention.

Existing processes for mitigating risk include a number of methods of alerting flight crews:

- The *FOQA /ASAP Reporter* is a newsletter put in pilot mailboxes.
- The *SAFEOPS Bulletin* is a small, brightly colored poster intended to deliver a brief message to passersby in crew ready rooms.
- Messages from Fleet Captains and Base Chief Pilots may be targeted at crews operating certain fleets or operating into certain airports.
- Recurrent training programs emphasize safety concerns.

Other steps for mitigating risk require more resources. Procedural changes, checklist revisions, and hardware acquisition need careful consideration of effectiveness and possible unintended consequences before large investments in manpower and money are committed. SafeOps escalates safety concerns through reasonable and cost effective risk mitigation steps on their way to an effective resolution.

Review questions

1. Discuss the importance of understanding the hazards associated with a risk to being able to assess the risk.
2. Explain why it is more appropriate to think of the severity or probability of occurrence of a hazard as an estimate of the distribution of potential severities rather than a single value.
3. Why is risk assessment the balancing of the potential for loss against the cost of controls?
4. Why can we never completely eliminate risk from an operation?
5. Explain how severity values are determined for risk assessment.

References

Federal Aviation Administration [FAA] (2006). *Introduction to Safety Management Systems for Air Operators.* Advisory Circular 120-92. Retrieved December 3, 2007 from http://rgl.faa.gov/Regulatory_and_Guidance_Library/rgAdvisoryCircular.nsf/0/6485143d5ec81aae8625719b0055c9e5/$FILE/AC%20120-92.pdf.

International Civil Aviation Organization [ICAO] (2006). *Safety Management Manual (SMM),* 1st edn. (Doc 9859 AN/460). Montréal, Canada: ICAO.

International Civil Aviation Organization [ICAO] (2007). "SMS Training, ICAO SMS Module 04—Hazards." Retrieved December 3, 2007 from http://www.icao.int/anb/safetymanagement/training/training.html

"risk". Online Etymology Dictionary (2007). Retrieved December 3, 2007 from http://www.etymonline.com/index.php?search=risk&searchmode=none.

Chapter 6

Controls

No great deed is done by falterers who ask for certainty.

George Eliot

Thus far, we have discussed the first two steps in Safety Risk Management (SRM)—hazard identification and risk assessment—in some detail. The third major component of SRM is *controls*. While SRM is perhaps the most important broad concept in SMS, controls are the most neglected part of SRM. But the *control* of hazards is the ultimate objective of SRM, so this step deserves considerable attention by SMS practitioners.

Principles of hazard control

Essentially, there are four steps involved in hazard control. They are as follows:

1. Ensure that the hazard is recognized and identified.
2. Determine and select hazard controls.
3. Assign responsibility for implementing control.
4. Measure and monitor the effectiveness of the control.

Ensure that the hazard is recognized and identified

This step was discussed in the previous two chapters, especially in Chapter 4. This chapter will focus on the remaining three steps.

Determine and select hazard controls

As we discussed earlier, both the ICAO and FAA sources present controls (also called mitigations) as, significantly, the last step in the sequence of SRM. First the hazards are identified, then the potential results of hazards described, then those potentials evaluated for risk, and then controls are considered to mitigate the risk. Finally a recalculation of risk is done to evaluate *residual risk* to determine whether it is acceptable. As we have noted in the previous chapters, this "standard" model of SRM is most appropriately applied when assessing risk for new situations, in which there is little historical information.

However, since aviation is not a brand new enterprise, another method can more quickly illuminate the relationship between existing hazards and controls. Controls have been built in to aviation from the beginning. Recall the discussion of the Selfridge accident in Chapter 2 where "the problems were corrected and the U.S. Army went on to purchase the airplane". That is the essence of reactive safety management—a problem occurs, and appropriate controls or safeguards are developed to (hopefully) prevent that problem from recurring.

Since we have the benefit of decades' worth of development of hazard controls in this industry, perhaps a more intuitively useful exercise is to enumerate hazards and controls together, since they almost always exist together already, and then evaluate the effectiveness of those controls in the initial process of risk calculation. Using this *hazard ↔ control* method, instead of describing this step in the hazard control process as *determine and select hazard controls*, we might call this step *identify existing controls associated with these hazards*.

This is not to discount the importance of keeping an open mind in identifying new hazards or inventing new controls. But since we already have languages to talk about hazards (for example, Threat and Error Management (TEM)) and with a bit more work can settle on a language for controls, it is a much more methodical approach to use that new TEM-based language, which includes those controls, to do our risk assessments.

Returning to our Gubbio scenario from Chapter 5 for a moment, it was clear in that example that in order to build an adequate model it was necessary to include controls from the beginning. In the Gubbio example, as in real life, we did not know the exact measure of the threat, or hazard. Nor did we know exactly the effectiveness of the simple control we chose to counter the hazard—that control being the guards. We had to create a table that described a distribution of our estimates of the effectiveness of the control.

That is the real world in aviation also. For example, aircraft are equipped with weather radar as a control to combat the frequently extreme hazard of thunderstorms. But sometimes the equipment fails; sometimes the crew is not fully trained on the use of radar. So the effectiveness of that control is not a fixed value (whether that value is a specific quantification we are using in a mathematical calculation, or a qualitative judgment we are making). Just as the severity of the threat of thunderstorms varies, so does the effectiveness of the control "use of radar". Our final estimates of reality—our risk assessments—have to take into consideration these relationships and especially these variances.

The Hazard ↔ Control Method

A comparison of the *standard* method to the *hazard ↔ control* method of risk assessment may be illustrative. We'll begin with the standard method, and then show how the hazard ↔ control method makes more sense.

Our example is the calculation of risk associated with the use of a certain aircraft that has been in service for a number of years. Suppose that an operator is considering starting scheduled operations into an airport they have never served, on a runway that is both relatively short and at high elevation. For this exercise we will only consider departures from that field.

The standard method would have us look at this from a blank slate, and list all hazards associated with the new operation. One of those hazards would be "short runway", and a risk associated with this hazard would be "inadequate climb performance" which credibly could lead to catastrophic loss. With this back-to-the-basics approach, we enter the risk matrix at the maximum elevation—as we now focus on applying controls to mitigate the risk, we focus on identifying methods to assure that the plane is operated within the certificated flight envelope. As we apply these controls, the likelihood of occurrence finally decreases to such a low point that we feel comfortable in proceeding with operations; that is, an acceptable level of risk.

There is nothing unsound about this approach, but as anyone in the business knows, it is quite theoretical. The process describes where the industry was 75 years ago, as standards for performance calculations were invented. Today's reality is that we already have controls in place for this hazard. If those controls are effectively applied, the risk of inadequate climb performance is quite low.

In contrast, consider the hazard ↔ control method: we know the hazard is a short, high elevation runway. We know that we have very well-defined controls in our performance calculation and management system, which includes load control, Minimum Equipment List control, and so forth. The hazard ↔ control method would have us ask "what controls do we presently have in place for controlling this hazard?", "what is the range of effectiveness of our controls for this hazard?", and "what is the residual risk in the controls' various failure modes"?

In the hazard ↔ control method, rather than concentrate on a problem that, at least intellectually, was solved 75 years ago, we have now concentrated on the system that is in place to mitigate the hazard. And, unfortunately, we know that this control system is not 100 percent effective. The SMS analyst would seek out data that would describe those failure modes, and describe the extent to which the system is compromised by those failures.

One known failure mode might be "failure of load control to provide accurate weight information to crew". In a good SMS data collection system, there would be information on rates of failure for this component, and measures of the inaccuracy of the information. These sources of data would also be distributions—the data might show that the load control system is accurate 99.95 percent of the time, but when it isn't the inaccuracies range from 100 to 30,000 pounds off.

Now we have information that we can use. If our control to meet the hazard of a short, high altitude runway has a 0.05 percent failure rate, and in those failures historical data indicates that 1 percent of the time the error is 30,000 pounds, then we can calculate the effectiveness of our control. In this case, we would experience 5 failures per 10,000 operations in which the aircraft could be as much as 30,000 pounds over weight.

Since our hazard is short and high, the residual risk for this failure is itself high indeed. By focusing on hazard ↔ control, we have uncovered a component of our safety management system that simply must be fixed before we can consider operations into such airports where margins are so slim.

Perhaps we would have arrived at the same conclusion if we would have used the standard method; perhaps not. The important point here is that the hazard ↔ control method allows us to focus our resources from the outset on the important questions concerning the effectiveness of our controls and the residual risk should the control(s) fail.

We have to constantly remind ourselves that we are not on new ground. Controls abound in this industry, many time tested and true, all of them not 100 percent effective. The hazard ↔ control method builds on what we already have, does not distract us from danger by erroneously focusing on what already works and, by concentrating our attention on methodically measuring the effectiveness of those controls, gives us a means to calculate our residual risk in the real world.

Assign responsibility for implementing control

Once the risk controls are determined, they should be:

- Described in clear, unambiguous language.
- Implementable—The control is of little value if it is not ready to be used in the organization to reduce risk.
- Documented—It is important to document the controls in sufficient detail so that someone not involved in the process could gain an understanding of how and why those particular controls were selected.

Work not assigned to someone is work not done. Once hazard controls are established, responsibility for implementing the control must be assigned to the appropriate person(s).

Measure and monitor the effectiveness of the control (safety assurance)

The final step in the principles of hazard control is *measuring the effectiveness of controls*.

When we measure the effectiveness of the controls we are performing *safety assurance*! The FAA states the following in AC 120-92 about controlling risk and techniques for ensuring that those controls achieve their intended objectives (FAA, 2006, p. 3):

> The safety management process described in this AC starts with design and implementation of organizational processes and procedures to control risk in aviation operations. Once these controls are in place, quality management techniques can be used to provide a structured process for ensuring that they achieve their intended objectives and, where they fall short, to improve them. Safety management can, therefore, be thought of as quality management of safety related operational and support processes to achieve safety goals.

This is a noteworthy statement which with we strongly endorse and, of course, is the reason why we included a section in this book as an introduction to quality management. Quality management is precisely the right way to set about monitoring and measuring the effectiveness of controls. This is typically accomplished through internal auditing, analysis, and evaluation systems so integral to quality management.

The FAA points out in AC 120-92 that the safety assurance function "need not be extensive or complex to be effective". In fact, organizations that have an Internal Evaluation Program (IEP) as discussed in Chapter 2 probably already meet, or nearly so, the requirements of an effective safety assurance function.

Quality assurance is focused on "demonstrating that the requirements for quality have been (and can be) achieved". Further, quality assurance gives us "confidence in the organization's products" (Juran & Godfrey, 1998, p. 11.8). The parallel is that safety assurance gives us the confidence that the risk controls, once designed and implemented, continue to be effective in maintaining risk within acceptable levels.

Quality is about data-driven decision-making, and SMS programs are no different. The sources of the data for the safety assurance function are numerous; for example, auditing and evaluation, employee reporting systems, safety investigations and, importantly, continuous monitoring of operations. As with other aspects of an SMS program, the amount of data that should be collected is a function of the size and complexity of the aviation operation.

Importantly, the FAA standard requires that feedback loops be established between the safety assurance functions described in Section 6 of AC 120-92 to evaluate the effectiveness of controls. These functions are: continuous monitoring, internal audits, internal evaluation, external auditing, investigation, and employee reporting and feedback system. The organization must ensure that mechanisms are established that enable these functions to exchange information or "data share" with one another.

Hierarchy of controls

The field of system safety has given us a categorization scheme for evaluating hazard controls. It is important that the SMS practitioner understands this scheme so that appropriate decisions about controls can be made. The following listing is in hierarchical order, from most to least effective in controlling the hazard (Brauer, 2006, pp. 99–103):

- Eliminate the hazard.
- Reduce the hazard level.
- Provide safety devices.
- Provide warnings or advisories.
- Provide safety procedures.

Eliminate the hazard

From a safety standpoint, the most effective way of controlling a hazard is to eliminate or avoid it. Our merchant from Gubbio had no means of eliminating the threat he faced, but he could have chosen not to make the trip and, consequently, foregone his potential profits. Our aircraft operator from a few paragraphs earlier could have decided not to fly that particular aircraft onto the short, high altitude runway. As we can see, eliminating the hazard has other possible consequences, often financial.

Reduce the hazard level

As we discussed in previous chapters, hazards possess two characteristics—severity and likelihood. Reducing either of these reduces the hazard level. Reducing the likelihood means that the probability of occurrence is lowered, so the chance of an incident or accident is less. Reducing the severity means that, if the event does occur, there will less injury and damage.

Provide safety devices

Safety devices do not remove hazards, but they can reduce their effect by providing features or controls that prevent the exposure of people to the potential hazards. Safety devices abound on aircraft, and include such items as weather radar, handholds, non-slip wing walk surfaces, switch guards for powerplant fire extinguishing system, traffic collision avoidance system (TCAS), and many others.

Provide warnings or advisories

Warnings and other advisories are provided to protect people from hazards. Warnings may be in a *visual* form, such as labels, signs, placards, and flashing lights; they may also be in an audible form, such as sirens, horns, bells, and whistles. And they may be a combination of both. We are all familiar with landing gear warning horns, stall warning horns, and stick shakers. Warnings are a form of communication; they are intended to send a message to the receiver that *human action must be taken* to prevent the hazard from occurring. Thus, great care must be taken to design the warning so that the possibility of misinterpreting the warning or failing to receive it is minimized.

Provide safety procedures

Procedures are actions that are taken to reduce the risk. Humans are trained to follow certain procedures at certain times. Not all procedures exist for safety reasons, but the aviation industry certainly makes great use of procedures for that purpose.

Residual risk

Once hazards are recognized and identified, and risk assessed, the safety risk must be controlled. Controls in the aviation field are generally well-known and effective, but they are rarely 100 percent effective. Often in SRM, we will find that there is some risk that remains after we've applied our controls; that risk is termed *residual risk*, and can be represented by the following equation:

Residual Risk = Hazard—Control Effectiveness

It is the residual risk that is evaluated to determine if the risks have been reduced to an acceptable level, or at least to a level that is as low as reasonably practicable. If the risks are still not acceptable, then other mitigations strategies and/or controls must be applied.

As always, it is important to quantify and document the residual risk in the SRM process.

Hazard control models

As we all know, the aviation industry is highly complex, involving relationships between people, technical systems, machines, organizations, and the environment. It is this complexity that makes the hazard control process so vexing. For example, many risk assessment efforts go awry because the analyst fails to take into consideration the use environment. Also, in some instances, we fail to properly consider the complex interactions among the elements potentially contributing to hazards. Fortunately, there are several models to help analysts visualize the interfaces of various elements acting on the system.

SHELL model

One such model is the *SHELL* model (see Figure 6.1). The SHELL model is named for its components—Software, Hardware, Environment, Liveware, and Liveware (again).

In the center of the model is *Liveware*, which refers to the person(s) in and affecting the system. The boxes in Figure 6.1 are straight lines, but it's useful to think of them as irregular shapes, underscoring that people do not interface perfectly with other elements of the system. When predicting hazards and planning controls, considerable care needs to be taken to anticipate how frequently and in what ways humans make mistakes, and how they interface with the other components of the system. This requires an understanding of physical (for example, height, vision, strength), physiological (stress, fatigue, health), psychological (motivation, judgment, risk attitudes), and psycho-social factors (personal financial issues, marital

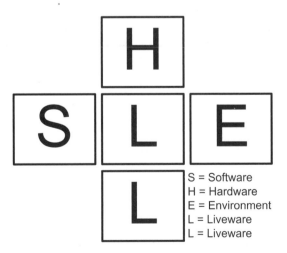

Figure 6.1   SHELL Model

problems) issues that all of us experience. As the model indicates, Liveware relates with all other elements of the system.

Liveware ↔ Software   We think of software as computer programs, but in the Liveware ↔ Software linkage we are also referring to the relationships between the human and non-physical aspects of the system, such as procedures, checklists, manuals, and symbology. An example of a potential hazard in this linkage area is misinterpretation of a checklist.

Liveware ↔ Hardware   Liveware ↔Hardware refers to the interface of man and machine. Consider all the ways in which we connect with our machines—a mouse, keyboard, steering wheel, control yoke, instrument panel, throttle quadrant, voice recognition devices, and so on—the list is nearly endless. Ill-designed or improperly used interface devices are a significant source of hazards in the aviation industry.

Liveware ↔ Environment   Aviation imposes special considerations for the interfacing of Liveware ↔ Environment. Examples include: oxygen for high altitudes, radiation exposure at altitude, ozone concentrations, sleep deprivation due to biological rhythms, spatial disorientation and illusions, and many others. Political and economic considerations are also part of our environment. Aviation is replete with examples of hazards and associated controls in this area.

Liveware ↔ Liveware   The interface between people is called Liveware ↔ Liveware. In aviation we relate to numerous people and groups in the workplace, including flight crews, air traffic controllers, management, airport authorities, regulatory authorities, airport screeners, flight dispatch, and others. We need to be concerned about communication styles and techniques, teamwork, and personality differences. There is standardized training for certain aspects of this area, such as crew resource management.

5M model

The *5M* model also enables the analyst to visualize the system (see Figure 6.2). The 5Ms stand for mission, man, machine, management, and media.

The *mission* is the central purpose of the system; in the case of the aviation industry, the mission is normally the transportation of people or goods. *Man* is the human element of the system. *Machine* represents both the hardware and software elements of the system. *Management* involves setting policy, rules, and regulations, and providing resources for the operation and maintenance of a system. Media refers to the environment in which the system will be operating.

Continuous improvement

In the final steps described in the ICAO process, it is clear that the "re-evaluate control strategies" and "collect additional hazard data" illustrate that ICAO is advocating continuous improvement through a feedback process. Though the FAA overview

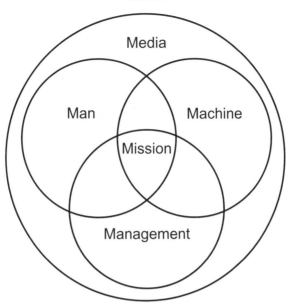

Figure 6.2   5M model

of SRM noted above does not explicitly list continuous improvement as a part of SRM, AC 120-92 is clear in its inclusion of quality feedback control mechanisms as a critical part of SMS. This is just a matter of presentation—both the ICAO and the FAA strongly state that continuous improvement is a necessary part of SMS.

Systems engineering and controls

The term "control" is one that has a somewhat variable definition, depending upon the level of process being examined. For example, one could reasonably state that the "point and shoot" procedure is a control aimed at mitigating the risk of altitude deviation. Another example of a perfectly legitimate use of the term is to designate an airline's load control department a control used in mitigating the hazards associated with inadequate climb performance or out-of-limit center of gravity states. For our detailed examination of controls, we're going to use the term more precisely.

The history of controls, from an engineering perspective

Controls have been engineered into systems since man began to build things, but a rigorous discussion of the principles of control was first published in 1868 by the physicist James Clerk Maxwell, in his treatise *On Governors*. In this work, which is recognized as the foundation of modern control theory, Maxwell analyzed a number of mechanisms already used in machines of the day, such as the centrifugal governor devised by James Watt in 1788. Maxwell's work described some of the mathematical theory behind control systems, and began the development of a taxonomy to describe controls. For example, he distinguished *moderators*, devices that control a system by slowing it down, from *governors*, devices that work by controlling the input of motive force (Maxwell, 1868). Control theory has since developed a detailed taxonomy that describes various types of control.

An in-depth examination of control theory is far beyond the scope of this book, but a review of the essential concepts will help in understanding how to best design controls into our SRM.

The two basic types of control   There are many methods used to control a system, but all of them fall into two basic types: open loop systems and closed loop systems. Hybrid systems incorporate both open loop and closed loop systems.

Open loop systems   An open loop control system uses only two inputs to determine its output, a measure of current system state (the trigger), and some sort of internal model of how the system behaves. Notably, an open loop system does not mediate its output based upon the performance of the system after the control is applied.

The classic example of an open loop system is a simple sprinkler irrigation system. One input is the model of the larger system it is installed to control. In this case the model is the design assumption underlying the irrigation system—this area of grass needs 1 ½ inches of water per week to thrive, and the irrigation system can deliver that amount by being turned on for 10 minutes each day. The other input in this case is time, specifically a timer system that opens a water valve at the same time each day, and then closes it 15 minutes later.

This is an open loop system because there is no effort in measuring the effectiveness of the system in achieving the real goal of installing the system in the first place, which is to maintain a fixed moisture level in the soil. This system will dutifully turn on and off, regardless of whether a monsoon is raging or if instead there is a prolonged heat wave parching the soil.

Open loop systems clearly have limitations, but they also offer advantages, primarily in cost of design and operation. In our sprinkler example, there is no need to install and maintain moisture sensors in the ground. If the model upon which the design is built accurately reflects the actual way the system works, open loops can be effective.

Open loop systems in aviation are more common than one might think. Let's look at one example, training. From a risk management point of view, one ever-present hazard is that an employee will get rusty concerning how to do a procedure that is seldom needed in the real world operation. One control aimed at mitigating the risk associated with this hazard is to require that employee to return to the schoolhouse every year to practice that procedure. There is an implicit model underlying that control. One could state that model as:

> Requiring employees to practice this procedure once a year will maintain a proficiency level sufficient to control the risk the procedure is designed to mitigate.

Thus, continuing qualification training would be an open loop control with this model as one input, and the "timer" of training scheduling as the other. Notice there is no measurement of system state here. The pilot who has just experienced 4 engine failures in the last month and is unfortunately very familiar with the engine failure procedure will go through the same training as his luckier counterparts. Maybe more importantly, there is no measure as to whether the assumptions of the model are correct. Is a one year period between practice sessions enough to maintain proficiency? It might be, but in this case there is no feedback mechanism to determine the answer to that question.

Another open loop control is the terrain avoidance maneuver. Once the signal to begin the maneuver is sensed (by hearing the Ground Proximity Warning System alert), the crew accomplishes the procedure, and does not moderate it through reference to the altimeter, for example.

Open loop control systems abound, and they are not necessarily a bad solution to controlling hazards, but the SMS practitioner should be suspicious of every one of them. Even when there is no direct feedback mechanism to a control (in other words, when it is an open loop control!), it is still possible to find some way to measure the state of the system downstream of the control in an aggregate way, to see if in general the control is effective. The SMS practitioner should strive to build in process measurements downstream of controls, especially open loop controls, in order to have a means of measuring the control's effectiveness.

In the example above concerning the "traditional" (non-AQP) model of continuing qualification training, the system was open loop, in that there was no means of modulating the frequency of the administration of the control based upon a measure of decay of competence in the maneuver. An astute SMS practitioner would seek to identify ways to measure this decay of performance and track that measurement, then put into place a means of changing the frequency of training based upon this measure.

Indeed, this is exactly what AQP is supposed to do, by measuring the success of "first-look" maneuvers in Continuing Qualification Training (CQT). First look maneuvers are performed at the beginning of the regular simulator session, without any coaching or prior refresher training administered. The maneuvers are "non-jeopardy" in that a pilot does not fail a simulator session because of a botched first look maneuver. Nevertheless, they are graded, and the aggregate measure of first look maneuvers across the pilot population is reviewed to determine whether the frequency of CQT sessions is adequate. If a downward trend is noted in first look maneuver grades, the training cycle can be shortened to attempt to decrease that decay of competence over time.

Closed loop systems (feedback systems)   Closed loop controls, on the other hand, substitute sensing of actual system state for the model input used in open loop systems. In a centrifugal speed governor, for example, the movement of the flyweights toward or away from the axis of rotation in turn modulates the position of a valve to control the amount of fuel introduced, therefore controlling speed.

Closed loop controls are also common in aviation risk management. One good example of a procedural closed loop control is the common practice of having the Pilot Monitoring (PM) issue callouts of airspeed and glideslope deviation during an approach. In this control the Pilot Flying (PF) is manipulating inputs or direction autopilot functions in order to achieve a particular airspeed and flight path (the target or reference values). Based upon the actual performance of the aircraft, the PM calls out deviations from the target airspeed or glidepath, and then waits to observe both a verbal acknowledgement of the deviation by the PF (usually in the form of the PF saying "correcting"), and also evidence of the airspeed or path actually correcting back to the desired targets.

Hybrid control types   Many systems have both closed loop and open loop controls as components (in this case the open loop component is often called a feed-forward control, as compared to the feedback control of the closed loop). This combination is the best of both worlds, in that the feedback system uses information from the real-world system state (which the open loop system is not designed to do). The feed forward mechanism also compensates for an untoward characteristic of closed loop controls—hysteresis.

Hysteresis describes the occasional tendency of a feedback system to cause oscillations around the reference value which is the target of the system control. Most of us have experienced hysteresis when we started older model cars and heard the engine revving up and down as the various mechanisms controlling fuel and air oscillated around their setpoints.

The SMS practitioner should look for ways to incorporate hybrid controls into risk management. For example, charter operator A always issues winter operations bulletins to its flight crews in early December, based upon an operational model that assumes retraining is a good thing to do just before crews need to start doing things they haven't had to do for six months (de-icing, calculating landing distances with clutter on the runway, and such).

This risk control used by charter operator A is an open loop control, and has great merit. They might consider modifying this open loop winter operations control into a hybrid control by adding a feedback mechanism. They could, for example, add a spot audit program that measures the effectiveness of their de-icing program, and have a protocol established such that when they measure an error rate above a set reference, they issue another more targeted set of bulletins. Adding the feedback mechanism now inserts a performance-based method of modulating the resources aimed at winter operations risk. Note, though, that they should not discard their feed forward mechanism, because it is preventing hysteresis in the system, which would show itself by an initial spike of operational problems. The feedback control would eventually damp that spike, but not until enough errors had been experienced to trigger the control.

Single Input Single Output System and Multiple Input Multiple Output System   In a sophisticated control theory description, a distinction is made between Single Input Single Output (SISO) systems and Multiple Input Multiple Output (MIMO) systems. Given that this is not a textbook on system control so there is no need here to belabor the intricacies of SISO and MIMO design. The short version, applicable to our focus, is in the difference in complexity between SISO and MIMO designs. SISO controls for risk exist in our domain, but certainly the closer you get to the flight deck, the more likely it is that any control will be a MIMO.

Let's examine, for example, a hypothetical "workload distribution" control (hypothetical only in the sense of identifying it as a recognized control—every crew exercises workload management techniques; we just have not achieved the level of sophistication in SMS yet to actually have a name for this set of behaviors). This control, owned by the captain but exercised by all flight crewmembers, has a plethora of inputs—aircraft systems management, communication, planning, stick and rudder flying,—the list of inputs to the control is long indeed, as are the outputs. Our take-away from systems control theory should be that MIMO systems are exceedingly complex, and require careful analysis of interactions between components of the control system. The danger of course is focusing on tight control of one output, only to experience the unintended consequence of another output getting out of control.

Process flowcharts and controls

Chapter 3 covered the seven basic quality tools. Among those tools is one that is especially important for the SMS practitioner to be proficient in applying; that is, the process flowchart. Process flowcharts are useful from a number of perspectives, but one of the most beneficial applications is in the understanding of controls. In the hazard ↔ control method of risk assessment, the flowchart becomes a critical tool.

Let's review the use of the flowchart to examine control effectiveness by revisiting one presented earlier, Figure 3.10. We will decompose the point and shoot control procedure with the knowledge gained from our brief discussion of system controls.

The first and most important thing to note is that by forcing us to think clearly about the process under study, the flowchart helps us to identify the components of the process, and understand exactly where elements of control are built in. Let's examine the first few steps in the flowchart, shown as Figure 6.3.

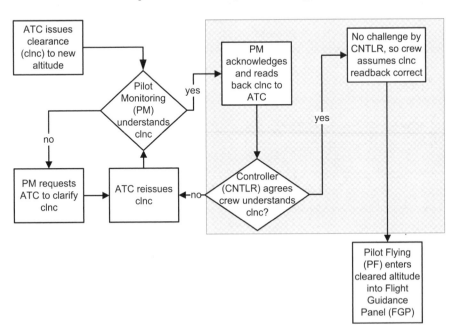

Figure 6.3 **First few steps of controls, risk of midair collision due to altitude deviation flowchart**

Notice that this part of the process, which we might designate *clearance reception*, has a closed loop control embedded in it (designated by the crosshatched area). The PM reads back the clearance to the controller, and based upon that new system state, the controller either corrects and reissues the clearance (in the case of a misunderstanding), or does not challenge the readback, and so the process proceeds to the next step.

Notice also that there is an open loop control in place. We can best see it if we remove the feedback loop (see Figure 6.4).

The diamond designating this control is an open loop, with error checking. The PM's understanding of the clearance fits in with the model in his head representing the set of all clearances that would make sense to receive in this phase of flight, and so when the input of the clearance comes in, it is checked against that model, and accepted as understood, or rejected and the PM asks for clarification. But of course we have removed the feedback loop for clarity in this case, so there is no closed system that is checking to see if the PM's understanding of the clearance is actually correct. (We might note that since readback is not a required action, it is somewhat ironic that the element that makes this set of controls into a closed loop us often discarded at airports or ATC facilities with high traffic volume, just when it is most important for there to be clarity in the understanding of clearances!)

Looking at another control component in this flowchart, something else becomes apparent. Figure 6.5 shows a simple SISO control, the only input being the PM's looking at the altitude set in the altitude select window, and then comparing that value with the reference for this control, that is, the PM's own understanding of the clearance. There is also only one output (with two states)—agree/disagree.

SISO controls have a simple clarity to them. In this case it would be important to assure that flight crew training emphasizes this clarity; if the PM agrees, they proceed with the altitude change, if the PM does not agree, they must clarify with ATC.

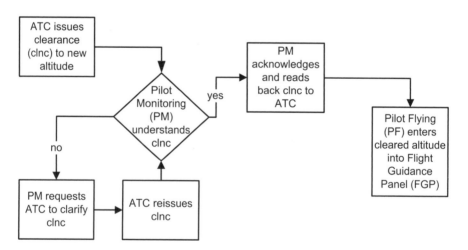

Figure 6.4   First few steps of controls, risk of midair collision due to altitude deviation flowchart, with feedback loop removed

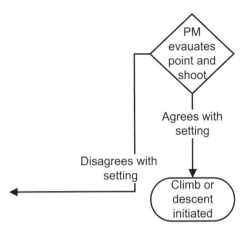

Figure 6.5 **Single input single output—agree/disagree**

The remaining control in the flowchart is shown in Figure 6.6, and it is also a SISO control, i.e., do the PF and PM agree on their understanding of the clearance?

Figure 3.10 diagrams the now widely accepted procedures of clearance readback and point and shoot. We can see that within these procedures (in the initial reception and readback) are one hybrid control composed of an open loop system with error checking, and a closed loop system. The point and shoot is also a closed loop system with two simple SISOs.

When exercised correctly, this is a very effective control system that can mitigate the risk of midair due to being off-altitude. Still, altitude deviations are the most commonly reported event in ASAP. A final benefit of using flowcharts to examine controls is that they can give the SMS practitioner guidance as to how to create a system to evaluate where controls might be failing. In general, there are four areas to examine for failure:

1. Are the inputs to the control unambiguous and clearly defined?
2. Does the internal working of the control adequately compare the inputs to the reference or target values?

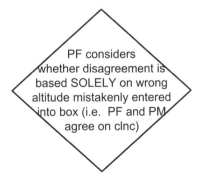

Figure 6.6 **Single input single output control—PF and PM agreement**

3. Are the reference values correct and well-defined?
4. Are the outputs of the control designed to definitively steer the course of the process flow?

For example, with the last control in the above process (see Figure 6.6), the SMS practitioner might examine whether the input to the control "PM Challenges PF", is clearly described in procedural documentation, and whether there are elements in the training program that emphasize assertiveness on the part of the pilot monitoring.

Review questions

1. What are the steps in hazard control?
2. Explain the hierarchy of controls provided by the field of system safety.
3. What is residual risk?
4. Explain open loop and closed loop control systems.
5. Explain the difference between SISO and MIMO controls.

References

Brauer, R. (2006). *Safety and Health for Engineers*. Hoboken, NJ: John Wiley & Sons.

Federal Aviation Administration [FAA] (2006). *Introduction to Safety Management Systems for Air Operators*. Advisory Circular 120-92. Retrieved December 3, 2007 from http://rgl.faa.gov/Regulatory_and_Guidance_Library/rgAdvisoryCircular. nsf/0/6485143d5ec81aae8625719b0055c9e5/$FILE/AC%20120-92.pdf.

Juran, J., and Godfrey, B. (1998). *Juran's Quality Handbook*, 5th edn. New York, NY: McGraw-Hill.

Maxwell, J. (1868). "On Governors." *Proceedings of the Royal Society*, No. 100. Retrieved December 3, 2007 from http://www.ee.adfa.edu.au/staff/hrp/historicalpapers/ongovernors.pdf

Chapter 7

Taxonomies[1]

The importance of taxonomies

We have made the point that SMS requires rigor and consistency in the classification of hazards. This need for standardization in classification is no less true for risks and controls. We will once again briefly review why this is true, and then suggest guidelines for selection of taxonomies in SMS.

Previously we emphasized the point that consistently applying a well-designed classification schema is an information gaining process. If the schema itself captures distinct and substantive measures of the mechanisms underlying the functioning of the system, then when one observes those measures reasonable conclusions concerning the underlying mechanisms can be made, and those conclusions can be applied to both individual events and aggregate analysis of those events. Let's now focus on the importance of taxonomies on that aggregate analysis. Remember, the SMS practitioner is continually evaluating that model of the functioning of the real world, and though individual events are informative, it is the aggregate that best describes the system.

In SRM, the SMS practitioner must create and use methods that produce repeatable and reliable measures of risk, so as to provide these measures to an informed decision support mechanism. Indices of risk are computed based upon measures of the severity and likelihood of hazards, and the effectiveness of controls. In the mature SMS, those measures are empirically derived. In order to have any hope of generating consistent results, the methods employed to derive those empirical measures of the indicators of hazards and controls must be carefully designed. The SMS practitioner must pay careful attention to how data are collected, and that means thoughtful consideration of taxonomies.

In order for calculations to produce repeatable results, the taxonomies used in the observational programs underlying the SRM process must be well-defined and, most- importantly, easily understood and applied by those responsible for recording the observations. It is incumbent upon the SMS practitioner to design mechanisms to measure inter-rater performance—in other words to validate the repeatability of results in classification.

And in order for those same calculations to be reliable, they must also be based upon measures that everyone agrees are realistic. We have previously discussed

---

1   A significant part of this section was composed with the assistance of our friend and colleague, Michelle Harper. Michelle has been a driving force behind the success of the application of threat/error taxonomies in self-reporting systems, and is continuing the pioneering work of Dr. Robert Helmreich and the rest of the Human Factors Research Project at the University of Texas at Austin (the UTHFRP).

some of the problems and pitfalls associated with reliably classifying severity. This is not an easy task, but it is one that must be squarely faced, or else we risk producing an SMS that looks wonderful on paper, but is ineffective.

Finally, it's worth stating the obvious one more time—the aggregate analysis of measures of a system such as ours in aviation, in which we can have thousands of employee self-reports per year, or millions of parametric observations from which events are detected, absolutely requires automation to support the analysis. Especially for larger service providers and data-sharing programs, the size of our datasets are much too big for manual analysis, and therefore standardization is a requirement; as we all know, computers are stern task-masters. We must be very clear and as precise as possible when feeding data to them, or, as the well-known axim goes, garbage-in garbage-out.

The following discussion presents the logic used in taxonomy selection as the UTHFRP team developed a pilot reporting tool to support ASAP, and as that same taxonomy became the standard for ASIAS.

Review of human factor and pilot error taxonomies

Research completed in the mid 1980s by Fleishman and Quaintance (1984) suggest that the most effective taxonomy for describing human factors in a given context is one in which the development of the taxonomy was based on information gathered from the targeted context and developed for a pre-defined goal. For the majority of human factor taxonomies the main goal of the use of the taxonomy is to support the identification of meaningful classifications in a body of information (Fleishman, 1967, pp. 1–10, 1982, pp. 821–834; Fleishman and Quaintance, 1984; Miller, 1967). The goal of the development and implementation of the ASAP Threat and Error Management (TEM) Taxonomy into the University of Texas (UT) ASAP Pilot Reporting Form and as a mapping structure for the DNAA (Distributed National ASAP Archive) Master List was to provide a classification system that could support the identification of contributing factors relating to why a reported ASAP event occurred.

With the objective of creating an interface to prompt pilots to provide information on factors that contributed to their reported event, a review of human factor and pilot error taxonomies was completed. Also completed was a review of taxonomies supported by airlines with active ASAP programs. A total of six human factor and pilot error taxonomies were identified that are in active use by the airlines or had been developed specifically with the goal of supporting ASAP programs. These taxonomies, as well as their theoretical basis and practical applications, were reviewed for potential inclusion in the structured interview process supported by the UT ASAP Pilot Reporting Form. The taxonomies were reviewed for the following criteria:

- The taxonomy had to be defined and actively in use by at least one airline and support a simple structure that could be presented to pilots without the need for training or explanation;
- The taxonomy had to be derived from language used by pilots;

- The taxonomy had to have an identifiable background in human factors research;
- The taxonomy had to result in data that could be used to feed an airline's SRM.

A total of 12 additional taxonomies were reviewed for inclusion in the UT ASAP Applications. Although efficient in identifying causal factors following the occurrence of an accident, these taxonomies were not based on terminology regularly used by pilots during their normal operations or actively used by either airlines or other groups in the air transportation system (Beaubian and Baker, 2002; D. A. Wiegmann, Rich, and Shappell, 2002). In general it was found that a large number of human factor taxonomies, most of which were derived from accidents, often included terms that would not be recognizable to pilots, but instead focused on higher order categorizations relevant to a specific area of research (Kirwan, 1998a, 1998b, p. 299). With the goal of developing a reporting form that could be used by pilots and reviewed by ERC members, many of whom are retired pilots, it was determined that only taxonomies that were developed with a pilot audience as the targeted users were relevant for use in pilot self-reporting systems.

The Aviation Safety Reporting Systems (ASRS) Anomaly Codes

ASRS is the longest standing and most recognized aviation reporting program in the air transportation industry. ASRS supports the following methodology for the review and categorizing of each ASRS report. First, all reports are screened for inclusion into the ASRS system. The reports are then reviewed and coded for hazards by at least two subject matter experts; the definition of a hazard being any issue, condition, action or set of circumstances that compromises the safety of an aircraft or a flight crew (ASRS, 1999). If the subject matter experts agree that the report is of a critical nature the report in its entirety is included in the ASRS database. ASRS supports a set of codes that are applied to each subject matter expert-approved report. A minimal amount of "descriptive characteristics" are retained by ASRS for all reports. This information includes the function of the person submitting the report, the place and time of the reported incident, and the written description of the occurrence. ASRS also collects a set of incident labels called anomaly codes. These codes are applied to a report by the ASRS subject matter experts and include a mixture of issues referencing weather, traffic aircraft positioning and pilot error (ASRS, 1994, 1999).

Following a review of the ASRS anomaly codes it was concluded that these codes could provide support for the identification of event type classifications but the taxonomy provided no distinction between event types and contributing factors. Also, to date there are no references available for defining the anomaly codes. An additional concern was the fact that the ASRS anomaly codes were used by a set of subject matter experts during group discussions, not by pilots submitting the ASRS reports. Although the ASRS anomaly codes have been used to categorize the largest aviation safety databases in the air transportation industry, there is no information presently available regarding the theoretical methods used for deriving the ASRS anomaly codes.

The British Airways Safety Information System (BASIS)

BASIS is one of the first and few software systems that support airlines in collecting and managing mandatory and voluntary pilot reporting (O'Leary and Fisher, 1993). The BASIS program was started in 1990 by British Airways and is now used by over 100 airlines and aviation companies. The BASIS system is now supported by a private company and information regarding the functionality supported by the tools includes automated reporting tools and risk assessment (Mercator, 2006).

Although several airlines that contacted the UTHFRP regarding the development of ASAP support tools were using the BASIS taxonomy for mandatory reporting programs, there is little information available on how the taxonomy was developed and no information on definitions or references on the BASIS taxonomy. What was identified from a review of the BASIS keywords, provided by one airline using the licensed BASIS tool, was an internal framework that supported a breakdown of key words into three main categories: Technical, Operational and Environmental. The key words referenced under each of these categories include more specific terms relevant to mechanical, technical or operational issues with an aircraft.

The review of the BASIS tools was restricted due to the proprietary control that the company supporting BASIS places on the tools and there is currently no published information on the theoretical or historical development of the system. These issues coupled with the fact that there was no information available on definitions for the BASIS taxonomy made incorporating information from this tool impossible.

ICAO Accident/Incident Reporting Data Reporting System (ADREP 2000)

The ICAO ADREP 2000 taxonomy is used predominately throughout the international aviation transportation community for classifying incident and accident data. This taxonomy is used to support a data collection tool commonly used in the European Coordination Center for Aviation Incident Reporting Systems (ECCAIRS). ECCAIRS is a mandatory reporting program that exists under a directive required by European Union States to collect mandatory reportable events. The ADREP 2000 Taxonomy is used through the ECCAIRS program by individuals within the aviation community that are elected and trained on the use for the ECCAIRS report tool.

The ICAO ADREP 2000 taxonomy includes a large and extensive list of event types that can be used to describe a wide range of events from minor incidents to more serious occurrences. This taxonomy was developed to be used by a third party member to collect information on a mandatory reportable incident and therefore supports an accident investigation methodology much too complex for a pilot to navigate for the submission of an ASAP report (Cacciabue, 1997, 2000).

Human Factors Analysis and Classification System (HFACS)

Unlike BASIS, the Human Factors Analysis and Classification System (HFACS) system is not supported by a software system that can be integrated into an airline's database. But regardless of this fact HFACS is one of the most commonly referenced tools for use in applying human factor assessments to accident investigations (Shappell and Wiegmann, 1997, pp. 269–291). HFACS was developed initially through the review of a large number of military and general aviation accident investigations (Wiegmann and Shappell, 2003). Most recently the HFACS methodology has been applied to commercial aviation accident investigations (Shappell et. al., 2007, pp. 227–242).

One of the benefits that HFACS holds over BASIS is the model's focus on human factors. HFACS is derived from James Reason's model of human error and Reason's distinction between active and latent threats (Reason, 1990). Active threats are referred to as unsafe acts that are committed by an individual, most often the pilot operating the aircraft. Latent threats are referenced as environmental issues or issues surrounding and contributing to the occurrence of an event.

HFACS was developed to support the completion of accident investigations and therefore supports a multi-level framework of connections of factors potentially contributing to an accident, starting with latent and active threats. The HFACS model is not meant to be completed in a short period of time but instead was developed for post-hoc investigations of accidents. The HFACS model was found to support many of the objectives needed for the ASAP Pilot Reporting Form taxonomy, including a theoretical model providing the basis for the human factor categorizations of pilot error, but the process for completing the HFACS methodology was found to be much too time consuming for a pilot to complete for submitting an incident report for ASAP. The fact that HFACS was developed to support accident investigations results in a methodology that is too complex for pilots to complete in a single report.

Aviation Causal Contributors for Event Reporting Systems (ACCERS)

The ACCERS taxonomy was developed by the American Institute of Research (AIR) at the request of the FAA Human Factors Research and Engineering Division. The request by the FAA was made to develop a set of contributing factors that could be used to support ASAP reporting. The resulting ACCERS taxonomy includes a set of seven primary contributing factors that were identified using a cluster analysis technique. The AIR subject matter experts reviewed 94 causal factors and sorted these factors into 9 groupings. These groups were then reviewed and it was found that only 7 groupings were identified as useful to the AIR researchers (Baker and Krokos, 2005, pp. 185–199).

The development of the ACCERS taxonomy was completed in June 2005 and therefore was not available at the time the UTHFRP review of taxonomies was completed. But, after a review of the 7 primary groupings it was determined that these categorizations did not appear to support a logical structure or framework that a pilot would use to describe an event. Although, cluster analysis provides a statistical measure of similarity among a set of classifications, the use of 7 groupings did not appear to support an intuitive representation of the potential factors that a pilot could encounter when handling a reportable event.

The Threat and Error Management Model

The Threat and Error Management (TEM) Model is both a theoretical model depicting the relationship between human and environmental factors that contribute to the occurrence of events as well as a working model that can be used to categorize these factors (Klinect, 2005). It has also been used as a training model for aiding pilots in preparing for and managing potential issues they may encounter during a normal flight (Helmreich, Klinect, and Wilhelm, 1999; Klinect, Wilhelm, and Helmreich, 1999; Phillips, 2000, p. 61).

The similarities between the TEM and HFACS model exist due to the fact that both models are based on Reason's theory of accidents and incidents occurring in a complex and inconsistent environments (Reason, 1997). The distinction between TEM and HFACS lies more in the practical application of the models than the theoretical background. TEM was developed through audits conducted during normal flight segments and therefore required a simple classification process that had to be completed in a short period of time and based on information available within the cockpit. HFACS supports data collection and categorization process as completed during accident investigations. This process is completed over a longer period of time and often includes multiple sources of information not directly available or observable in the cockpit.

The primary factors represented in the TEM Model are threats, errors and undesired states. Threats are issues that crews encounter that they must manage during a flight. Threats are defined as issues that occur beyond a pilot's control but require attention and management in order for the pilots to complete their required duties. Threats are not caused by a crew but by external events or errors outside the crew's control.

A critical part of what a crew must handle when operating an aircraft occurs beyond its completion of normal operating procedures. Both Reason's model of human error and the TEM Model promote the safety principals of crews being aware of potential threats to completion of required duties or how such threats can act as distracters and lead to pilot error. The idea that a safe crew is one that prepares for potential threats and communicates such awareness is based on the principles of crew resource management (CRM) (Helmreich, 1997, pp. 40–45, 1999; pp. 6–29; Helmreich and Foushee, 1993). Started in the late 1970s to promote better communication between pilots, CRM has evolved into what is now considered a crew's ability to properly avoid errors, trap errors, or manage the consequences of an error (Helmreich, Merritt, and Wilhelm, 1999). CRM has expanded to include principles of error management as it became evident during non-jeopardy observations completed through programs like Line Operations Safety Audit (LOSA), this expansion includes the premise that a safe crew had to not only be prepared for completing tasks in complex environments but they also had to be able to properly mitigate errors that they committed (Helmreich, Klinect et al., 1999; Helmreich, Klinect, and Wilhelm, 2001).

Pilot errors are mistakes that pilots make that lead directly to a deviation from intentions or expectations. Pilot errors can be hard errors like mistakes in handling the aircraft or programming the automation systems or soft errors like communication errors with ATC or procedural errors like incomplete or rushed briefings. TEM is based on the assumption that it is a combination of the ability of a crew to prepare for threats and properly manage errors that will enable them to efficiently handle complex, non-standard or heavy workload situations.

The final main factor of the TEM Model is undesired aircraft states. An undesired aircraft state is defined as an incorrect position, location or configuration of an aircraft. An undesired state is the result of a crew error or mismanagement of a threat. Undesired states can be considered a condition in which the aircraft is placed in an unsafe or unplanned for position or location.

TEM when applied as a working model can be used to categorize factors contributing to a wide range of aviation safety events, from normal operations to accident investigations. TEM as a working model and taxonomy of pilot errors, threats and undesired states evolved through the development and refinement of the LOSA methodology (Klinect, 2005; Klinect, Helmreich, Wilhelm, Tesmer, and Maurino, 2002, pp. 12–15; Klinect et al., 1999). In LOSA these observations are completed by trained line pilots who observe crews from the jump seat under voluntary agreement by the airlines and pilots being observed. The TEM Model and its supporting taxonomies have been empirically derived from the information gathered by these observations. The methodology used to develop the model is considered an applied methodology because it was not developed through simulator assessments or from a cognitive modeling approach commonly used in human factor error research, but through the collection and analysis of pilot derived terminology and pilot identified issues. Through the use of pilot experts, identification of the formal and informal process that crews use to manage various types of distractions including planned and unplanned issues they encounter during a flight, as well as errors they may have committed is recorded. As a result the database supporting the development of the TEM Model is composed of a range of descriptors of pilot behavior that pilots use to counteract adverse situations and descriptions of the observed external issues. The TEM Model has been developed from over 3,000 flight segments and is based on a set of taxonomies of pilot observed and pilot described errors, threats and countermeasures (Klinect, 2005).

TEM as a working model developed through the direct observation of pilots in their normal operating environment includes a rich source of factors that include a range of descriptors of pilot error that would not normally be seen or described in training or in traditional regulatory safety programs. Therefore the TEM taxonomy as developed through LOSA provided descriptions of factors that were the closest to what pilots would experience and describe first hand. The Threat and Error Management Model provided a framework for Reason's model of human error and starting point for the development of a list of contributing factors relevant to events that pilots are likely to submit to ASAP.

Of the six taxonomies reviewed, the TEM Model met the majority of the criteria needed for inclusion into the UT ASAP Pilot Form in that it was developed through direct observation of pilots, has retained the terminology that pilot-observers use to describe events they observe in the cockpit, is based on a human factor framework and based on the success of LOSA throughout the industry, can be used by an airline to feed an SMS program (Klinect, 2005). Following the completion of this review it was determined that the Threat and Error taxonomy was best suited for the development of a structured interview process to be used by pilots to self-report their own errors and describe their working environment when managing a reportable event. Table 7.1 provides an overview of the reviewed taxonomies.

Airline-developed taxonomies

One additional task that was completed during the review of the airline ASAP program was a review of the taxonomies that the airlines supported. Most airline taxonomies were based on either the BASIS model of aviation incidents or they were internally derived. Several airlines reported using the BASIS model due to the fact that no other taxonomies for incident data were available at the time their ASAP program was started.

One of the problems that was evident for many airlines is that their ASAP taxonomies had grown over the years. This growth occurred as analysts or managers changed positions; new personnel brought new perspectives on what was important to collect. As a result many airlines were maintaining "organically" grown taxonomies. Although these taxonomies were regularly added to as new issues or human factor theories arose the airlines did not support a way for the factors in the taxonomies to be systematically collected at either the pilot, ASAP manager or analyst level. Without a consistent way for applying their taxonomies to the pilot reported narratives the airlines can not reliably query their ASAP databases.

Summary of the review (see Table 7.1)

Table 7.1   Review of human factor and pilot error taxonomies

	Actively in use	Taxonomy used directly by pilots	Taxonomy supports human factors model of pilot error	Terms derived from pilot language	Provides data that could support an SRM system
ASRS Anomaly codes	YES	YES	NO	NO	NO
ACCERS	YES	YES	NO	NO	YES
ADREP	YES	NO	YES	NO	YES
BASIS	YES	YES	NO	NO	YES
HFACS	YES	YES	YES	NO	YES
TEM Model	YES	YES	YES	YES	YES

The UT ASAP threat and error taxonomy

Through the use of the TEM Model and the structured interview process supported by the Pilot Reporting Form, the UT ASAP Applications enable ASAP reports to be categorized by pilots, reviewed and confirmed by the ASAP manager and ERC members and archived for future analysis. The critical expansion of these tools beyond what airlines were previously using is that the tools prompts pilots to provide categorized information on not only what type of event occurred but also why the event occurred and what contributed to this occurrence. Although this information was being discussed in the airline ERC meetings it was not being retained in the airlines' ASAP databases. The UT ASAP Applications provide an interface for this information to be gathered, reviewed and retained for future analysis.

Following the completion of the review of human factor taxonomies and the review of airline supported taxonomies, UTHFRP completed a review of the TEM taxonomy as it was supported by LOSA. The purpose of this review was to customize the TEM taxonomy to support a self-report framework as the goal for the use of the UT ASAP taxonomy was to enable it to be used directly by pilots. This review included a set of subject matter experts who voluntarily participated in two-hour review sessions completed once a week over a period of six months. This working group of airline subject matter experts systematically reviewed each item of the LOSA TEM taxonomy. The goals for the group were to review the LOSA TEM taxonomy and make adjustments to the wording used in taxonomy so that the taxonomy would be appropriate for pilots to use when self-reporting event types, threats and errors they encountered. The working group members were also instructed to identify additional factors that they believed to be missing from the LOSA TEM taxonomy or items that they felt were not appropriate for the UT ASAP Pilot Reporting Form interface.

One structural change that was made to the LOSA TEM taxonomy was a change in reference to Undesired Aircraft States. Similar to a reported ASAP event, a LOSA observation takes place during a flight, somewhere between the point where the pilots take command of the flight during pre-flight activities and the end of the flight where the pilots perform their post-flight briefing. But unlike LOSA, each ASAP report is being submitted due to the pilot's incentive for reporting an event that occurred during the flight. This is not true with LOSA, where observation could be completed without the occurrence of an event or undesired aircraft state. Therefore the UT ASAP TEM taxonomy includes an expanded set of undesired aircraft states that are referenced as Event Types.

The other departure from the LOSA TEM taxonomy was an expansion of the threats and errors. As part of the review process that the working group completed, each member was asked to review their airline supported taxonomies and determine if additional factors that they collected within their internal systems were missing from the LOSA TEM taxonomy.

The result of this review process by the airline subject matter experts is the ASAP TEM taxonomy. At its initial structure the UT ASAP TEM taxonomy is based on language and an initial set of factors derived from LOSA and has been customized by pilot subject matter experts to support the self-report requirements of ASAP.

From our review of airline ASAP programs we concluded that the current process for collecting and reviewing ASAP data creates a narrowed focus on addressing one report at a time and one individual pilot error at a time. Although this process may keep that single pilot from making a similar mistake in the future it is not addressing larger system problems that may contribute to the future occurrences of the event and, most importantly, will not help the next pilot who encounters a similar situation. Although ASAP as a growing safety program holds tremendous potential, airlines developing these programs must be careful that they manage their data collection process so that the information contained in reports can be used to identify and proactively address factors contributing to potentially critical safety issues, not focus solely on addressing one individual pilot-reported error at a time.

The integration of the ASAP TEM taxonomy into the UT ASAP applications marked the completion of the first two goals for supporting airlines with ASAP programs:

- Provide airlines with a set of tools that can be used to collect, categorize, and analyze factors contributing to ASAP events.
- Incorporate a taxonomy based on human factors into the Pilot Reporting Form to support the categorization of issues contributing to ASAP events.

The result of these studies clearly demonstrates that the TEM taxonomy is well suited for application in aviation Safety Risk Management.

Why TEM is uniquely suited to SRM   We have left the most fundamental reason why TEM is a good choice for use in SRM for last. It is a solid choice because aviation operations around the globe have quickly adopted it into their data collection methodologies, and have integrated TEM concepts into their training.

> Since our LOSA, we have introduced a 1-day TEM course for our pilots. The overwhelming response has been positive, and there's a recognition among pilots that in TEM, the academic community is using language we understand and feel. Additionally we are using TEM as a debriefing tool for training events. Once again this makes sense to the pilots, and the common reaction is one of dawning; penny-dropping; eureka!

> *(FAA, 2006).*

From one perspective it is easy to see why TEM has quickly been incorporated: the reason is exactly that—its perspective. TEM conceptually requires the adoption of the reporter's perspective; a threat is classified as a threat because of its potentially hostile relationship with the reporter, errors are naturally those mistakes committed by that reporter, undesired states are those experienced by the one writing the report.

Of all the data collection programs, self-reporting programs are the most beneficial for the continued development of SMS. In their association with the promise of a non-punitive approach to the control of error, self-reporting programs give proof to the organization's commitment to the development of a safety culture. And, through their inherent first person perspective, they encourage ownership and accountability. The language of TEM, similarly, is a language of ownership and accountability. "These were the hazards I saw", "here are the errors I made", "this was the undesired state I was responsible and accountable for". Front line workers understand the value of self-reporting systems, and they intuitively understand TEM. It makes sense to integrate TEM into self-reporting, and to use TEM's methodology to identify hazards, controls and risks.

Review questions

1. Describe the TEM model.
2. What are the characteristics that a self-reporting system taxonomy needs?
3. Explain why TEM is suited to SRM.

References

Aviation Safety Reporting System [ASRS] (1994). ASRS Database Statistics. *ASRS Directline*. Retrieved March 3, 2007 from http://asrs.arc.nasa.gov.

Aviation Safety Reporting System [ASRS] (1999). Aviation Safety Reporting System: Program Overview. *Program Briefing*. Retrieved March, 3, 2007 from http://asrs.arc.nasa.gov.

Baker, D., and Krokos, K. (2005). Development and Validation of Aviation Causal Contributors for Error Reporting Systems (ACCERS). *Human Factors, 49*(2).

Beaubian, J., and Baker, D. (2002). *A Review of Selected Aviation Human Factors Taxonomies, Accident/Incident Reporting Systems, and Data Collection Tools.*: American Institute for Research.

Cacciabue, P. (1997). *Human Reliability Assessment: Methods and Techniques*. London: Butterworth-Heinemann.

Cacciabue, P. (2000). *Human Factors Insight and Reliability Data from Accident Reports: The Case of ADREP-2000 for Aviation Safety Assessment*. Paper presented at the International Conference on Probabilistic Safety Assessment and Management.

Federal Aviation Administration [FAA] (2006). *Line Operations Safety Audit*. Advisory Circular 120-90. Retrieved December 3, 2007 from http://rgl.faa.gov/Regulatory_and_ Guidance_Library/rgAdvisoryCircular.nsf/0/013a142c839ea74086257162006cc27d/ $FILE/AC%20120-90.pdf.

Fleishman, E. (1967). Development of a Behavior Taxonomy for Describing Human Tasks: A Correlational-Experimental Approach. *Journal of Applied Psychology, 51*(1).

Fleishman, E. (1982). Systems for Describing Human Tasks. *American Psychologist, 37*(7).

Fleishman, E., and Quaintance, M. (1984). *Taxonomies of Human Performance: The description of human tasks*. San Diego, CA, US: Academic Press.

Helmreich, R. (1997). Managing Human Error in Aviation. *Scientific American, 276*.

Helmreich, R. (1999). CRM Training Primary Line of Defense Against Threats to Flight Safety, Including Human Error. *ICAO Journal*.

Helmreich, R., and Foushee, H. (1993). Why Crew Resource Management? Empirical and Theoretical Bases of Human Factors Training in Aviation. In E. L. Weiner, B. G. Kanki and R. L. Helmreich (Eds.), *Cockpit Resource Management*. New York: Academic Press.

Helmreich, R., Klinect, J., and Wilhelm, J. (1999). *Models of Threat, Error and CRM in Flight Operations*. Paper presented at the Tenth International Symposium on Aviation Psychology, Columbus, OH.

Helmreich, R., Klinect, J., and Wilhelm, J. (2001). *System Safety and Threat and Error Management: Line Operational Safety Audit (LOSA)*. Paper presented at the 12th Annual Symposium on Aviation Psychology, Columbus, Ohio.

Kirwan, B. (1998b). Human Error Identification Techniques for Risk Assessment of High Risk Systems—Part 2: Towards. *Applied Ergonomics, 29*(5).

Klinect, J. (2005). *Line Operations Safety Audit: A Cockpit Observation Methodology for Monitoring Commercial Airline Safety Performance. (Doctoral Dissertation, University of Texas, 2005)*. University of Texas.

Klinect, J., Helmreich, R., Wilhelm, J., Tesmer, B., and Maurino, D. (2002). LOSA —Managing Human Error. *ISASI Forum, 35*(3).

Klinect, J., Wilhelm, J., and Helmreich, R. (1999, 2002). *Threat and Error Management: Data from Line Operations Safety Audits*, The Tenth International Symposium on Aviation Psychology: Vol 2. Columbus, Ohio.

Mercator. (2006, 01/07/2007). Safety Information Reporting Tools. from http://www.sentinel.aero/solutions/sentinel.asp.

Miller, R. (1967). Task Taxonomy: Science or Technology? In W. T. Singleton, R. S. Easterly and D. C. Whitfield (Eds.), *The Human Operator in complex systems*. London: Taylor & Francis.

O'Leary, M., and Fisher, S. (1993). *British Airways Confidential Human Factors Reporting Programme: First Year Report (April 1992–March 1993)*. Hatton Cross: British Safety Services.

Phillips, E. (2000). Managing Error at Center of Pilot Training Program. *Aviation Week and Space Technology, 153*(3).

Reason, J. (1990). *Human Error*. New York, NY, US: Cambridge University Press.

Reason, J. (1997). *Managing the Risks of Organizational Accidents*. Aldershot: Ashgate.

Shappell, and Wiegmann, D. (1997). A Human Error Approach to Accident Investigation: The Taxonomy of Unsafe Operations. *International Journal of Aviation Psychology, 7*.

Shappell, S., Detwiler, C., Holcomb, K., Hackworth, C., Boquet, A., and Wiegmann, D. (2007). Human Error and Commercial Aviation Accidents: An Analysis using the Human Factors Analysis and Classification System. *Human Factors, 49*(2).

Wiegmann, D., and Shappell, S. (2003). *A Human Error Approach to Aviation and Accident Analysis*: Ashgate Publishing, Ltd.

Wiegmann, D., Rich, A. and Shappell, S. (2002). *Human Error and Accident Causation Theories, Frameworks and Analytical Techniques: An Annotated Bibliography*. Oklahoma City: Federal Aviation Administration.

Chapter 8

Process-Based Safety Risk Management/ Safety Assurance

If you can't describe what you are doing as a process, you don't know what you're doing.

… Learning is not compulsory … neither is survival.

W. Edwards Deming

The SMS practitioner knows that true SMS goes well beyond the components described so far, encompassing the entire organization, with continuous improvement through constant application of the quality Plan-Do-Check-Act cycle. It is a complex process, one that is difficult to encapsulate in a brief description of SMS. The explanations of how to actually *do* SMS in the ICAO and FAA documents must be understood in the light of this complexity. Both sources describe the relationship between Safety Risk Management and Safety Assurance (SRM/SA) and present this model as outlining how the work of SMS is accomplished. Their purpose is to present the 30,000 foot view of the topic in order to assure that the basic principles are understood. Our purpose is to dig deeper.

The "standard" model of safety risk management/safety assurance

AC 120-92 relates SRM and Safety Assurance (SA) in the following way (FAA, 2006, p. 10):

> **Integration of Safety Risk Management and Safety Assurance.** [Figure 8.1] shows how the safety risk management and safety assurance processes are integrated in the SMS. The safety risk management process provides for initial identification of hazards and assessment of risk. Organizational risk controls are developed and, once they are determined to be capable of bringing the risk to an acceptable level, they are employed operationally. The safety assurance function takes over at this point to ensure that the risk controls are being practiced and they continue to achieve their intended objectives. This system also provides for assessment of the need for new controls because of changes in the operational environment.

A review of this diagram reveals that the simplified description of SRM depicted is the same as what we earlier described as *new* process designs. And that is what the descriptive text also indicates—in the AC's understandably abbreviated presentation, SRM is a process accomplished once at the system design point, and then again on

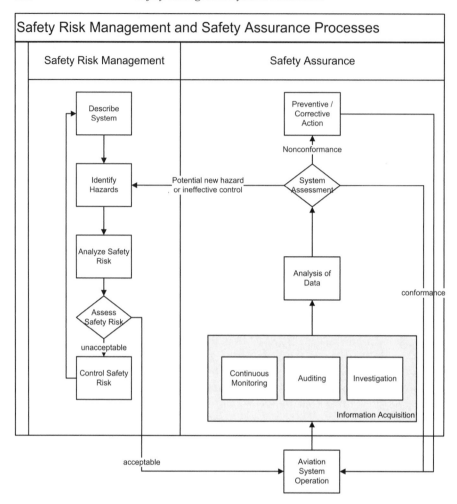

Figure 8.1   Safety risk management and safety assurance processes

an as-needed basis, only when new hazards or ineffective controls are identified. Note this statement in the description above:

> Organizational risk controls are developed and, once they are determined to be capable of bringing the risk to an acceptable level, they are employed operationally.

But the preceding chapters have established that much, if not most, of the SRM that will be conducted will be associated with already existing processes. We have argued that this standard model described in the ICAO and FAA documentation will continue to hold an important place as *one* method in a larger toolset available to the SMS practitioner. It will be helpful to put together another, more expanded version of SRM and SA, which will capture in a summary form that larger toolset.

The description in the advisory circular begs questions that must be understood before SRM/SA can be done. For example, what exactly is the "system" that must be described, before one can accomplish SRM? What is it, exactly, that we should be continuously monitoring in SA? Against what standard should audits be accomplished in SMS? What should an SMS-oriented investigation finding focus upon? How does one go about judging that a control is ineffective?

The answers to these detailed questions go beyond the scope of high-level summary documents, but are essential to address before we can put together a plan of action for SMS implementation. A serious look at the very first question, concerning the system that must be described, will lead us to the answers.

> What is a system? A system is a network of interdependent components that work together to try to accomplish the aim of the system. A system must have an aim. Without an aim, there is no system. The aim of the system must be clear to everyone in the system. The aim must include plans for the future. The aim is a value judgment.

> *(Deming, 1993, p. 50)*

In the discussion of quality in Chapter 3, frequent mention was made of Deming, and it is not surprising that this giant of the quality discipline can provide guidance to assist us in understanding how to do SMS. We will keep Deming's definition in mind as we describe the basis of SRM/SA to assure that we have satisfied all of his criteria.

As the first quotation at the beginning of this chapter indicates, Deming was a very strong proponent of the assertion that activities must be clearly described as processes. It is *only* through the exercise of process description that the true extent, detail, dependencies, contingencies and outputs of an activity can be understood. We will take Deming's words as truth and at face value—in managing safety, we can't afford to not know what we are doing, therefore we must understand, embrace, and *do* that which is necessary to produce high-quality process descriptions. In Deming's definition of system above, processes comprise the "network of interdependent components that work together to try to accomplish the aim of the system". SRM/SA in a mature SMS is based upon well-designed process descriptions.

Process-based SRM/SA

The required elements of a complete process description

In order to be a component of a mature SMS, a process description should contain *all* of the following:

1. Purpose,
2. Scope,
3. Interfaces,
4. Stakeholders,
5. Responsibility,
6. Authority,
7. Procedure description/flowchart,

8. Materials/equipment/supplies,
9. Hazards,
10. Controls (production and protection),
11. Process measures (production and protection),
12. Targets (production and protection),
13. Assessment (production and protection),
14. Change management,
15. Qualifications required for participants in process,
16. Documentation/record-keeping.

This is not to suggest that every organization must adopt this specific outline and enumerate process characteristics in exactly this order. As mentioned many times, SMS implementation is quite flexible, and operators can choose their own format for most components. But to be effective, any process description should contain within it the elements above.

1. Purpose

The purpose of the process should be described as clearly and concisely as possible. This explanation can help guide the rest of the description. For example, if the purpose of a process is well-defined, it will be easier to set performance targets so that stakeholders can measure whether the process is working correctly. A well-formed purpose statement can also guide the creation of training materials used to educate stakeholders involved in the process.

2. Scope

The statement of scope for a process is an extremely important component. A well-defined scope statement is helpful in a number of ways. For example, a scope statement for a lower-than-standard approach minimums process might include a clause indicating that the process applies for Category II or III Instrument Landing System (ILS) approaches when reported crosswinds are no more than 10 knots. Suppose at some point the operator finds it necessary to accomplish a safety investigation concerning low-minimums approaches. If a common factor in the incidents requiring investigation were reports of a 15 knot crosswind, then the existence of the scope statement (and evidence of effective training concerning that limitation) would guide the investigator towards failures in more fundamental controls, such as decision-making, judgment or crew coordination. Scope identifies limits, boundaries, and restrictions for the process at hand.

3. Interfaces

Readers familiar with ATOS will recognize the interfaces component as one of the five "safety attributes" that a process must have, as defined in the FAA's Air Transport Oversight System documentation. (The others are responsibility, authority, procedures, controls, and process measurement, all of which are included in this list.) Interfaces are listed last in the FAA documentation, a position that does not imply anything about their relative importance, but nevertheless the interface topic is often neglected in process descriptions. It is important because the concept of interface includes two of the most important components of Deming's descriptions of process (see Figure 8.2).

This simple and intuitive process diagram is still revealing when viewed with quality in mind. Unless the inputs to a process are well controlled and possess the needed characteristics, the process is unlikely to work well. Equally, it is important to view the process from the customer perspective—from the point of view of the output—in order to understand what the process must accomplish.

By exhaustively listing all the interfaces to a process, one can determine what the inputs to the process are, who the customers are, and what those customers need delivered by the process, information essential to establishing targets. This is why interface considerations should be third on the list when designing the process.

4. Stakeholders

Establishing the list of stakeholders in a process is an important step. Typically the stakeholder list is composed of those people or parties who actually accomplish the work, but also contains an enumeration of the interfaces to the process—the suppliers and customers. The interrelationship digraph described in Chapter 3 can be used to help understand the connections and interdependencies between stakeholders, which will be helpful when the process is mapped out later. Another quality tool, the power versus interest grid described in Chapter 9, can help to understand stakeholder relationships.

The stakeholder list will also be used in one of the last steps in the process description, when qualification and training issues are addressed.

5. Responsibility

Next it is essential to assign responsibility for the conduct of the process. This responsibility needs to be clearly and overtly spelled out in the process documentation. Typically a process has a number of parts, each of which must be assigned to someone, or some party, to accomplish. Each of those areas of responsibility must be again clearly described. The responsibility attribute will later be used as an input to another part of process design—specifying and documenting training requirements.

6. Authority

Responsibility and authority attributes are frequently confused. Someone who has authority over a process has the ability to manage the process itself—stop it, start

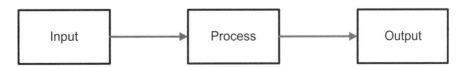

Figure 8.2   Process

it, or (within specified procedures described below) change it. Responsibility and authority might or might not be shared by the same person or group.

The party *responsible* for a process is the one that is accountable for the accomplishment of that process as it is outlined in the process description, and is accountable for the output of the process and the meeting of the target outcomes of the process during the time he or she participates in the process. The party with *authority* over the process is accountable for process design and overall success of the process.

When a process is not working, it is necessary to examine both the responsibility and authority elements. It might be that the responsible party is not accomplishing the process as specified in the design document. On the other hand, it might be that the party with authority over the process has designed it so that it can't succeed, or has set unrealistic performance targets.

As will be described in Chapter 11, assigning both responsibility and authority to the same party is a very effective way to assure that the process is designed well—who knows better how to design a process for success than the ones doing the process, and from our perspective, who knows better the areas of risk?

7. Procedure description/flowchart

The procedure description and the process flowchart are the components usually associated with the idea of a process description. It should be clear by now that the description/flowchart component is only a part of a complete process description. But it is an essential one, the one that describes how things are actually going to get done.

When a new process is being built from scratch, it is highly recommended that a quality tool, the process workflow diagram, be used to fully depict the process before descriptive text is written. If instead the task is the review of an existing process, it again makes sense to first use the process workflow diagram to draw out all parts of the process, and then evaluate the textual description. (A very effective technique for the SMS practitioner is to create the process workflow diagram by interviewing the stakeholders of a process *before* reviewing the documentation describing the process. This technique can illuminate areas where the existing process description is in error or lacks sufficient detail.) The visual aid of the chart is a great help in assuring all parts of the process are accurately described.

As discussed in the previous chapter, the use of the process workflow diagram helps to identify where controls already exist, or need to exist. A complete diagram will list every component of the process, including interfaces, controls and process measures.

Up to this point, the sequence of action in creating a process description should follow the order presented, establishing the purpose, scope, interfaces, stakeholders, responsibility and authority. But especially starting with procedure description and flowcharting, the rest of the task is iterative in nature. It will probably be necessary to work a while on the flowchart, then devote time to hazard identification, then risk analysis and controls (for new processes, or control analysis and residual risk evaluation for existing processes), and possibly even return to the stakeholder or interface step as greater understanding of the process is gained. By being flexible and moving back and forth from working on the flowchart to hazard identification to control description, to process measurement creation, as needed, the final product is most likely to incorporate all requirements.

8. *Materials/equipment/supplies*

When planning a new process, it is natural and intuitive that the planning team would give close consideration to the materials, equipment and supplies. Except for the most basic of processes, these are the tools for and inputs to the work at hand. For example, a team working on the ramp arrival process at an FBO would list tie downs and chocks as supplies necessary for the process, and once listed they would then identify the quality requirements for those supplies, and quickly realize that those requirements are dependent upon the size of aircraft being marshaled in.

Once complete, the aggregated list becomes a "specifications document" that describes all of the quality requirements needed by this process in order to be successfully, and safely, accomplished. It is likely that once all of these specifications are complete, the interface step might have to be revisited, since it would now become apparent that the entity within the organization obtaining the tiedowns is an important player. In fact, once the organization has well-documented processes for all of its activities (no small task), the specifications document for the ramp arrival process (for example) feeds into the output requirements for other interfacing processes.

Consideration of equipment requirements is equally important for a successful and safe process design. These considerations can certainly define what equipment needs to be purchased for a process to function properly, but equally important is the definition of acceptable operational parameters for that equipment. Maintainers are well aware of this part of process design; for example, any maintenance process that involves measurement tools will need to have a specification addressing the calibration of those tools.

Note that in this suggested order, materials/equipment/supplies occurs after the process workflow. There is nothing hard and fast about this order, but it might help to do the process workflow first, so that when considering what materials, equipment and supplies are needed, the team can walk through the workflow diagram and identify what is needed for each step.

On the other hand, when a team is taking an existing process and creating a complete process description for it using this outline, it might be beneficial to move this step before workflow, so that the team can ask themselves the question "if we had a free hand in specifying any materials, equipment or supplies we might like, how would that change our existing process?"

9. *Hazards*

Another quality tool is the method of choice for working on the hazard identification component of a process description. It is the process decision program chart (PDPC), described in Chapter 3, and used liberally in both ICAO and FAA documentation. Hazard identification is covered thoroughly in previous chapters, so there is no need to repeat that discussion. The important thing to emphasize is that in the mature

SMS, hazard identification is an integral part of process description, and conversely, the process description is a critical resource to have available when accomplishing hazard identification.

The team doing the hazard identification should have available all of the notes used to create the process description up to this point. The notes and quality tools used to identify the inputs and outputs to the process are helpful in identifying hazards. The team should pay particular attention to the inputs—poorly controlled input quality is always a hazard, and should always be listed as such on the PDPC used to list hazards. The interrelationship digraph used to describe the connections between stakeholders is also useful in hazard identification, especially hazards associated with faulty information flow. And of course, the process flowchart is a primary resource for hazard identification, in that the team can walk through the process step by step and consider what hazards exist along the way.

Another quality tool useful for this step is the Ishikawa or cause-and-effect (C-E) diagram (also known as a fishbone diagram). The typical C-E diagram uses the "5M method" (see Chapter 6) devised by T. P. Wright at Cornell University to assist in root cause analysis of accidents in the transportation industry. A 5M C-E diagram defines the "bones" of the diagram as Mission, Man, Machine, Management, and Media (environment). Using the 5M fishbone in hazard identification assures that the team considers each of these potential contributing factors.

10. Controls (production and protection)

The topic of controls has also been covered thoroughly in previous chapters, and the reader is referred to those chapters for a review of the subject. It's important to emphasize that the SMS practitioner should be the resident expert concerning controls for the team creating or evaluating process descriptions, and should be prepared to explain the differences and relative advantages and disadvantages of open and closed loop controls, and how SISO and MIMO controls differ.

The iterative nature of creating or evaluating a process description is especially evident as the team examines controls. For new process design, the PDPC hazard form is used as explained earlier, and as described in the "standard" model of SRM in ICAO and FAA documentation. For existing processes it is more efficient to use the hazard ↔ control method discussed in Chapter 6. In either case, the PDPC hazard form is used to record the team's work, but at the same time the team makes frequent reference to, and perhaps modification of, the process workflow diagram.

Another important clarification to keep in mind is that controls are used *within* the process, to assure that an outcome of an action meets design parameters. Therefore the inputs to the control (on the process flowchart, the lines coming into the decision diamond) must be very clear and well-defined. These are the signals that the control needs in order to determine the desired path. Just as a process depends upon high quality inputs, a control depends upon high quality signals, so the team should closely examine how the quality of those signals is going to be assured.

The astute reader no doubt noticed that the parenthetical phrase *production and protection* was appended to the topic of controls, as it is for the following three topics. It is time to emphasize another critical point that the SMS practitioner needs to always keep in mind. Processes exist in order to accomplish an outcome that adds value to the organization. The "gate departure process" is accomplished in order to get paying passengers on the airplane, load up the plane with revenue-producing cargo, and leave the gate on time. Thus, on the production side of the production-protection axis, it is critical that process descriptions have effective production controls built in, just as it is important that safety controls are built in so that protection needs are met. Both sets of controls need to be understood in order to accomplish SRM. The team responsible for the design of a process should be accountable for both the production and the protection aspects. This assures that safety is built in.

11. Process measures (production and protection)

A process cannot be managed from either the production or the protection aspect without having process measures built into it. The simplest of process measures can be done (and always should be done) at the output of the process—for example the gate departure process can be measured by recording time-out-of-gate, by number of passengers enplaned, by cost of damage occurring during the process, or by number of injuries to employees occurring. But a well-designed process has process measures identified throughout the workflow.

In order to create efficient and meaningful measures, a process design team needs to identify key performance indicators, or KPIs, along the workflow path. KPIs are just that, the *key* measures indicative of the functioning of the process. Measuring a few well-placed KPIs is more valuable than measuring a hundred poorly thought out metrics.

Both production and protection KPIs should be illustrated on the workflow diagram, at the point in the workflow where the measurement will be made. In addition to clarifying exactly how, when, where and by whom the KPI will be measured, annotating the KPI on the workflow diagram drives home another important point. Process measurement is (generally) not free—resources are required to measure KPIs, and sometimes the measurement process can interfere with other important duties. A good example of this was engine performance monitoring in the days before FOQA. Flight crews were once frequently required to record engine parameters such as exhaust gas temperature (EGT), low-pressure compressor (N1), high-pressure compressor (N2), exhaust pressure ratio (EPR), and fuel flow a certain number of minutes after setting cruise power. These were certainly good KPIs to measure, but on short legs the task removed one crew member from the loop during times when other duties were pressing. It's again important to remember that a few good KPIs are better than a bunch of them, for each one generates another chore to accomplish.

Identifying KPIs is not enough, of course. One must figure out how to record them, and how to maintain those records. Automated measurement is by far the best option, but is not always available. Process measurements do not have to be taken continuously—it is perfectly acceptable to include a measurement schedule into a process description such that a KPI is measured every 10 cycles, or 7 days, or any reasonable interval. If this approach to KPI measurement is taken, it's important to make sure that the sampling is done on a schedule so that the aggregate statistics represent the real process as closely as possible. It's not acceptable for sampling to be done just whenever someone feels like doing it.

Safety assurance (SA) cannot exist unless those processes under scrutiny have KPIs defined. It is through the monitoring of KPIs that risk is managed. It's therefore critical that the correct KPIs are chosen. The PDPC form used to document hazards, risks and controls is a good reference to use to help identify where and how to best measure the process.

The team accomplishing the process definition has the freedom to define a process measure in any way that makes sense. It could be a measure of a particular type of occurrence, such as the rate of Traffic Collision Avoidance System resolution advisories (TCAS RAs) in a particular approach airspace. Or it could be a parametric measure, such as zero fuel weight at dispatch. Or it could be a derived risk measure, such as a risk index aggregated from ASAP reports concerning a particular event type. As long as there is a consistent method used to generate the process measure, any of these options can be used.

Since the purpose of SA is to measure the effectiveness of controls, a logical place to put KPI measurement is downstream of controls in the workflow diagram. But don't forget to consider measuring hazards. In fact measuring hazards is a very good approach to determining the effectiveness of controls. For example, using FOQA to create a tailwind component KPI during landing is a good method to measure the effectiveness of crew briefing, decision-making and/or monitoring controls (by studying the percentage of landings with tailwind components above the limit established by the standard operating procedures (SOPs), for example).

Once again the SMS practitioner should keep in mind the nature of the controls used in the process. It's a good idea to try to create a KPI downstream of an open loop control, because otherwise no one will know whether the control works or does not.

While it is true that KPIs are necessary components of a process description in order for SA to be accomplished, they are not sufficient. SA requires that a standard is established, against which to compare the KPI records. This leads to the discussion of the next very important but often neglected component of process design.

12. Targets (production and protection)

In SMS, SA is not a casual, loosely organized evaluation of the state of safety in an organization. It has a very specific definition—SA is the process of measuring the effectiveness of controls. And the determination of the judgment as to whether a control is effective is a disciplined procedure in itself. In SMS SA, a control is judged to be effective or ineffective based upon a comparison to a pre-defined *target*. In some references, ICAO and the FAA refer to this concept as a target level of safety, or TLS. Whatever one calls it, the association of targets to process measures is an important part of what makes a process definition useful in SMS.

Obviously the target chosen as the standard against which a KPI will be evaluated must be consistent with the process measure itself. If an operator chooses to monitor the number of errors in flight crews' zero fuel weight calculations in a load planning process, the target would need to be expressed as "no more than X errors per 1,000 departures" or some similar statement.

What can be confounding is establishing a target when the KPI being measured has a hard and fast limitation associated with it. In our example of zero fuel weight (ZFW) calculation monitoring, the operator is of course mainly interested in assuring that its crews never allow an exceedance of maximum ZFW. It would be inappropriate for a target for such a KPI to be expressed such as "no more than 5 maximum ZFW exceedances per 1,000 departures"— maximum ZFW is a limitation, and it's not acceptable to state that you will be satisfied with any exceedances of this limitation. In cases like these, probably the best approach is to use historical data to establish the average number of exceedances in the past, and then set the target as a fixed percent reduction in the historical error rate.

It is again worthy of note that targets should be set for both production and protection KPIs. A well-run operation will be closely monitoring performance and measuring that performance against targets, such as on-time departure rate, or turn time (time between gate arrival and gate departure for a particular aircraft). It's particularly valuable for the team that sets production targets to also be responsible for setting protection targets because activities in a process that are aimed at satisfying one type of target can directly influence the other type. For example, a production target for flight attendants might be associated with a measure of time required to deliver snacks and drinks to every passenger. Setting a very high standard for this production target (meaning a short wait for beverage delivery—a good thing), might very well negatively influence safety-related measures, in this case such as number of times the service cart is left unattended. Having one team responsible for setting both targets maximizes the likelihood that such interactions will be understood and dealt with.

13. Assessment (production and protection)

A complete process description will contain guidance to help stakeholders answer a very basic and important question—how do we know when we have succeeded? For those responsible for accomplishing the process, there should be no doubt about whether their work meets expectations, and for the process owner there should be a well-defined protocol that regularly assesses the level of success achieved by the process.

From the safety perspective, assessment means risk assessment. The differences between methods used for new-process risk assessment and established-process risk assessment have been detailed in previous chapters. As described in the ICAO and FAA documentation, new-process risk assessment can be thought of as a one-time task (though it should be returned to any time new hazards arise). But established-process risk assessment is much better thought of as a muscle in need of regular exercise. The evaluation of the effectiveness of controls accomplished in SA is a relatively blunt instrument—the KPIs either meet target expectations or they don't. The analysis accomplished in SRM is more finely detailed and will be needed to make adjustments to the process to improve performance, even when the overall targets are being met as determined by SA.

14. Change management

After this much hard work, the team will be highly motivated to assure that the system they so diligently constructed does not decay because of uncoordinated action by individual stakeholder members. This is accomplished by building into the process description the steps required to change the process itself. Central to this change process is the need to coordinate changes with all stakeholders *before* the change takes effect, and in most circumstances it is best to give stakeholders input into the design of the change itself. None of this is rocket science, and change management verbiage will be quite similar from one process to another. The safety department is well situated to facilitate the inclusion of a standard template for change management into each process description, and the safety representative on the team should be sure to provide the template and whatever coaching is necessary to assure that once in place the change management procedure is followed.

15. Qualifications and training

After the immersion in process required of their task, the team is now well positioned to establish the qualifications required to perform the process, and the schedule of training necessary to maintain those qualifications. The stakeholder list can assist in identifying who needs training, and of course the purpose statement and workflow diagram can assist in outlining training content. Particular attention should be paid to the training needs of the party responsible for the conduct of the process. Training can be something as simple as requiring a stakeholder to read the process description, or as complex as that undergone by flight crews. Whatever the training, it must be documented.

16. Documentation/record-keeping

Another oft-neglected but essential detail of any process description is the enumeration of what documents are needed to perform the process, and what record-keeping is necessary. For example, a process might require that employees use one or more work instruction documents when accomplishing the task. And of course since KPIs are defined in any well-designed process, it is necessary to describe how those measurements will be recorded. Check sheets, as described in Chapter 3, are the obvious choice for this task.

Where to start?

For both ICAO and the FAA, there is no mistaking the importance assigned to process descriptions. It is also clear that the FAA understands the challenge of assuring that good process descriptions exist—process documentation as an element in SMS implementation first appears in phase 2 of its suggested deployment schedule, and continues through phases 3 and 4. While the eventual goal of a mature SMS is to transform all of its processes to incorporate the elements necessary to allow SRM and SA to be efficiently employed, this is a large assignment, and it is universally acknowledged that this transformation will take long term commitment, and, frankly, patience.

Where should an organization start when re-engineering its processes for SMS? That is, again, left up to the organization to decide. And the organization is free to define its processes any way it wants, so different organizations will choose different sets of activities. For an airline, one way of thinking about how to group its many functions into systems and processes is to adopt the structure used in the FAA's Air Transport Oversight System (ATOS). In ATOS, an airline operation is divided into seven "systems" and within those seven systems are 107 subsystems, another way to say processes. The excerpts below will illustrate this means of classification:

1.1.3 Special Flight Permits (AW)

1.2.1 Airworthiness Release/Logbook Entry (AW)

1.3.5 MEL/CDL/Deferred Maintenance (AW)

1.3.6 AD Management (AW)

1.3.16 Fueling (AW)

1.3.17 Weight and Balance Program (AW)

1.3.18 De-Icing Program (AW)

1.3.19 Lower Landing Minimums (LLM) (AW)

3.1.7 De-Icing Program (OP)

3.1.9 Aircraft Performance Operating Limitations (OP)

3.1.10 Lower Landing Minimums (LLM) (OP)

3.2.2 Flight/Load Manifest/Weight and Balance Control (OP)

3.2.3 MEL/CDL Procedures (OP)

(AW = airworthiness, OP = operations)

One strategy an airline could adopt would be to review all 107 subsystems in the ATOS inventory, and choose a short list based upon an evaluation of which areas hold the highest risk, or are the most easily transformed. (Here is another opportunity to use a quality tool, the prioritization matrix, and combine the evaluation of high risk and easy transformation into one effort.)

From the list above, let's choose two subsystems, 1.3.18—the maintenance component of the airline's de-icing program, and 3.1.7—the operational side of the de-icing program. We'll use these to walk through how to do SRM/SA.

Process-based SRM

Our airline has chosen these two ATOS items to build their first SMS-compliant SRM/SA because their existing safety program has concluded that de-icing holds the potential for high-risk outcomes, and their historical data from audits and ASAP indicate that problems exist within the process. In addition, the SMS champion within the airline wants to use this project as a means of breaking down barriers and silos between departments, and these two ATOS subsystems provide the opportunity to get maintenance and flight operations at the same table working together to generate one process description covering the entire de-icing activity.

The cross-functional development team follows the outline for the creation of process descriptions above, and first develops a purpose statement for the de-icing process that encompasses all of the stakeholders at the table. Next the team develops the scope statement, and in doing so they realize that the scope of this process extends beyond their corporate borders, allowing their maintenance department to provide de-icing services to other carriers. They record this observation in their notes, which become useful in the next step, the identification of stakeholders. They also realize that dispatch is a stakeholder in this discussion, and invite a representative from that department into the fold.

The team decides that a member of the flight operations team will assume the role of a flight crew from another carrier, so that their efforts can include a representative from this stakeholder group, if only by proxy. Once the stakeholder list is complete (for this iteration) the team tackles the task of deciding responsibilities within the process, and finally who will have the authority to control the overall process. After much discussion (some of which is still anchored in the old stovepipe management paradigm) the team decides that flight operations will be the owner of the process. This is a significant decision, because it assigns the accountability for the success of the overall process to flight operations, and removes some autonomy for process control from maintenance for their elements within the overall process. This is not an easy political decision for anyone, but is wise nevertheless.

The procedure description and flowcharting step is next, and here the team decides to split into workgroups primarily organized by functional unit—a workgroup for maintenance, and a workgroup for flight operations. Again wisely, they decide that there will be maintenance representatives on the flight operations working group, and vice versa.

The tedious work of this step begins, and the team decides to create the flowchart first, using input from interviews with subject matter experts from each stakeholder in order to obtain a real-world understanding of how de-icing is actually conducted. Subsequent review of the existing documentation reveals that their talk and their walk align pretty closely, but they note the few areas where the documentation is weak for future reference, when the graphic depiction of the flowchart is translated into the verbiage of the process description.

With the first draft of the process flowchart complete, the team takes on the challenge of listing all of the materials, equipment and supplies necessary for accomplishing this process. Once beginning this brainstorming session, they are surprised at how extensive the list becomes. For example, one of the maintenance team members starts listing all of the clothing needed for the deicers, and the team realizes that there are special requirements for shoe soles in a deicing environment. In fact the maintenance reps remind the rest of the team that one of their team members was seriously injured the previous winter when he lost traction on a surface covered with slippery deicing fluid, and fell, breaking his arm.

They also realize that they need to specify minimum requirements for both the deicing fluid, as it is delivered to them, and also the measurement requirements for stored fluid, which of course begs the question of equipment calibration. The materials/equipment/supplies step takes them quite a while to complete, but the team is quite proud of the comprehensiveness of their work.

Next the team identifies the hazards associated with de-icing. As the team works through the constellation of hazards associated with de-icing, one member realizes that one possible flight crew error involves forgetting to turn off the air conditioning pack valves before de-icing commences. An FMEA analysis of this error reveals that the cabin crew has been so far neglected as recognized stakeholders—they would immediately become players as soon as an aerosol of deicing fluid begins circulating in the passenger cabin. The oversight is corrected, and a representative from the flight attendant department joins in the effort.

The team wisely uses the risk assessment method appropriate to the question at hand. For the de-icing fluid aerosol issue just described, the team realizes that this is an area they have not explored, and therefore decides that the "standard" method of risk assessment is appropriate. Hazards are identified, the range of potential outcomes for each hazard or hazard-set is described, initial risk is assessed, controls are devised, and residual risk is evaluated. The process continues until as low as reasonably practicable (ALARP) is achieved, and the controls created by the risk assessment are incorporated into the flowchart.

For those aspects of the process that have an existing process in place to control risk, the hazard ↔ control method is used. Historical safety data is reviewed to assess the existing residual risk for each hazard ↔ control set, and those measures are noted for reference in the next few steps of their work.

It's now time for the team to step back from its draft flowchart and determine the best means of measuring the system. They settle on the following list of measures to support KPIs:

- De-icing fluid quality records, from maintenance.
- Continuing qualification training records relevant to de-icing, from maintenance.
- Date/time that de-icing procedures were declared in effect, and date/time they were cancelled, from dispatch.
- Flight numbers of flights that departed the station while de-icing procedures were in effect from dispatch.
- Flight number/time of beginning of de-ice application procedure, from maintenance.
- Actual time of start of takeoff roll for affected flights, from dispatch.
- Computed time interval between start of de-ice application and beginning of takeoff roll, from previous two KPIs, and comparison of that measure to maximum hold-over time for type of de-ice fluid and temperature.
- ASAP reports from the pilot, maintenance, dispatcher and flight attendant programs.
- A representative from the safety department notes that flight ops has one control in place that is open loop—the yearly de-icing bulletin issued to flight crews at the beginning of the winter season. An additional KPI is added in which line check airmen administer a short non-jeopardy quiz on de-icing procedures to a representative sample of crews undergoing a routine line check. The purpose of the KPI is to monitor the effectiveness of this open loop control.

The team next sets the targets for each KPI:

- All de-ice fluid quality records current and in limits within 6 hours prior to start of de-icing.
- Overall error rate for de-ice fluid quality records decreased 10 per cent over previous year.
- All designated de-icers trained before start of season (which is itself a specific date).
- No flights departing beyond established holdover time limits.
- 80 per cent of flights departing within one half maximum holdover time limit.
- Aggregate analysis of ASAP reports concerning de-icing does not indicate increasing error trend.
- 90 per cent average score for flight crews quizzed about de-icing procedures by line check airmen.

The team then decides to incorporate monthly internal audits of these KPIs as measured against their targets, accomplished by each relevant stakeholder department. In addition, the team leader coordinates with the IEP manager to assure that an audit of this process, to include a review of KPI records, is included in the regular IEP audit schedule.

The team reviews its work and uses a template provided by the safety department to write the change management procedure into the process description. Use of the template assures that procedures will be in place to notify all stakeholders any time a change to the process is about to occur.

The team examines the workflow a final time to determine exactly what training and qualification measures are needed by each stakeholder, and records this in the process description. Finally, the team reviews their work, and determines what work instruction documentation is necessary, and how the KPI measurements will be recorded.

For the SMS practitioner, it's important to realize that the parts of this work directly dealing with hazards, controls, and risk assessment—the parts often assumed to be the entirety of SRM—are essential components of the work just described, but there is much more to the complete task. Every step is needed, and should exist, in a mature SMS.

Process-based SA

With the foundation built by this top-notch team, safety assurance associated with this process is now well-defined. The right half of Figure 8.1 illustrates the SA process, and the first steps of this process are shown in Figure 8.3.

The continuous monitoring component of SA information acquisition is now directly guided by the process description. In our example, the dispatch function is tasked with collecting the information necessary to compute the time between start of de-icing and takeoff, and the carrier's ASAP programs are assigned the task of ascertaining whether there is evidence for trends in de-icing problems, and reporting the results of that study to the process owner. The other stakeholders assigned KPI data collection are similarly tasked with providing their information to the owner.

Note the difference between this model of continuous monitoring and the kind typically found today. For example, a typical FOQA program generates a wide

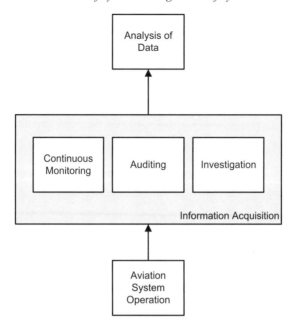

Figure 8.3   First steps of safety assurance process

variety of operational analyses, and then goes out shopping to find someone in the organization who will be interested in using the data. In process-based SA, it is the process design team that goes shopping—they are the consumers, and programs like FOQA shape their output to the needs of those consumers. This results in a much more focused set of programs. In this model, the FOQA, ASAP or other program analyst will be able to answer the question when asked why a particular report is created.

Similarly the audit component of information acquisition becomes customer-driven in a mature SMS. A set of audit questions is asked not just because they are interesting, but because the owners of the process need the information in order to do their work. And when an organization makes the commitment to have its process descriptions meet rigorous standards consistent with SMS needs, the IEP auditor has firm ground upon which to stand when critiquing process documentation.

The remaining component of information acquisition, investigations, also benefits from a process-based approach to SA. With detailed and well-documented process descriptions, the job of the incident investigator to identify weak processes or failed controls becomes much easier.

The risk management plan

In the FAA's diagram of SRM/SA, the final steps to SA just above information acquisition and analysis are shown in Figure 8.4.

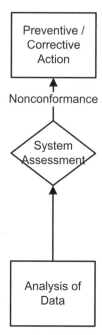

Figure 8.4   Final steps of safety assurance process

System assessment can be thought of as applying just to our one example process of de-icing, but of course the reality is that a mature SMS will have tens of similar processes, similarly designed, similarly being consumers of intelligence provided by information acquisition and analysis. But taken together the whole is greater than the sum of its parts. Taken together the system can and should be assessed at the organizational level. This again is another key feature of SMS, the integration of safety management into the highest levels of organizational management.

The nuts and bolts of how to do this integration is provided again by the hard work accomplished at the individual process level. The measures, KPIs, targets and analysis at the process level become the details of the larger organizational level risk management plan. In Chapter 11 we will discuss the highest level management structure within SMS, the Safety Council (SC). It is the SC that sits in the middle of the SRM/SA diagram. The individual performance of the various processes monitored by the SMS provides the basic data the SC needs in order to determine the overall priorities for the organization, and in order to determine the overall risk the organization is exposed to.

The SC is also the only part of the organization positioned to coordinate the various safety targets adopted by the designers of individual processes. The aggregate of these targets organized and prioritized by the SC constitute the organization's risk management plan (RMP). With the SC's wider view of the organization, and with the detailed performance data that process-based SRM/SA provides, the RMP plan can serve as the roadmap that leads the organization into safer operations.

The ERP as a component of the RMP

The authors resisted the temptation to add another item to the list of required components of a solid SMS-based process description—16 items is enough. But it is worthwhile to briefly discuss the connection between a good emergency response plan and good process descriptions.

Chapter 1 presented an overview of emergency response as a component of an SMS. From a documentation point of view the way to recognize whether an SMS has incorporated emergency response planning is to examine the organization's emergency response plan, or ERP. The first chapter in this book enumerated the components of a well-designed ERP, and indicated some of the reasons why an SMS needs to have such a document.

An ERP represents a top-down look at emergency response planning. There is another perspective, and that, of course, is from the bottom-up. That is, how does each process within the organization support the ERP?

Since the ERP, when exercised at its extremities in dealing with a major event, requires the resources of the entire organization, the primary level of construction of the ERP has to be at the institutional level. This assures that the people involved with the creation of the plan are those who can mobilize the resources when necessary. But from another perspective all emergencies are local: a station has to deal with a crash on landing; a gate has to deal with a fuel spill; a flight attendant manager has to deal with the grieving family of a co-worker.

Chapter 3 covered quality tools, and once again we find that quality is the place to look to find the best way to integrate top-level emergency planning with the real-world operational side of the enterprise. We suggest that the reader review the section on Hoshin planning. Briefly, Hoshin Kenri is a process used to assure that the entire company is aligned and coordinated to accomplish a task. There is no more important use of Hoshin planning than its application to emergency response.

The SC should have the responsibility for, and authority over, the ERP. Just as the SC is best situated to manage the RMP, there is no other part of the organization better connected with the safety component of each of the processes within the organization. It makes sense—the SC should be the owners of two documents: the Risk Management Plan, and the Emergency Response Plan.

SRM/SA in the Real World

Those who have been involved in the aviation industry for some time immediately recognize that the hypothetical scenario described above does not represent the existing state-of-the-art in process documentation, inter-departmental collaboration, or directed safety risk management and safety assurance. There is unfortunately a great danger that an average line manager in an average operation might perceive a complexity to SMS that immediately discourages participation or adoption. This is not just a *potential* problem—it already exists today, and the only way to overcome this understandable resistance is for disciples of SMS to patiently explain that one does not impose SMS. Rather, it is best grown in place, step by step, with small steps at first. Expecting any organization to transition to a mature SMS within a short period of time is both unrealistic and self-defeating. We will grow a successful and mature SMS by identifying one or two risk areas at a time, and working on those processes to incorporate the essential components that allow SRM and SA to develop to their potential. It is, and should be, a slow, methodical effort, but it is one worth the wait, and worth the work.

Note: After such an exhaustive coverage of process descriptions the authors cannot help but wonder whether a few readers will think that it is overkill to suggest that an SMS based process description needs to go into such detail. Our answer is a resounding *yes*, and we offer the following anecdote as support.

A few years ago one of us obtained certification as an ISO 9000 Lead Auditor. The topic of process descriptions, workflows, inputs, outputs—all the usual quality stuff—was extensively covered in this training. One morning we all came in to the classroom to see one whole wall of the room covered by a spectacularly detailed process workflow diagram. One of the fellow-students, the quality manager at a small manufacturing firm, had spoken with the instructor the night before, and with her permission had come in early to put up the workflow diagram he and his team had created that described *all* of the production processes existing in his company.

The workflow diagram was remarkably detailed. At every line coming in to a process from outside the company, there was a reference to a supplier quality document that described the specifications of the input, and how that quality was controlled. KPIs were highlighted throughout the map. Major controls were emphasized, and a smaller insert described a management review cycle.

This student was understandably proud of this work, but someone of course asked whether it was worth all the work. He simply pointed out that since embracing quality, the company had shown a consistent rise in profits and customer satisfaction, and that they were seriously considering going for the Baldrige Award.

Our question to the worried reader is: do our customers deserve less than those of a widget manufacturer?

SMS in Practice

Jack Kreckie, Deputy Fire Chief for Massport Fire Rescue (retired), offers his insight into emergency management at airports in an SMS environment:

> Effective and efficient management is best achieved when the stakeholders themselves are involved in developing, testing and implementing a plan. This is true in every case, whether it be management of an aircraft arrival at the gate, an aircraft accident, an airport security plan, or a *Safety Management System*.

> When a team approach is used for developing safety policy and objectives, a number of benefits are quickly realized, including the development of important relationships. Aviation is highly competitive, but when these business adversaries meet at the safety table, there is one primary goal. The stakeholders in safety share

methods and ideas, working together to develop inter-operative plans, which better serve the airport community as a whole. The benefits to this approach include:

1. The development of a "Safety Culture", which universally raises safety awareness and results in a reduction of accidents and injuries.
2. The tendency of the "Safety Culture" to interface naturally with the "Security Culture" which already exists at most airports.
3. Enhancement of emergency operations through established relationships, communications, asset sharing and a spirit of cooperation.

The most significant lessons learned through the management of the most challenging events in the last decade relate to interoperable emergency management models. The terrorist events of September 11, 2001, and the devastating havoc caused by Hurricane Katrina and Rita clearly outlined the need for a standard template for emergency management and Incident Command, which resulted in the National Incident Management System (NIMS). This system requires that all emergency responders be trained to the same incident management model, i.e., everyone is readily reading from the same script and speaking the same language during the active phase of emergency management.

For a number of reasons, airlines and airport support companies deal with rapid turnover of employees. This increases the challenge in maintaining updated contact lists, and keeping employees trained in emergency procedures. A successful SMS requires constant interaction with representatives from every employer. Safety Committees conducting risk analysis, training, safety audits, and safety promotion continuously keep a line of communications open throughout the airport community, working together in problem solving. Each group learns and better understands the culture of the other stakeholders. The Police, Fire and Airport Operations Departments are critical members of this team.

Similar to NIMS on the national level, an effective SMS provides an environment for the stakeholders to reap benefits for emergency managers at the airport level, who depend upon instant communications, immediate response for information and assets, and "mutual aid" from other airport stakeholders.

Review questions

1. Describe Safety Risk Management in terms of a process.
2. Explain the importance of key performance indicators in Safety Assurance, and in measuring processes.
3. What is the fundamental purpose of Safety Assurance?
4. Describe the interplay between production and protection measures, targets and assessments.
5. Describe how equipment specifications in one process become output requirements for another.

References

Deming, W. (2000). *The New Economics for Industry, Government, Education*, 2nd edn. Cambridge, MA: MIT Press.

Federal Aviation Administration [FAA] (2006). *Introduction to Safety Management Systems for Air Operators.* Advisory Circular 120-92. Retrieved December 3, 2007 from http://rgl.faa.gov/Regulatory_and_Guidance_Library/rgAdvisoryCircular.nsf/0/6485143d5ec81aae8625719b0055c9e5/$FILE/AC per cent20120-92.pdf.

Chapter 9

Managing the SMS

Where no counsel is, the people fall: but in the multitude of counselors there is safety.

Proverbs 11:14, King James Bible

SMS in Practice

Cpt. Hugh Schoelzel, former VP—Corporate Safety at TWA, discusses how building partnerships in safety allowed his airline to solve a potential safety problem:

> The grand delusion: Most professionals will tell you "the more we know, the more we know we don't know", but the converse is the true grand delusion. The less we know, the less we know what we don't know. For example, industry wide it is accepted that for safety reasons approaches must be stabilized by a given altitude, typically something between 500' and 1000' above touchdown. Next, a tale of success that emanated from deluding ourselves into thinking we knew something about stabilized approaches.

> From ATC reports, we knew our B-757 fleet was making far more go-arounds than other aircraft types. Compared to the others, the B-757 is known as somewhat of a "glider", or put in other terms, its lift-drag profile makes it more difficult to descend. This would explain why so many approaches were abandoned in this airplane, simply because the descent rate and airspeed were unstable more often than in other types at the 500' hard floor. But wait, there is more. At this stage of our development, the B-757 was the only aircraft in our fleet with an active FOQA program. Could it be that our ever-so-sharp B-757 pilots knew their unstable approaches would immediately be detected by FOQA, whereas pilots of other aircraft types knew a little use of their superior skill here and there would never be noticed? If that was the case, then all types were probably experiencing unstable approaches at a somewhat equal rate, only 757s were going around, and our problem was much larger than shown by the data. Through some intensive interviewing, we determined that in fact that was the case.

> We now knew the problem, but needed to know its cause. Our computer gurus back-traced many FOQA descent profiles from the runway to the top-of-descent. We then tried to see how early we could predict an unstable approach at 500'. Airplanes have a lot of variability in their descent profiles, including aircraft configuration, pilot technique, wind, ATC procedures and traffic. Before describing what we found, a review of the offending runway configuration is in order. The airport being studied was St. Louis Lambert, which had parallel runways oriented SE-NW. Most unstable approaches occurred on the southern-most runway as expected, since it typically

handled most arrivals due to proximity to the terminal (less taxi time). Normal ATC procedures dictated that departures crossing under arrivals level off at 6000'. Inbound flights to this runway were held at 7000' until clear of the departure paths. Typical profiles assumed an ILS approach and three nautical miles to lose each 1000' of altitude, so rounding off to a 1000' field elevation, 18 miles to touchdown would be required from 7000' in a clean configuration. (There are more operational complexities, but these numbers are fine for this discussion.) As long as a full ILS approach was conducted, this worked fine. The devil entered the picture when pilots rightfully started worrying about fuel consumption and on-time performance. The incentive became the least flight time which equates to the shortest flight path. ATC controllers knew this as well, and offered close-in turns to the airport when traffic and weather permitted, with perhaps only 12 miles to lose 6000'. Pilots are typically "can-do" people who accept the challenge. Unfortunately, the vagaries of wind and other performance factors are more art than science, so a percentage of these flights approached the 500' floor in an unstable condition. So there was the cause, apparent when studying FOQA data, and confirmed through pilot interviews.

The solution was not so obvious, as it is very fuel inefficient to prepare all flights for the close in approach, or "slam-dunk" as pilots call it. We needed expertise from other disciplines. So far, this analysis had been done by our safety department, which included FOQA experts and highly experienced pilots. We asked our pilots' union safety representatives to supply line pilots for actual-use interviews, and they were very cooperative. An important point is that trust had previously been established, so line pilots felt comfortable telling us things they may not have otherwise revealed. Not many people will self-incriminate themselves unless they have a high degree of confidence in management protecting their confidentiality. This may be one of the more important points in this entire discussion. Next we involved FAA personnel from our Certificate Management Office. This also required a high degree of trust, as we wanted to solve this problem without regulatory action against our airline or our pilots. Because of previous efforts on both sides, we were able to rationally lay out a joint game plan. We decided to take a team of airline safety experts, pilots' union safety specialists, and FAA CMO personnel to the TRACON facility. Our goal was to educate ATC on safety aspects of stabilized approaches, the limits of aircraft performance for different types, and efficiency factors for fuel conservation and on-time arrivals.

Our safety department prepared a PowerPoint presentation with supporting FOQA data and visual depictions. We had a strategy session with our three presenting parties, clarifying the issues and who would present what. We wanted to be sure our presentation was clear and succinct, to assure ATC buy-in and quick movement to solutions.

After a brief tour of the new TRACON facility, we met with a similar grouping of ATC people. Because we had set the ground rules of non-punitive action, the group moved rapidly and openly from our presentation to solutions and an implementation plan. It turned out that ATC was unaware they had been causing a problem, presuming it had been a pilot issue, with some being better than others. While that may be true to some extent, we worked toward a team solution that worked for everyone.

It turned out to be simple and effective. With heavy traffic, the efficient 3:1 (three miles per thousand feet) rule was used to assure a fuel- saving idle descent arriving over the outer marker at the initial approach altitude. When ATC could see gaps coming in the approach lineup, they lowered the level-off altitude of departing traffic and/or vectored them away from arrival traffic, thus allowing a lower than normal altitude for arriving flights planned for close-in base legs. Savvy pilots quickly realized what this meant, and prepared for the "slam-dunk". We gave ATC the appropriate requirements for close-in approaches, which we had tested in our flight simulators. ATC trained their controllers and implemented these new procedures rapidly, with the end result being a considerable dollar saving in fuel for all airlines, better on-time performance, and elimination of hazardous unstable approaches and expensive (in dollars and time) go-arounds.

Bear in mind that by solving this problem for a single airplane type, we also did so for our entire fleet and all other airlines. The payback was immense.

So what should you take away from this discussion? Building personal relationships and trust between management, operators and regulators cannot be over emphasized. None of this could have happened without all of us pulling on the same end of the rope. Then there is marketing. It is inefficient and expensive to merely come up with great ideas. Once the data speaks, and you truly hear what it is telling you (rarely is anything as it first appears), spend some time on a "marketing" plan. This may be the most important part of this discussion; your brilliant vision and analysis won't mean much if you can't sell it to the implementers. A formidable approach is a stake-holder partnership, with all singing the same tune. Go for it, and enjoy your new position in marketing!

There are several good reasons why we need to strive to achieve safety (Brauer, 2006, p. 21). First and foremost, our society places a high value on human life, so it is considered humane to attempt to preserve that life. This *humanitarian* reason is the moral basis for safety.

Second, many governments have adopted laws requiring organizations to identify and manage risks. We readily think of *laws and regulations* of this nature applying to transportation systems such as aviation.

Third, there are *financial* considerations for safety. Irrespective of which industry one belongs to, it is simply bad business to be regarded as "unsafe". Being unsafe brings with it significant financial costs associated with accidents, legal fees, replacement of equipment, higher insurance costs, fewer customers, and so on.

In aviation, perhaps even more than in other industries, management has an important role to play in achieving safety, and thereby protecting the humanitarian, legal, and financial interests of the organization. A well-developed and effective SMS provides management the best opportunity to meet its fundamental obligations regarding safety.

Management's responsibility for safety

SMSs are predicated on top management's strong and visible commitment to safety. No SMS will be effective without senior management devoting the attention, time, and resources to safety as a core value of the organization.

Safety as a core value

The core values of an organization are those ideals that form the foundation on which the organization conducts itself. They are not transient in nature; rather they are constants that define the organization and govern its processes, behavior, relationships, and decision-making. Core values are deeply ingrained in the organization and are non-negotiable.

Core values are integrated into all levels and all functions of the organization. It has been said that if you can find anyone in the organization who is unable to tell you, even generally, the organization's core values, they aren't really core values. Top leadership has a responsibility to establish those core values, and to promote them throughout the organization.

Senior management establishes safety as a core value by making it an integral part of the organization's management system. Once the core values are established, management must set objectives and goals that support the safety value, and hold workers accountable for achieving the goals. No discontinuity can exist between values and these objectives and goals; the first indication of management compromising a safety value in order to achieve an operational or financial goal will undermine a great deal of work to culturalize safety in the organization.

Accountability versus blame

After the safety goals and objectives are established, management must establish a plan for accountability. Many people confuse the terms *accountability* and *blame*; these terms have substantively different meanings. In practice, accountability means that someone is responsible *and* answerable for an activity. This means that someone may need to produce an account of their knowledge of the activity in question. That accounting may be used for understanding the circumstances of that activity and, hopefully, used to improve the system that produced that activity.

Plans for accountability should be formal, specific, and comprehensive. All significant safety activities should be clearly assigned to someone who is responsible and accountable.

Blame goes further. Blame is accountability deserving of censure, discipline, or other penalty. Brenner (2005) suggests that blame and accountability differ in at least four dimensions:

1. Learning vs. punishment—As stated earlier, an accountability culture seeks to learn from the situation so that it is not repeated. Blame simply seeks to identify the culprit, and the process often goes no further.
2. Incidence of fear—If someone is fearful of being held accountable, blame is probably involved. There should be no fear in being held to account for something.
3. Organizational chart altitude distribution—Responsibility and accountability are found at all levels on an organizational chart. When most of the people we find accountable are concentrated at the bottom of the chart, it is likely that we are actually assigning blame.

4. Acknowledging interdependence—When we seek the learning opportunities that are afforded by exercising accountability, oftentimes there are numerous people accountable. When we seek blame, we're usually satisfied with finding just one person to punish.

Recognition of management's role in systemic failure

Dr. Deming, our well-known quality guru cited frequently in this text, estimated that 85 per cent of quality problems are created by management. He professed that the vast majority of behavior and performance comes from the system, not the individual. So, if we want to change our circumstances, we must change the system, not the worker. Who controls the system? Management! Managers must recognize that the system is the culprit, and that they alone can change the system.

As discussed earlier in Chapter 1, aviation accident investigations in the past were characterized by finding the cause and blaming the individual(s) involved, usually the pilot. Of course, we now know that this long-standing but misguided approach to improving safety had multiple deleterious consequences, including discouraging individuals in the system from reporting anything for which they might be subject to blame, and failure to improve the system in which the event occurred.

Management plays a vital role in establishing a safety ethos. Safety culture is discussed throughout this book, and especially in Chapters 1 and 11.

Management is vested with the authority and responsibility for managing safety risks in the company. This is best accomplished through a robust quality management-based risk management system. Management controls the resources, so it is management's job to ensure that the safety function has what it needs in terms of personnel, expertise, funding, time, and organizational support to satisfy its vital function.

Stakeholder identification and analysis

A stakeholder is "any group or individual who can affect or is affected by the achievement of the organization's objectives". The analysis of stakeholders involves the identification of the stakeholders and the determination of their needs. This would seem a rather simple task with respect to aviation safety, but it is not always so.

We could all agree that the flying public is a primary stakeholder in aviation safety. So, too, is the general public, the air carrier, code share partners (if any), the aircraft and component manufacturers, the regulator(s), airports, other government agencies, firefighters, police, civil defense, first responders, medical personnel, hospitals, family members, government officials, and on and on. It is not sufficient in practice, though, to just simply list every entity that comes to mind and be done with it. Some stakeholders are more concerned about some aspects of an aviation operation than others. The persons responsible for ramp safety have more immediate concern about a service cart running into the side of the airplane than does the general public. (It probably would never come to the attention of the general public and, if it did, they would likely be pretty forgiving of the incident as long as proper repairs were made.)

Stakeholder analysis should not be done without a purpose that is clearly defined and well-known to everyone involved.

Usually, stakeholder analysis begins with one or more individuals doing a preliminary assessment of stakeholders using, for example, the *basic analysis technique* (Bryson, 1995) or *power versus interest grid*. The basic analysis technique works through a multi-step process that includes: brainstorming a list of potential stakeholders, determining what criteria each stakeholder would use to judge the organization's performance, identifying what can be done to satisfy each stakeholder, specifying how each stakeholder influences the organization, and rank-ordering the stakeholders according to their importance to the organization. Power versus interest grids array stakeholders on a two-by-two matrix based on the stakeholder's interest in the organization and the stakeholder's power to affect the organization's future (see Figure 9.1). This analysis produces four categories of stakeholders: players (those who have interest and power), subjects (those who have interest but limited power), context setters (those who have power but little direct interest), and the crowd (those with little interest or power) (Eden and Ackermann, 1998, pp. 121-125, 344-346).

Generally, the *crowd* requires minimal effort, but their comments should be respected, their actions monitored, and care should be taken in giving them representation in the process. Often the *context setters* have the most insight into problems and, thus, they should be empowered. This is a very important group and at some point may become powerful. The *subjects* can provide objective feedback and critique, and it is important to manage them well. The *players* are the most critical stakeholder group, and it is important to have their representation on the team and to collaborate with them.

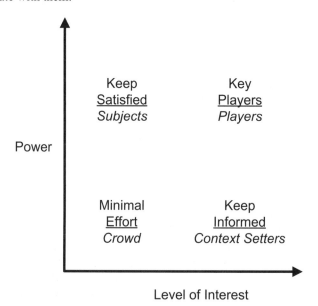

Figure 9.1   Power versus interest grid—stakeholder matrix

Unfortunately, stakeholder identification is often overlooked in the planning and execution of strategy. According to Bryson (1995), there are a number of reasons for this omission, including not knowing how to do it, assuming they already know who the stakeholders are and what their interests are, lack of time, and concerns about what the analysis might reveal.

Regardless of the issue, aviation in general is a complex endeavor, and aviation safety is both complex and vital. Managers must recognize the need to understand who has interest in the safety function, what their priorities are, and what their relative importance to the organization is. Managers would be well-advised to engage in stakeholder identification and analysis to inform the strategy and execution process.

Regulatory oversight

ICAO

As we mentioned in Chapter 1, the International Civil Aviation Organization (ICAO) is a specialized agency of the United Nations created in 1947 to carry out the principles established at the *Convention on International Civil Aviation* (i.e., Chicago Convention). ICAO has the responsibility and the authority to "ensure the safe and orderly growth of international civil aviation throughout the world". One of the primary means ICAO uses to achieve its mission is through the development of Standards and Recommended Practices (SARPs), which reflect the best operational experience of the states. SARPs are contained in the annexes to the Chicago Convention.

In an effort to improve global aviation safety, ICAO has mandated that its member states develop and achieve an acceptable level of safety in aviation operations. This mandate was implemented by amending 3 of the 18 annexes of the ICAO statutes: Annex 6 Parts 1 and 3—*Operation of Aircraft*, Annex 11—*Air Traffic Services*, and Annex 14—*Aerodromes*. ICAO has stated that amendments to other annexes may be implemented in the future.

Because SMS thinking has grown out of various committees, sectors of the industry, and even countries, the need to harmonize the global approach to SMS was recognized by ICAO. ICAO believes that harmonization will lead to a better and common understanding of SMS, more adaptable regulations, increased information and data sharing, more rapid expansion of SMS throughout the industry, and common training and education material. This effort led to various amendments to Annexes 6, 11, and 14 which took effect on November 23, 2006, and to the publication of ICAO's *Safety Management Manual* (Document 9859) in 2006 as a resource for those involved in development of SMS programs.

FAA

In the U.S., the governing authority for aviation is the FAA. At present the FAA's approach to SMS implementation is non-regulatory, however, the FAA opened a Rulemaking Project Record in November 2006 and a Rulemaking Project Team was assigned a month later. The proposed strategy of the rulemaking effort is to: 1.) align regulations with ICAO, 2.) draft acceptance criteria in policy documents, and 3.) set implementation milestones in regulatory language. Rulemaking aside, the FAA is moving rapidly to introduce SMS, to support pilot studies to develop and implement these programs, and to develop the infrastructure to support them.

Often a first step toward a regulation, the FAA issued an advisory circular, AC 120-92 *Introduction to Safety Management Systems for Air Operators*, on June 22, 2006. The AC introduces the concept of a safety management system (SMS) to aviation service providers (e.g., airlines, air taxi operators, corporate flight departments, pilot schools), and provides guidance for SMS development by these organizations. The AC applies to both certificated and non-certificated air operators that desire to develop and implement an SMS. Shortly after the AC was issued, the FAA followed with Order 8000.1 on August 11, 2006. The order is entitled *Safety Management System Doctrine*, and is intended to enable the agency to implement a common SMS in the Aviation Safety (AVS) organization, standardize SMS terminology, set forth management principles to guide AVS offices in their safety oversight activities, and explain SMS principles and requirements.

With respect to airports, the FAA issued AC 150/5200-37 on February 28, 2007, entitled *Introduction to Safety Management Systems (SMS) for Airport Operators*. The agency also recently commenced a rulemaking project to consider a formal requirement for SMS at airports certificated under 14 CFR Part 139. The FAA anticipates issuing a notice of proposed rulemaking (NPRM) for public comment in 2008. A final rule may be adopted after the agency has considered all of the public and industry comments received on the NPRM. The rulemaking process can take anywhere from several months to several years.[1]

Oversight systems

ICAO distinguishes *safety oversight*, which is a function of the state, from *safety performance monitoring*, which is a responsibility of the operator and service provider. Oversight, then, is considered a function of the regulatory authority. In Doc

---

1   FAA Rulemaking. The FAA's rulemaking process is complex and requires input from the various stakeholders. Generally, the process involves:

- a petition to change a rule,
- publication in the Federal Register,
- FAA considers comments and decides whether or not to proceed with rulemaking,
- an aviation rulemaking advisory committee (ARAC) is sometimes formed to assist in developing the rule,
- departments within FAA review draft rule; FAA assigns a priority number,
- FAA studies economic impact and legality of new rule,
- other agencies (e.g., Office of Management and Budget, DOT) review proposed rule,
- draft rule is published in Federal Register as Notice of Proposed Rulemaking (NPRM) with comment period,
- comments are reviewed and NPRM is accepted as-is or revised and becomes final rule, or rewritten and prepared as a new NPRM,
- final rule is published in Federal Register,
- FAA prepares for rule's requirements, e.g., training of inspectors.

9734-AN/959, ICAO identifies eight critical elements for a state oversight system (ICAO, 2006, p. iii). These are:

1. Primary aviation legislation.
2. Specific operating regulations.
3. Civil aviation structure and safety oversight functions.
4. Technical guidance material.
5. Qualified technical personnel.
6. Licensing and certification obligations.
7. Continued surveillance obligations.
8. Resolution of safety issues.

In the case of the United States, the regulator is the Federal Aviation Administration. While some of the functions identified by ICAO occur at the national level, many of them occur at the operational level. In 2005, the FAA had an inspector workforce of nearly 3,200 inspectors; almost 1,700 inspectors were dedicated to airline operations and the remaining 1,500 oversaw general aviation. Much of the effort of the FAA's inspectors is dedicated to surveillance activities. How surveillance is conducted depends on the type of organization, the size, the nature of its operations, and other factors.

The oversight of the nation's airlines is an important responsibility of the FAA. In the past, FAA oversight of the airlines (and other operators) involved an inspector, checklist in hand, watching the work of an employee at specified intervals to ensure the work was being done properly. This method of oversight had serious limitations, including the fact that it was outcomes-oriented, labor intensive, inefficient, and it didn't tend to foster a collaborative approach to safety management.

From 1985 until the late 90s, the National Work Program Guidelines (NPG) had been the basis for the FAA's inspection of airlines. NPG established a set of required and planned inspection activities for airlines to ensure compliance with safety regulations.

Following the 1996 crash of a ValueJet transport into the Florida Everglades, the FAA determined that its existing approach to surveillance was inadequate to detect systemic safety problems in the airline industry, and that a new approach was needed. Thus, in 1998 the FAA began implementation of the Air Transport Oversight System, which was developed based on system safety principles, safety attributes, risk management, and structured system engineering practices. Initially, ATOS was implemented at ten airlines, and now includes the nation's largest 15 commercial airlines and cargo carriers; eventually all airlines and cargo carriers will be included.

In 2002 the FAA introduced another component, the Surveillance and Evaluation Program, to the inspection process. This change incorporates some of the principles of ATOS into its inspection process of some airlines not yet under ATOS, adding system safety concepts to inspections.

The FAA has developed these new oversight tools to overcome the deficiencies inherent in inspections. (Recall from our discussion on quality management that quality can't be inspected into the product!) These new oversight methods are an unambiguous departure from the "over the shoulder" methods of the past, and are based on system safety principles.

Safety oversight is one of the cornerstones of an effective SMS program. Safety oversight has several purposes:

- Demonstrate compliance with rules, regulations, standards, procedures, and instructions.
- Provide an additional method for proactively identifying hazards.
- Validate the effectiveness of safety actions taken.
- Evaluate safety performance.

ICAO and the state share oversight responsibilities. ICAO carries out its responsibility via the ICAO Universal Safety Oversight Audit Program (USOAP). Launched in 1999, the USOAP is a monitoring program that enables authorities to ensure that all states implement the operational safety standards, recommended practices and related procedures which appear in the Annexes of the Chicago Convention.

As stated above, the state engages in oversight through rulemaking, standard-setting, accident investigation, enforcement (sanctions or fines), education, inspection (no-notice and formal or scheduled), safety audits, and surveillance activities.

Organizations employ numerous methods for monitoring their safety performance. These methods vary widely based on the size and complexity of the organizations. Primary means include:

- Quality assurance (QA). QA provides evidence that quality-related activities are being performed effectively. QA is a part of quality management and includes quality control. QA provides fact-based assurance that it has in place the necessary elements to ensure that a product meets the needs, expectations, and other requirements of customers and other stakeholders. An effective QA program enables an organization to meet its product or service requirements, improve its efficiency, and reduce risks.
- Vigilance. As obvious as this may seem, vigilance on the part of all persons exposed to the operational areas can make a dramatic difference in achieving a higher level of safety performance. Organizations should train their personnel in being vigilant—what it means, how to do it—and strive to make it part of the work culture.
- Inspections. Inspections are an integral part of safety oversight, just as they are in the oversight functions of quality management. Inspections afford both regulators and the organization the opportunity to observe actual work practices and performance as well as and assess safety conditions. Generally, the most valuable inspections will reveal any systemic safety conditions that may exist.
- Surveys. A properly constructed survey can reveal systemic hazards that may compromise safety. Surveys can be an excellent means of assessing attitudes of personnel regarding safety.
- Data analysis. In the airline sector, data-based programs such as Flight Operations Quality Assurance, Aviation Safety Action Programs, and Line

Operations Safety Audits provide valuable data about the operations of the airline. Flight schools have data collected during stage checks and practical tests. Airports have numerous data collection programs. And so on. In sum, all aviation organizations can establish methods for collecting data that can be used by managers to determine the safety performance of the organization.

- Safety audits. Develop identified safety performance indicators and targets.
- Monitor adherence to safety policy through self-auditing.
- Allocate adequate resources for safety oversight.
- Solicit input through a non-punitive safety reporting system.
- Systematically review all available feedback from daily self-inspections, assessments, reports, safety risk analysis, and safety audits.
- Communicate findings to staff and implement agreed-upon mitigation strategies (14 CFR Part 139 already requires this for actions covered by that regulation).
- Promote integration of a systems approach to safety into the overall operation of the airport.
- Safety studies, and others.

Relationships between production, SMS-P and SMS-O

Figure 9.2 represents the FAA's view of the relationship of system for certificated operators. On the "protection" side of the model are the FAA's SMS-O (oversight), with its objective of public safety, and the operator's SMS-P (provider), with its objective of controlling safety risk. These systems interact with one another through *audits* and *approvals*.

On the "production" side of the model are the process activities that produce products and services, with the objective of serving customer requirements. These processes interact with the SMS-O through *direct sampling* such as *surveillance*, and with the SMS-P through *internal safety assurance*, *risk management*, and *safety promotion* (see Figure 9.2).

SMS programs implemented by organizations and by the FAA should be developed with the objective of relating to one another from the outset. For example, both the SMS-O and the SMS-P have responsibilities to audit the processes to ensure quality and safety. Audit tools and processes can be developed for joint use by the organization and the FAA. As well, procedures for data collection, information sharing and protection, and voluntary disclosure can be incorporated into the organization's and FAA's SMS programs, serving as "hooks" that will connect the programs and allow a greater degree of interoperability and harmonization. This should benefit all involved and serve to strengthen the relationship between the regulators and the aviation service providers.

Roles, responsibilities and relationships

Aviation systems today are highly complex and complicated structures involving numerous stakeholders, and a high degree of interaction among various organizations

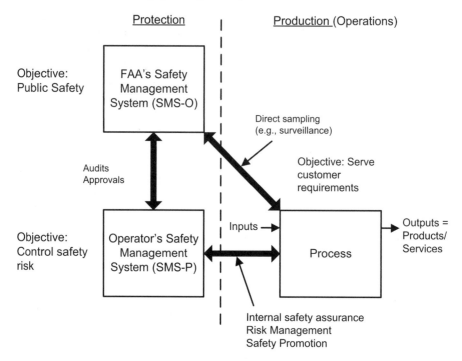

Figure 9.2   System relationships—certificated operations

and agencies. Not just one, but many entities share in the burden of maintaining high levels of safety in the aviation industry. SMS acknowledges this shared responsibility, and specifically describes the roles, responsibilities, and relationships between all stakeholders involved in maintaining safe operations. In SMS, each interface between production and operation on the one hand, and oversight on the other, is clearly identified, and each subsystem is designed to provide the interfacing agency or organization everything it needs to perform its role.

The FAA has a statutory obligation to conduct safety oversight of aviation product/ service providers, regardless of their size. The agency fulfills that obligation through the issuance of regulations, standards, orders, and policies, and the certification and surveillance of aviation service providers.

The aviation product/service providers are responsible for managing safety for their operations. The management of these providers direct and control the resources of their organizations. Thus, management is the only entity that can effectively control safety risks faced by the organization and thereby manage safety.

In its doctrine on SMS (FAA Order 8000.1) the FAA describes three levels of interaction with the air transportation system and its components (FAA, 2006b, pp. 10-12). The first is the *National Air Transportation System* level. At this level the FAA has responsibility for safety management in the National Airspace System, the commercial aviation system, and general aviation. The FAA evaluates the effectiveness of regulations, policies, and standards in maintaining safety performance and takes corrective action as necessary.

At the *organizational* level, the FAA interacts with aviation product/service providers primarily through certification and surveillance activities. The FAA's role is to ensure that the SMS is comprehensive and functioning properly, and that the SMS performance, process design, verification functions, and organizational safety attributes are adequately accounted for. The FAA's role is *not* to ensure a safe product; rather it is to ensure that the organization has the *capability* of delivering a safe product. The organizations retain the responsibility for safety management, and for integrating SMS into their business model.

Individuals and aircraft that are certificated, authorized, or otherwise directly controlled by the FAA's safety oversight process constitute the most basic, *individual* level. Interactions between the FAA and the individual occur most often through certification, surveillance, or safety promotion. Again, individual operators are responsible for safety risk management. Since individuals generally do not participate in a formal SMS program, the FAA's role is primarily safety oversight of performance and safety promotion rather than the design and performance of SMS systems.

The three levels of safety risk management

As we discussed earlier, ICAO categorizes safety management methods as follows:

*   Reactive—incident analysis, determination of contributory factors and findings as to risks.
*   Proactive—mandatory and voluntary reporting systems, safety audits, and surveys.
*   Predictive—confidential reporting systems, flight data analysis, normal operations monitoring.

Reactive

Reactive safety management is often equated with the well-known "fly-crash-fix-fly" adage. There is an accident or incident, and we use investigative tools to try to determine what the contributory factors were that caused the problem. It is forensic in nature; that is, we apply scientific methods to understand the relevant factors and offer those to the public debate or discussion (the etymology of the Latin word *forensis* means public forum). ICAO uses the term *reactive* safety management to include "incident analysis, determination of contributory factors and findings as to risk".

Proactive

We have all heard the expression, "don't go looking for trouble!". Proactive safety is exactly that: actively looking for trouble, or more accurately, actively looking for potential safety problems through trend analysis, hazard analysis, and other methods of scientific inquiry. In the airline world, statistical analysis, visualizations, and reporting applied to so-called proactive safety programs such as FOQA, LOSA, ASAP, IEP, and others, have contributed much to improving safety. ICAO includes "mandatory and voluntary reporting systems, safety audits, and surveys" in its description of *proactive* management.

Predictive

Predictive safety is more. Today aviation is operating at such a high level of safety that breakthroughs in safety improvement will be hard-won, and will require higher levels of analysis and increasingly sophisticated tools and methods. That's not to say that we should abandon the approaches that helped us achieve our enviable safety record. Incident analysis will always be important, although we hope there will be fewer and fewer incidents available to analyze. Though relatively new on the aviation safety timeline, proactive safety has enabled us to make substantial gains. But if we wish to move safety to an even higher level, the aviation industry must begin to embrace methods that allow us to better assess complex systems and *predict* where the failures will be. Predictive safety methods will enable us to find those failure points and eliminate them; in effect, predictive safety will allow us to *change the future*. ICAO includes "confidential reporting systems, flight data analysis, and normal operations monitoring" in its description of *predictive* safety. We argue that, in order for the industry to make substantive improvements in safety, predictive safety management must be more than those items identified by ICAO.

Figure 9.3 depicts a Safety Management Continuum using the ICAO terms of reactive, proactive, and predictive management. A sampling of safety activities and programs are placed on this model continuum based on the discussion above. It should not be inferred that a program is limited by this representation; in fact, many of these concepts have greater potential than is currently realized. Also, no two organizations have identical programs—they vary widely in sophistication, philosophy, and intent. Some organizations, for example, might use confidential reporting systems as a proactive tool while others limit their use to reactive applications. Finally, as depicted in the figure, there is no hard distinction between these "categories" of safety risk management; depending on how it is used, a program can span more than one. For example, flight data analysis—generously characterized by ICAO as

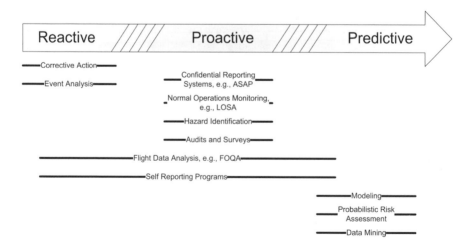

Figure 9.3   Safety management continuum

predictive safety management—can be reactive if it is used to examine past events one at a time, proactive if they perform aggregate analysis to determine trends, and predictive if the analysis feeds more scientific methods discussed below. Actually, we assert that predictive safety must involve more than the *routine* analysis of flight data and monitoring of routine operations because those activities primarily focus on the current state and what that implies about the future. Predictive safety risk management seeks to understand the existing system and, through the use of various forms of modeling, determine where and when the system is likely to fail.

Models are excellent tools to help us predict the future. They are used in predicting weather, financial markets, and aviation safety. While there are many modeling techniques that can be used in the aviation safety arena, two of particular interest and worth are presented in Chapter 10: Probabilistic Risk Assessment and data mining.

SMS in Practice

FAA Associate Administrator for Aviation Safety, Nicholas Sabatini, discussed moving from a 'forensic' approach to a predictive approach to safety management in this excerpt from testimony before Congress:

To continue to improve aviation safety we must use every tool at our disposal. The most effective way to improve safety is through Safety Management Systems (SMS). Safety Management Systems enable organizations to identify and manage risk far better than before. With this formalized approach, we can identify issues, fix them, and ensure they stay fixed.

Operating under a Safety Management System assures a disciplined and standardized approach to managing risk. The best part is we can review past experience and address known hazards, and at the same time we can look ahead and rigorously apply Safety Risk Management principles to any changes or introduction of new elements.

Furthermore, under an SMS, the whole process—identifying potential problems and putting corrections in place—is ongoing and the procedure is continuously assessed to make sure it is working.

In short, SMS formalizes risk management, which is imperative as we move from a forensic, or after-the-fact accident investigation approach, to a diagnostic and more prognostic, or predictive, approach. With the accident rate as low as it is, we must get in front of information, analyze trends, and anticipate problems if we are to continue to improve on an already remarkable record of achievement. Operating under a Safety Management System will allow airlines, manufacturers, and the FAA to do this better than before. So that we are all operating from the same approach, FAA must apply the same high standards to ourselves that we require of the entities that we regulate.

Source: http://www.faa.gov/news/testimony/news_story.cfm?newsId=7395.
(Excerpted statement of Nicholas A. Sabatini, Associate Administrator for
Aviation Safety, FAA, before the committee on Transportation and Infrastructure,
Subcommittee on Aviation, on FAA Safety Oversight, September 20, 2006.)

Review questions

1. What is the difference between accountability and blame?
2. Explain the power versus interest grid method of stakeholder analysis.
3. What roles do ICAO and the FAA play in safety oversight?
4. Describe the relationship between an SMS-O and an SMS-P.
5. Describe the three levels of Safety Risk Management.

References

Brauer, R. (2006). *Safety and Health for Engineers*. Hoboken, NJ: John Wiley & Sons.

Brenner, R. (2005). "Is it Blame or is it Accountability?" Point Lookout, 5 (51). Retrieved December 3, 2007 from http://www.chacocanyon.com/pointlookout/051221.shtml.

Bryson, J. (2003). "What to do when Stakeholders Matter: A Guide to Stakeholder Identification and Analysis Techniques." A Paper Presented at the National Public Management Research Conference. Retrieved October 15, 2007 from http://www.pmranet.org/conferences/georgetownpapers/Bryson.pdf.

Eden, C., and Ackermann, F. (1998). *Making Strategy: The Journey of Strategic Management*. London: Sage Publications.

Federal Aviation Administration [FAA] (2006a). *Introduction to Safety Management Systems for Air Operators*. Advisory Circular 120-92. Retrieved December 3, 2007 from http://rgl.faa.gov/Regulatory_and_Guidance_Library/rgAdvisoryCircular.nsf/0/6485143d5ec81aae8625719b0055c9e5/$FILE/AC per cent20120-92.pdf.

Federal Aviation Administration [FAA] (2006b). *Safety Management System Doctrine*. Order VS 8000.1. Retrieved August 1, 2007 from http://rgl.faa.gov/Regulatory_and_Guidance_Library/rgOrders.nsf/0/6aae93ff516cd6fd862571fb00661605/$FILE/VS per cent208000.1.pdf.

International Civil Aviation Organization [ICAO] (2006). *Safety Oversight Manual: Part B: The Establishment and Management of a Regional Safety Oversight System*, 1st edn. (Doc 9734 AN/959). Montréal, Canada: ICAO.

Chapter 10

Tools and Analysis Methods

You can't expect to meet the challenges of today with yesterday's tools and expect to be in business tomorrow.

Author Unknown

SMS requires reliable, repeatable processes that produce data used for decision-making in a structured, engineered environment. An effective SMS is based on a quality management system, and has elements of quality, safety, and reliability engineering, project management, and other disciplines. One of the significant challenges for organizations implementing SMS programs is to acquire or train personnel who possess the skills and knowledge in these disciplines, and an understanding of the tools and analysis methods used in them.

Unfortunately, these are not skills that the typical aviation manager currently has.

Admittedly, tool and method usage will vary widely in different segments of the industry, and in different organizations within those segments. Consider that a very diverse set of organizations will implement SMS programs, from large commercial air carriers to very small fixed-base-operators, and everything in between. Obviously, not every organization will need to use every tool. Certain tools will be appropriate to the process of investigating safety related events, determining corrective actions, and tracking the implementation of those actions. Other tools may be most appropriate for the analysis of past events, trend monitoring, and the identification and quantification of potential safety risks—that is, proactive safety management.

The size of the organization will certainly play a role in the depth of knowledge SMS practitioners must have in tools and methods. It is unlikely that safety practitioners in small organizations will require the expertise in more sophisticated tools used by larger, more complex organizations.

It is recommended, though, that the practitioner of SMS gains a familiarity with the concepts and use of the tools discussed in this text, as this will lead to a more standardized, best practices approach to problem-solving and decision-making. Without a doubt, some of these tools are already used effectively in some safety programs. The purpose of presenting these tools here is to expose these tools to a wider aviation safety audience.

Several important tools have been discussed in other parts of this book and, in the interest of brevity, won't be repeated here. We'll simply list the tool and refer to the chapter where that tool is discussed. For some of the tools, an example is provided for its use; for others we refer the reader to other sources. Three tools in particular, Failure Mode Effects Analysis, Fault Tree Analysis, and gap analysis are presented first and receive a more extensive treatment than the other tools due to their value in safety management in all organizations.

Finally, a more extensive discussion is provided for two tools and methods that should be highly valued as *predictive* safety management: Probabilistic Risk Assessment and data mining. Examples of the use of these tools are provided in this chapter.

Tools

1. Failure Mode Effects Analysis (Proactive)

One of the fundamental concepts of quality is that quality should be built into a product or process rather than inspected in. Another way to state this is that quality problems should be "designed out" of a product or process. One of the tools that has been helpful in achieving this goal is failure mode effects analysis (FMEA). The purpose of the FMEA is to reduce the risk of failure. It accomplishes this by providing a systematic means of identifying and assessing potential failure modes, understanding the root causes of those failures, and determining the actions necessary to eliminate the potential failures.

The FMEA is a "bottom up" approach. The practitioner begins this process with a list of potential failures, typically developed either through a detailed analysis of the diagram of a system or the results of brainstorming potential failures with experts on the system. The effect on the system of each potential failure is then considered.

The FMEA uses a numerical system, usually a scale of 1 to 10, to rate the severity of the effects, the likelihood of occurrence for the failure, and the likelihood of the engineering controls detecting the failure should one occur. These factors are multiplied together and the product is the risk priority number (RPN); that is, severity x occurrence x detection = RPN.

In Chapter 5 we discussed the use of the risk matrix in SMS, which uses the first two of those factors (severity and occurrence), but not detection in assessing risk. However, it is clear that the ability to detect failures is an important component of risk assessment, making the FMEA an excellent addition to the traditional risk matrix used by many aviation organizations.

Often the most difficult aspect of employing the failure and reliability tools discussed in this book is obtaining the appropriate values for reliability and failure. Some sources for this data include:

- Manufacturer's data;
- Industry consensus standards;
- Simulation and testing;
- Delphi estimates;
- MIL standards;
- Historical evidence;
- Other industry-specific sources.

2. Fault Tree Analysis (Reactive / Proactive)

Fault Tree Analysis (FTA) was developed at the Bell Laboratories in the early 1960s to evaluate the safety of an ICBM launch control system, and was later adopted and refined by The Boeing Company, among others. Today FTA is used by many organizations in their system reliability and safety programs.

FTA is a graphical tool for analyzing complex systems to determine potential failure modes and the probabilities that these failures might occur. FTA uses a logic block diagram with symbols to indicate various states. It is built from the top-down, beginning with a potential failure mode, which might be an accident, an incident, a near-miss, or other negative event. Pathways are used to interconnect events that contribute to the failure. These pathways use standard logic symbols, such as AND, OR, and others.

FTA can be used for accident investigation purposes. For example, NASA used FTA to examine every conceivable chain of causation that led to the loss of the Space Shuttle Columbia, STS-107, in 2003. Seven interdisciplinary teams composed of NASA personnel, contractors, and other experts developed fault trees for each of the shuttle's six major components (orbiter, space shuttle main engine, reusable solid rocket motor, solid rocket booster, external tank, and payload) and one for systems integration. Some of the fault trees developed contained hundreds of unique elements (CAIB, 2003).

The FTA is an event-oriented method and, because of this, it has several advantages over other methods, including FMEA. Some of the strengths of this tool relative to other methods of system analysis include:

- FTA has the ability to discover failure combinations that might not be evident using other methods.
- This tool has the ability to combine human error contributions and hardware failures in the same analysis, provided detailed task analysis information is available. This feature makes the FTA a powerful tool for the reliability (or safety) practitioner.
- FTA is by nature proactive. It is a structured process that can help identify potential causes of system failure *before* the failures occur.
- FTA leads to the understanding of all possible combinations of low-order events that will cause a system failure. This is infinitely more important than knowing the impact on the system of the failure of a single component. Since FTA assumes the failure of the top event, and examines the lower order events to determine the combinations that can lead to failure, it is regarded as a *deductive* approach.
- FTA is graphical, which makes it relatively easy to understand by all interested parties, including management.
- FTA works with both quantitative and qualitative analysis. This is an important feature since quantitative data is frequently unavailable or unreliable for some safety events.

There are numerous symbols used in fault tree construction. Table 10.1 provides a listing of the most common used gates in development of FTAs.

The most commonly used fault tree events are displayed in Table 10.2.

A simple example of a fault tree is provided in Figure 10.1 using just a few symbols.

Table 10.1   Commonly used gates in fault tree analysis

Symbol	Name	Description
	OR Gate	The event above this gate occurs if any of the events below the gate occur. OR signifies union of events.
	AND Gate	The event above this gate occurs if all the events below the gate occur. AND signifies intersection of events.
	Exclusive OR Gate	The event above this gate occurs if only one of the events below the gate occur.
	Priority AND Gate	The event above this gate occurs if all the events below the gate occur in the order specified.
	Inhibit Gate	The event above this gate transpires if the event listed within the Inhibit gate is satisfied and the event below the gate takes place. (This is a special type of AND gate.)

Table 10.2   Commonly used events in fault tree analysis

Symbol	Name	Description
	Basic Event	The lowest level of failure possible.
	House Event	A house event is a type of event employed for specific uses, such as representing an event that is expected to occur, or to disable parts of the fault tree to make them non-functional. In general, these events can be set to occur or not occur; that is, they have a fixed probability of 0 or 1.
	Undeveloped Event	The event has not been defined.

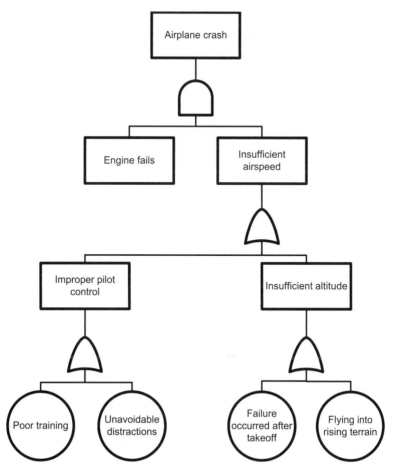

Figure 10.1 Example of Fault Tree

There are only two gates used in this simple FTA—an AND gate (top), and three OR gates. If the probabilities of failure of each component are known, a quantitative analysis can be performed.

3. *Gap analysis*

Gap analysis is a term used to describe a broad range of techniques to examine and describe the difference between current conditions and desired conditions. The purpose of the gap analysis activity will determine the technique to be used. Generally, the steps to performing a gap analysis include the following:

- Define the scope of the gap analysis.
- Review all information about the issue under study.
- Determine the criteria, standards, regulations, performance measures, or other factors that represent the desired conditions.

- Possess a thorough understanding of current conditions.
- Determine the appropriate instrument upon which to record the differences.
- Perform the analysis.
- Record and document the results.
- Analyze the results.
- Take the appropriate action on the information gained as a result of the analysis.

Sometimes the determination of the desired conditions is rather straightforward. For example, an organization wishing to determine its readiness for an ISO 9000 quality audit has multiple resources from which it can obtain an off-the-shelf gap analysis tool. The tool may be a series of compliance-based questions to which the responses are simple "yes" or "no" answers.

In other instances, such as when performing a gap analysis against best-in-class performance, the determination of objective performance measures can be considerably more complex, and a process must be developed to accomplish that task. That process may involve cross-functional teams using quality-based tools such as brainstorming, affinity diagramming, and others. This leads to the development of a set of criteria that represents the "desired condition".

As with many other techniques including auditing, planning a research study, or planning a project, the preliminary work for performing a gap analysis is often the most time-consuming and challenging step in the process. But a well-planned gap analysis will make the downstream tasks so much more manageable, and the results more reliable, that it's worth the extra effort.

We'll use the FAA's draft SMS Audit/Gap Analysis Tool as an example of a useful gap analysis tool. Appendix 1 of AC 120-92 *Introduction to Safety Management Systems for Air Operators* provides "a uniform standard for SMS development by aviation service providers". By extension, the FAA will be able to use this standard to determine how fully an organization's SMS comports with the FAA's SMS standard. To facilitate this, an objective statement for each of the major sub clauses of the standard has been written and incorporated into the tool. Figure 10.2 depicts a small portion of the gap analysis tool.

So in this example, the FAA's draft tool is based directly on the standard they have written. The tool includes the objective based on the standard in Appendix 1 of the AC, the documentation source used to determine conformity, and an assessment of conformity. By completing this tool an assessment can be made on how fully the aviation service provider meets the requirements of the standard, and a plan can be developed for the remediation of any shortcomings.

(Note: A primary reference for many of the tools described below is the Federal Aviation Administration Air Traffic Organization Safety Management System Manual, Draft, Version 2.0, dated March 2006.)

4. *Accident/Incident Analysis*

The purpose of an Accident/Incident Analysis is to use existing risk data to prevent future accidents from occurring. There are many ways that this analysis can be

DRAFT

SMS Standard AC 120-92 Objective	Detailed Audit/Gap Analysis Tool	Documentation Source	Assessment
4.9 Documentation and Records			
Has the organization clearly defined and documented safety policies, objectives, procedures, and a documented maintenance process that may be in paper or electronic format?			
5. Safety Risk Management			
Does the organization understand the critical characteristics of its systems and operational environment and apply this knowledge to the identification of hazards, risk decision making, and the design of risk controls?			
5.1 System and Task Analysis			
Has the organization analyzed its systems, operations and operational environment to gain an understanding of critical design and performance factors, processes, and activities to identify hazards?			
5.2 Identify Hazards			
Has the organization identified and documented hazards that are likely to cause death, serious physical harm or damage to equipment or property in sufficient detail to determine associated risk and acceptability?			
5.3 Analyze Safety Risk			
Has the organization determined and analyzed the severity and likelihood of potential events associated with identified hazards and identified factors associated with unacceptable levels of severity or likelihood?			
5.4 Assess Safety Risk			
Has the organization assessed each identified hazard and defined acceptance procedures and levels of management that can make safety risk acceptance decisions?			
5.5 Control Safety Risk			
Has the organization designed and implemented a risk control for each identified hazard with unacceptable risk to reduce the ... or damage to			

Figure 10.2   Example gap analysis tool

accomplished, but the objective is always to better understand the current trends and causal factors associated with accidents. The factors associated with accidents and incidents are recorded in a database, and then examined for trends and patterns, such as distribution among subgroups, locations, time of day, activities occurring in conjunction with the accidents, and others. This data can be a rich source of information that should be mined on an annual or semi-annual basis.

5. Cause and Effect Tool ✗

PG 64

The Cause and Effect tool was discussed in Chapter 3.

6. Change Analysis ✗

The purpose of Change Analysis is to look systematically at possible risks in situations where change is occurring. This tool examines the differences from normal operations configuration, or activities that have occurred due to planned or incremental changes. It is used for proactive hazard and risk assessment in changing situations and during accident investigations to understand changes that have occurred in the system.

7. Hazard and Operability Tool

The Hazard and Operability Tool (HAZOP) is a brainstorming technique for identifying hazards and operability problems at the completion of process design or for planned modifications. An experienced, interdisciplinary team normally conducts a HAZOP in order to identify all possible deviations from an intended design as well as the consequences of the deviations. HAZOP is particularly useful for new operations where other methods that rely on experienced operational personnel are less effective. HAZOP is regarded as the most highly structured of the hazard identification methods. The team uses probing questions based on a series of standard guidewords to generate the list of possible deviations. The deviations are determined by combining the guideword with a variable parameter or process term; that is:

$$\text{Guideword + Parameter = Deviation}$$

8. *Human Error Analysis*

The purpose of a Human Error Analysis (HEA) is to identify, analyze, and mitigate safety hazards associated with human error. Everyone commits errors. HEA seeks to identify hazards related to human error during the development of complex systems. Various tools can be used by human factors practitioners to understand how human decisions impact the system if an error is made. Controls can then be determined for these hazards.

9. *Interface Analysis*

The purpose of an Interface Analysis is to uncover potentially hazardous interfaces among seemingly unrelated activities. An Interface Analysis examines potential energy exchanges between two activities to identify potential hazards. This tool is useful when a new activity is being introduced and there is a chance that an unfavorable interaction could occur as a consequence.

10. *Job Safety Analysis*

The purpose of a Job Safety Analysis (JSA) is to identify, analyze, and document the steps involved in performing a specific job, to identify potential hazards associated with the job, and to identify controls for the hazards identified. This task begins by breaking jobs down into individual steps. Hazards can be identified using tools such as the What-If Analysis and the Scenario Analysis.

11. *Job Task Analysis*

A Job Task Analysis (JTA) identifies, analyzes, and documents human tasks within a system, with the goal identifying hazards and risk factors requiring intervention. A JTA analyzes each task in terms of physical and mental demands of the human in the system. The JTA identifies what people do on the job, and is informed by flow charts and diagrams, system descriptions, and brainstorming on the part of those doing the job.

12. *Management Oversight and Risk Tree*

Management Oversight and Risk Tree (MORT) is a comprehensive and detailed method for the analysis or investigation of accidents and events. It uses a fault tree diagram (and FTA symbology) where safety program elements are arranged in a logical, orderly manner, beginning with the top event which is an accident or system failure. It is then progressively broken down using the fault tree method. For example, if a failure occurs and it is categorized as a management failure (as opposed to the failure of a control), it might then be determined to be a failure of a management policy, then a risk assessment method, then a hazard analysis, and so on. The analyst works through this predefined tree in sequence until the diagram is fully developed. A full MORT diagram may contain more than 10,000 blocks; less involved MORT analyses can consist of fewer blocks. Because a MORT is so labor-intensive, its primary disadvantage is that it is time-consuming and costly to complete; therefore, it is typically used on the most risk-critical projects. MORT is primarily reactive in nature, but can be used to proactively consider hazards.

13. *Preliminary Hazard Analysis*

The purpose of a Preliminary Hazard Analysis (PHA) is to provide a listing of possible hazards that may be present in a system. As its name implies, PHA provides a *preliminary* listing of hazards and, as such, is usually broad but not particularly deep. PHA is useful in ensuring that all hazards are considered before becoming overly focused on any particular hazard. Hazards are then ranked according to their severity, and controls for the hazards are determined.

Hazards are identified by examining existing documentation on the system (such as flowcharts), reviewing previous hazard analyses, considering interactions between system components, brainstorming with others, involving subject matter experts, considering human machine interfaces, performing What-If analyses, and so on. A risk matrix can be used to assess the risk.

14. *Scenario Analysis*

The purpose of Scenario Analysis is to identify hazards by visualizing scenarios, or possible outcomes, that could happen in an operation. Scenario Analysis provides a structured means of viewing the flow of events in an operation and considering the scenarios that lead to risk.

15. *What-If Analysis*

A What-If analysis is a brainstorming approach that uses loosely structured questions to identify hazards. The technique is typically used by a team of experts with diverse backgrounds to generate a comprehensive review of hazards. It is a particularly effective tool to use following a Preliminary Hazard Analysis to focus on the hazards that need additional investigation. A What-If analysis is an extremely effective and powerful tool, partly because it is so simple to perform.

The What-If analysis can be used to further explore the hazards in an operation by developing short scenarios that reflect the worst credible outcome from the compound effects of multiple hazards in the operation.

Predictive safety risk management: through modeling

Many of the tools and methods presented in this book have focused on decomposing systems to better understand the component parts. The goal of modeling is to represent the system under consideration as a whole since, as the great philosopher Aristotle once said, "the whole is more than the sum of its parts". How to perform complex, engineering modeling is far beyond the scope of this book and, in many cases, would require expertise in mathematics, statistics, computer science, systems engineering, and other fields. While these tools have a place in safety science, it is certainly not the intent of the authors to suggest that predictive safety management cannot be performed without such sophisticated methods! In fact, there are numerous methods that can be employed by SMS practitioners, depending on the size and complexity of their organizations.

This section will present the most cursory introduction of an increasingly popular tool—probabilistic risk assessment (PRA).

16 . *Probabilistic Risk Assessment*

There are two kinds of models used in problem solving and prediction in the engineering world—deterministic and probabilistic. Many problems cannot be solved using deterministic methods due to variability and uncertainty in the dimensions of the problem; PRA is specifically designed to cope with these uncertainties. PRA is a systematic methodology to assess risks associated with a complex engineered technology entity (for example, airplanes, spacecraft, or nuclear powerplants) for the purpose of improving its safety and performance. PRA generally deals with events that have low probabilities of occurring and high consequences if they do occur. PRA helps managers decide how to allocate resources to improve safety; to wit, it is a decision support tool. These factors make PRA a useful tool for risk assessment in our highly complex transportation systems.

PRA answers three basic questions: what can go wrong? How frequently does it happen? What are the consequences?

Also known as quantitative risk analysis (QRA) or probability safety analysis (PSA), PRA has become widely used in the chemical, transport, energy, aerospace, military, and financial management fields. The nuclear industry, in particular, embraced the concept of PRA many years ago and, along with other industries including petrochemical and defense, developed it into a valued and respected method of safety assessment. In fact, PRA has excelled in uncovering safety flaws in the nuclear sector that deterministic and statistical methods have overlooked.

The first full scale application of PRA was undertaken in the nuclear sector. This resulted in the publication of the *Reactor Safety Study*, WASH-1400, published by the U.S. Nuclear Regulatory Commission in 1975. While some of the methodologies in this initial report were later deemed to be flawed, the underlying principles of probabilistic analysis were gaining acceptance.

The nuclear industry has made a very strong commitment to PRA. The nuclear industry, in its *Procedures Guide*, describes three levels of PRA analyses: 1.) systems analysis—focuses on potential release of hazardous substances and/or energy from a facility; 2.) containment analysis—evaluates pathways into the biosphere, and examines parameters relative to transporting the substance into the biosphere; and 3.) consequence analysis—pathways—such as dispersion through the atmosphere and water, and the food chain—by which the hazardous substance can reach man are investigated.

NASA is a notable proponent of PRA. The agency began developing PRA tools in the 1960s, but the approach fell out of favor and was abandoned until the Challenger accident in 1986. The reason the approach was discontinued until Challenger is a subject of some debate, but it is clear that the political consequences of publishing failure probabilities that were "too high" might threaten the space program. After the Challenger accident, Recommendation Number 6 of the Slay Committee's report stated, in part, that PRA approaches be applied to the Shuttle risk management program at the earliest possible date (NASA, 2002, p. 2). This is certainly a compelling endorsement of the value of such methods.[1]

The first step in a PRA study is to identify the undesired top event and, using event trees (ETs), map out all the hazards that could lead to that event. For the initiating event (IE), or trigger event, and all subsequent events, fault trees (FTs) are normally used. The basic events in the FTs are assigned probabilities, and these probabilities are propagated up the tree to establish the probability of the undesired top event.

NASA's approach to a scenario-based PRA process is as follows (NASA, 2002, pp. 10–13):

- Objectives Definition—The objectives of the risk assessment are defined.
- Systems Familiarization—Familiarization with the system is important, including all design and operational information.
- Identification of IEs—These events perturb the system from its present state. FMEAs are one tool used to identify IEs that lead to end states.
- Scenario Modeling—Using inductive logic and probabilistic tools, ETs are used to model accident scenarios.
- Failure Modeling—Each failure is modeled with deductive logic and probabilistic tools called FTs. FTs are composed of three parts: the top part is the event defined in the accident scenario; the middle part is the intermediate events or failures causing the top event; the basic events are the failures that

---

1   Following the Challenger accident in 1986, a report entitled, *"Post-Challenger Evaluation of Space Shuttle Risk Assessment and Management,"* was produced by the Committee on Shuttle Criticality Review and Hazard Analysis Audit, National Research Council. The Committee, chaired by Retired General Alton Slay, issued 11 recommendations, including using PRA, establishing an agency-wide Systems Safety Engineering function, and performing FMEAs on software (and including human factors considerations in the FMEAs).

cause the top event to occur. The basic events and the intermediate failures are linked through logic gates, such as AND and OR gates.

- Data Collection, Analysis, and Development—Various types of data are collected and utilized through the process.
- Quantification and Integration—FTs are linked and quantified, and scenarios are grouped. End states are then grouped.
- Uncertainty Analysis—Monte Carlo simulations are often used for uncertainty analysis.
- Sensitivity Analysis—Sensitivity analyses help determine which analysis inputs cause the greatest change in risk results.
- Importance Ranking—The lead contributors to risk in accident scenarios are determined and ranked.

Developing these scenarios is not a trivial undertaking, and locating the input data for the model can often be the most difficult part of the process. Once developed, these scenarios serve to map complex reality into a set of logical relationships that can be analyzed by probabilistic software tools.

As explained in NASA's PRA guide (NASA, 2002, p. 28):

A scenario contains an IE and (usually) one or more pivotal events leading to an end state... As modeled in most PRAs, an IE is a perturbation that requires some kind of response from operators or pilots or one or more systems. The pivotal events include successes or failures of these responses, or possibly the occurrence or non-occurrence of external conditions or key phenomena. The end states are formulated according to the decisions being supported by the analysis. Scenarios are classified into end states according to the kind and severity of consequences, ranging from completely successful outcomes to losses of various kinds, such as:

- loss of life or injury/illness to personnel;
- damage to, or loss of, equipment or property (including software);
- unexpected or collateral damage as a result of tests;
- failure of mission;
- loss of system availability; and
- damage to the environment.

It is well-established that the largest contribution to the probability of system failure in complex systems is from human error. A risk assessment method of any value in aviation must consider human interactions and errors on system reliability. Human Reliability Analysis (HRA) addresses an important aspect of PRA; that of modeling human behavior to better understand human interactions with the rest of the system. HRA attempts to assess failure probabilities through an error classification scheme. A well-known taxonomy of performance is based on the work of Rasmussen, et. al. (1981), who describes performance as skill-based, rule-based, or knowledge-based. Reason (1990) has built on Rasmussen's work, and describes several failure modes for each of these performance levels, such as interference errors and omission for skill-based performance, information overload and redundancy for rule-based performance, and overconfidence and problems with complexity for knowledge-based performance. He also introduces an error-modeling system that distinguishes between monitoring failures and problem-solving failures.

A popular method used for human performance reliability prediction is the ✳Technique for Human Error Rate Prediction (THERP). THERP grew out of a need to quantify probabilities of human error in a U.S. bomb-assembly plant. Based on the use of event trees, THERP is a technique for predicting human error probabilities and system degradation based on human errors. In a THERP, the paths of human action that can lead to failure are determined, and are modeled into an event tree. The nodes of the event tree correspond to human action, and the branches correspond to operator success or failure in executing that action. Probabilities are assigned to these actions, and performance-shaping factors are used to make judgments about particular situations. THERP commonly involves five steps:

1. Define the system or process.
2. Identify and enumerate all human operations performed and their relationships to the system.
3. Predict error rates for each human operation.
4. Determine the effect of human errors on the system.
5. Make changes that will reduce the system failure rate.

PRA has been used in numerous safety applications where safety is a function of interactions between multiple factors—for example, human operators, technical systems, and procedure—all of which are highly distributed. Safety is about ensuring that all of these elements function properly but, importantly, it's also about understanding the interactions among these factors and their effects on safety performance. As Charles Perrow noted in his 1984 book, *Normal Accidents*, interactive failures, or hidden flaws, occur when components in complex systems interact in unexpected ways (Perrow, 1984, pp. 75–84). Perhaps the greatest gains we'll make in aviation safety in the years ahead will be in employing better methods for addressing these interactions. PRA can help us understand and cope with these interactions.

17. *Monte Carlo*

Perhaps the most widely used probabilistic method, Monte Carlo methods are popular in many disciplines of science and in many industries. Monte Carlo Analysis (MCA) uses computer simulation to combine multiple probability distributions in a risk equation.

There are many appealing characteristics of an MCA as opposed to point estimate methods. For example, MCA provides more information than a deterministic point estimate calculation. While a point estimate provides the central tendency of exposure of risk, it does not indicate the uncertainty of the estimate, which is useful for decision-makers. The probability distributions created by MCA provide the location of any particular risk estimate. This allows us to select a level of exposure or risk that corresponds to the desired level of protection.

MCA can be performed on Microsoft® Excel using commercial add-on software such as Oracle's® Crystal Ball or Palisade's® @Risk. Either of these software programs allows variables to be treated as probability distributions and permits random distribution of events over specified time intervals.

In an MCA, the analysis software selects a value at random from the probability density function for each exposure variable and calculates the corresponding risk, and the inputs and the resulting estimate of risk is saved; this is called an *iteration*. This process is repeated many times, perhaps 1,000 to 10,000 times; the set of iterations is a *simulation*. Each iteration is stored and the entire simulation is represented as frequency distributions, tables, and other reports.

Depending on the objective of the risk analysis, risk modeling typically provides the following outputs:

- *Estimates of risk* at predetermined levels of confidence.
- A *risk profile* that ranks risk events in order of decreasing risk values.
- An *exposure profile* indicates the range of consequential costs for risk events.

MCA is mathematical in nature, and proponents of the method argue that it injects much needed science into risk assessment. Of course, like any method presented here or elsewhere, it should only be used when its use is justified. An assessment should be made as to the areas of aviation risk assessment where probabilistic methods, including MCA, will be most useful to decision-makers.

A discussion of MCA was given in Chapter 5 when introducing risk assessment. An exemplar aviation safety study is presented in the following section.

A hypothetical demonstration   Accident investigations and literature have taught us that there are usually prior alerts or signals that, if recognized, could have averted the undesired event from occurring. These alerts or signals are called leading indicators because they precede the undesired event and, since these signals can be monitored and identified in advance, they have value in predicting the occurrence of that event.

While *lagging indicators* serve as measures of whether the organization has achieved its goals, leading indicators act as predictors of an organization's ability to meet its future goals. Leading indicators are an important part of successful SMS programs, and are developed from safety objectives established by the organization. They are monitored routinely, and are used to influence short- and long-term strategy.

Once the leading indicators are determined, it is important that ongoing assessment of the indicators is accomplished to ensure that the indicators correlate well with safety performance. If the indicator is not a good measure of safety performance, better data may be needed, or the indicator may need to be modified or eliminated. Correlation analysis using common statistical tests, such as Pearson Product Moment Correlation Coefficient, the Spearman Rank-Difference Correlation Coefficient, and t-test, should reveal the strength of the correlation between the indicator and safety performance.

In our simple hypothetical example of the use of MCA, let us assume that we've determined that there are several valid leading indicators of safety performance in a flight training organization. The purpose of this simulation is to gain a better understanding of the impact of changing performance associated with various indicators of safety performance, and to observe how simulation can help us better understand the environment in which we are operating.

Our fictitious flight training organization has been managing safety and collecting data for years, and is now beginning to implement an SMS program. Through data analysis and expert judgment, the managers have determined that there are six primary leading indicators of safety performance; specifically, success on stage checks, performance on safety audits, level of safety culture, budget for safety-related activities, retention rate of flight instructors, and composite experience level of instructional staff. (It should be noted that some of these indicators may well serve as lagging indicators in other areas of study. For example, "success on stage checks" could be thought of as a lagging indicator in the assessment of quality of flight instruction; that is, it is an after-the-fact measure of that quality.) For some of the indicators, historical data can be used to select the appropriate probability distribution for the model from a gallery of distributions that include: normal, triangular, uniform, lognormal, gamma, Weibull, logistic, exponential, binomial, Poisson, beta, and many others. Crystal Ball examines the data and determines a mathematical fit based on several standard goodness-of-fit tests, and selects the best distribution as a result. For example, using data collected on "success on stage checks", Crystal Ball's Fit Distribution function was used to select a beta distribution with minimum of 0, a maximum of 100, an alpha of 13, and a beta value of 4. This process was repeated on other indicators where historical data were available; where data were not available, expert judgment was used.

Expert judgment was also used to establish importance weightings for these factors. For our organization, "experience of instructional staff" was weighted most important at .25, and "performance on safety audits" and "measurement of safety culture" were lowest at .10 each. Table 10.3 lists our indicators, importance factors (weightings), and distribution shape.

A cursory examination of the indicators suggests that they are not entirely independent factors; that is, the value of one may have influence on the value of one or more of the other indicators. For example, "success on stage checks" may be related to "composite experience level of instructional staff"; that is, the more experience our instructors have the higher success rate their students have on stage

Table 10.3 **Indicators, importance factors, and distribution shape for Monte Carlo example**

Variable	Leading Indicators	Importance Factors	Distribution Shape
A	Success on stage checks	.20	Beta
B	Performance on safety audits	.10	Triangular
C	Measurement of safety culture	.10	Lognormal
D	Budget for safety related activities	.15	Uniform
E	Retention rate of flight instructors	.20	Beta
F	Composite experience level of instructional staff	.25	BetaPERT

checks. And clearly the "retention rate of flight instructors" is fairly strongly related to "composite experience level of instructional staff"; the longer we retain our instructors the more experience they gain.

The model we're building must take into account these relationships and their relative strengths. Therefore, we will next build a matrix that provides our estimates of the correlations among these leading indicators expressed as correlation coefficients (see Table 10.4).

The general equation for solving this problem is as follows:

$$[v_1...v_6] = [v_1...v_6]\begin{pmatrix} \rho_{11} & & \rho_{16} \\ & & \\ \rho_{61} & & \rho_{66} \end{pmatrix} + [w_1...w_6]$$

where   v = our variables or leading indicators,
             ρ = correlation coefficient,
             w = random variables,
and where $\rho ii = 0$,
             $\rho ij = \rho ji$.

With this model input into Microsoft Excel, the Monte Carlo analysis was deployed using Crystal Ball. Five thousand trials were run in the simulation. Crystal Ball produces a forecast chart for each forecast cell in the model; the information can be displayed both graphically and numerically. We will not present all of the charts and graphs produced by this simulation, but rather we'll focus on one leading indicator—"success on stage checks" and the aggregate of these indicators.

Figure 10.3 depicts a frequency distribution for "success on stage checks". This distribution assumed an approximate shape of the beta distribution used in the assumption.

Figure 10.4 depicts the frequency distribution for the aggregate of the six indicators. (Note that out of 5,000 trials (upper left hand corner of the figure), 4,983 are displayed, indicating that 17 fell outside the display range of the chart.)

Table 10.4   Correlation coefficients of leading indicators

	A	B	C	D	E	F
A	0.00	0.15	0.10	0.20	0.25	0.30
B	0.15	0.00	0.30	0.30	0.15	0.02
C	0.10	0.30	0.00	0.25	0.15	0.10
D	0.20	0.30	0.25	0.00	0.25	0.20
E	0.25	0.15	0.15	0.25	0.00	0.50
F	0.30	0.02	0.10	0.20	0.50	0.00

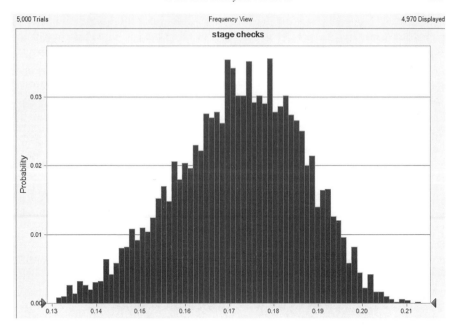

Figure 10.3 Frequency distribution for 'success on stage checks' (screenshot)

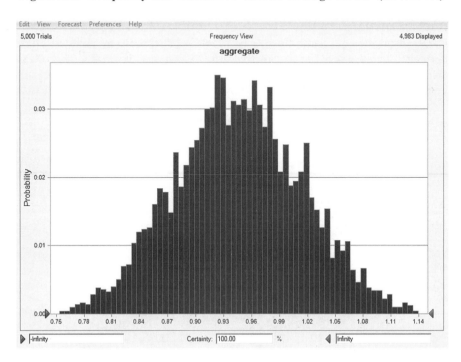

Figure 10.4 Frequency distributions of the aggregate of the indicators (screenshot)

Figure 10.5 depicts an overlay chart for the six leadings indicators. This chart is useful for displaying the relative characteristics of multiple variables on one chart. Notice the "success on stage checks" distribution in the rear center of the figure.

Sometimes it is useful to understand how much certain assumptions influence the results. A sensitivity chart depicts each leading indicator's contribution to the variance. In Figure 10.6, we see that "success on stage checks" contributes only 11.2 percent to the variation we observe. This figure tells us that "retention rate of flight instructors", "composite experience level of instructional staff", and "performance on safety audits" account for 83 percent of the variation.

This simplistic, hypothetical example demonstrates how a Monte Carlo tool can be used to help an organization understand the behavior of its safety system based on changing leading indicator values. Obviously, for this model to be truly useful and practical it would need further development and customization to a particular organization. The model does, however, show how managers might prioritize and allocate resources to improve its overall performance by addressing areas that have greater influence and are not performing as well. The managers in our hypothetical organization desire a balanced, continuously improving score on each of the indicators and its overall performance, while achieving maximum return on investment in its safety program. Monte Carlo simulation is one tool in the arsenal of the managers to help achieve those goals.

10. Data Mining

Data mining (DM) has become an increasingly popular analytical method in numerous industries, including science, finance, homeland security, business and marketing, transportation, and nearly every other industry. Those applying DM methods seek to make greater use of existing databases to learn more about the problem or issue

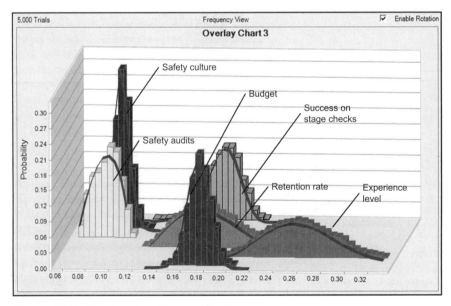

Figure 10.5 Overlay chart (screenshot)

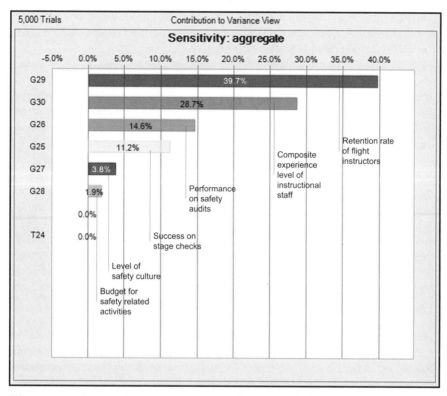

Figure 10.6   Sensitivity chart for aggregate (screenshot)

at hand than more traditional methods have afforded. Given the vast data collection efforts that are occurring in aviation safety, DM has the potential to unlock secrets hidden in that data.

This chapter will explore the essential information about DM, including methods, steps, and crucial concepts. Finally, an exemplar DM modeling project is presented.

Applying these methods to aviation safety is not a new concept. For example, an exploratory study on a FOQA database at a major air carrier took place in 2005 (GAIN, 2005). The cooperative study involved the air carrier, the FAA, the Global Aviation Information Network and a DM software provider, and was intended to provide guidance on tools that may be useful in enhancing the current analysis of airline digital flight data. This study focused on principal components analysis, correlation of different events, conditional (Trellis) graphics, tree-based models, and neural networks. In part, the DM study found that certain methods showed promise in improving efficiency by automating some of the query and output process. Principal components analysis and clustering methods were deemed helpful for data reduction and characterization of correlation structures. Tree-based models provided a modeling structure for understanding the relationship between flight events and flight parameters, and for assessing the importance of variables. Neural network models were deemed less useful due to their inability to distinguish between landing approaches that resulted in a successful landing from those that resulted in a go-around. The study also noted an additional disadvantage that neural networks are more difficult to interpret than tree-based models.

Another similar study funded by the FAA involved the analysis of FOQA data on the airline's Boeing 777 and 747 fleets. The objective of this study was to determine whether DM techniques can help improve airline or system safety by identifying risks, and assess the effectiveness of operational changes. Three learning algorithms, that is, decision trees, clustering and association rules, were applied to the data. In general, the DM tools identified many interesting patterns and associations beneath the surface that had not been identified by the air carrier's flight data monitoring program (GAIN, 2004).

Helicopter health and usage management systems also generate large amounts of data that are used mainly for diagnostic purposes to detect helicopter faults. An initiative by the Ministry of Defense in the United Kingdom has been to apply tools that improved analysis capability, increase levels of automation, and provide enhanced use of resources. The study evaluated several supervised and unsupervised methods, and also explored fusing the results of unsupervised techniques with the judgments of other mathematical and artificial intelligence tools, such as logic, fuzzy logic, and Bayesian networks (Knight, Cook, and Azzam, 2005, pp. 507–524).

What is Data Mining?   Data mining is an analytic process designed to explore large amounts of data in search of consistent patterns and/or systematic relationships between variables (StatSoft, 2003). It is used for such broad areas as accurately evaluating insurance risk, predicting customer demand for goods and services, predicting the prices of stocks and commodities, monitoring expensive and critical equipment, conducting yield analysis and quality control, and predicting credit risk.

Traditional statistical techniques are not as useful on very large databases because all mean comparisons are significant and standard measures of variability are extremely small. Due in part to this limitation, DM techniques increased in popularity in the mid to late 1990s. DM tools are based on standard statistical techniques and artificial intelligence analysis techniques, and are applied to large databases for the purpose of finding otherwise undiscovered data attributes, trends and patterns. There are numerous methods of DM; the following is only the most cursory overview of several of the more popular methods.

Regression modeling normally begins with a hypothesis which is tested by this common statistical technique. Linear regression (commonly used for prediction) and logistic regression (used for estimating probabilities of events) are two examples of regression modeling.

Visualization is an important concept in DM. Through the study of multidimensional graphs the analyst is able to detect trends, patterns, or relationships.

Cluster analysis is an exploratory data analysis tool that consists of several different algorithms and methods for grouping objects of similar kind into respective categories. The goal of cluster analysis is to sort different objects into groups in a way that the degree of association between two objects is maximal if they belong to the same group and minimal if they do not. Cluster analysis can be used to discover structures in data without explaining why they exist.

Decision trees are very popular classification models. They are called decision trees because the resulting model is presented in the form of a tree structure. The visual presentation makes the decision tree model very easy to understand. Decision tree methods include Classification and Regression Trees (C&RT) and Chi-squared Automatic Interaction Detection (CHAID).

Neural networks are analytic techniques that are intended to simulate cognitive functions. These techniques learn with each iteration through the data, and are capable of predicting new observations (on specific variables) from other observations (on the same or other variables).

Steps in DM   There are three basic stages to most DM projects, as depicted in Figure 10.7: initial exploration; model building and validation; and deployment. Initial exploration refers to the preparation of the data, which may include cleaning of the data, (limited) data transformations, selecting subsets of records, and performing feature selection operations. Model building and validation involves evaluating various models for predictive performance and choosing the most appropriate one for the project. Deployment refers to the application of the chosen model or models to generate predictions or estimates of the outcome.

Crucial concepts in DM   Of course, not all projects are the same and few involve the full range of DM tools and methods, but some familiarity with the crucial concepts in DM is important. These concepts are summarized below (StatSoft, 2003; Wang, 2003).

Data preparation, cleaning, and transformation   Many times this is the most time-consuming aspect of the project, and one that is often given little attention. Data that is collected via an automatic process, which probably includes most input data in DM projects, frequently contains data that contain out of range values, impossible data combinations, and other irregularities. Various methods are employed to clean the data to make it usable, or to eliminate the data from the analysis.

Feature selection   A feature selection technique enables the analyst to include the best variables for the project when the data set includes more variables than can be reasonably used.

Feature extraction   Feature extraction techniques attempt to aggregate the predictors in some way in order to extract the common information contained in them that is most useful for model building. Typical methods include Factor Analysis and

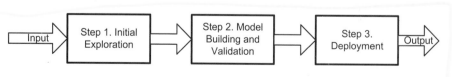

Figure 10.7 Steps in Data Mining

Principal Components Analysis, Multidimensional Scaling, Partial Least Squares methods, and others.

Predictive DM This type of DM project is intended to develop statistical or neural network models that can be used to predict objects of interest.

Sampling, training, and testing (hold-out) samples In most DM projects, only a randomly chosen subset of the data is used. This enables the analyst to evaluate multiple methods using different samples, and then test these methods to gain insight into the predictive capability of the results.

Over-sampling particular strata to over-represent rare events (stratified sampling) Sometimes it is necessary to employ stratified sampling to systematically over-sample rare events of interest. This precludes predictions of a no response for all cases if simple random sampling were used when, in fact, these (rare) events are present.

Machine learning Machine learning refers to the application of generic model-fitting or classification algorithms for predictive DM, and reminds us that the emphasis in DM is *accuracy* of prediction rather than having a clear and interpretable understanding of the prediction.

Deployment Deployment is the application of a trained model so that predictions can be obtained for new data.

An Exemplar Case Study[2]

The exemplar case study is an example of how data mining can be used in an SMS program. This example makes use of a particularly rich source of objective data—that found in a FOQA program.

Fuel is a major expense for air carriers and must be managed wisely. This case study involves a fuel consumption analysis using DM methods applied to FOQA data. This is important topic in safety analysis as well, including Extended-range Twin-engine Operational Performance Standards (ETOPS) flights where fuel consumption can be critical. Of course, fuel consumption should be considered just one of a plethora of studies that can be performed using FOQA data, and just one of many more that can be performed using other sources (or combinations of sources) of data.

The purpose of this study was to develop parsimonious models for fuel consumption using DM methods applied to FOQA-derived data, with the objective of being able to identify outliers (specific flights) with respect to fuel consumption. A range of DM methods and techniques was used to ascertain the optimum method(s).

---

2   The following exemplar case study was published in the *Journal of Air Transportation* in 2007 (see Stolzer, A., Halford, C., "Data mining methods applied to Flight Operations Quality Assurance (FOQA) data: A comparison to standard statistical methods." *Journal of Air Transportation* 12(1), 2007). Portions of that article are reprinted here with the permission of the publisher.

One significant advantage DM methods have over traditional statistical methods is that DM methods are generally robust to non-linear data, complex relationships among the variables, and non-normal distributions. With traditional methods, the analyst would need to spend a significant amount of time in examining, pre-processing, and (potentially) transforming the data to ensure that the violations of the particular statistical tests are not present in the processed data. In this case study, the examination of the data set was limited to ensuring that the data was within allowable ranges; no transformations were accomplished even though exploration indicated that some of the data were irregular.

The data used for the study were provided by a major air carrier, and consisted of nearly 2,000 routine passenger-carrying flights on Boeing 757 aircraft. The data set includes dozens of parameters, some of which are engine-independent (for example, airspeed, altitude, temperature) and some of which are engine-dependent (n1, n2, oil pressure); thus, we decided to create a separate model for each engine.

STATISTICA, a suite of analytic software products produced by StatSoft® (2003), was employed to run the analysis for this case study. *STATISTICA* provides a comprehensive array of data analysis, data management, data visualization, and DM procedures. Its techniques include a wide selection of predictive modeling, clustering, classification, and exploratory techniques in a single software platform. *STATISTICA* includes an extensive array of analytic, graphical, and data management functions, as well as DM and machine learning algorithms, including: support vector machines, EM (Expectation Maximization) and k-Means clustering, CART, generalized additive models, independent component analysis, stochastic gradient boosted trees, ensembles of neural networks, automatic feature selection, MARSplines (Multivariate Adaptive Regression Splines), CHAID trees, nearest neighbor methods, association rules, random forests, and others (StatSoft, 2003).

The project was accomplished using three analytical techniques: Classification and Regression Trees; Advanced Comprehension Regression Models; and Intelligent Problem Solver.

Standard recursive partitioning (that is, tree) methods called *Classification and Regression Tree Models (C&RT)* were performed first. *STATISTICA* contains numerous algorithms for predicting continuous or categorical variables from a set of continuous predictors and/or categorical factor effects. Each child node in the tree diagram represents a bivariate split on one of the predictors. Terminal nodes indicate actual predicted values for sets of cases. The dendrograms created in this process are quite easy to review and interpret to understand the sets of if/then statements created by the model.

The C&RT method was run using V-fold cross-validation (a technique where repeated (v) random samples are drawn from the data for the analysis). The variables contained in the tree diagram for the Engine 1 model included CAS, GWeight, ENG1n1, ENG1egt, and ALT. A goodness of fit test performed on this model yields the results as depicted in Table 10.5.

The C&RT analysis was also performed on the ENG2ff model. The tree diagram for ENG2ff included CAS, GWeight, ENG2n1, and ENG2n2. A goodness of fit test performed on this model yields the results as depicted in Table 10.6.

Table 10.5   Summary of goodness of fit—engine 1 fuel flow

Factor	Predicted
Mean Square Error	13449.18
Mean Absolute Error	89.06
Mean Relative Squared Error	0.00
Mean Relative Absolute Error	0.03
Correlation Coefficient	0.92

Table 10.6   Summary of goodness of fit—engine 2 fuel flow

Factor	Predicted
Mean Square Error	13674.90
Mean Absolute Error	89.25
Mean Relative Squared Error	0.00
Mean Relative Absolute Error	0.03
Correlation Coefficient	0.91

An Advanced Comprehensive Regression Models (ACRM) project was performed next. This STATISTICA tool has several pre-arranged nodes for fitting linear, nonlinear, regression-tree, CHAID and Exhaustive CHAID, and different neural network architectures to a continuous dependent variable, and for automatically generating deployment information.

The next method used was *STATISTICA's* ACRM project. This model fits several DM methods to a continuous dependent variable, and automatically generates deployment information. Figure 10.8 depicts the *STATISTICA* workspace as it is configured to run this project.

Table 10.7 contains the summary output from goodness of fit tests on the various methods explored by the ACRM tool on ENG1ff.

Both the Generalized Linear Model (GLM) and the Multilayer Perceptron (MLP) had very high correlation coefficients exceeding 0.995 and relatively low error measures. Figure 10.9 depicts a plot of the predicted variable versus the observed, and Figure 10.10 depicts a plot of the residuals versus the observed variable for the GLM for ENG1ff.

Figure 10.11 depicts a plot of the predicted variable versus the observed variable, and Figure 10.12 depicts a plot of the residuals versus the observed for the MLP.

Table 10.8 contains the summary output from goodness of fit tests on the various methods explored by the ACRM tool on the ENG2ff model. As with the ENG1ff model it can be concluded that the GLM and the MLP models provided the best predictive capability for ENG2ff of the models tested.

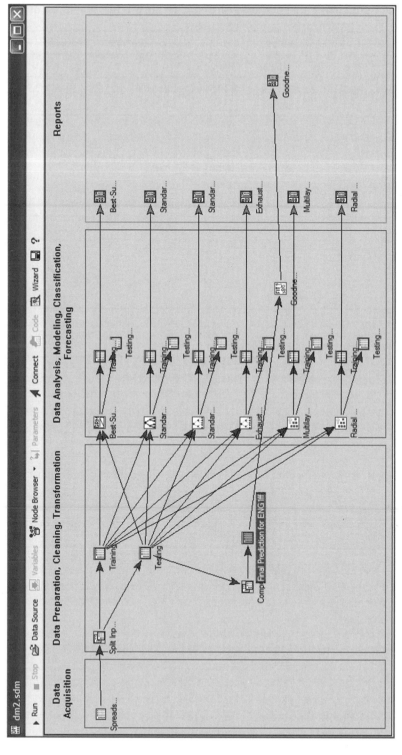

Figure 10.8 STATISTICA workspace for advanced comprehensive regression model project (screenshot)

Table 10.7   Summary of goodness of fit for engine 1 fuel flow: advanced comprehensive regression model

Factor	GLM Predicted	Trees Predicted	CHAID Predicted	ECHAID Predicted	MLP Predicted	RBF Predicted
Mean Square Error	670.201	9025.980	56545.54	46538.480	553.511	55059.900
Mean Absolute Error	19.253	71.926	181.990	166.860	17.7905	181.690
Mean Relative Squared Error	0.000	0.001	0.000	0.000	0.000	0.000
Mean Relative Absolute Error	0.006	0.021	0.050	0.050	0.005	0.050
Correlation Coefficient	0.996	0.941	0.530	0.640	0.997	0.550

GLM—Generalized Linear Model; CHAID—Chi-squared Automatic Interaction Detection Model; ECHAID—Exhaustive Chi-square Automatic Interaction Detection Model; MLP—Multilayer Perceptron Model; RBF—Radial Basis Function Model

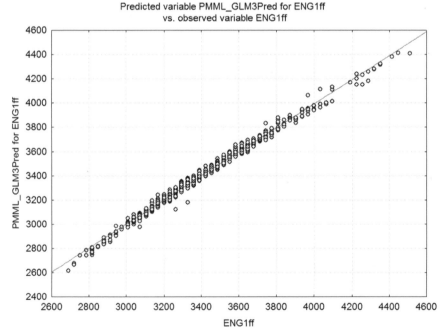

Figure 10.9   General linear model of engine 1 fuel flow: predicted versus observed

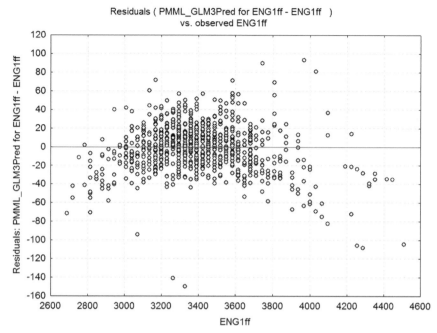

Figure 10.10 **General linear model of engine 1 fuel flow: residuals versus observed**

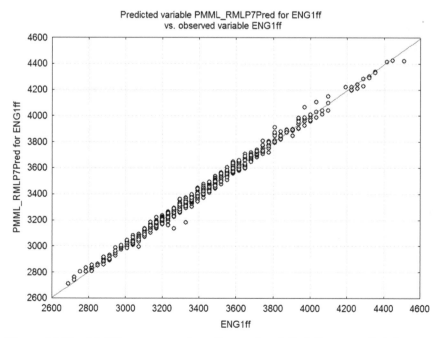

Figure 10.11 **Multilayer perceptron for engine 1 fuel flow: predicted versus observed**

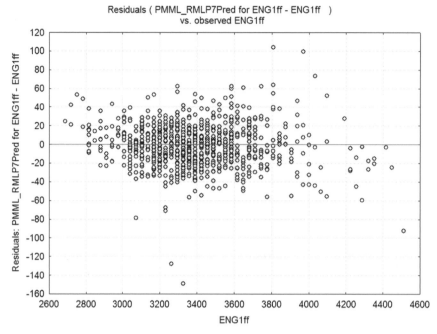

Figure 10.12   Multilayer perceptron for engine 1 fuel flow: residuals versus observed

Table 10.8   Summary of goodness of fit for engine 2 fuel flow: advanced comprehensive regression model

Factor	GLM Predicted	Trees Predicted	CHAID Predicted	ECHAID Predicted	MLP Predicted	RBF Predicted
Mean Square Error	633.783	8899.214	42906.560	38836.210	786.319	32815.580
Mean Absolute Error	18.734	68.991	159.980	150.560	19.877	129.160
Mean Relative Squared Error	0.000	0.001	0.000	0.000	0.000	0.000
Mean Relative Absolute Error	0.006	0.020	0.050	0.040	0.006	0.040
Correlation Coefficient	0.996	0.945	0.690	0.720	0.995	0.770

GLM—Generalized Linear Model; CHAID—Chi-squared Automatic Interaction Detection Model; ECHAID—Exhaustive Chi-square Automatic Interaction Detection Model; MLP—Multilayer Perceptron Model; RBF—Radial Basis Function Model

Finally, *STATISTICA's Intelligent Problem Solver (IPS)* procedure was used. The IPS is a sophisticated tool for the creation and testing of neural networks for data analysis and prediction problems. It designs a number of networks to solve the problem, copies these into the current network set, and then selects those networks into the results dialog, allowing testing to be performed in a variety of ways. Like the ACRM tool, the IPS allows the numerous DM algorithms to be run simultaneously on a dataset.

Tables 10.9 and 10.10 are summaries of goodness of fit analyses for the five models retained for ENG1ff and ENG2ff, respectively.

Figure 10.13 presents a composite graph of all five models evaluated depicting observed versus residuals for the ENG2ff model. This graph shows a fairly tight pattern of observations with only few possible outliers, which are mostly found in Models 4 and 5—the two Radial Basis Function (RBF) models.

In summary, the recursive partitioning method, C&RT, produced excellent results, that is, correlation coefficients of .92 and .91. Further, the dendrograms produced by the C&RT are easy to interpret. For example, it can easily be determined that the first node generated in the ENG2ff dendrogram is based on variable CAS, the bivariate nodes from CAS are GWeight and CAS, the nodes from GWeight are ENG2n1 and GWeight, and so on. This information enables the analyst to better understand the classifications being determined by the algorithm.

The ACRMs also produced excellent results on the data. The correlation coefficients reported by each of the models were very high. The GLM reported correlation coefficients of .996 for both ENG1ff and ENG2ff, and the MLP reported correlation coefficients of .997 and .995 for ENG1ff and ENG2ff, respectively. These values significantly exceed those obtained by standard multiple regression methods. The error values for the GLM and the MLP models were also low relative to the other models examined.

Table 10.9   Summary of goodness of fit for engine 1 fuel flow: intelligent problem solver

Factor	ENG1ff Model 1 GLM	ENG1ff Model 2 MLP	ENG1ff Model 3 MLP	ENG1ff Model 4 RBF	ENG1ff Model 5 RBF
Mean Square Error	683.411	690.712	711.707	6043.053	4424.089
Mean Absolute Error	19.061	19.030	20.130	48.525	50.813
Mean Relative Squared Error	0.000	0.000	0.000	0.000	0.000
Mean Relative Absolute Error	0.006	0.006	0.006	0.014	0.015
Correlation Coefficient	0.996	0.996	0.995	0.961	0.971

ENG1ff—Engine 1 Fuel Flow; GLM—General Linear Model; MLP—Multilayer Perceptron Model; RBF—Radial Basis Function Model

Table 10.10 Summary of goodness of fit for engine 2 fuel flow: intelligent problem solver

Factor	ENG2ff Model 1 Linear	ENG2ff Model 2 MLP	ENG2ff Model 3 MLP	ENG2ff Model 4 RBF	ENG2ff Model 5 RBF
Mean Square Error	736.102	600.180	660.567	1802.759	1706.794
Mean Absolute Error	20.319	18.778	19.273	29.733	28.654
Mean Relative Squared Error	0.000	0.000	0.000	0.000	0.000
Mean Relative Absolute Error	0.006	0.006	0.006	0.009	0.008
Correlation Coefficient	0.995	0.996	0.996	0.988	0.989

ENG2ff—Engine 2 Fuel Flow; GLM—General Linear Model; MLP—Multilayer Perceptron Model; RBF—Radial Basis Function Model

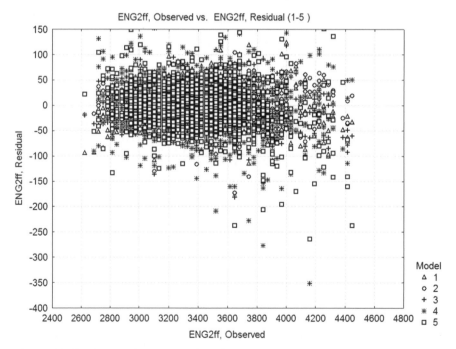

Figure 10.13 Composite graph of all five models evaluated depicting observed versus residuals for the engine 2 fuel flow model

The IPS model produced five models with no correlation coefficients less than .961. As with the ACRM results, the GLM and MLP models were the best performers, with all correlation coefficients exceeding .995.

Review questions

1. What is a Failure Mode Effects Analysis and when is it used?
2. What is a Fault Tree Analysis and when is it used?
3. What is a gap analysis?
4. Describe Probabilistic Risk Assessment.
5. What is Monte Carlo Analysis?
6. Describe the steps in data mining.
7. Why is data preparation important in data mining?

References

Columbia Accident Investigation Board, [CAIB] (2003). Report of the Columbia Accident Investigation Board, Volume 1. Retrieved September 1, 2007 from http://anon.nasa-global.speedera.net/anon.nasa-lobal/CAIB/CAIB_medres_full.pdf

Global Aviation Information Network [GAIN] (2005). *Application of Insightful Corporation's Data Mining Algorithms to FOQA Data at JetBlue Airways: A Technology Demonstration in Partnership with the Federal Aviation Administration and the Global Aviation Information Network.* Retrieved July 1, 2006 from http://www.gainweb.org

Global Aviation Information Network. [GAIN] (2004). *Application of Smiths Aerospace Data Mining Algorithms to British Airways 777 and 747 FDM Data: A Technology Demonstration in Partnership with the Federal Aviation Administration and the Global Aviation Information Network.* Retrieved July 1, 2006 from http://www.gainweb.org/

Knight, P., Cook, J., and Azzam, H., (2005). "Intelligent Management of Helicopter Health and Usage Management Systems Data." *Proceedings of the Institution of Mechanical Engineers 219* (Part G: Journal of Aerospace Engineering).

National Aeronautics and Space Administration, [NASA] (2002). *Probabilistic Risk Assessment Procedures Guide for NASA Managers and Practitioners*, Version 1.1. Retrieved September 15, 2007 from http://www.hq.nasa.gov/office/codeq/doctree/praguide.pdf.

Perrow, C. (1984). *Normal Accidents*. New York, NY: Basic Books.

Rasmussen, N., Pedersen., O., Carnino, A., Griffon, M., Mancini, C., and Gagnolet, P. (1981). *Classification System for Reporting Events Involving Human Malfunctions*, Report M2240, Roskilde, Denmark: Risø National Laboratory.

Reason, J. (1990). *Human Error*, Cambridge University Press.

StatSoft. (2003). *Statistica Data Miner (version 70)* [computer software]. Tulsa, OK.

Wang, J. (2003). *Data Mining: Challenges and Opportunities*. Hershey, PA: Idea Group Publishing.

Chapter 11

Implementing an SMS

Knowing is not enough; we must apply. Being willing is not enough; we must do.

Leonardo da Vinci

SMS in Practice

Jerry Dennis, Executive Director of the Medallion Foundation, provides some lessons learned regarding SMS implementation:

The Medallion Foundation, Inc. is a non-profit aviation safety organization funded by a grant from the Federal Government and limited to the State of Alaska. In the development of the Medallion Foundation Five Star Shield program in 2002–2003, every Safety Management System (SMS) currently available was reviewed and where possible best practices were incorporated. At this writing, there are 75 operators enrolled in the program, more than half have achieved one or more of the five stars.

Here it must be emphasized that most aviation SMS's are focused on large air carrier operations or government organizations such as the FAA Air Traffic Organization. The focus of the Medallion Foundation is small Part 121 and even smaller Part 135 operations.

We are pleased that the National Institute of Occupational Safety and Health (NIOSH) has recognized the contribution of the Medallion Foundation in reducing the accident rate in Alaska. That agency stated in its most recent report that the Medallion Foundation was the only program that had a statewide impact. Statistics also indicate those operators with more stars were safer than those with fewer stars. It is interesting to note that the Five Star Shield program has also influenced a change in the aviation safety culture of Alaska.

The Medallion Foundation was the first to introduce ASAP to the Part 135 community. It has now become a goal for the operators to move to that level. It is in essence, a voluntary program within a voluntary program. Our MOU is also unique in that it can address ANY employee. Currently we have six operators in the program with that many more seeking to join. Both the operator and the employee benefit and the information is invaluable. We were able to move from a 'just culture' to a 'learning culture' through the introduction of ASAP.

While the program has been successful in reducing the accident rate in Alaska there are some valuable lessons learned that can be passed on to others going down this road:

- Without the support of top management the program is doomed to fail! This we have observed time after time.
- Top management does not want to get involved in the program or training. Without this training, management will "assign" the responsibility to someone else and will not be accountable.
- The economics of the program must be emphasized and demonstrated. This is the only way you can retain management buy-in.
- There is not enough emphasis in the FAA AC 120-92 or ICAO document on change management. An SMS is a process of continual improvement (change) which differs considerably from traditional compliance based programs.
- There is a definite need for a formalized operational risk management program that is based on something more than a risk matrix.
- There is a need for a viable database that can provide information not only to the operator, but operators of like equipment as well.
- The SMS must be standardized to the point that an appropriately trained individual can accomplish the program. Just as important, the standardization must be sufficient that an individual moving from one operator to another can recognize the SMS at the new carrier.
- The program must be a profit center, not a liability to the company.
- The internal audit is invaluable to the health and wellbeing of a company.
- There is a lack of continuity within most companies because of a constant change in personnel, specifically safety personnel. We have observed this far too often—in one instance the operator changed the safety officer six times over a three year period.

If a student of SMS were to read no further than this point, we hope that he or she would have profited from the study, leaving the effort with a greater understanding of and appreciation for the discipline. But SMS is not an intellectual or academic pursuit, and our goal is not mere understanding. In our business, when risk is not managed successfully, people can die, careers can be destroyed, and companies can vanish. Ours is a very serious business.

We have referred to the object of our study as the *discipline* of SMS. One need not stretch the term too far to realize that the intended readers of this book will be, we hope, *disciples* of SMS. So what is it that the SMS practitioner believes?

Safety change management

There are many ways to approach this question of belief; we have touched upon some of them. We could discuss the belief in the commitment to empowerment and accountability for front line employees. We could discuss believing in the importance of fact-based decision-making, a fundamental tenet of quality management and safety management. We could discuss believing in the value of devising and utilizing a structured approach to the assessment of risk in routine operations. Such an approach is a central component of SMS, so much so that if it doesn't exist in an organization, the SMS practitioner would have to assert that no SMS existed.

But even if an organization has the most logical fact-based decision-making process in the most empowered workgroup using the most sophisticated risk assessment tools, but is still missing one thing, SMS is not yet in their possession. That one thing is at the core of the SMS practitioner's belief system—the passionate commitment to effectively managing a safety change process.

Without the commitment to effective safety change management, no other aspect of SMS matters, regardless of how well-developed it might be. In our discussion of quality management, we have described the classic approach to change management in the field of quality: Plan-Do-Check-Act (PDCA). We stand by the assertion that the mastery of this simple quality technique is at the heart of SMS, and that the SMS practitioner needs to be able to engineer processes that have this continuous improvement spiral built in. But it is important to understand that PDCA is a technique, and falls into that realm of knowledge to which Leonardo refers in the quotation that introduced this section. The knowledge of how to do PDCA is necessary but not sufficient for SMS. We have to be very clear about the essential element: it is the *passionate commitment* to effectively managing a safety change process.

The ability to *implement* an SMS is vital. We suggest that everything else in this book, or in any other resource for SMS implementation, is secondary to the development of this attribute in the SMS practitioner, especially in the champion—that individual chosen to lead the effort in an organization. All of the rest of SMS will follow if this one attribute is nurtured and developed; without it, SMS will wither and die, or ossify into just another ill-fated program.

We recommend that the SMS champion (in fact all SMS practitioners) read two books concerning techniques, challenges, and personal risks associated with achieving organizational change. The first book, *Leading Change*, by John P. Kotter, describes eight steps that constitute a blueprint to successful organizational change. The other work, *Deep Change*, by Robert E. Quinn, contrasts the various types of change that can occur in individuals, between members of a group, or within an organization. The primary distinction Quinn makes is between *managerial change* and *transformational change*. Kotter offers step-by-step directions to use to effect organizational change, while Quinn suggests that a realistic assessment of the challenge in front of us is in order; for in most organizations the adoption of SMS will be in the nature of transformational change.

The SMS champion

The prerequisite for beginning down the path that both Kotter and Quinn illuminate is the appointment of a champion; for us, that champion is the individual who will lead the SMS implementation effort—our disciple. That champion must be empowered so as to have the authority to transform the organization. That is a substantial statement, worth pondering. Transformation can be a costly process, perhaps costly in the expenditure of resources, but especially in the expenditure of political capital.

The nature of some of the changes necessary to implement a complete SMS requires not only the re-engineering of systems and processes within the organization, but also the adjustment, and sometimes overthrow, of managers' long-held beliefs about how to manage, or employees' beliefs about responsibility and accountability.

For example, the belief in the effectiveness of punitive action to control error can extend all the way up the managerial food chain, indeed in many organizations these beliefs were the norm a few decades ago, when present-day managers were at the beginning of their own careers and being mentored by bosses of the "old school". In some organizations one might not want to proclaim it too loudly, but the fact is that SMS is antithetical to that approach. Empowerment, accountability, and self-reporting of error all depend upon a non-punitive approach to managing people, and all are important components of a well-designed SMS.

The CEO's support of the champion

The champion of SMS can expect to encounter the challenge of dealing with powerful people who do not agree with some components of SMS. If indeed the upper echelons of company management are resistant to the changes the adoption of SMS brings, it will be very difficult to succeed without the clear and direct support of the CEO. There is good reason for ICAO and the FAA to state unequivocally that support from the highest levels of management is necessary for SMS to succeed. Understanding that SMS-induced change can be transformational also helps to understand that this high level support must not be in name only. The CEO must not just sign a policy document endorsing the principles of SMS. He or she must be ready to support the SMS champion even against forces in the boardroom or executive suites.

As an industry, we need to give careful thought to the issue of what a CEO needs to know about SMS, because it is central to the initial steps in successfully launching an SMS in any organization. The fact of the matter is that it will be the rare organization in which the CEO is the initial visionary who grasps the importance of SMS and personally takes on the mantle of SMS champion. That being the case, whoever that visionary is will need all the help we can offer. Our SMS champion must be able to quickly, concisely, and accurately communicate to the CEO why SMS will require some of the organization's precious resources, including time of the CEO. We must provide to that champion a Cliff Notes version of SMS that a CEO would be willing to learn.

Our CEOs do not need to understand Probabilistic Risk Assessment, or Fault Tree Analysis, Monte Carlo simulations, or other profundities of SMS. They do need to understand that SMS is a business process approach to safety. They need to understand risk indices and the appropriate, graduated management responses to those indices when a report crosses their desks. They need to understand the requirement to provide adequate resources for risk assessment. They need to understand their role in incorporating SMS management review into their regular schedule. They need to understand the cultural changes that SMS entails, such as the cross-functional teamwork required to manage risk, and especially the need to develop non-punitive methods to control human error. And they need to understand that the primary responsibility for safety promotion is in their own job descriptions.

Our champion is faced with quite an educational challenge, but there are resources available to help. Both ICAO and the FAA are developing SMS implementation handbooks aimed squarely at educating both top and line management in the basics of SMS. Our SMS champion will need to stay abreast of the development of these resources, and will need to become very familiar with them.

The question of discipline

Moving from a philosophy of the necessity of disciplinary action to the expectation of accountability is perhaps the most difficult cultural issue facing SMS implementation. The guidance for SMS development issued by ICAO, FAA, and the International Air Transport Association (IATA) is very clear on this matter. SMS is by its very nature non-punitive.

For many companies, punitive disciplinary action is so ingrained in the culture that it is hard to imagine how the transformation to responsibility and accountability at all levels can be made. Nevertheless, this is the challenge that many of our SMS champions face. It might help to know the history of the evolution of thought on the subject, and to also be aware of resources available that can help make the slow turn toward a more effective management practice.

Theory X, Theory Y

In the 1960s, Douglas McGregor at the MIT Sloan School of Management published a description of two commonly held approaches to the management of human behavior in the workplace. He called these two opposing alternatives *Theory X* and *Theory Y*. Each described the underlying assumptions held by the organization concerning the characteristics and motivations of the average worker. Theory X held that the average worker would rather avoid responsibility and work if at all possible, and that the manager's role in the workplace was to create an environment in which this avoidance was too costly for the employee; in effect to make the employee decide that it was more advantageous for the employee to work than to not work.

In contrast, Theory Y asserted that human beings naturally want to contribute, and are naturally responsible. Given the right circumstances, they will exercise self-control and self-direction. In a workplace governed by Theory Y, the manager's role is to assure that the work environment encourages such behavior, and empowers the employee to exercise these naturally productive tendencies.

McGregor was not naïve, and understood that the real world was full of a mix of people that considered as a whole would fall along a continuum between the extrema represented by Theory X and Theory Y. His assertion to businesses was that the preponderance of employees was better explained by Theory Y. Equally importantly, he asserted that the management structure required by Theory X was of necessity top heavy, bloated, and incapable of rapid change or adaptation. A Theory X manager's day is busy indeed, just keeping the workers' noses to the grindstone. If the Theory X manager can accomplish this, then that is in itself a success story, and so production goals or safety targets become icing on the cake rather than the actual goal. The combination of the distributed nature of responsibility in Theory Y, along with the fact that most people do actually want to do good, makes Theory Y the better choice for companies that need keep their eyes on the ball in order to perform in today's fast-paced and quickly evolving business environment.

It is very important to understand the distinction between Theory Y and a Pollyanna view of human nature. Theory Y does *not* assert that everyone will always be responsible and do the right thing, but rather that the organization will be more productive by creating management structures which assume that the employee workforce, when taken as a whole, will act responsibly. McGregor asserted that Theory Y was the better choice not because it was more moral, but because it was more productive.

SMS is a Theory Y approach to risk management. The SMS practitioner holds a deep belief that a non-hierarchical and non-punitive approach to managing risk is the better one, but he needs to have the language to be able to relate the basis of that belief in terms that a hard-nosed business manager can understand. The message to relate to the CEO and to recalcitrant managers is that SMS is better not because we have this deep belief in the righteousness of humanity, but simply because it works.

Still, the champion of SMS needs to be prepared to address the concerns of those front-line managers who have had the misfortune of being disappointed in the level of responsibility of some employees. It is of course an unfortunate fact of life that not everyone performs responsibly, and some managers who have to deal with this type of behavior routinely will balk at new policies that explicitly state that the organization is adopting a non-punitive approach to the control of human error.

Rather than focus on the punitive versus non-punitive argument, the SMS champion will find better traction if the discussion is guided into the topic of accountability. Punitive/non-punitive actions are means to an end, but accountability in all levels of the workforce is a goal in itself, one that any manager can agree with. There are very good tools to assist in this discussion.

We introduced the concept of a safety culture in Chapter 1 and we'll add to that discussion later in this chapter. You will recall that one aspect of a safety culture is that it is also a just culture (it is more than a just culture, but here we will focus on this aspect). Simply stated, a just culture is one that expects every member of that culture to accept responsibility for his or her own actions and be accountable for them, and in turn each member of that culture expects that he or she will be dealt with fairly. The concept of fairness is a cultural norm, and is shaped by the members' common agreement on what can realistically be expected of them, and what should happen to those members who do not perform according to that self-generated norm of realistic expectation.

In a just culture, bad things can happen to the individual that does not conform to the cultural norm of reasonable expectation, and that bad thing can resemble in many ways the same outcome as might have happened were that individual to have been disciplined in a hierarchical, punitive environment. The difference is that in a just culture, as part of fulfilling its safety promotion obligations, management invests significant time and effort to assure that standards for behavior are well-known, that they are realistic, and that to the greatest extent possible, everyone buys in to that expectation. The manager in a just culture plays the occasional role of the enforcer of the cultural norm, rather than the imposer of an external will.

If the just culture component of SMS is presented correctly, the harried front-line managers should find that SMS supports their need for appropriate behavior rather than undermining it by depriving them of punitive means of control, because even in the difficult times of dealing with problem behaviors, they remain members of a team that includes not only the bosses, but also the entire culture that supports, or rather *expects*, normative behavior.

Our champion should become familiar with resources available to assist in developing just cultures. An excellent example of such a resource is JustCulture.org. JustCulture has developed a straightforward and clear set of guidelines for managers to use when dealing with human error: the Just Culture Algorithm.

It is not within the scope of this book to give a detailed account of the principles underlying the Just Culture Algorithm, but prospective SMS practitioners should acquaint themselves with the concepts. Moreover, an SMS champion who is confronted with the challenge of transitioning the organization from punishment to accountability would do well to utilize this valuable resource.

The SMS champion and "the accountable executive"

There is some confusion as to the origin and definition of the term "accountable executive" as it applies to SMS. The origin of the term is in regulations issued by Transport Canada (TC) that define how an SMS must be structured. Following is the TC definition of the accountable executive (AE) (TC, 2007c):

The accountable executive (AE) is the agent for cultural change. Cultural change, by definition, starts at the top of the organization. For example, Transport Canada operates a government air service, Aircraft Services Directorate, for which the Deputy Minister of Transport Canada is the Accountable Executive.

The responsibilities of the AE are defined in the regulations and have everything to do with effective control of resources. In most cases, despite having a large budget, this will not be the chief operating officer (COO) but someone higher in the company/organization who provides the COO with their operating budget.

TC provides useful flowcharts that assist certificate holders in determining the appropriate person to appoint as the AE (see Figures 11.1 and 11.2):

In the TC model, there is no lack of clarity about who the AE is for any organization; it is the chief executive. If one examines the flowcharts in any detail, it is clear that the position of director of safety in U.S. airlines does not have the clout to act as AE, nor does the director of operations. The TC model, echoed by ICAO, is that the AE is at the very top of any organization.

Accountability is the cornerstone of the ... model. The nomination of the accountable executive is intended to provide the direction and leadership required to foster an appropriate "safety" culture and provide adequate resources to successfully manage the safety risks inherent to the organization

(ICAO, 2006, p. 2).

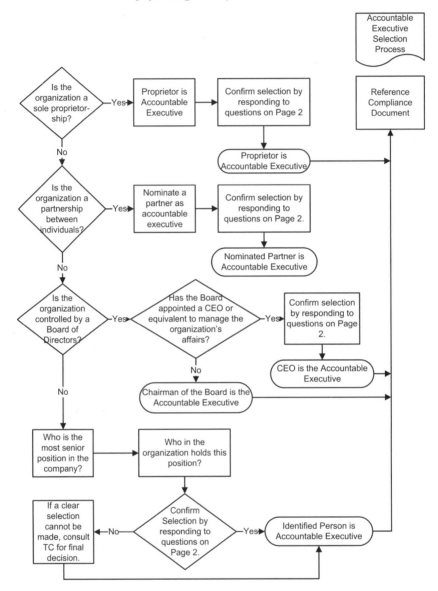

Figure 11.1 Accountable executive selection flowchart

It's important for the SMS practitioners and potential champions in the U.S. to keep this distinction in mind. Almost certainly the champions we discuss in this section will not have the power inherent in the Canadian or the international model of SMS, as represented in the person of the AE, nor is there a regulatory requirement for those above the champion's position to make the same affirmative statement of support for SMS as the position of AE requires. What this means for the U.S. SMS champions is that their model requires more persuasion and

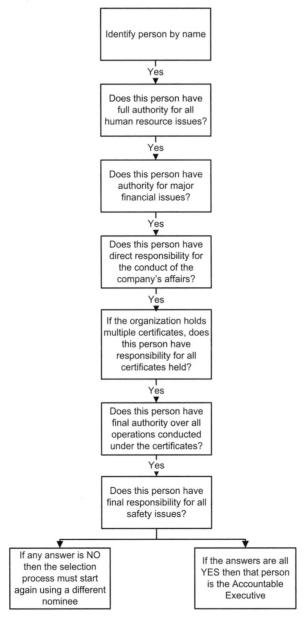

Figure 11.2 Accountable executive selection question list

gentle education than does the international model. For many reasons (probably not the least of which is the litigious nature of U.S. society) the FAA has chosen, for the moment, to not require the designation of an AE in an SMS. Time will tell which model of top-level SMS management is more successful in assuring that the resources necessary for implementation and continuing operation are available.

Positive safety culture

One of the challenges for the organization implementing SMS is to assess and develop a positive safety culture. Let's take a look at some aspects of a safety culture a bit more in depth. The term *safety culture* can be traced to the 1986 Chernobyl nuclear accident and, since then, has become a term widely used to characterize the values, beliefs, and norms shared by a group of people regarding safety. In Chapter 1, we defined safety culture as a fusion of several cultures—informed, flexible, reporting, learning, and just—and we briefly defined each of those cultures. Let's examine some attributes of a positive safety culture:

- A positive safety culture is generated from the top down. Like so many of the other issues we've discussed in this book, senior leadership must set the stage for a positive safety culture. Through words (verbal *and documented*) and actions, management at all levels must clearly demonstrate its commitment to safety in all its decisions. This includes directing the resources of the organization to address safety concerns. Senior management establishes safety as a core value, and provides strong safety leadership.
- While this may sound obvious, the organization must acknowledge the nature of its activities as high-risk and high-consequence. Some have termed this as "maintaining a sense of vulnerability".
- Trust permeates the organization. All involved must believe that trust is an essential ingredient in safety management, and that they will be supported by the organization when they make decisions in the interest of safety.
- Hazards and safety risks are actively sought, and there is no thought of shooting the messenger. Everyone in the organization is vigilant and wary about the organization's activities, and is predisposed *and trained* to recognize and respond to the hazards identified. Further, when those hazards are identified, prompt action will be taken to investigate and mitigate them as practicable.
- The responsibility for safety is shared. There may be a safety department or a designated safety officer in the organization, but *everyone* knows that they bear responsibility for safety. Further, individuals in the organization will challenge others when they observe unsafe acts.
- High standards of performance are established, and there is constant monitoring of that performance.

Establishing a positive safety culture

There is no single approach to establishing a positive safety culture, but no effort to establish a safety culture will succeed without *top management commitment and leadership*. First and foremost, top management commitment is a fundamental and necessary requirement of building a positive safety culture.

The next step in establishing a safety culture is to assess its current culture, which is not a trivial task. In 2000 Professor James Reason presented a safety culture checklist to the assembled masses at the Manly 2000 conference, an initiative of the Australian Aviation Psychology Association. The checklist, which is currently published on Transport Canada's website (http://www.tc.gc.ca/CivilAviation/ systemSafety/Brochures/Tp13844/menu.htm), includes 20 issues, such as *mindful of danger, accepting setbacks, regular meetings, data, money vs. safety, reporting encouraged, trust, blame, acknowledge error*, and others. An integrated scoring system rates the user's responses to the issues; scores range from 0 (interpreted as "Jurassic Park") to 16-20 ("so healthy as to be barely credible") (TC, 2007d).

The Keil Centre, a private company of chartered psychologists located in the United Kingdom, has developed a Safety Culture Maturity® Model that has been applied in several industries, including aviation. Patterned after the Capability Maturity Model, a process model developed for the software industry and now used in other domains, the Safety Culture Maturity Model has five levels: (1) Emerging, (2) Managing, (3) Involving, (4) Cooperating, and (5) Continually Improving. The model enables organizations to determine their current level of maturity and develop plans to reach the next level.

There are numerous other readily-available tools for assessing safety culture in an organization, including self-assessment tools. These normally include interviews, questionnaires, observations, and review of documentation.

An organization needs to understand its safety performance in order to establish a positive safety culture. If it is not crystal clear to the organization how its safety *performance* ranks against its competitors, then a *benchmarking* study is in order (see Chapter 3 for a discussion on benchmarking). A properly designed benchmarking study will reveal a great deal about the current state of the organization's safety program as well as that of its competitors.

A safety *policy statement from top management* is vital to establishing a positive safety culture. The statement should be direct, clear, and unambiguous about what the organization's expectations are and who is responsible for achieving them. The policy statement should be widely disseminated throughout the organization. This creates an awareness of the importance of a positive safety culture, and this awareness must continually be fostered by communication.

Responsibility for safety should be established at the appropriate levels throughout the organization. Usually this means that operations personnel should be tasked with safety. And, good management dictates that if people are responsible for something they also should be held accountable. That means that job descriptions and performance reviews should reflect that responsibility.

To establish a positive safety culture, operations managers have to buy-in to the concept and its importance before they can sell it to others. These managers are trained to be focused on their areas of responsibility. Making safety one of "their areas of responsibility" as discussed above is an important step. Another key is to *link the safety culture with the operations* and processes with which they're most familiar. Establishing that linkage will enable the managers to define their roles in safety on-par with their roles to deliver high quality flight instruction, operate an excellent airplane fueling program, provide excellent aircraft maintenance services, or whatever their task may be.

In large, more complex operations, it might be useful to *form a team* or teams to assist with the transition. Unions and other working groups should be involved in this process from the outset to build trust and support for the effort. This team should be tasked to create a blueprint for culture change that will cascade throughout the organization. The blueprint is designed to engage successive layers of management and workers in the change process in a deliberate, structured manner. The relationship between the transition team and the operations managers must be made clear, and it should be understood by all that the operations managers, not the transition team, retain responsibility for safety.

Eventually, the worker on the "shop floor" sees that management is committed to safety. When workers observe that management communicates safety information frequently, aggressively attempts to discover the root causes of safety problems, and makes decisions that are in the best interest of safety (even when some expense is incurred or profit foregone), culture will begin to change. Once that change starts and workers see evidence of improved safety, the momentum for change increases. Therein is the inextricable link between a positive safety culture and SMS.

Getting on with it: The work of the SMS Implementation Team

So let us assume that our champion has successfully briefed the CEO, and has received the commitment of support necessary for success. Let's also assume that the champion has gathered together the resources necessary to begin the long road toward the cultural changes necessary for SMS to flourish in a non-punitive environment. Let's look at what Kotter recommends as a roadmap for change.

The eight-stage process for creating major change

Kotter identifies eight stages in the evolution of any successful change management process:

1. Establishing a sense of urgency.
2. Creating the Guiding Coalition.
3. Developing a Vision and Strategy.
4. Communicating the Change Vision.
5. Empowering Broad-Based Action.
6. Generating Short-Term Wins.
7. Consolidating Gains and Producing More Change.
8. Anchoring New Approaches in the Culture.

Kotter convincingly describes why the order of these stages must not be significantly modified; each step is dependent upon the preceding one and builds upon former success. It will be worthwhile to examine each stage as it relates to SMS implementation. A successful SMS program at its maturity will necessarily have gone through each of these stages.

Establishing a sense of urgency   Since transformational change is by its very nature difficult, there has to be a strong motivation to stick with the effort. This motivation must exist throughout the team assigned to achieve the goal of the project, but Kotter's point at the beginning of the process is that this sense of urgency must exist at the very top of the organization. Our SMS champion must to the greatest extent possible convince the CEO that not only should the organization do it, it has to do it.

Of course there are a variety of ways to establish urgency. One way is the issuance of new rules by a governing agency such as ICAO or the FAA. To "hang" a phrase here from the 18th century English writer Samuel Johnson, "Depend upon it, sir, when a man knows [a new regulation will be issued] in a fortnight, it concentrates his mind wonderfully." Our SMS champion should not be shy about reminding the leaders of the organization that ICAO has mandated SMS in its member States, and that each of those States is in the process of accomplishing that mandate. No matter what their initial level of support for SMS, business people understand the wisdom of quick adoption of programs they are going to eventually have to do anyway.

Creating the guiding coalition   We have discussed the importance of selecting a champion who is passionate about building an effective change management process. It is equally important for the champion to be empowered to select members of the SMS Implementation Team from across all of the operational departments who will be affected by SMS, which is, frankly, the entire operational side of the enterprise. The members of the SMS Implementation Team do *not* have to be top level managers, in fact there is much to be said for team members to not have the level of un-delegatable responsibility that senior managers usually have. The team needs to focus on this task, and not be constantly pulled away.

While the implementation team members should not be the executive VPs, they should have a high degree of respect within the organization, because they are going to be leading their coworkers into a new way of doing business. Leaders exist within all levels of an organization, and the SMS champion needs to populate the team with them.

If the organization's workers are represented by one or more unions, it is also extremely important to bring them into SMS planning. In some organizations SMS will be asking employees to do things that might be very different from traditional roles, such as self-reporting of error, participation in process design, and evaluation of corrective action effectiveness. As threatening as these changes can be for some managers, so can it be for some employees. Having union representation present from the beginning will minimize the potential for misunderstanding and conflict as SMS begins to change long-held processes.

Finally, the SMS champion should strongly consider inviting the regulator to participate in implementation planning. Doing so will build the lines of communication between SMS-O and SMS-P, and will insure that the regulator is comfortable with the progress that is being made. Folding the regulator into the process also provides further resources for the team—federal agency training presentations, documentation, and of course the knowledge that an experienced member of the FAA or similar agency can provide.

There are quality tools that can assist in selection of members for the implementation team. An excellent tool for this purpose is the *power versus interest grid* which was presented in Chapter 9 (see Figure 9.1).

The organization itself will probably insure that high interest/high power representation is provided, but it is important to not ignore the high interest/low power group. Front-line workers are typically in this cluster. To ignore them is to ignore the best information source available concerning how things *really* work. Additionally, it is a mistake to think that their power is limited because they are not officially high in the command food chain; in reality they have a tremendous amount of influence on processes.

A final concern about selection for the SMS Implementation Team is that this project is going to be a long term one. Some turnover is inevitable and probably good, but longevity on the team will give consistency and build institutional knowledge of what works and what doesn't.

Once the team has been selected, the champion's goal must be to make every member of the team equally knowledgeable about SMS as the team leader is. Investment in training, in a reference library, and simply in time spent discussing SMS principles will provide payoffs later in the project. Productivity can wait a while—first get everybody well-educated!

The next four stages of Kotter's plan are: 1.) Developing a Vision and Strategy, 2.) Communicating the Change Vision, 3.) Empowering Broad-Based Action, and 4.) Generating Short-term Wins. This is the core work of the implementation team. We hope that the previous chapters in this book have been helpful for the reader in forming the ideal, central vision of what an SMS is. That collection of ideas, the "vision thing", is critical for all members of the implementation team to possess. But Kotter is considerably more concrete and practical when he discusses vision and strategy; the team must take the essential elements of that generic vision and make it a reality relevant for that particular organization. That takes considerable planning.

The other thing that it takes is an honest assessment of the present state of safety management in the organization. This fact is the primary reason why no two SMS deployment strategies are going to be alike. Both the vision and the strategy must be real-world oriented, and identify not just the ideal, but what is realistically achievable. Whatever the specific path the implementation team chooses, there will be two components to every implementation strategy that are common to all plans. Both components have to do with assuring that safety change management is built into the process. We'll call those components *vertical change management* and *horizontal change management*.

Vertical structure in an organization refers to a defined chain of command that exists to control and accomplish action. This is the traditional "looking downward are the direct reports, looking upward is the boss" structure that exists in nearly every organization. Information flows both ways in a vertical structure, but upward flow tends to be *summarized* performance-related information (e.g., the job is done, we were on time, slightly over budget, and encountered these problems), while command information and resource allocation tends to flow downward (e.g., good, do it faster next time, don't spend money, cope). Without question, vertical control is needed and is here to stay, no matter how flat the design of an organization might be.

In contrast, horizontal structures are composed of teams. Information flows across the team and is relatively real-time, and control is determined more by procedure than authority. Resource allocation decisions are tactical rather than strategic—how to use these existing resources, rather than long term planning for those resources. Collaboration is the common style of interaction. Most complex processes are accomplished by teams, and so SMS must include a focus on this level of organizational action.

The first tasks of the SMS implementation team will be to build a framework that supports both the vertical and horizontal components. Since the product of SMS is safety change management based upon risk assessment, the team will have to bring together these two attributes of SMS for both the vertical and the horizontal.

Vertical change management

It is tempting for an SMS implementation team to jump right in and begin work on the horizontal components of SMS, which are frequently (though by no means exclusively) represented by safety programs such as ASAP, FOQA, IEP, or sometimes by cross-functional Safety Action Teams assigned to solve specific operational problems. That would be a mistake. An organization could have state-of-the-art examples of every one of these programs, but without integration into a functioning vertical change management component, the result would not be SMS. In fact this description is close to what exists today in many organizations. As described in Chapter 2, the recent history of safety management evolution has been characterized by the growth of the various types of safety programs described above. That is not a criticism of those organizations that have created such programs. They are extremely valuable, and will serve the organizations well during phases 2 and 3 of SMS development (described below). But the key question to ask is whether the output of those programs is risk-oriented, and whether that output serves as an input for an *institutional level* risk management strategy.

SMS must plug in to the organization's vertical command structure in order to be effective. In small organizations with few employees, that vertical structure might not be extensive, and so the vertical integration might be relatively informal. But given the specialization inherent in aviation, a service provider of any size at all quickly becomes organized according to those specializations, sometimes even to the extent of creating the stereotypical stovepipe structure with which we are unfortunately all too familiar. An effective institutional risk management strategy must be able to reach across these specializations with ease to assure that risk mitigation actions can be supported and directed within each specialization's chain of command, while simultaneously being coordinated with the actions of other departments. This requires that a structure be built in which the tops of the food chain in each operational specialty are a part of SMS.

The first order of business for the SMS implementation team, therefore, is to create a Safety Council. A Safety Council (SC) can be called anything the organization wants, of course, but all of them will be comprised of either the leadership of each operational department, or representatives of those departments who have direct access to and significant influence in each department's leadership circles. The SC will be the place where the big-picture activities of the organization's SMS take place—the global risk assessments and prioritizations, the institutional resource allocations, the management reviews.

For ICAO and especially Transport Canada (TC) (that is, in SCs other than those in the U.S.), the AE is a member of the SC. Translated, that string of acronyms means the chief executive officer's routine schedule must include activities with the Safety Council. In the U.S. these default recurring calendar appointments are perhaps not as clearly mandated by regulation, but it is hard to imagine how an organizational structure can guarantee access to resources without the CEO being very closely associated with at least some of the activities of the SC, if not necessarily in the thick of the action. To put it another way, the Safety Council counsels the accountable executive. Call it what you will—the CEO must be in the loop. Our SMS champion is the *facilitator* of this counseling process.

So our new SMS implementation team must create the structure in which the SC can perform this role. This does *not* mean just sending out the meeting reminders to the group. We will discuss phase 1 SMS development below, and detail the extent of the work necessary prior to the first SC meeting. It is extensive.

Horizontal change management

As the implementation team builds the vertical dimension of the SMS structure, it must also begin preparing for the construction of the other dimension. Details of this construction will be explained in phases 2 and 3, but it's important for the team to understand what's coming so that what they construct in the vertical dimension during phase 1 will fit nicely with their horizontal efforts in later phases.

While vertical change management concentrated on using the existing command structure of the organization to accomplish the goals of SMS, the horizontal dimension spotlights the front-line teams where the work of the organization is actually accomplished. Each dimension has its particular strengths and uses within SMS. Since we are all used to the idea of a chain-of-command structure addressing and solving problems in an organization, the concept of vertical change management is intuitive and pretty easy to accept. Perhaps not so with horizontal change management, therefore an example might help the discussion along.

For those who have been associated with an aviation service provider for any length of time at all, almost certainly some untoward event has occurred. If that event was of high severity, the organization probably got both serious and creative, and appointed a working group to examine the circumstances around the event. That working group was probably purposely designed to be cross-functional, so as to have representatives on that team from all of the major stakeholder groups involved in the event.

During that group's deliberations, it was able to draw from the individual expertise of all of the specialists on the team, and this combined expertise was able to see the larger processes surrounding the event in ways not usually available in routine operations. Especially valuable was the team's ability to elucidate the interfaces between the various specialties, a frequent source of failure for any system.

If the group accomplished its work well, the product was probably a set of recommendations that reached across all of the individual components of the team, resulting in changes to controls within sub-processes that when taken as a whole addressed the factors contributing to the event, decreasing the level of risk for future operations.

What that group did was horizontal change management. The essence of horizontal change management is sensitive understanding of the realities of the operation from multiple perspectives, with a coordinated effort to problem-solving across the entire set of stakeholders. Virtually every organization has some experience and success in doing this. The challenge in front of the SMS implementation team is to create procedures, practices, even expectations, that encourage the development of the horizontal dimension of safety change management.

When viewed together, it is clear that one dimension of change management is crippled without the other. The vertical has power and resources, but lacks the deep insight into problems or potential solutions. The horizontal has knowledge and

---

SMS in Practice

Bruce Tesmer, former Manager, Flight Crew Performance/Safety at Continental Airlines, and President of the Foresight Bias Collaborative, explains:

As a *program*, SMS must be an integral part of every level in the entire management structure of the company. However, SMS as a *process*, will not survive if it is reviewed and impacted individually by every organizational level. Historically, the larger the organization, the more vertical is the management structure. It is not uncommon to have 10 or more levels from the front-line employee who delivers the product or service of the company, to the top position of the organization, the CEO.

For effective SMS, only two levels need to remain as they currently exist: the top and bottom levels. To avoid interference with the SMS process of safety, the remaining layers of Middle Management need to be represented by a Safety Change Process which will limit their ability to deny, delay or "spin" the need for safety change. An interactive and proactive SMS process requires that the CEO be directly involved in that process.

The CEO needs to know what is happening in normal everyday front-line operations that negatively impact safety. The data and analysis supplying that information come from safety data collection programs belonging to the Measurement Department —(Safety). Armed with that information, the CEO can manage safety through the company's highest oversight theater; the Corporate Safety Review Board. That body is responsible for approval and oversight of each division/department's Safety Action program of front-line employee Safety Action Teams.

The data and analysis are directly presented by the senior Safety Department official to the CEO in the form of Safety Change Targets. Measurement sums the entire reason for a safety department. The real work at providing possible solutions comes from the front-line employee Safety Action Teams. The task of organizing the Safety Action Teams, prioritizing valid solutions, requesting approval & funding, and installing funded solutions belongs to the layers of middle management and is directed by the Safety Change Process, thereby limiting the impact of eight management levels into one input.

Structured in this manner, the CEO has the initial and final say as to what changes are funded, knowing the priority of each safety change target. The front-line employees know that they are impacting the safety in their environment by providing the research for best safety solutions for each safety target. Of equal significance is the coordinated but limited impact that each level of management can exert on implementing a solution. Any one level will be unable to drag its feet, shoot from the hip, redirect responsibility or use other forms on management friction to have it their way.

The process of SMS is best served by a flat organizational structure in order to be effective.

---

ideas, but little influence over the larger operation. Together, they reinforce each other's strengths. Together they constitute SMS.

So now we have a vision of what it is that the implementation team must do. Let's return to Kotter's list, and see how the first two phases of SMS development can proceed.

So far our SMS champion has established the appropriate sense of urgency and achieved buy-in for the project from the executive suites. The SMS implementation team has been created and, with support from top management, has become the guiding coalition. They understand vertical and horizontal change management, and especially understand that their mission is not to solve a specific safety problem, but rather to create the structure that can solve many problems. They have read Kotter, and understand that stages 2 through 5:

2.   Developing a Vision and Strategy,
3.   Communicating the Change Vision,
4.   Empowering Broad-Based Action,
5.   Generating Short-Term Wins,

are best considered as one sentence:

Developing a *specific* vision and a *specific* strategy, communicating that change vision, and empowering broad-based action, *in order to* (initially) generate short-term wins.

They have identified their target, determined that it is achievable, and are going after it. Nothing will help create long-term success better than a short-term win.

Going after that short-term win is exactly the objective of the ICAO and FAA descriptions of a phased approach to SMS development. In our next segment we will examine the FAA outline for a four-phase plan for SMS implementation, and how that plan relates to what we have thus far presented.

The next four parts of this treatise are each preceded by tables whose elements have been extracted from draft FAA guidance documents (Arendt, D. personal communication, September 9, 2007). Each element explains what an auditor might examine to determine whether an SMS has matured to a phase 1, 2, 3, or 4 status. A detailed list of questions associated with each element is provided later in this chapter; at this point we will examine these tables in order to understand the developmental progression through the four phases. The "new to phase" column in each table provides information on elements that did not exist in the previous phase, and therefore are important markers for that progression. (Note: All elements in Table 11.1 are marked as new to phase because, well, it's phase 1!)

Phase 1: Laying the groundwork

Notice that in phase 1, no mention is made of hazard identification, risk assessment, or the creation of any risk management plan. Phase 1 is clearly a preparation for things to come. Planning and the creation of policy and procedure documentation is the content of phase 1, and the focus of those policies and procedures is vertical change management. This is the chance for the implementation team to design Safety Council processes that guarantee appropriate representation and empowerment, and describe the activities of the SC.

Table 11.1   Phase 1 implementation

Source: Arendt, D. Personal communication, September 9, 2007

PHASE 1	
ELEMENT	**New to phase**
4. Policy	■■■■■
4.1. General Requirements	√
4.2. Safety Policy	√
4.3. Quality Policy	√
4.4. Safety Planning	√
4.5. Organizational Structure and Responsibilities	√
4.6. Compliance with Legal and Other Requirements	√
4.7. Procedures and Controls	√
4.9. Documentation and Records Management	√
7. Safety Promotion	■■■■■
7.1. Safety Culture	√
7.2. Communication and Awareness	√
7.3. Personnel Requirements (Competence)	√
7.4. Training	√

The existence of a healthy safety culture is a necessary attribute of the fully developed SMS, and part of the first phase of SMS development is focused on the safety culture's growth. The evolution of the organization's culture cannot be neglected as the other aspects of SMS are developed, and so if one imagines the growth of SMS in the organization as a process of moving from one phase to another—at each stop leveraging the tools associated with that stage to mature the SMS just a bit more, at each stop raising the level of safety, then moving on to the next stage—it would probably be best to imagine returning frequently to this topic.

A mature SMS has all the tools to support a Learning Culture, a critical component of the larger concept of a Safety Culture. A Learning Culture is one that has the information necessary to manage risk available any time it is necessary, and also knows how to use that information. The informed and motivated member of a Learning Culture can say "I know what my job is because I know where to find the policies and procedures that govern the job, they are consistent and relevant to my task at hand, and I have continuing training to assure that I can accomplish them. In addition, I know where the risks are in what I do, both from a theoretical perspective, and from current information about what is happening in the real operation." Developing this level of Learning Culture is needed in a fully functioning SMS.

A Safety Culture, in addition to being a Learning Culture, is also a Just Culture. We should directly and explicitly acknowledge to ourselves that creating a Just Culture often, usually, requires transformational change, both in the managers and in the employees themselves. Managers have to be trained to not only act, but believe, that control of human action through punitive means is antithetical to the culture the organization is trying to establish. Employees have to step up and accept a new, higher level of responsibility and accountability for actions. This is hard work, and long work.

Phase 2: Test runs; finding and controlling risk

Phase 1 implementation created the foundation upon which to begin building SMS. Phase 2 (see Table 11.2) continues the effort by building SRM/SA in one targeted area or program, and by reviewing and if necessary modifying the organization's ERP.

Implementing while operating   If we had the luxury of starting with a clean slate, our approach might be somewhat different than the following argument. Perhaps some readers will be doing just that—starting up a new aviation service provider. For such a reader, the challenge of creating an SMS might be similar to that of designing a new product for manufacture. The manufacturer-entrepreneur has a considerable advantage over our SMS creator—the road to quality in manufacturing has been well paved, using time-proven quality principles. Before that manufacturer's first die is used to stamp the first component part, the full system would be outlined and codified in the company's Quality Manual, procedures, and job aids. Perhaps the management team would decide on a Quality Function Deployment, coordinating customer requirements with design requirements in a combined process that allows them to focus in on product quality. Statistical process control techniques would be designed right into the production line, so that measures of quality performance can

Table 11.2   Phase 2 implementation

Source: Arendt, D. Personal communication, September 9, 2007

PHASE 2	
ELEMENT	**New to phase**
4. Policy	■
4.7. Procedures and Controls	
4.8. Emergency preparedness and Response	√
4.9. Documentation and Records Management	
5. Safety Risk Management	■
5.2. Identify Hazards	√
5.3. Analyze Safety Risk	√
5.4. Assess Safety Risk	√
5.5. Control Safety Risk	√
6. Safety Assurance and Internal Evaluation	■
6.1. General Requirements	√
6.3. Information Acquisition	√
6.4. Analysis of Data	√
6.5. System Assessment	√
6.6. Preventive/Corrective Action	√
6.7. Management Reviews	√
7. Safety Promotion	■
7.1. Safety Culture	
7.3. Personnel Requirements (Competence)	
7.4. Training	
7.5. Safety Lessons Learned	√

be analyzed with the very first production run. Employee reporting systems would be ready for the first timecard punch, standing by to relay problems in process design to regularly scheduled management reviews. From the beginning, cross-functional quality teams would be responsible for, and accountable for, system design and performance.

Our widget manufacturer friend can approach his startup business with this level of sophistication because of the decades of theoretical development, trial and error, successes, failures, and finally the maturation of a discipline, all of which constitute the history of quality.

We stand at the beginning of the evolution of SMS into a professional discipline in its own right. Our present moment in the development of SMS is quite similar to the early phases of the development of the quality movement, when Deming and Juran reoriented management attention from product to process. As Deming frequently stated, "quality comes not from inspection but from improvement of the process".

So the reality for the industry is that we are going to have to jump in to SMS development mid-stream. Few operations can afford to stand down while a new system is put into place. During our ramp-up into SMS, planes will continue to fly, employees will continue to be trained, and the operation will continue to be managed, hopefully with regular internal reviews of successes and failures in achieving corporate objectives. Few organizations will have a turnkey experience in adopting SMS. Most will undertake a process in which the eventual goal is a fully functioning SMS program, but which, during the interim growth phases, choices must be made concerning where to focus energy, people and resources. We need to think carefully about this interim period, and choose the evolutionary path that maximizes continuous safety improvement on our way to fully functioning SMS systems.

Begin with reality   We know now from our theoretical discussions of SMS that a fully functioning system has strong and consistent policies in place, has clear, concise procedures that describe the work to be accomplished, and promotes a safety culture among its employees. But one could spend massive amounts of time and money perfecting documentation, and still have tragedy beset the operation. One could preach inspirationally to the masses about the benefits of safety, and still expose workers and customers to unacceptable levels of risk. So the first place to start in the development of any SMS is, not surprisingly, reality. Having a perfect manual system is less important than investing in programs that give accurate information as to what is really going on. Investing in a training system that produces perfection in the schoolhouse is much less valuable (initially) than creating and maintaining a system that gives decision-makers current and truthful information about the daily operation.

So the task of phase 2 implementation is to choose a process to concentrate on, and develop SRM/SA for that process. Keeping in mind Kotter's recommendations, the choice for that first area of implementation should be important, yes, and meaningfully impact safety, yes, but even more important is that it be *achievable*. It would be very valuable to consider the entire operation and choose an area that represents a significant portion of the organization's risk exposure. But the team is going for a win here, and going after too big a program, or the highest risk area, can itself be risky for continued success.

Since SMS is a risk management system, the obvious place to start re-engineering for SMS is in creating reliable tools with which to measure risk. There are many such tools available, and in any one organization the specific tools to select for initial re-engineering would depend upon existing strengths. Therefore, the implementation of each SMS is unique—there is no single correct method. There are commonalities, though, and it is helpful to review our previous discussion of hazard assessment in order to begin clearly thinking about and planning for implementation strategies.

Recall that we have previously made the distinction between two approaches that identify hazards: identification through observation of the operation, and identification through process analysis. Once again we emphasize—*both* must exist in order for an organization to legitimately claim having an SMS. But for phase 2, it will probably be the case that the implementation team will primarily focus on operational observations.

Functional safety teams In the ideal organization horizontal change management is embodied by Functional Safety Teams (FSTs). FSTs ideally exist throughout the operation. They cross traditional stovepipe management structures, and by their nature require employees from diverse crafts and classes to cooperate in system design and process accountability.

If FSTs do not already exist within the organization, the SMS implementation team identifies phase 2 focus, and creates them in the relevant operational sectors. The teams are taught the fundamentals of quality management, are empowered by management (through direct support from management levels higher than the team members' direct supervision), and are held responsible for process design and accountable for process performance.

FSTs are responsible for the process they accomplish, and are accountable for its results. With risk assessment information from operational assessment programs, and with the responsibility for process (re)design assigned to the FST, it is here that the SRM in SMS occurs. The FST (with expert facilitation from a source such as the safety department) takes the risk assessment information extracted from operational assessment programs and evaluates whether the present procedures adequately mitigate that risk, or if not, how to best modify those procedures. The FSTs are by far the best teams to assign this job—they are the closest to the work those processes are designed to accomplish, and are usually the ones who bear the consequences of risk.

Chapter 7 described the foundation of SMS: process-based SRM/SA. The astute reader will remember that a comprehensive process description was at the heart of SRM/SA, creating the KPIs and targets that SA depends upon. And in the work of creating the detailed process description, the FST is able to comprehensively understand the relationships between hazards, controls and risks.

But a detailed and rigorous process description such as presented in Chapter 7 is no small task. The work of phase 2 does *not* include the creation of such a comprehensive task analysis and process description, simply because of the complexity of the job. That is left for phase 3 development. Instead, phase 2 concentrates on the basics: understanding hazards, controls and risk, identifying how best to measure, and implementing this basic process so that SA can function, and so that the vertical change management process embodied in the Safety Committee has input and can begin to exercise its responsibilities.

A sound phase 2 implementation will have created the FST structure for the process selected, and that FST will have begun the task of creating the complete process description by concentrating on hazards, controls and risk, by identifying basic KPIs and a first cut at targets, and process measurements will begin to feed into the SA and be managed by the SC.

The final part of phase 2 SRM/SA development depends upon the connections being made between horizontal and vertical change, and this is the point at which an SMS can legitimately begin calling itself an SMS. That final piece is enumerated in Table 11.2, item 7.5, in the identification of safety lessons learned.

It is in phase 2 that the organization reviews its emergency response plan to assure it meets all regulatory requirements, and is scheduled to be exercised at regular intervals. As noted in Chapter 8, the logical place to assign the authority over the creation and maintenance of the ERP is the Safety Council (SC). The SC is the part of the organization most connected with the safety component of all of its processes, and will have the greatest knowledge of areas of organizational risk.

If an organization embraces the recommendations contained in Chapter 8, and seriously takes on the challenge of building process-based SRM/SA, then a very important component of success in this area will be the development of skills in creating comprehensive process descriptions. That being the case, the creation or review of the organization's ERP is a great first project. If the SC is accountable for the ERP, then it would be the SC that would manage and participate in the creation of that comprehensive process-based ERP. This is an excellent way to hone the skills required in phase 3, where the bulk of work is in building process descriptions, by having the SC itself be the first to apply those skills, during the building of the ERP in phase 2.

Phase 3: Expansion and process analysis

Phase 3 of SMS implementation takes the skills developed in the targeted phase 2 development, and begins to use this short-term win by applying the skills to other parts of the operation. But significantly there are new components in phase 3, as shown in Table 11.3.

The third phase introduces system and task analysis, and the FAA standard includes such elements as considering the system's interactions with other systems in the air transportation system, the hardware and software components of the system, the environment, and any assumptions made about the system, system interactions, and existing safety risk controls. We suspect that many people who have studied systems theory will examine that list and think of two words: systems thinking. Systems thinking is a handy skill to have to approach this phase of SMS implementation. For those that have not had such exposure, the following very brief discussion based primarily on the work of an expert in organizational learning, Peter Senge, should be informative.

First, the term *systems* is derived from the Ancient Greek word *synistanai*, which means "to bring together or combine". *Systems* is not a new term or concept—it has been used for centuries. In his famous quote, "the whole is more than the sum of its parts", Aristotle is in fact arguing against the notion of reductionism (that is, that the nature of complex things can be reduced to the nature of sums of simpler or more fundamental things) as a means of explaining complex systems. It was not until the 19th and 20th centuries, though, that formal recognition of the "systems"

Table 11.3   Phase 3 implementation
Source: Arendt, D. Personal communication, September 9, 2007

PHASE 3	
ELEMENT	**New to phase**
4. Policy	■
4.7. Procedures and Controls	
4.9. Documentation and Records Management	
5. Safety Risk Management	■
5.1. System and Task Analysis	√
5.2. Identify Hazards	
5.3. Analyze Safety Risk	
5.4. Assess Safety Risk	
5.5. Control Safety Risk	
6. Safety Assurance and Internal Evaluation	■
6.1. General Requirements	
6.2. System Description	√
6.3. Information Acquisition	
6.4. Analysis of Data	
6.5. System Assessment	
6.6. Preventive/Corrective Action	
6.7. Management Reviews	
7. Safety Promotion	■
7.1. Safety Culture	
7.3. Personnel Requirements (Competence)	
7.4. Training	
7.5. Safety Lessons Learned	

approach to management, philosophy, and science emerged (Whitehead 1925, pp. 88–90; von Bertalanffy 1968). Then, beginning in the late 1930s, Karl Ludwig von Bertalanffy, an Austrian-born biologist, established (general) systems theory as a science by publishing numerous works on his theories. According to von Bertalanffy, systems theory involves examining structure and properties of systems in terms of relationships from which new properties of wholes emerge.

In his seminal book, *The Fifth Discipline: The Art and Practice of the Learning Organization*, Peter Senge explains that businesses are "bound by invisible fabrics of interrelated actions, which often take years to fully play out their effects on each other" (Senge, 2006, p. 7). Because these patterns are difficult to see, we tend to focus on snapshots of the parts of the system rather than the whole. This, he explains, is why our deepest problems never get solved. And this, we argue, is why SMS practitioners need to be well-prepared and broadly educated.

In aviation the accident rate has seemingly reached a plateau, and new methods are needed to drive the rate down. SMS recognizes that this will only happen when we clearly see safety as *part of the system*, and understand how safety interacts with the other elements of the business system; this is called systems thinking.

Systems thinking Systems thinking is a way of viewing systems from a broad perspective that enables one to see the overall patterns and events in systems, rather than seeing only specific events in the system. It is this broad view managers must have in order to diagnose problems in an organization.

Systems thinking has emerged as a powerful tool for organizations to guide change and make decisions. Many organizational change experts assert that all employees in the organization should have an understanding of systems thinking and the methodologies and tools associated with the philosophy. In the past, it may have been sufficient for only the top-level managers to receive training in the discipline, but contemporary organizations are subject to much more rapid and complex changes. That has resulted in organizational structures that are generally flatter and decision-making that occurs at lower levels in the organization. Thus, middle-level managers, directors, and supervisors are now more active in the decision-making process, and this necessitates that they have a deeper understanding of the complexities of the organization, the interdependencies of its component parts, and the respective environment in which it interacts.

Systems thinking is somewhat antithetical to the way many of us have been taught to solve problems, including in the safety realm. Usually when faced with a problem we try to break it down into smaller, more manageable pieces; that is, we decompose it. This approach allows us to get our minds around the problem, analyze various facets of it, and begin to formulate solutions. The trouble is that when we decompose the problem we are unable to see the interactions between that problem and the larger system in which it (normally) operates. In contrast, systems thinking uses tools and methodologies that enable us to focus on how the issue being studied interacts with the other constituents of the system of which it is a part. When those interactions are kept in view, the results of our problem solving efforts are often much different than they would be using conventional methods. Systems thinking is most effective with problems that are complex or dynamic, recurring, and where actions affect the environment within which the issue exists.

Imagine a hypothetical, but not so unrealistic, Safety Risk Management scenario where there was a hazard identified in an aviation service provider's organization. After a root cause analysis ineffectively accomplished, a control was determined and applied to mitigate the risk. For a short time, it seemed that the control was having a positive effect, but then it was determined through risk analysis that the hazard was even greater than before. Then, after a thorough and in-depth analysis of the problem using quality tools and methods, it was determined that the initial control that was applied actually eliminated an existing control that was keeping the risk somewhat in-check. Thus, implementing the new control removed an even more effective control the team had not considered, and the safety problem grew worse. Once this was discovered, other more effective controls were applied with much better results.

The moral of this story, aside from selecting risk controls carefully, is that it is important to see the whole picture before taking action. Failing to do so may result in our actions actually having the opposite effect of what was intended. Thus, it is important that those involved with the implementation and operation of an SMS program develop the ability to raise our thinking to the level necessary to achieve the results we desire. There are some practical tools and methods used in the discipline of systems thinking; the following will provide a very brief introduction to those areas.

Tools and methods Various authors list and categorize these tools and methods in different ways (see Richmond (1993), Kim (1994)). Causal loops are a way to view the interrelationships of the organization. In the causal loop diagram, nodes represent variables—things that change over time, and the relationship between the variables is depicted by arrows that are turning right or left, and increasing or decreasing in size. *Reinforcing loops* are ones in which the interactions are such that each action adds

---

SMS in Practice

Mont Smith, Director of Safety at the Air Transport Association, talks about the value of being a systems thinker:

Once upon a time in another life I was told by a senior federal civil service manager, who held an Ed.D. in organizational leadership, that I was what was known in the literature as a "boundary spanner". He reassured me this was a "good thing". I was told that I had an innate characteristic that involved looking beyond my own turf to see interfaces and opportunities to link and coordinate horizontally across department or division boundaries. This provides several advantages. You become aware of problems others have had, so you have an opportunity to be sure that history does not repeat itself! You get to see and evaluate how other people deal with problems similar to yours, a methodology commonly called "benchmarking". Maybe more importantly, you subconsciously and voluntarily begin to normalize your efforts toward a collective cross-functional approach. This is not to be confused with a *standard* imposed by the regulator. The normalization process encourages voluntary improvement beyond the minimum performance mandated by a standard, because it permits adaptation to a unique company organizational and safety culture, while maintaining relevance. Some people rush to label the result a "best practice", but in my opinion it is not optimized until it demonstrates true transparency together with a high degree of experiential effectiveness. Oh, and one more thing. My friend advised me never to implement a process I had devised until I had "walked it through" to completion. Why? Because my view of how the process would be accomplished might just not be the common or universal view. As they say, "the devil is in the details".

to or reinforces the other. *Balancing loops* are ones which have the effect of bringing variables into agreement. It is worth highlighting the fact that circles are used for these depictions rather than straight lines; this is consistent with systems thinking, which is moving away from the linear and toward systems patterns at work.

In many instances it can be beneficial to visualize our actions in terms of a looping process. This process enables us to view our actions not as linear, action-reaction events, but rather the looping process offers us a more flexible paradigm for system modeling.

Archetypes is a term used by Senge (2006, pp. 92–112) to describe the common patterns of behavior in organizations. Senge asserts that archetypes are structures and patterns that control events in our lives, and that these structures can be used to gain insight into patterns of behavior, and predicting future behaviors. Once archetypes are understood and the leaders can identify which seem to characterize their organizations, they are far better equipped to employ specific strategies to deal with the problems of the organization.

Systems modeling and simulation is another tool that is used in system thinking. A model can be thought of a simplified representation of a system with the goal of achieving a greater understanding of the system. There are many forms of simulation, of course, but typically simulations are run on computer software to explore the implications of changes and interactions over time before they are implemented.

Finally, in some organizations many people will ultimately be involved in the implementation of SMS and, as we discussed earlier, there will no doubt be resistance from some to the program. Through education and evidence produced by the model, systems thinking and modeling offers an additional means of overcoming the deep-seated beliefs that cause some to resist changing policies and strongly held emotional beliefs.

With this background, we can begin to see that the challenge put in front of the FST is larger than just handing them an outline showing them what a complete process description looks like, and then expecting them to produce one. What we're really asking the FST to do in phase 3 is to take the basic work accomplished in phase 2 and apply systems thinking to the task. The *output* of that systems thinking is that disciplined format of the process description—the systems thinking has to come first. A thorough SMS Implementation Team will give considerable thought to how they want to train the FSTs to accomplish phase 3, and included in that training should be a distillation of Senge's work.

Phase 4: Maturity—is it working?

Phase 4 marks the maturation of the SMS, and the checked item in Table 11.4 describes the essential question to be answered at this phase of development, and continuously as the SMS becomes an integral part of the organization: is there evidence of continuous improvement? Without continuous improvement there is no point in maintaining the SMS.

The new element in Phase IV is continual improvement—a term close to the heart of any quality advocate. Continual improvement is directly connected to the life cycle of the safety management process. As we've stressed throughout the book,

Table 11.4   Phase 4 implementation

Source: Arendt, D. Personal communication, September 9, 2007

PHASE 4	
ELEMENT	**New to phase**
4. Policy	████
4.1. General Requirements	
4.2. Safety Policy	
4.3. Quality Policy	
4.4. Safety Planning	
4.5. Organizational Structure and Responsibilities	
4.6. Compliance with Legal and Other Requirements	
4.7. Procedures and Controls	
4.9. Documentation and Records Management	
5. Safety Risk Management	████
6. Safety Assurance and Internal Evaluation	████
6.3. Information Acquisition	
6.8. Continual Improvement	√
7. Safety Promotion	████
7.1. Safety Culture	
7.3. Personnel Requirements (Competence)	
7.4. Training	
7.5. Safety Lessons Learned	

an SMS program is a continuous process with feedback loops, based on audit results, safety reports, operational data, lessons learned, and so forth. This, then, enables the evolving, learning, growing, maturing SMS, and it is in this phase that the processes for a relentless continual improvement program are fully implemented.

So here is the fully functioning SMS—built on quality principles incorporated into FSTs, managed by an SC that is championed by the very highest levels in the organization. The SMS first establishes methods, and then continuously uses those methods to incrementally raise the level of safety, measuring its success against clear targets. It interfaces with regulators through portals designed to assure that the regulatory agency has a clear and accurate picture of operational risk, but even more importantly, those portals are designed to assure that the regulator is fully aware of the organization's plans to mitigate that risk.

A successful SMS must have built into it mechanisms that assure that the system is adaptive. Being adaptive, of course, means that there is an innate capability to change in ways that make an organism or an organization more likely to survive and succeed in its environment. This ability to adapt must go well beyond a simple and classic feedback control loop. Indeed, an SMS is full of feedback control loops, designed to detect and subsequently control variation from an established standard of safety. But the truly well-designed SMS is able to identify when that very standard is in need of adjustment. While the former is mere (but absolutely necessary) control, the latter is adaptation. Stated in the language of interpersonal and organizational change, an SMS is able to transform itself.

SMS in Practice

Darryel Adams, SMS Program Manager for the FAA's Airport Safety and Operations (AAS-300), offers the following perspective on SMS implementation at airports:

> When considering the logistics of implementing Safety Management Systems (SMS) at airports the existing operation should be evaluated first. It's important to identify those components of the airport operation that meet the intent of SMS in order to not duplicate effort. Many airports have robust safety programs that fit well within the construct of SMS. Once the existing system has been described and compared against the elements of SMS the next step is to identify the "Gaps." Typical gaps reported during a SMS pilot study sponsored by the Federal Aviation Administration for Airports were:
>
> 1.   A defined safety policy.
> 2.   Integration challenges of existing safety programs.
> 3.   A defined visible non-punitive safety reporting system.
> 4.   Safety risk management process.
> 5.   Defined methods to document safety risk management.
>
> It's important to note that these airports were, in most cases, doing much of this work, but informally and without sufficient documentation. Another common gap deals with integrating these existing informal and independent safety programs into one safety system, or SMS.
>
> Integration requires buy-in from everyone in order for the system to function properly. For example: in order for the ramp SMS to be effective, air carriers, baggage handlers, and vendors must be included as part of safety committees and be accountable to respond to identified safety hazards. It would be difficult for a safety committee made up of only airport operations personnel to identify and mitigate hazards on the ramp without the input from those who actually work there.
>
> Another key element of a safety system is a positive safety culture; a culture free from fear of reprisal and supported by top management. Top management must be accountable and has the responsibility to communicate a safety policy outlining the fundamental elements of the SMS. A visible non-punitive safety reporting system, as

defined by the airport's safety policy, will provide the foundation for such a culture to evolve.

The last challenge to integration I would like to mention is scalability. SMS is not a one-size-fits-all solution. An effective SMS can be quite simple for an airport that has only one air carrier operation each day or it can be very complex for a large international airport.

The air transportation system in the United States is the busiest and most complex in the world. It is estimated that the volume of air traffic will increase three-fold by the year 2025. SMS is a forward-thinking approach that will enable system growth to accommodate this additional load while improving upon the current level of safety.

Review questions

1. Describe Theory X and Theory Y management.
2. What is an accountable executive in SMS?
3. Give some examples of how to foster a safety culture.
4. What is the difference between vertical and horizontal structures in an organization?
5. What are Functional Safety Teams and what are they used for?
6. Describe why proficiency in systems thinking is a prerequisite to building comprehensive process descriptions.
7. Describe in as much detail as possible Kotter's eight stages to transformational change.
8. Briefly describe the objectives of each phase of SMS development.
9. How do you know when an SMS has reached maturity?

References

International Civil Aviation Organization [ICAO], (2006). *Directors General of Civil Aviation Conference on a Global Strategy for Aviation Safety.* (DGCA/06-WP/15). Retrieved on August 16, 2007 from http://www.icao.int/icao/en/dgca/wp/dgca_06_wp_15_e.pdf

Kim, D. 1994. *Systems Thinking Tools.* Cambridge, MA: Pegasus Communications.

Richmond, B. 1993. Systems Thinking: Critical Thinking Skills for the 1990s and Beyond.

Senge, P. (2006). *The Fifth Discipline: The Art and Practice of the Learning Organization.* New York, NY: Doubleday.

Transport Canada [TC], (2007a). *Appendix D—Accountable Executive Selection Flow Chart.* Retrieved October 21, 2007 from http://www.tc.gc.ca/CivilAviation/SMS/tp14343/appendixD.htm

Transport Canada [TC], (2007b). *Appendix E—Accountable Executive Selection Question List.* Retrieved October 21, 2007 from http://www.tc.gc.ca/CivilAviation/SMS/tp14343/appendixE.htm

Transport Canada [TC], (2007c). *II. Accountable Executive*. Retrieved October 21, 2007 from http://www.tc.gc.ca/civilaviation/SMS/FAQ/AE/Q6.htm

Transport Canada, [TC] (2007d). *"TP 13844—Score Your Safety Culture."* Retrieved October 3, 2007 from http://www.tc.gc.ca/CivilAviation/systemSafety/Brochures/Tp13844/menu.htm.

Von Bertalanffy, L. (1968). *General System Theory: Foundations, Development, Applications*, New York: George Braziller.

Whitehead, A. (1925). "Science and the Modern World Lowell Lectures." New York, NY: The Macmillan Company.

Epilogue—Quest Airlines Story

.

Note to Reader: We left the story of the mysterious power loss on 123 with the ERC meeting about to convene.

Boston: 12:00 UTC (07:00 EST) QAL Headquarters—'ERC Meeting'

Day 3

Following Seyfat's lead of getting the lesser items out of the way first, Joe began the ERC meeting by discussing the three other matters on the agenda prior to moving to Flight 222.

"Okay, on to 222," Joe stated. He offered a recap of the events that culminated in the pilots filing ASAP reports. The three representatives from the company, the union and the FAA, along with one of the department's best analysts, reviewed the reports in detail, and then turned their attention to the results of the maintenance probe.

Joe walked through the reports from the contractor and also those from QAL's maintenance go-team. He explained that the airplane, with its original crew, was dispatched to Miami to return to service. The group read the detailed entries of components that were tested and replaced.

"Let's get the captain on the phone," the union rep said.

"I sent a message to him last night and he responded saying he and his F.O., Evans, were both available," Joe responded. "He's at the hotel—I'll call him on his cell."

Sanders, Evans, and the ERC had a lengthy conversation about the power loss event in which the captain assured the ERC that the event was in no way caused by the crew. He stressed the point that his primary concern was ensuring that the airline gets to the underlying cause so neither 'he nor his compatriots ever has to do an impromptu audition for the television show *Survivor*'.

"I'm glad to hear that, Bob. It's your call how broadly we can share information but, obviously, the more we can share the greater likelihood we solve this puzzle."

Sanders was very familiar with the ASAP program and Joe's management of it. He knew that Joe worked hard to build trust and a positive culture.

"What's the FAA's stance on this thus far?" asked Sanders.

"Our POI, Sandy Peters, is saying all the right things. He wants us to figure this out and said he'll go with what the ERC decides."

Sanders and Evans conferred with each other, and gave Joe the green light. "We'll authorize you to share the report at your discretion," Sanders responded.

After more discussion, Sanders and Evans signed off the call. The ERC continued, turning its discussion to the maintenance contractor at Gander.

"We know our maintenance guys have conferred with the contractor in Gander, but maybe there's something we could find out if we talked with them. Any chance we can talk with the mechanic who gave it the initial look?" asked the FAA member.

"We can try," Joe responded. "We might be able to pull them in under the ASAP, agreement, not sure how that would work across national borders. I propose a short break while I run the line and see if we can get the approvals necessary to even talk to him. It's about 10 a.m. in Gander; I don't know what shift he works, but let's see what happens."

After a short break, the ERC reconvened. Joe reported the inconclusive result of his inquiries.

"Well, our read, shared by the union, is that despite the best good will in the world, we're not there yet—it's just too complex to try to provide coverage to external employees when they're certificated by another country." said Joe. "If this were a crash it might be different, and we could get quick action on such a consideration, but thank God it isn't. On the other hand, our illustrious DOS has spoken with the folks at DA Aviation Services, and they value our business. Everyone has agreed to allow the employee to discuss the matter with us."

Joe punched in the numbers on his conference phone, and within a few minutes, Jim Jacobs from DA Aviation Services was on the line.

"Jim, this is Joe Quick, and I manage the Aviation Safety Action Program for Quest Airlines. Around the table are members of the Event Review Committee, and we're trying to dig into this problem we had with our 757 a couple of nights ago. I believe you were called back in after your shift to work on it?"

"Of course, I remember it. What a mystery. But I put everything in my maintenance entry. What else do you need?" Jim asked hesitantly.

"Jim, we would just like to talk to you in more detail about the actions you performed, and hopefully that will help us uncover what happened."

"Okay, what do you want to know?"

Over the next several minutes, Jim detailed the procedures he followed to assess the hobbled 757. His supervisor had brought into the conference room a laptop with the 757 maintenance procedures loaded on it to refresh his memory.

"It had to be puzzling that the crew noted a power loss on both engines," stated one of the ERC members. "What did you think of that?"

"Obviously, unusual. I did think about the points of commonality in the system. Hell, I even checked the throttle quadrant." Jim replied.

"Really, what did you find?" Joe asked.

"Some residue from something, that's all," Jim stated.

Joe looked at his colleagues with a puzzled expression. "I didn't see that on the write up, Jim, how specifically did you check the throttle quadrant?"

Realizing that he was about to admit performing a maintenance check without having logged it, Jim hesitated. His supervisor, who had walked into the room a few moments earlier, motioned to Jim to cut off the conversation.

"Listen, guys, I'm due back on the floor. I probably shouldn't answer more questions until I have some union representation with me. Okay?"

"Okay, Jim. I understand," said Joe. "When you talk to your people please tell them our interest is in sharing information and solving this problem, not creating problems for you. To that end, we'll be happy to discuss our intentions with any of them."

"Okay, Joe. Thanks."

After disconnecting the call, Joe turned to the others in the room. "Well, obviously, this guy did some things he didn't document. Who knows whether it's related, but we've got to find out. Everyone agree? I'll get the process started. I'll also update Don, Todd, and Glenn on where we are."

Boston: 12:00 UTC (07:00 EST) QAL Headquarters—'Morning Call'

Day 4

"Bring us up to date, Joe," Seyfat began.

"Not much new since the ERC meeting yesterday, Glenn, except for politics. Our union rep talked with the union guys at DA Aviation, and it appears that the mechanic has been given a three day vacation. We won't get any more direct information from him."

Seyfat sighed.

"I've talked with the go-team about the throttle quadrant issue," Todd stated. "There's nothing in the troubleshooting procedures they didn't look at it. We need more information. 123 is back in service and on its way to SFO right now. It's due for a B check tonight anyway, so we've arranged for a spare to take the rest of its schedule today, and we'll just start the check early. I've ordered that the quadrant be examined. Nothing against our friends at Gander, but I'll be more comfortable after we've taken a peak."

Seyfat leaned back in his chair and paused. As an experienced manager, he knew that people sometimes get caught up in the minutia of something and lose sight of the big picture. He believed it was senior management's responsibility to support his team, but also to keep their eyes focused on the ball. "Let's assess. We are investigating the incident following our company procedures, correct? The investigation is protected under ASAP, and we've gotten an important clue from Gander. There is no known reason to keep the plane out of service, but we're continuing to assess that situation as information becomes available. Our FAA partners have been involved every step of the way, correct Sandy? We've been documenting our findings. Let's all be evaluating this to see how we can improve our processes. In accordance with our SMS, we want to make sure we're continuing to evolve. I'll be asking for input in the near future; in the meantime, let's continue to focus on our *entire* operation. Remember, our SMS demands that we look forward—that we hunt down and eliminate problems before they occur. Let's get to work."

By the time Seyfat had wrapped up his work day dealing with the routine of an active flight operation, it was the middle of the evening. As he punched the elevator button, Lisa Tada, the FOQA manager, rounded the corner.

"Glenn—good deal, you're still here. Do you have a minute?" said Lisa.

"Go home, Lisa." Glenn said.

"I will, but you need to see this. It's about 123."

Glenn followed Lisa back to the skunkworks, as they called the FOQA office. It was filled with the most sophisticated hardware and software the company possessed, a point that had made IT jealous on more than one occasion.

"I told you about that weird transient that we saw right around the same time the event occurred. We've been playing around with our new data mining tool—remember, the one I had to beg and plead with you to purchase?" Lisa grinned.

"OK, prove that you were right," Glenn said, as he looked over her shoulder at the multi-screen setup on her desk. Glenn was glad some of the more penny-pinching members of the Board never saw the skunkworks.

"We looked back through 123's data, and saw that there were similar spikes before the incident. Very transient, and we found it only because Bob is the best analyst in the business. We didn't have an existing data view that would lead us to it, but he created one once he saw what was happening. Here's a trace of all of the parameters that have anything to do with gizmos in the quadrant." Lisa brought up a flight data view with tens of squiggly lines on it, and virtually every one had a spike at the same time.

"Here's where the incident occurred. Everything associated with the quadrant went crazy at the same time."

"Fascinating," said Glenn.

"And here's the results of DataMiner," Lisa said triumphantly. "This pattern is definitely unique, and 123 has only been experiencing it for four days."

"Do you mean …" said Glenn. Lisa interrupted, "That's exactly what I mean. Whatever caused this happened during an overnight four days before the incident. In New Orleans."

"Lisa, the next time you need new toys, just tell me and you got it." Glenn thanked her again, and started toward his office.

"Just a minute," Lisa said, as she opened her top desk drawer, pulled out a piece of paper, and handed it to Glenn. "Here's the list. Substitutes won't do."

As Glenn entered his office, his phone was ringing. On the other end of the line was Ken Tiller, the CEO.

"Glenn, glad I caught you. Burning the midnight oil again I see. I just wanted an update on 123. Are we any closer?"

"We might have just had a breakthrough, Ken." Seyfat explained what the FOQA department had found, and couldn't resist explaining why they were able to find it, praising both Bob the analyst and the expensive software that even his enlightened CEO had complained about purchasing.

"So what do you think happened in New Orleans?" Ken asked.

"Well it's not a maintenance station, and we didn't see any writeups, so no crew noticed anything funny on the inbound. It must be something associated with the station. I'll give them a call first thing in the morning," Glenn offered.

"Before you do that, let me make a few calls and throw some roses down on the path in front of you," Ken interjected. "I smell something here—somebody screwed up, and we can't afford to not manage this correctly. Before you make any move, I want to talk to the GM at New Orleans, and our corporate contacts at every vendor we use there. I want to make sure we don't start the whack-a-mole game, where someone gets disciplined or fired before we fully understand what happened. If someone down there shoots first and asks questions later, they'll have to answer to me."

"Yes, sir," Glenn acknowledged. Tiller didn't intervene frequently in safety investigations, but when he did it was usually to give operational managers an attitude adjustment. Glenn suspected the calls would go smoothly tomorrow.

Boston: 16:30 UTC (11:30 EST) QAL Headquarters

Day 4

"Okay, everybody, thanks for calling in so soon after the morning call," Glenn said to the group. "We have some news concerning our little incident the other night. By the way, joining us is our CEO, Ken Tiller. Ken, any words before I start?"

"Nope, not a peep. Your show."

Glenn summarized for the group the findings of Lisa's FOQA team, then asked Todd Jacks to review what the maintenance folks had found overnight.

"Well, as expected, all the boxes we R&R'd from 123 checked out fine. But SFO line maintenance opened up 123's quadrant last night during the overnight, and found some interesting stuff. Our unfortunate Gander mechanic had done an excellent job of cleaning. But we pulled the throttle position sensors and learned something interesting. First of all, the bottoms of them were covered with a thin film of sticky goo. Most of us on the line have kids, so you'd all recognize it—mostly dried up soda; Coke, Pepsi, Mr. Pibb, who knows. The interesting thing we didn't know is that both sensors share a common ground, established through that interface where the goo was. Nobody is supposed to pour a soft drink down the quadrant of course, but if they do, we have a single point of failure here. We've been talking to our manufacturer contacts all morning about this. I bet we'll have at least a Service Bulletin addressing this problem."

Glenn continued. "Now let me tell you what happened this morning on our end. After Ken spoke with the folks in New Orleans, we had excellent cooperation from all parties. It turns out that four days before our incident a brand new employee of our cleaning contractor at MSY found the cockpit door to 123 open, and went up front for some flight deck familiarization—alone."

"What?? How did he ..." Doppermeyer, the Director of Operations exclaimed.

"Hold it, Don, we'll get to that," said Seyfat. "Our ASAP guys were able to talk to the kid who did it. Working himself through college, wants to fly. He told them the whole story, after Mr. Tiller spoke with the owner of the cleaning service and persuaded him to not fire the guy."

Tiller interjected, "The owner was very cooperative after I indicated to him that we would need to see that new employee's training records, especially the part that taught him to never enter the cockpit without escort. After a good heart-to-heart, I think we'll forgo that audit right now, but I'm eager to hear about their new training program when we visit them in a month. Can we schedule that, Glenn?"

"Already done," Seyfat reassured. "So the kid didn't know—okay maybe he should have been smart enough anyway, but the point is he wasn't directly informed of what his responsibilities were. I'm glad he has a second chance—sounded like a good kid."

Doppelmeyer could wait no longer. "Now to the main point. How did he get in the cockpit? Why wasn't the door locked?"

"I'll answer that," the pilot union ASAP representative stated. "The kid told us that when he walked past the cockpit door on his way out of the aircraft, he saw that a Styrofoam cup had been made into a doorstop and was blocking the door from closing. I later called the inbound crew, and the captain ... well, I strongly suggested that he submit an ASAP report."

"This is going to test our definition of 'intentional disregard' isn't it?" asked Joe, the ASAP manager. "Yeah, I guess it will," replied the union rep. He knew already that he could not in good conscience argue that this report should be included in ASAP.

"OK, here we are," said Seyfat. "We now know the proximate causes were the captain's breech of procedure in not assuring the door was locked before departing the aircraft, coupled with the lack of training at our vendor. I don't see that we have a process problem concerning the cockpit door. Don, what do you think?"

"I personally speak to every new captain about security. I make them tell me what they are supposed to do. He knew." Donn sounded disgusted.

"I'll have to speak to IEP about how the training issue slipped past us. It's probably because we only did a documentation review." Glenn stated.

"Let's talk offline about supply chain management," the CEO offered. "Back at the old car company we stubbed our toes more than once on this one."

"It's time to wrap this one up," said Seyfat. "Sandy, as the Federale in charge, tell me what you think."

Peters replied, "Don, keep me posted as to your actions regarding the captain. First we wait for ASAP, of course. Let's review the IEP plan in a week or two. And Todd, we're especially interested in your single point of failure comment. Thanks for keeping us informed this morning.

"Other than that, I think we're good over here," Sandy indicated.

"Okay that's it. Lisa, once again, fine detective work, and thanks by the way for the new list. And Lisa, since you're doing the RMP review next Monday, let's make this one a bit more detailed than usual, and talk about lessons learned.

"Thanks, everybody. Let's get back to work," Seyfat said, and the call ended.

Later that evening, as Tiller and Seyfat sat at a local brew house sampling their second, or third, local brew, Tiller said "You know Glenn, we were lucky—my wife and I were lucky. This could have been bad.

"What do you think? You guys are not using slide rules any more, but do you think your fancy systems can yet measure the fate of one man against another's?"

"Not yet, Ken, not yet. But I will say this, we're not going to sit still and be the hunted. We are now the hunter."

Postscript

(*Note to Reader:* The story is for illustration purposes only and the authors make no claim as to the technical feasibility of the malfunction.)

Some readers may recognize the triggering event of the story as borrowed from the 1961 classic book, *Fate is the Hunter*, by aviation author Ernest K. Gann.

While the story we've presented in this book is a reactive investigation of an operational event, we've tried to stress throughout the book that SMS is primarily looking forward and managing safety by predicting where the problems are and eliminating them. In that sense, the purpose of SMS is to find fate, and change it in our favor. The subtitle to this SMS book could very well be … *Fate is the Hunted*!

Discussion questions

1. Where is SMS exhibited in this story?
2. Is there evidence of a safety culture? Where, and where not?
3. What were the key elements that solved this mystery? Don't think about tools or software, rather think about processes.
4. Identify the management interventions that led to the successful conclusion of this case.
5. Describe the role of oversight in this case. Name the components of oversight.

Index